Serial Mexico

CRITICAL
MEXICAN STUDIES

CRITICAL MEXICAN STUDIES
Series editor: Ignacio M. Sánchez Prado

Critical Mexican Studies is the first English-language, humanities-based, theoretically focused academic series devoted to the study of Mexico. The series is a space for innovative works in the humanities that focus on theoretical analysis, transdisciplinary interventions, and original conceptual framing.

Serial Mexico

Storytelling across Media,
from Nationhood to Now

Amy E. Wright

Vanderbilt University Press
Nashville, Tennessee

Library of Congress Cataloging-in-Publication Data
Names: Wright, Amy E., 1974– author.
Title: Serial Mexico : storytelling across media, from nationhood to now /
    Amy E. Wright, Vanderbilt University Press.
Description: Nashville : Vanderbilt University Press, 2023. | Series:
    Critical Mexican studies; 10 | Includes bibliographical references.
Identifiers: LCCN 2023002346 (print) | LCCN 2023002347 (ebook) | ISBN
    9780826505613 (paperback) | ISBN 9780826505620 (hardback) | ISBN
    9780826505637 (epub) | ISBN 9780826505644 (adobe pdf)
Subjects: LCSH: Serialized fiction—Mexico—History and criticism. |
    Storytelling in mass media. | Narration (Rhetoric) | Digital
    storytelling.
Classification: LCC PQ7207.S46 W75 2023 (print) | LCC PQ7207.S46 (ebook)
    | DDC 863--dc23/eng/20230317
LC record available at https://lccn.loc.gov/2023002346
LC ebook record available at https://lccn.loc.gov/2023002347

For my son, Rahm, who reminds me every day that I am an author.

Contents

Acknowledgments

I want to acknowledge the vast number of individuals who helped me along this exhilarating journey. (Please forgive any unintentional omissions.) First and foremost I thank my entire family and the many students, friends, and colleagues who have offered their great enthusiasm and encouragement for this project.

I am deeply grateful to those I met during my early years at university and who molded and shaped my thinking during that time. At the University of North Carolina at Chapel Hill, I remember the guidance of Marcia Collins (Spanish), Jonathan Hartlyn (political science/Latin American studies), and John Chasteen (history/Latin American studies). The support I received from the John Motley Morehead Foundation, under the aegis of Chuck Lovelace and Megan Mazzocchi, was essential. Gabriel Evens and his family were instrumental in my development. From my time at Brown University I thank Wadda Ríos-Font and Geoffrey Ribbans (QEPD), who guided my early navigation of the labyrinth of nineteenth-century popular literature. From the days of my first job at NC State University I appreciate the excellent leadership of Dr. Ruth Gross, and a deep friendship with Shelley Garrigan, with whom I have now enjoyed some twenty years of conversation on matters both personal and professional. I also met Billy Acree, now a colleague in Saint Louis, then finishing his PhD at my alma mater. From my earliest trips to Mexico, I have lifelong friends—Cynthia Viveros, Adriana Alcántara, Maira Vaca, Mauricio Dussange, Gabriela Pérez, and Marimar Patrón Vázquez—who first welcomed me into their homes and families. And from the same period dates a friendship with Brenda Campos, who twenty years later in New York City would usher me into the world of entertainment-education, and the groundbreaking work of storytelling pioneers such as Ev Rogers, Arvind Singhal, and Miguel Sabido.

Since arriving in Saint Louis, I am especially grateful to my long-term friend and mentor Christopher Conway for his enduring interest in my work, his intellectual generosity, and the many talks we have shared without which this book would hardly be possible. I gratefully acknowledge the early support of Saint Louis University (SLU) and my then-department chair Kathleen Llewellyn in graciously providing the sabbatical that allowed for the bulk of this project's archival labor. My thanks go out as well as to SLU's College of Arts and Sciences (CAS), under Dean Donna Lavoie's leadership, for the Mellon and Stolle Awards, and to David Borgmeyer and the Office of the Vice President for Research, for the Beaumont Award and for support of my NEH application. I am deeply appreciative for our SLU graduate students (in particular former graduate research assistants Mariela López and Angela Blash) and colleagues (Ellen Crowell, Pascale Perraudin, Ana Montero and others who participated in our CAS research groups). Colleagues from nearby Washington University—in particular Ignacio Sánchez-Prado, Colin Burnett, Elena Dalla Torre, and again, Billy Acree—have been exceptionally supportive over the years.

I am wholly indebted to Mexico City researchers and librarians at the Hemeroteca UNAM (Fernando Lizárraga and Alfredo Bramlett Ruiz), the Fondo Reservado UNAM (Rosario Páez and Alberto Octavio Partida Gómez), the Biblioteca Miguel Lerdo de Tejada (Jorge Corona García Pina), the Museo del Estanquillo (Ana Laura Peña Aguilar), the Fonoteca Nacional (Pável Granados), the Protele Foundation (Nadia Elizabeth Rosas Pineda and Edgar Gerardo Hernández Alonso), the Academia San Carlos (Elizabeth Fuentes Rojas), the Biblioteca Nacional (Colección Personal Monsiváis), and to scholars Virginia Medina Ávila, Maricruz Castro Ricalde, and Juan Manuel Aurrecoechea, among many others, for sharing their deep knowledge and personal attention during my time in Mexico. In Austin, Texas, I thank the scholar Charles Ramírez-Berg as well as expert librarians Adrian N. Johnson and Dylan J. Joy, for their skillful stewardship of the resources of the Nettie Lee Benson Latin American Collection (UT-Austin); in Harlingen, Texas, my thanks go out to Rogelio Agrasánchez and Xóchitl Fernández of the Agrasánchez Film Archive. Alejandra Monroy of Mérida provided key help with translation during a time when I was far too busy to take care of that single-handedly. (Indeed, nearly all of the Spanish-to-English quotes in this book are the result of that collaboration.) I am very pleased to have participated in the excellent CONACYT working group led by Yanna Hadatty Mora and Viviane Mahieux, which brought together a top-notch group of scholars to collaborate on Culture and Press in Mexico (1880–1940). I am also extremely grateful for the many fortuitous life connections that allowed me to consult with Juan Pablo O'Farrill Márquez, Surya MacGrégor, C'Cañak Weingartshofer, Sergio Villegas, and Gabriela Rodríguez on various materials that I have used in this book.

A huge thank you goes out to the National Endowment for the Humanities. I am honored and humbled by that award for this project. I offer profuse thanks to Efraín Navarro in Mexico City and my editors Gianna Mosser and Joell Smith-Borne of Vanderbilt University Press—as well as my stellar copyeditor, Peg Duthie—for their extraordinary assistance and considerate attention.

Last but not least, I thank my dear parents, Gerald and Jean Wright, for the unconditional love and support they have offered me throughout life. I thank Kunal Rehani for cheering me on through the last lap of the book preparation marathon. And I thank my sweet son, Rahm, for bringing immense delight into each of my days: proof of some of the finest joys to be found in repetition.

Introduction

This is a book about one of the most enduring and fundamental exercises in human communication—storytelling. Narrative plays a core role in the ways that we define ourselves, individually and communally: we use and share stories to structure and transform our realities. Storytelling about our world offers patterning and predictability to existence, prompting certain questions: What happens next? What's in this story for me? Once these questions are raised, we are hooked, and we keep following the stories to find answers. That level of engagement is not reached through just any story, however. The most compelling tales include transformative elements of "what is" and "what could be."

If storytelling has the power to shape our individual and collective identities over time, serialization is storytelling on steroids. Serialization, or the sharing of a story as a sequence of installments, is a vital feature of narrative that traditionally has been overlooked. Yet today, across the globe, serialization is more prominent and participatory than ever, proliferating through blogs, podcasts, and on-demand shows, in relative independence from broadcast media conglomerates. Serialization allows for stories to be repeated and continued over long periods of time, cultivating an "in-progress" mentality with a lack of completion that may activate desire and existential longings for resolution.

In Mexico consumers have been presented with the "what is" and "what could be" of their country through two hundred years of serial narrative. It is through "serial time" that they have come to understand themselves and their trajectories. *Serial Mexico: Storytelling across Media, from Nationhood to Now* traces this robust tradition from the country's beginnings into the twenty-first century. This story has not been told, in spite of the fact that Mexico's first novel, still read today, was issued in installments on the eve of Independence, while its twentieth-century soap operas have been exported to every corner of the world. Indeed, Mexico has received little recognition for its groundbreaking path within the global phenomenon of serialization.

This book will help widen the lens of history by highlighting places, people, and events that deserve more credit for their primary roles in shaping national and international phenomena. We will access the continuity of worlds and characters made familiar to generations of Mexicans through two centuries of serial repetitions and reiterations. We will read these repeated articulations as a critical elaboration of identities, a trove of national nostalgia, and above all a source of pleasure—of a joy in repetition. We will also see how foundational narratives of the nineteenth century—presented in the form of serial novels, themselves drawing on oral traditions—live on in the series and technologies proliferating in the twenty-first century, ensuring the influence of these texts in contemporary Mexican culture.

Taken in their totality, serial enunciations of identity have gradually defined Mexico over time, as repeated drops of water etch the surfaces of a rock. Yet serialization practices and products have generally escaped critical conversation from within Mexican studies, perhaps because of their ephemerality, their subsequent republication in a single-volume format (masking episodic origins), or a devaluation of popular culture that has resulted in intellectual neglect. I argue here that exploring serialization, as well as its incipient intermediality and transmediality, is in fact essential to understanding the novel's place in twentieth- and twenty-first-century popular culture, and most importantly the myriad ways serial repetitions have shaped the national repertoire.[1]

Scholars on Latin America have touched on the presence of seriality in popular culture in salient ways since the 1980s, when Jesús Martín Barbero wrote *De los medios a las mediaciones: Comunicación, cultura y hegemonía* (1987). It describes the three-century progression by which the popular classes became a historical subject in Latin America, and the key role that mass media played in that process. The masses consume media, according to Martín Barbero, in the ways that they find most "useful," exploiting their power as consumers of narratives to modify form and content, giving voice to their own interests. Using *telenovelas* among his examples, Martín Barbero demonstrates how the television industry recycles viewers' demands into programming appealing to mass audiences, offering stories that provoke intense identification in their consumers. He shows how the most popular stories are strongly connected to traditions of oral narrative.

William Rowe and Vivian Schelling's equally provocative 1991 work examines the interactions of diverse twentieth-century Latin American cultural productions (ranging from *carnaval* to samba to *telenovelas*) with technology and globalization. *Memory and Modernity: Popular Culture in Latin*

America focuses on the masses' agency to reinterpret and reappropriate mass media using collective memory and an organic blending of tradition with modernity that is unique to Latin America. Rowe and Schelling explore the region's hybridity through a lens of remembering: modernity is embedded in the memory of a past that lives on in the present through popular practices. The authors show how mass media and technology are important sites for the storing and processing of the *pueblo*'s collective memories.[2]

With serialization's rapid intensification in the twenty-first century, seriality studies worldwide have correspondingly intensified. First defined by Henry Jenkins in 2003 as the flow of narrative across multiple media platforms, transmediality is most often tied to a twenty-first-century "convergence" in which new technologies bring different media together in a redefined media environment, where manufacturers as well as consumers influence products; in Jenkins's view, seriality plays a role in contemporary texts' transmediality. There has subsequently been an uptick in scholarship on serial "expansion" as a condition of transmediality, with Marie-Laure Ryan (2004) and Carlos Scolari (2009) investigating the intersections of narrative and new media in relation to transmedial storytelling.

More recently, Rob Allen and Thijs van den Berg (2014), Carlos Scolari, Paolo Bertetti, and Matthew Freeman (2014), and Frank Kelleter (2017) have examined seriality on its own terms, reflecting on assorted media and case studies from all over the world. Kelleter in particular has historicized seriality's function within transmediality as "a storytelling practice that shapes all media of popular culture."[3] In doing so, he makes a case for understanding serials' materiality in terms of cause and effect, showing how its special structures of repetition and variation, as well as specific contexts and conditions, make a difference in narratives' form and content. This conceptual framework engages ambitious overarching questions, such as: "What *is* culture if not a realm of repetition and variation, the desire to practice reproduction as innovation?"[4] What happens to the narrative experience when resolution is denied? Kelleter arrives at a key conclusion: culture itself is dependent on serial reproduction, in spite of humans' seemingly existential need for closure. The spread of culture-defining stories across media is a time-honored phenomenon, even as that media continually takes on new forms, as we will see in the specific case of Mexico.

It is crucial to take seriality not as a given or a happenstance but instead to foreground it as a critical object of scrutiny. Earlier studies dealing with Latin America did not concentrate on seriality per se, paying attention to it mainly in relationship to oral culture and soap operas. They were also geographically broad: their authors examined multiple artifacts from various countries and periods to make general arguments about the nature of popular culture and its reception in Latin America. This book focuses specifically on multiple narrative media from Mexico, presenting seriality as a form that deeply affects the structure and reception of numerous products, and considering its socio-semiotic role in the creation and sustenance of Mexico's discourse communities. By focusing on a single key country with a robust serial and narrative tradition, I probe the particularly Mexican themes, motifs, characters, and storylines that have resonated over time. Such reiterations and repetitions reveal ongoing dialogues within the serial space regarding national identities (past and present), gender roles, family, cultural and even political models, extended to the broadest possible range of interlocutors through the widest possible range of media, given seriality's propensity toward transmediality. Looking at selected artifacts against a large backdrop and through media-specific contexts brings out structural similarities that might not be otherwise visible.

The following questions undergird the methodology at this project's core: How has serialized storytelling functioned and developed over time? What accounts for seriality's pervasiveness in the development of Mexican narrative? How can we better understand the relationship of seriality to transmediality through different case studies? How does the serial form define Mexican storytelling? Which stories (and which characters, themes, storylines, and storyworlds) have circulated repeatedly? How have those stories defined Mexico? This panoramic project explores not only the topic of serialized storytelling, but also how national identities are imagined and reinforced through narrative, with crucial cultural and sometimes political implications. It identifies culturally specific and historically hierarchical storytelling practices—the motifs, formulas, and ideologies most widely disseminated to vast sectors of the Mexican public through the mass culture industries of printing, radio, and television. Within the above, it highlights the interconnected nature of storytelling through transmediality; the ways serialized storytelling differs from the individuated forms of authorship tied to so-called literary fiction; and linkages between national identity, nostalgia, populism, and storytelling. The overall framing question of "What *is* popular seriality in Mexico, and how does it function?" leads to interdisciplinary gains that become apparent as we survey the diverse collection of narratives included here: pamphlets, novels, comics, radio dramas, and soap operas (*telenovelas*).

The five snapshots that follow highlight five key moments in this two-century-long trajectory of Mexican serialized storytelling, focusing on the ways serial form defines Mexican storytelling and seeking out the specific stories (characters, themes, storylines, and storyworlds) that have repeatedly circulated, coming over time to shape Mexican culture. We begin our review of those two centuries with Chapter 1, initiating our exploration of the recurrent serial metaphor of nation as family with Mexico's first novel, *El Periquillo Sarniento* (1816), published on the eve of Mexican nationhood (1821). This picaresque-style narrative was first distributed in serialized pamphlets addressed to a diverse "family" of readers and listeners, its author a rebel journalist who hoped to evade censorship through publishing fiction. Lizardi intuited that serializing this foundational narrative would transmit its progressive messages to the largest possible number of interlocutors, who would see themselves depicted within his novel as a family dispossessed, led by a *pícaro* whose lessons learned in his failed family of origin gave way to his fatherly teachings for future generations.[5]

Chapter 2 studies the nineteenth-century practice of revisiting the past to interpret the present and shape the future, as accomplished through the serialized historical novels popular in Mexico's Restoration and corresponding cultural movement El Renacimiento (1867–1876). Serialist Vicente Riva Palacio was a well-known and well-loved general who, after rescuing Mexico from French invaders, seized an opportunity to rewrite Mexico's history through best-selling fiction prolifically published within the pages of a prominent newspaper. The two novels that captivated audiences most were lively history lessons that serialized the nation's highly contested colonial past to show how the collective hero (and historic underdog), the Mexican *pueblo*—a motley family led valiantly within the novels by Martín Garatuza, the historical *pícaro-espadachín* (swordsman)—was on an ascendant path toward progress.

Chapter 3 further probes the metaphor inaugurated by Lizardi of Mexico as family and its need for education. In the era following the Mexican Revolution, newspapers continued to serve as an important space for cultural imaginings, national consolidation, serial narratives, and a referendum on the common man's participation in Mexican cultural and political life. In the 1920s, cultural editor Salvador Pruneda proposed a homegrown version of the US "family comic strip." The result was the long-running *Don Catarino y su apreciable familia* (1920s–1960s), which showed the education and modernization of an amiable cowboy (*charro*) and his family, in a visually accessible series that encouraged Mexican families to pursue the same.

Chapter 4 traces the seemingly endless trajectory of Mexico's first transmedial hero, Chucho el Roto, focusing on his most popular iteration in Televisa's longest running *radionovela*, *¡Chucho el Roto!* (ca. 1965–1975).[6]

The bandit folk figure Jesús Arriaga (1858–1885) was first celebrated in oral legends during the nineteenth century in exploits that have been compared to those of Robin Hood, and then in serial novels from the early twentieth century, during which time the focus fell on the honorable bandit's family. The effects created by this *radionovela*'s sound and suspense were so real, so transformational, that listeners consistently confused the series' star, Manuel López Ochoa, with the noble outlaw that he portrayed. The radio serial, which ran for a decade, took the family theme and expanded on its melodrama, inaugurating a transmedial boom in which Chucho the Urban Bandit became the protagonist of comic strips, *fotonovelas*, film series, and television series that captivated Mexican audiences through the rest of the twentieth century.

With Chapter 5 we come full circle, revisiting family themes from Riva Palacio's historical serial novels (Chapter 2) that entered Mexican television through a 1980s neobaroque revival. This chapter investigates the rebirth of the colonial-baroque aesthetic in two Televisa *telenovelas*, *Martín Garatuza* (1986) and the iconic cult classic *El extraño retorno de Diana Salazar* (1988–1989). The remixing and rebooting of the colonial baroque through 1980s TV series demonstrate how foundational Mexican serial novels live on in nostalgic content, form, and aesthetics through transmedial productions from the late twentieth and early twenty-first centuries. The staging of scenes in a time previous to the present, often with prelapsarian overtones, allows for the examination of both origins and contemporary dynamics in less threatening ways. The frequent appearance of this nostalgia for historical settings is not accidental; it speaks to possibilities within these narratives for creating communality—a shared national nostalgia. To close, we turn our gaze to twenty-first-century on-demand serial viewing practices, new media tendencies, interactive user-generated serialized media, and groundbreaking series that upend traditional images of the Mexican family, such as the subversive matriarchy represented in *Las Aparicio*, which appeared first as a soap opera (2010) and then as a film (2015).

The analysis presented through these five chapters is the product of years of conferencing, peer collaboration, investigation, and careful archival collection of data and images at Mexico City's Fundación Televisa, Fonoteca Nacional, the Universidad Nacional Autónoma de México (UNAM) libraries, Biblioteca Lerdo de Tejada, Biblioteca Vasconcelos, and El Museo del Estanquillo. It weaves current considerations of seriality and intermediality into its review of their evolution in the Mexican context, from the foundations of nationhood into the late twentieth century, across a variety of different yet complementary genres. The interdisciplinarity surrounding the phenomenon of seriality from within Mexican studies—in particular a refashioning and reinvigorating of discussions on nationhood and foundations—is especially relevant to our era, in which seriality is a crucial means of transmitting and consuming social messages. In acknowledging that the devaluation of serialized texts has stemmed in part from an association with marginalized groups, I offer an entry point into a vibrant web of seriality outside of the English-speaking world, and a more inclusionary (and thus more accurate) understanding of the historically long and geographically vast phenomenon of seriality as a meaning-making form.

The history of serialization in Mexico has been continuous since the nineteenth century.[7] During that foundational period, most Mexican novels were initially published via pamphlets, newspaper/magazine installments (*folletines*), or chapters released in intervals (*entregas*).[8] These were sold in bookstands or delivered to subscribers, only later to be bound into books. Through these modes of publication, serial novels forged crucial links between print media, narrative, and temporality as cognitive tools that could organize Mexican society on a timeline toward progress—a form of pedagogy that could be used to determine interlocutors' subjectivities. With the nineteenth-century emergence of periodicity-as-marker-of-modernity, serial novels embodied a new cultural dependence on consistency and efficiency as keys to advancement, producing corresponding changes in societal notions of linear time and rational futurity. Serializing a novel in a periodical made its content more timely to consumers, as it appeared simultaneously with news and could be distributed with that news on a daily or weekly basis. Serialized time-structure generated a segmented manner of reading, postponed by everyday life and porous both to quotidian experiences and to consumers' input. These narratives needed to take interlocutors' preferences into account to survive, and they allowed for perceived dialogue and influence in a highly stratified society.

On the eve of Independence, print was not accessible to all. Books were expensive and generally unavailable. Putting installments in pamphlets or newspapers offered an early workaround, as their means of transmission was nonexclusive. Quickly passed from person to person (*de mano en mano*) and easily read aloud in public spaces, serialized novels tapped into a more democratic oral culture that reflected the zeitgeist of the early nation. Words were performed in community as a part of social as well as intellectual life, and social spaces proliferated in which to hear and discuss public readings or performances. These early serial narratives had the potential to bring largely illiterate communities into print culture and to generate transmedial conversions via reading.

The serial format linked novels to Mexico's traditional oral and visual cultures, placing novels in a key position of mediation between orality and print, and between popular and erudite narrative. The oral repertoire served as Mexico's earliest collective cultural experience, defining the larger group's identity. It contained popular style and content, with folksy speech and slang, local heroes, and themes with which listeners were already familiar and associated with their own life experiences. These stories, which spoke to the realities of the Mexican world, involved telling (reflecting the oral world of America) as much as reading (the written world of Europe). Prior to 1816, no written text had attempted to represent that repertoire.

Serialization played a definitive role in the conception and success of Mexico's very first published novel, *El Periquillo Sarniento* (1816). Its author, José Joaquín Fernández de Lizardi (1776–1827), was a rebel journalist evading censorship of his newspaper by publishing fiction in its stead. On the eve of Mexican nationhood, gazettes such as his *El Pensador Mexicano* were already an important source of everyday information, so Lizardi circulated his novel as a series of pamphlets (*cuadernos*) with ongoing storylines that hooked the "serenísimos lectores" (and listeners) to whom his work was dedicated. Its chapters were brief and easily read aloud, inspiring group discussion as well as promoting literacy. Lizardi's convincing descriptions of the late colonial world placed characters and author on the same plane as consumers, exemplifying key strategies now associated with twenty-first-century transmediality—narrative proliferation, recursive repetition, world-building, metafictionality, intermediality, and interlocutor engagement, as Lizardi communicated with his public through a feedback loop in which alternative outcomes were requested. The engraved illustrations of *El Periquillo*'s early book editions supported listeners' memory over time, as well as additional entry points into the story for people at various levels of literacy.

A defining feature of Mexican print culture has been the availability of affordable ephemera in contrast to books, expensive to print and purchase. Throughout the nineteenth century, beginning in the 1830s and 1840s, novels published in periodicals were increasingly accessible through a burgeoning of independent periodicals that incorporated greater orality and visuality to cultivate and increase their audiences. Editors and printers such as Mariano Galván Rivera (1791–1876) or Ignacio Cumplido (1811–1887) took advantage of technological advancements to enhance the quality and quantity of images in their publications, while reading clubs, reading rooms (*gabinetes de lectura*), literary circles (*tertulias*), literary salons, and bookstores offered access to texts and stories across social classes.[9] Illustrations made texts more easily accessible to those not yet able to read the written word.

No strategy for increasing reach was more successful than the serialization of novels, often with accompanying lithographs. Beginning in the mid-1830s, French newspapers such as *La Presse*, *La Siècle*, and the *Journal des Débats* had witnessed leaps in sales by publishing installments of long-form fiction at the base of their front pages, an area known as *le feuilleton*. After Eugene Sue became an international phenomenon with *Les mystères de Paris* (1842–1843), *le feuilleton* became a coveted space for aspiring novelists. In Mexico, the equivalent *folletín* proved particularly useful to editors who wanted to please and expand the consumership of their papers, beginning with translations of novels by Sue, Alexandre Dumas, Sir Walter Scott, and Frédéric Soulié. (The term *folletín* is used not only for the location but also for the text.)[10]

It took some time for Mexican novelists to find their own voice in the new format, but Justo Sierra O'Reilly (1814–1861) and Manuel Payno (1810–1894) eventually became Lizardi's successors.[11] Their novels imitated European forms while portraying authentic Mexican customs, exploring the country's past and present to create original national mixes. Palpable throughout was the high melodrama associated with *el folletín* and *lo folletinesco*—the nineteenth-century aesthetic of extreme sensation and sentiment that foregrounded emotional and ethical dilemmas, frequently offering a satisfying moral resolution. Romantic melodrama's exaggeratedly Manichaean struggles were reminiscent of Mexico's colonial theatre and tumultuous post-Independence political divides. Their stark binaries of good versus evil captivated audiences and marked novels well into the twentieth century. Sierra serialized his melodramas in newspapers from Mérida to Campeche during Yucatán's Caste War, at a time when the peninsula was considering secession. Sierra completed his first *costumbrista* novel, *Un año en el Hospital de San Lázaro*, over four long years (1845–1849), through irregular installments in his regional newspaper *El Registro Yucateco*.[12] Sierra's second novel, *La hija del judío* (1848–1851), was a drama of origins with a dose of Jesuit intrigue, published weekly in his literary newspaper *El Fénix*. Payno, a Mexico City journalist, wrote reviews praising Sue when *Les Mystères* first appeared in Spanish translation (1844). One year later, in the *Revista Científica y Literaria de México*, Payno began his serial publication of *El fistol del diablo* (1845–1846). This portrayal of Mexico's contemporary vices and virtues, left incomplete when the *Revista* was suspended, was continued later in two Payno publications, *El Eco del Comercio* (1848) and

El Federalista (1871), becoming a thirty-year work-in-progress. Payno's second novel was also initially unfinished: as nineteen installments in the short-lived *La Independencia, El hombre de la situación* (1861) focused on allegorical family dynamics from the colonial period to Independence. In the cosmogonies of Mexico's early novels, from Sierra to Payno, we find the collective melodramas of anagnorisis—cathartic recognitions of true origins and identities—ready-made for twentieth-century *radionovelas* and *telenovelas*. This period closes with Luis G. Inclán (1816–1875), a self-described *charro impresor* (country printer) specializing in newspapers, *corridos* (ballads), engravings, and novels. His *Astucia* (1865–1866) was an illustrated "novela histórica de costumbres mexicanas" (historical novel on Mexican customs) seemingly inspired by Dumas. Inclán issued it to sub-scribers in the form of booklets, featuring a total of thirty-three engravings. Its first-person narration by its characters was a metafictional trick that put interlocutors on an equal footing with the author-as-narrator and charac-ters, all of whom were "listening" to these stories-within-their-story.

The next generation to take up Lizardi's mantle called itself El Renaci-miento. The innovative labor of that movement's principal novelists dur-ing Mexico's Restoration (1867–1876)—Manuel Payno, Ignacio Altamirano (1834–1893), Vicente Riva Palacio (1832–1896), and Juan A. Mateos (1831–1913), among others—ushered in the Golden Age of Mexico's national novel.[13] This generation practiced serialization as a way to educate and enter-tain the *pueblo*, employing cliffhangers, vertiginous plots, high emotions, and resounding moral resolutions in their project to rewrite and massify national history. As printing technologies steadily advanced, Restoration periodicals featured increasingly sophisticated images, ads, and artwork. The lithographs of Hesiquio Iriarte (ca. 1820–1893) adorned the pages of *El Renacimiento*, the Sunday literary magazine co-founded by Altamirano, the movement's chief architect. Altamirano's informal essays, published serially in *La Iberia* (1868), championed the intimate connection between litera-ture and journalism: "The novel instructs and delights the poor *pueblo* that doesn't have access to libraries. . . As long as there is a reduced circle of supe-rior intelligence, the novel, like popular song, journalism, the grandstand, will be a link that unites the classes, perhaps the strongest."[14] Altamirano's first novel, *Clemencia* (1869), was published in weekly installments in *El Renacimiento*; his third novel, *La navidad en las montañas* (1871), appeared as an eleven-part *folletín* in *La Iberia*.[15]

During the Restoration, the melodrama permeating serial novels and theater stages offered shared pleasure and nostalgia to the public. Mateos and Riva Palacio led the charge in both genres. Mateos began advertising the installments of *El cerro de las campanas* (1868) in *Siglo XIX* at the start of the Restoration, initiating a long career of authoring multiple serials and series. His friend and frequent collaborator Riva Palacio was a popular general who, after helping rescue Mexico from French invaders, began rewriting national history through prolifically published serialized novels from 1868 to 1872. These were advertised in Carlos Casarín's *Orquesta*, a liberal newspaper famous for political caricatures (the lithographs of Constantino Escalante in particular). Riva was its editor when his first novel was promoted there; under pseudonym he distributed *Calvario y tabor* (1868) to *La Orquesta*'s subscribers in weekly installments printed by Manuel C. de Villegas. Riva's *Monja y casada, vírgen y mártir* and *Martín Garatuza*, accompanied by evocative illustrations from *La Orquesta*'s renowned caricaturists, were issued in the same format later that year.[16]

Whether embraced or rejected, the serial novel and its aesthetic associations formed a legacy to be reckoned with, as seen in the end-of-century swan songs of the indefatigable serialist Payno. In 1887, while on diplomatic assignment in Europe, Payno expanded the scope of *El fistol del diablo* from 1845 to 1846, augmenting its oral register by adding long sections of dialogue, elements of irony and meta-reflection, and promising subscribers yet another continuation.[17] It was redistributed in installments through Juan de la Fuente Parres, a Barcelona publishing house with ties to Mexico City. In 1888, Payno began his last novel, a monumental masterpiece containing allusions to its own seriality. Parres released the installments of *Los bandidos de Río Frio: Novela naturalista, humorística, de costumbres, de crímenes y de horrores* in both Mexico and Spain, likely between 1888 and 1891.[18] This encyclopedic chronicle of melodramatic *mexicanidad* catalogued Mexican popular culture from 1810 to 1830. Accompanied by color lithographs and a glossary of *mexicanismos*, it showcased the author's deep nostalgia for his *patria*.

Unlike later novelists of the Porfiriato, Heriberto Frías (1870–1925) was eager to educate in the hard scrabble spirit of Lizardi, to explore controversial social problems, and to sympathetically portray the marginalized and oppressed. Frías strode onto the literary scene with *¡Tomóchic! Episodios de campaña: Relación escrita por un testigo presencial*. At the age of twenty-two he participated in the government's near extermination of a Chihuahuan town and was said to have penned his manuscript the following week. Three months later, *El Demócrata* published *¡Tomóchic!* in twenty-four anonymous installments (1893), a bombshell leading to the author's eventual imprisonment and the newspaper's temporary closure. In 1895, *El Demócrata* serialized Frías's accounts of prison life, as well as his less-fortunate second novel of eighty-eight installments (*Naufragio: Novela del autor de Tomóchic; Costumbres mexicanas*). The broad popularity of Frías's next project, however, was remarkable, generating five full series of publications: *Las leyendas históricas mexicanas* (1897–1898), serialized in *El Imparcial*, spawned a long-running children's version entitled *La biblioteca del niño mexicano* (1899–1901), published by Mexico's Maucci Brothers: the effect of each individual sixteen-page pamphlet was intensified by full-color covers and smaller color lithographs within.[19] At the Revolution's beginning, Frías continued his serial stories of *Tomóchic* protagonist Miguel Mercado in a 1911 sequel, *El triunfo de Sancho Panza: Novela de crítica social mexicana; Continuación de Tomóchic*). *Tomóchic*, however, remained Frías's most popular novel, garnering four reissues before 1910, at a time when few novels were printed in multiple editions. After another decade, Frías embarked upon a Revolution trilogy, interrupted by his death at the age of fifty-five.

Though naturalist-leaning novelists such as Frías would eschew sentimental tendencies, they nonetheless used the serial form to establish themselves and reach a wider public. Many availed themselves of the new "cultural supplements" spearheaded by publishing magnate Rafael Reyes Spíndola in *El Universal* (founded in 1888) and *El Imparcial* (founded in 1896). By the century's end, these heavily illustrated dailies were attracting significantly larger audiences.[20] The authors within their pages were among the first writers to work in the nation's mass culture industries.

From Independence to the Porfiriato and beyond, strategies pioneered by Lizardi fostered the reproduction, remixing, and recycling of Mexican novels into other genres, formats, and media. The social instability of the Mexican Revolution (1910–1920) prolonged serialization's utility and range. Newspapers such as Felix Palavicini's *El Universal* (founded in 1916) and its prominent weekly cultural supplement *El Universal Ilustrado* (founded in 1917) serialized and illustrated the period's most important revolutionary narratives as *folletines*.[21] In 1914, provincial doctor Mariano Azuela (1873–1952) began writing *Los de abajo: Cuadros y escenas de la revolución actual*, as well as its two sequels (*Las moscas* and *Los caciques*). *Los de abajo* was published in twenty-three episodes by the little-known Texas newspaper *El Paso del Norte*, shortly after Pancho Villa's defeat (1915). In 1925, *El Universal Ilustrado* republished the twenty-three episodes by combining them into five uneven parts (some ending mid-syllable) that catapulted its author to fame. The novel's notoriously fragmented structure might well have come from its original serialization: Azuela wrote it while fleeing with Villa's defeated troops and had already agreed to its publication in installments when he hastily penned its ending section in the offices of *El Paso del Norte*.[22]

Another influential writer of the Revolution, Martín Luis Guzmán (1887–1977) wrote about *folletines* early in his career, in a newspaper series on film criticism (1915–1916) during his first European exile. Upon his return to Mexico in 1920, Guzmán founded his own evening daily and a radio station. His paper *El Mundo* (1922–1923) featured serialized novels (such as *Chucho el Roto*), complemented by serial radio, before Guzmán was forced back into exile. From Spain, Guzmán continued to write in installments for *El Universal* (Mexico City), *La Opinión* (Los Angeles), and *La Prensa* (San Antonio); his memoirs "De mis días revolucionarios" was first released as a serial in *La Opinión* and *La Prensa* (1926). At the end of the year, the same text appeared with illustrations on the first page of *El Universal*'s Sunday section. In 1927, *El Universal* began publishing *El águila y la serpiente* (1927–1928) in some sixty illustrated installments—a *folletín* both in style and format.[23] Its follow-up, *La sombra del caudillo* (1929), was announced as Part 2 of Guzmán's trilogy on the Revolution, bringing its author instant notoriety once President Plutarco Elías Calles threatened to ban the work. *El Universal* continued Guzmán's success by serializing his *Memorias de Pancho Villa* in 1936.

Journalists Gregorio López y Fuentes (1895–1966) and Rafael F. Muñoz (1899–1972) were also prolific serialists for *El Universal Ilustrado*. López y Fuentes was discovered through a contest for "La Novela Semanal" (The Novel of the Week); his first novel, *El vagabundo*, appeared in *El Universal Ilustrado* with illustrations by Andrés Audiffred.[24] Muñoz had been writing weekly installments about the Revolution when *El Universal* hired him to complete memoirs of the recently assassinated Villa: Muñoz's illustrated *Memorias de Pancho Villa* (1923) preceded Guzmán's identically titled serial. From 1928 to 1929, *El Universal Ilustrado* published a story by Muñoz each Sunday in a series entitled "Los seis leones de San Pablo," illustrated in color by Francisco Gómez Linares. These installments formed the foundation of Muñoz's first novel, *Vámonos con Pancho Villa* (1931), an immediate bestseller and the source for one of the first films about the Revolution (1935). In addition, Muñoz's work inspired Villa-related *radionovelas* in the 1940s, numerous comics during the 1950s and 1960s, and Paco Ignacio Taibo II's graphic novel *Pancho Villa toma Zacatecas* (2013). Azuela's *Los de abajo* reappeared in comics (1983), films (1940 and 1976), and a *radionovela* (1980–1981). Guzmán's controversial *La sombra del caudillo* was filmed by Julio Bracho in 1960 and released some thirty years later; *El águila* and *la sombra* both became *radionovelas* (1960s–1980s).

The end of the Mexican Revolution heralded sea changes: significant migration accelerated the growth of Mexico City, where an audiovisual boom began early in the 1920s, and cultural productions began to circulate more fluidly among the masses whose cultural presence had been trumpeted by the Revolution. The arrival of urban technologies such as cinema and radio decentered serial print culture, but it remained influential, surviving in a rich new *convivencia* (coexistence) with innovative formats that amplified its reach. Through the 1930s, newspapers and magazines remained the best way to garner Mexican audiences, but transmediality in the form of comics, *radionovelas*, and *telenovelas* became a hallmark of serialized narrative from the Revolution onward.

Postrevolutionary comic strips featured ongoing stories that, like serial novels, expanded newspapers' readership. The ratio of visuals to words invited semiliterate populations to consume stories through illustrations, affording comics an important role in the extension of literacy; short episodes and simple everyday language accommodated the working classes' limited reading skills and fragmented leisure time. Comic books streamlined familiar tales and updated themes while retaining the exaggerated expression, high suspense, and dramatic face-offs between good and evil that had made their novelistic antecedents so engaging. After a Golden Age of Mexican comics (1930s–1950s), the industry reached its apex in the 1960s and 1970s, when Mexicans were among the biggest consumers of comic books in the world, collectively purchasing millions per week.[25]

In the 1920s and 1930s, reading serials aloud in groups had been subsumed by long-running live *radioteatros*, easily accessible to anyone near a transmitter, and recording advances soon improved radio's diffusion and distribution. The earliest 1960s *telenovelas* were themselves adaptations of Golden Age radio serials, which had been derived from a substrate of Mexican storytelling with foundational heroes, iconography, and imagery, as well as legends from oral tradition. Attracting a massive fanbase, *telenovelas* held the entire nation rapt over scores of episodes, with viewers bonding over family melodramas that were appealing and relatable to all tiers of society. In sheer numbers, *telenovelas* reached more people than any media that had come before. These "novelas" became a national pastime with the potential to smooth over vast disparities across regions and classes, through the collective, sustained consumption of stories channeling significant differences into improbable feelings of togetherness. In a process spanning both the nineteenth and twentieth centuries, serialized narratives also played a key role in making the Mexican masses culturally visible, effectively protagonizing the common man—perhaps even the underdog—as the good guy whom one most desires to see succeed.

Twentieth-century Mexican comic strips, film series, *fotonovelas*, and *radioteatros* drew heavily from nineteenth-century serial novels to increase

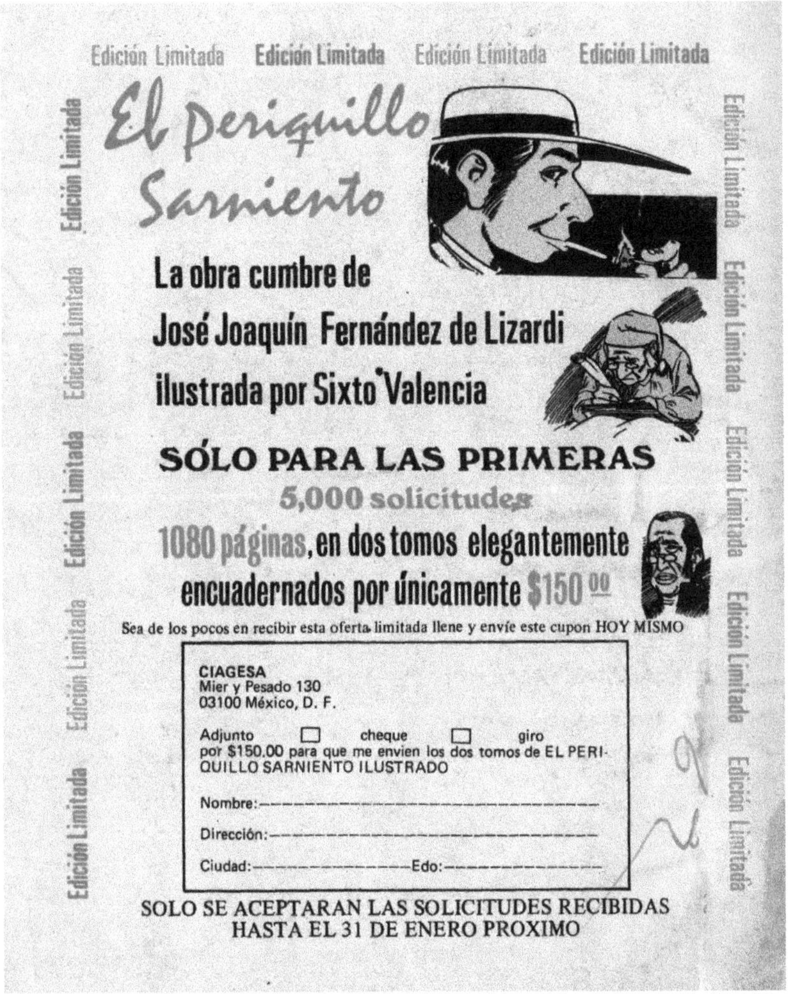

FIGURE 0.1. Back cover (1981) of the SEP comic *El Periquillo Sarniento*, illustrated by Sixto Valencia Burgos. Lizardi's masterpiece was reissued in an adapted serial format, illustrated by one of Mexico's most popular cartoon artists of that time. The first five thousand subscribers would receive their installments elegantly bound in a two-volume set, in an offer "available for a limited time only." Image courtesy of Christopher Conway.

their national nostalgic appeal, inviting the masses to consume familiar storylines and characters in new formats. What follows is a highly incomplete list. Payno's *Bandidos*, for example, saw numerous iterations, including a film loosely based on the novel (1938), a two-part adaptation starring Luis Aguilar (1956), 1960s comics, Edmundo Báez's *telenovela* (1976), and a 2013 graphic novel by F. G. Haghenbeck and Bernardo Fernández ("Bef").

Radio versions of Payno's *Bandidos* and *El fistol del diablo* (itself a movie in 1961) have also appeared. Inclán's *Astucia* has had a similarly prolific transmedial life: a children's theater piece written and directed by Salvador Novo performed fifty-three times at the Palacio de Bellas Artes (1948); an eighteen-episode radioseries (1981) rereleased by Radio Educación in 2016; and Mario Hernández's film starring Antonio Aguilar and Ignacio López Tarso from 1986. Riva Palacio's *Monja y casada* debuted on the silver screen in 1935 under director Juan Bustillo Oro, and reappeared as a *telenovela* in 1986 with the title of *Martín Garatuza* (1986), *Monja*'s original sequel. From 1981 to 1983, the Secretary of Public Education (SEP) sponsored comics based on novels by Lizardi, Payno, Inclán, Altamirano, Riva Palacio, and others; installments of *El Periquillo Sarniento*, illustrated by Sixto Valencia Burgos, kicked off the series.

Generational nostalgia has continued to remix earlier presentations into new productions, such as the recent live musical and variety show *La Hora Radio Roma 1 y 2*.[26] From the mid-twentieth century on there have been pastiches (and frequent parodies) of the forms consumed by creators in their youth. Some works play on serialization and its impact through their titles and references, while others imitate its stereotypically archaic tone and content. Emilio Carballido's novel *Las visitaciones del diablo: Folletín romántico en XV partes* (1965; emphasis mine), released as a movie in 1968, pays tribute to Payno's *El fistol del diablo*. In Luis Zapata's *Melodrama* (1983; emphasis mine), Mexico's Golden Age is a prominent inspiration, its film stars serving as Zapata's muses; *Melodrama* was converted into a regional *radionovela* in 2012. Laura Esquivel's *Como agua para chocolate: Novela de entregas mensuales con recetas, amores y remedios caseros* (1989; emphasis mine) was adapted by its author into a film (1992) replete with nineteenth-century references, including the phrase "monthly installment novel" in its title.

Historical novels saw a resurgence in the last quarter of the twentieth century, their serial heritage visible in prominent uses of metafiction, beginning with Fernando del Paso's masterpiece, *Noticias del imperio* (1987). Enrique Serna's *El seductor de la patria* (1999) delves into the life and times of nineteenth-century strongman Santa Anna, while his parodic *Los ángeles del abismo* (2004) dialogues with the nineteenth-century serial novel in general and Riva Palacio's *Monja y casada, vírgen y mártir* in particular.[27]

Mexican detective and police series also pay homage to serial influences, stretching back to the narratives of justice and criminality found in Altamirano, Payno, and Frías. Taibo's long-running series about detective Héctor Belascoarán Shayne began with *Días de combate* (1976) and ended with

Adiós Madrid (1993), generating several films along the way; Bef's Andrea Mijangos and Lizzy Zubiaga, characters who first appeared in *Tiempo de alacranes* (2005), are the protagonists of *Hielo negro* (2011), *Cuello blanco* (2013), and *Azul cobalto* (2016). Crime novels now serve as Mexico's *novela costumbrista por excelencia.*[28]

Since the second half of the twentieth century, Mexican novels have thrived in dialogue with popular culture and lighter genres—a clear reflection of their nineteenth-century origins, when novelists aspired less to winning elite critical favor and more to reaching readers across a wide range of social classes. Contemporary Mexican novelists have inherited their predecessors' distinctive rhythms of orality, vernacular expressions, and neologisms, beginning with Lizardi. This legacy of strategies, styles, and subjects supports the successful television and streaming series of today, with serials proliferating like never before. While series produced in Mexico from the twentieth century onward have hardly been limited to literary adaptations, their tone and content, as well as their format and reception, are fruits of a robust popular tradition refined over two centuries of experiments, to the great pleasure and engagement of ever-widening audiences.

These were drawn from a body of popular orality that defined serial narrative well into the twenty-first century. Some of the most distinctive features of this subjective mode of storytelling were emotions over logic, melodrama over erudition, folk heroes and historical characters (such as bandits and outlaws), regional *costumbrismo*, folksy speech and local slang, and episodic structure. Consumers were already acquainted with these elements from oral stories circulating within Mexican folktales, *literatura de cordel* (popular chapbooks), street theater, bullfights, puppet shows, circuses, *corrido* ballads, and *carpa* (tent shows akin to vaudeville in the US). These tales spoke to and reflected Mexicans' everyday realities, communicating a sense of togetherness and belonging to their audiences, alongside moral lessons for navigating common struggles. These stories became so familiar, their protagonists so believable, and their worlds so recognizable as to produce (unexpected) metafictional effects, blurring the lines between reality and fiction. Repeated and reiterated over long periods of time as demanded by the public, serial stories skillfully sustained the paradoxical dynamic essential to their appeal: these were stories told as continually in progress, incomplete, and unresolved, yet dependable, stable, and long-lived at the same time: their very lack of resolution offered a sense of continuity to loyal interlocutors.[29]

In this archaeology of serial storytelling, I trace a throughline from older practices to newer examples of transmediality by identifying a set of consistent and interdependent narrative strategies, carried over from oral tales into the very first serial novels. These elements, when present, allowed stories to cross over easily into other texts of the same medium (intermediality) as well as into other media (transmediality). First among these strategies is proliferation, on which seriality's very existence is predicated: the potential for unlimited expansion of content as well as length. Closely related to proliferation comes repetition, and its related modes of recycling and reiteration, which serve to intensify interlocutors' engagement and desire. Popular literature's dependence on repeated schema can be compared to the mnemonic devices relied on by the ancient bards, or Vladimir Propp's categorization of fairy tales into thirty-one functions.[30] In the world of oral storytelling, listeners are less concerned with originality and more with the feelings generated by recognizable themes, characters, plots, spaces, and forms. The recycling and reiteration of familiar elements bring pleasure, satisfaction, and even a sense of mastery to interlocutors as they enjoy the repetitions that express their experiences. Repetition and proliferation underpin serial storytelling's transmediality—its potent and sometimes simultaneous expansion and extension within texts and across media.

Proliferation is itself dependent on a strong storyworld—a highly detailed and believable space evoked across a sequence of installments, with the capacity to unify multiple storylines. This vast fictional universe remains constant, providing a connective backdrop for the characters (with enticing origin stories or incomplete back stories) and the storylines (with loose ends, hinting to a larger narrative) that come and go within it. This recognizable storyworld lends coherency to the potentially endless creation and to the elimination of elements that occurs during narrative proliferation.

The survival of a serial directly depends on the level of identification and participation, or desire, that its stories inspire.[31] In oral storytelling, engagement relies on the degree to which listeners identify with the characters. A strategic and predictable "hook" of suspense is manipulated between episodes to entrance consumers and ensure their continued participation over time. These cliffhangers may become increasingly calculated as the story progresses, with the promise of resolution perpetually deferred. Exciting and ever-more-complicated plot developments encourage audiences to stay tuned on a regular basis and keep interlocutors coming back for more. The desire for both resolution and continuance is the very tension fueling successful seriality.

Identification and desire are further intensified through metafictional strategies that implicitly merge the fictional storyworld and its characters with the consumers' own world and lives. This sensation is facilitated by serial narratives' general porousness to life outside the text, a quality exacerbated by the multiple pauses and interruptions inherent to seriality. The convergence of intra- and extra-diegetic experiences may culminate in staged events or spectacles in which the public "interacts" with the narrative's characters, creating the illusion of their migration from the fictional text to the real world.

In Mexico, an intense level of identification has been elicited through seemingly endless variations of the distinctively melodramatic family stories, near and dear to the hearts of audiences, which constitute numerous origin texts in Mexican storytelling. Martín Barbero posits that in Latin America "the family" operates symbolically in opposition to materialism and commodification, and that family melodramas become key repositories for transmitting and reinforcing shared memories of the social group.[32] Since one single, seamless popular memory is not possible, serial storytelling performs a necessary continuance through ongoing episodes.

The family has remained in Mexico as the sole most important meaning-making unit—the most intimate source of foundational encounters with group belonging, identity, and authority figures.[33] Indeed, serial narratives have been vital to the cultivation, consolidation, and continuation of national identities as family identities: communicative practices such as reading and listening to the same stories offer opportunities to develop the sense of simultaneity, to experience a universalized timeframe, that is created through an omniscience shared with the narrator and the other (imagined) readers, together as a national family.

Throughout this book, I argue that, with the help of serial narratives, Mexico imagined itself into being, particularly into the potent (and malleable) image of a national family. These serial narratives could also be conveniently fostered from within the real family as society's nucleus. Since the nineteenth century, reading had eased its way into some Mexican families' social lives, as an interactive group activity mediated by discussion of and comments on the story. Group readings were at times performative, with reader(s) acting out the parts of the narrator and different characters in novels with copious dialogue, reinforcing familial bonds through the shared experience of interpreting (and even altering) the written text, taking on the roles of characters portrayed within the family melodrama.

Melodrama, a mood frequently present in Mexican serialized narrative, became the recurrent emotional state associated with these family dramas, and the filter through which affect could be passed. In its earliest Victorian manifestations, melodrama entailed the essential act of anagnorisis, an intense recognition, that served as a revelation of truth, often in the spheres of family, kinship, or community. In most melodrama, this truth perseveres in the face of great obstacles—usually false appearances and evil influences that prevent true identities or sincere virtues from shining through. In their portrayal of Mexican family models, melodramas of identity and recognition circulated and propagated metaphors surrounding the Nation-as-Family, a community achieved through immense struggle against internal and foreign enemies. Interlocutors were encouraged to employ their intimate knowledge of their own families to understand more abstract concepts such as citizenship, nationhood, and participation in the nation as a membership in "one big family," the *gran familia mexicana*. The families portrayed in serial narratives would conform to or contest familiar patriarchal models, often featuring the protagonism of fathers, sons, and brothers as heads of family or heroes to society—principal sources of power and authority—with women in a supporting role. At minimum "family" functioned as an organizing principle throughout the twentieth century, often as a symbol of unity aligned with masculine nationalist sentiment, and at times as the basis for an emergent cultural politics.

Male hero characters serve as an entrypoint into a vast Mexican storyworld whose topography is already well known to consumers. Could this shared world also be the imaginative space of the patriarchal nation, inhabited by a multitude of recognizable figures, spawning different storylines that explore its diverse areas? The structures of serial storytelling allow for the creation and proliferation of a corpus of narratives, which over time accumulate into one grand mythology—a seemingly indefinite continuation of the storyworld of Mexico through serialized episodes. How did popular Mexican male protagonists evolve, within texts and across media, to inhabit and expand this larger (metaphorical) storyworld? How did the figure of the prototypical Mexican hero (or antihero) change over time, while remaining recognizable to consumers over the course of multiple textual permutations? As the nation evolved, its narratives multiplied in response to interlocutors, market, and context, with a constellation of figures and themes becoming culturally definitive in the course of being recycled and repeated over time.

With the accumulation of a character's appearances across multiple texts, his collective mental image is gradually created, unbound from any single iteration, similar to a folkloric motif. Formed from and between these texts, Periquillo, Garatuza, Catarino, and Chucho share an "everyman" status in their everyday struggles for survival. They enact certain long-held masculine values such as brotherhood, loyalty, solidarity, and kinship, performed

EN LA PAGINA 131, OTRO EPISODIO DE:

Vida y hechos de Periquillo Sarniento escrita por él para sus hijos

por
Don José Joaquín
Fernández de Lizardi
"El Pensador Mexicano"
ADAPTACION : Gonzalo Martré
DIBUJO : Sixto Valencia

Año I -- No. 32

NOVELAS MEXICANAS ILUSTRADAS. Una Producción de la D. G. P. B./SEP. Se publica semanalmente. Es una coedición de la Secretaría de Educación Pública, Dirección General de Publicaciones y Bibliotecas y del Grupo Sayrols, Compañía General de Ediciones, S. A.: Mier y Pesado 130, México 12 D. F. Editor Responsable: Lic. Jorge Velasco Félix. Certificados de licitud: de título 998 y de contenido, exp: 11432 "80" 12059, expedidos por la Comisión Calificadora de Publicaciones y Revistas Ilustradas. Reserva al uso exclusivo del título núm. 297 expedido por la Dirección General del Derecho de Autor. Impresa en los talleres de: Editormex Mexicana, S. A., Av. de la Luz núm. 58, México 12, D. F. Distribuida en la ciudad de México por la Unión de Expendedores y Voceadores de los Periódicos de México; en el interior de la República Mexicana y en el extranjero: Libros y Revistas, S. A. Mier y Pesado 128, México, D. F. Miembro de la Cámara Nacional de la Industria Editorial. Precio por ejemplar: $12.00 M.N. Editada e impresa en México. Printed and made in Mexico.

FIGURE 0.2. Inside cover (1981) of the SEP comic *El Periquillo Sarniento*, illustrated by Sixto Valencia Burgos. Announcement of the upcoming episode of Periquillo's "life and times, written by him, for his children." Each installment was available for 12 pesos, distributed via Mexico City's street vendors association (the union of *voceadores* founded in 1923), with regional and international subscriptions also available. Image courtesy of Christopher Conway.

in opposition to corrupt, false, often elite and sometimes foreign institutions—weak replacements for the support and daily sustenance provided by an ideal Mexican family. Each hero's ongoing adventures replay, remix, restore, repudiate, and otherwise respond to significant family archetypes found deeply embedded in the national consciousness.[34] The character acquires a legendary, myth-like aura as his adventures are told across different media, each portrayal offering more details about the deeds that reflect his deep values in the larger fight of good against evil, which in turn both informs the *pueblo* of its genealogy and generates its "history." Such figures are frequently incarnated as leaders of a family that is also in the process of transformation and evolution.

These serials' repetitive focus on patriarchal families originally allowed interlocutors to link familiar units to national culture on a traditional allegorical level: the nation is a family; heads of state are fathers; citizens are children. It presented models for them to assess: how well were male authority figures living up to societal expectations as fathers and as leaders? Models of mothers, children, family relationships, and domestic daily life similarly circulated through these narratives, reinforcing a gender-based system rooted in long experience. The male-centric Nation-as-Family metaphor, repeated and reexamined through the first serialized family melodramas, helped interlocutors imagine their own responsibilities to the *patria*. It construed nationhood as a family bound in shared lineage, heritage, and a highly subjective sense of belonging.

This exploration of archetypal realms is part and parcel of popular narrative: in their exaggerated rendition of good versus bad, darkness versus light, lies a space as cathartic as it was recognizable, in which passions, patriotic history, adventures, and betrayals could be processed as shared experiences across disparate societal sectors—a community of feeling established through a collective emotional experience. Consumed simultaneously, melodrama's emotional excesses became a national family pastime over the course of two centuries, inviting pleasurable participation in deeply shared sentiment—a democracy of feeling, exalted as profoundly meaningful. Serialized melodramas were key to providing the common cultural experiences that could consolidate Mexico into a single national market, offering a semiotic-symbolic unification that obviated heterogenous Mexico's vast divides, at least superficially. And so serialized narratives became a necessary tool in the country's long, slow process of making the masses visible—no longer subordinate as the cultural underclasses—and essential to the creation (i.e., imagining) of a mass national culture. Throughout this centuries-long process, serial storytelling performed itself as an essentially modernizing and democratic practice deeply rooted in Mexico's past, elemental to a modern liberal society, and in constant need of continuation and renewal. As the nation slowly evolved into a strangely sustainable collective, serial narratives evolved and expanded at its side, encouraging collective practices of consumption to preserve faith in the persistence of Mexico and the patrimony of its *pueblo*.

The concept of *pueblo* has been elaborated on by Paul K. Eiss, *In the Name of El Pueblo: Place, Community and the Politics of History in Yucatán* (2010), in ways that inform my use here. Eiss demonstrates how *pueblo* has a tangible existence in the sociomaterial world, persisting as a framework for explaining relations in Mexico's Yucatán Peninsula, where contentious acts of constructing or claiming that entity have been both externally and internally directed. In this book I look toward the most expansive meaning of the *pueblo* as a (proto-)national identity and a collective social-political subject—however heterogeneous, conflictive, and internally contested— existing in both time and space, with an extended temporal reach, from Mexico's colonial period to the present. This idea of the *pueblo* presumes awareness among its constituents of its enduring existence in the past, pres- ent, and future; a historical consciousness based in collective memory; and, most important for this work, an archival repertoire of texts and narratives, histories, and representations of the past that play a critical role in its con- struction as a collaborative entity. Shared stories about the past and ways of telling those stories (storytelling) exist, giving a coherent and mutually intel- ligible form, through narrative, to aspects of the community's experiences. This repertoire of experiencing, telling, feeling, and performing stories is crucial to the *pueblo*'s understanding of itself as a community over time.

While it may be tempting to regard transmedial storytelling as radically new and revolutionary, in Mexico the multimedia treatment of popular sto- ries—narratives whose longevity is considered essential to the identity and the survival of the group—stretches back to the beginnings of nationhood. This book interrogates the earliest forms of mass culture (such as serialized novels) to identify their traces in contemporary culture industries, and the possibilities for collective memory that these spaces provide. In Mexico, that repertoire has constituted a *pueblo*, past and present.

At its most generative and productive, serialized storytelling continues to demonstrate its capacity to transform twenty-first-century realities into more meaningful narratives—sometimes national, sometimes global, always human—that allow for the reinterpretation and reinvention of alienated modern everyday lives. Serials can bring disparate and detached interlocu- tors together into conversations that imagine different worlds and generate new options for existence while remaining a predominant source of sym- bols for the community, even in the fragmented age of online streaming. Seriality's ongoing episodes provide an interpretive dimension to everyday life that transforms and elevates meaning, providing comfort and stability in their continuation, extendable seemingly infinitely over time, weaving an endless web of never-ending stories based deep in oral culture, tradi- tion, and nostalgia, presented through ever-modernizing media formats. In sum, effective serial storytelling has the power to preserve living cultural repertoires. Serialization generates confidence in the continuation of Mex- ico's collective story, against and alongside new global realities. *Continuará.*

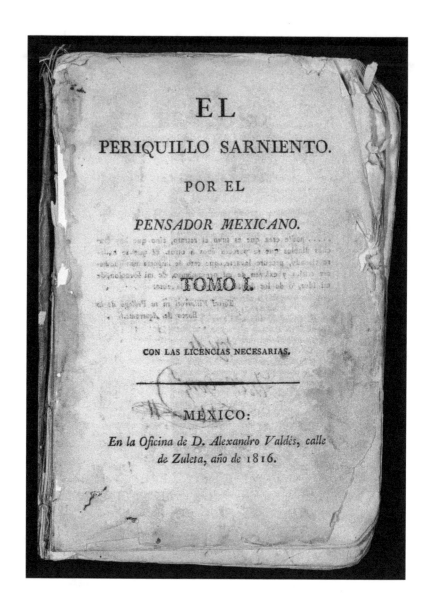

FIGURE 1.1. Mexico's inaugural serial. Title page from the first edition of *El Periquillo Sarniento* (1816). Image courtesy of Benson Special Collections, UT-Austin.

Nation as Family in Mexico's First Novel

Lizardi's *Periquillo* (1816) as Pamphlets

In 1816, Spain's three-century rule over the Mexica was creeping torturously toward its end, although it would be another full decade before the colonials began to call themselves *mexicanos*. From the beginning of this struggle in 1810 until 1821, the Spanish crown, desperate to forestall the imminent collapse of empire, repeatedly revoked and reinstated freedom of the press. It was from these vicissitudes that *El Periquillo Sarniento* was born. Mexico's first novel rose directly from the revolutionary anti-colonial journalism appearing on the front pages of newspapers and in pamphlets or broadsheets distributed in the streets.

From the start, the two births—of the Mexican nation and of the novel[1]—were linked. The genre of the novel arose out of this moment of discursive possibility, and then provided a symbiotic space in which writers could experiment with the linguistic politics that would shape the nation. *El Periquillo Sarniento*—first published as a series of pamphlets—can be seen as one of the principal midwives in the birthing process of the nation-to-be. How its author, José Joaquín Fernández de Lizardi (1776–1827), used it at a politically strategic moment in Mexico's history to encourage education and reform illustrates not only the liberating effects of decolonization on literary production, but also the reverse—how novels could decolonize minds, promoting independent Mexico to newly "nationalize-able" interlocutors as a viable and desirable entity.

We must examine Lizardi's work within the context of its initial publication, as a serial, if we are to fully comprehend its importance to and function for the young nation of Mexico. The ritualized distribution of a linear, horizontal storyline with which consumers regularly and repeatedly "interacted" was especially potent in the reconfiguration of time and space that Benedict Anderson theorized as necessary for the nation. In this chapter I show how the material realities of *El Periquillo Sarniento*'s publication may have affected Lizardi's desired audience, an audience that expressly included the *pueblo*.[2]

El Periquillo Sarniento was, in fact, the first new novel of the nineteenth-century Spanish-speaking world, preceding the 1840s debut of original novels in Spain by a full two decades. (The first novels published in Spain after *Don Quixote* [1605/1615] appeared in the late 1830s as translations of French and English works.)[3] The debut of serialized fiction in Mexico rather than Spain has been attributed to efforts both to avoid censorship and to ameliorate the high cost of producing full-length books in the colonies. On both sides of the Atlantic, however, the widespread practice of pamphleteering in England and France during the latter part of the eighteenth century can be regarded as a forerunner of the Hispanic world's publication of narrative fiction in pamphlet or installment form.

Newspapers had begun to change colonial ways of thinking as early as 1805, with the appearance of *El Diario de México* (1805-1817), the first Mexican daily and the first successful alternative to Spain's government-controlled gazette. Characterized by literary scholar Jefferson Rea Spell as "the most important organ of aspiring Mexican writers in the early years of the nineteenth century," Lizardi contributed to *El Diario*'s editorial exchanges. It was in the *Diario* where he first announced his intention to write a novel based on a character he would call Periquillo Sarniento (February 14, 1812). He would later appropriate its commercial and highly participatory template when he began his own newspaper.[4]

Bibliographer Paul Radin reports that by 1810 Lizardi owned a private printing press and was earning a meager living as a publishing "maverick," selling poetry for a few cents per pamphlet—with pamphletry being "the most effective form in which to reach the public ear" at that time.[5] When freedom of the press was officially granted to New Spain in 1812, Lizardi was well positioned to take advantage. That year, he launched himself into notoriety with a weekly newspaper, christened with his nom de plume, *El Pensador Mexicano* (The Mexican Thinker).

In contrast to *El Diario de México*, which Spell describes as a forum "judiciously tempered to the requirements of censors, civil and ecclesiastical," Lizardi's newspaper and pamphletry served as a space where real educational and social reforms could be discussed freely for the first time. According to Spell, "In the work of no other writer are political, social and religious conditions in Mexico in the early years of the nineteenth century subjected to such scathing criticism as in the many pamphlets issued by El Pensador Mexicano, who therein outlined for Mexico a constructive program, which, if adopted, would have placed the country a century sooner in the ranks of modern nations."[6] Putting similar polemics to work in *El Pensador Mexicano*, Lizardi served as author and editor of each issue, exercising sole control over style and content.

His paper enjoyed immediate success. The overwrought viceroy responded to the rising fervor that newspapers stoked by revoking freedom of the press within two months of its proclamation. Circa 1815, Lizardi decided to find a different venue for his ideas. He turned to the novel to avoid censorship, an interpretation corroborated by his rapid return to journalism upon Mexico's independence.[7]

Lizardi's choice of the novel as his new forum was not coincidental. Beyond relative safety, the open territory of the novel offered other discursive possibilities. It was, as neoclassical literary critics deemed it, a "bastard genre," undefined in its use of multiple discourses, and ripe for experiments in both form and content.[8] Through his journalism, well before his brief four-year period of novelistic activity, Lizardi had honed narrative skills that he would deploy in his novels. Many of the political pieces he wrote between 1810 and 1816 relied on conversational dialogue, suggesting Lizardi's early interest in the polyphony and heteroglossia later foregrounded by Mikhail Bakhtin as essential aspects of the modern novel. Lizardi used didactic dialogues throughout *El Periquillo* to create the effect of increased polyphony and "double voice."[9] Lizardi's journalistic writings from this time also evidence innovative handling of fictional personae. In newspapers that were shorter-lived and more experimental than *El Pensador Mexicano*, Lizardi tried his hand at verse, dramatic invention, allegory, dialogue and satirical fiction—forms that would be put to good use in his first novel.[10]

In a formative discussion of the symbiosis of nation, novel, and newspaper, Benedict Anderson posits that the creation of newly "national" identities depends on three (re)imaginings: readers must (re)imagine space, time, and their belonging to a community. In *El Periquillo*, he sees the "national imagination at work in the movement of a solitary hero through a sociological landscape [. . .] that fuses the world inside the novel with the world outside."[11] Yet Anderson's analysis (of *El Periquillo* and other nation building novels) tends to separate the book and the newspaper into two distinct spaces, overlooking serial publications such as the *folletín* as their unique and particularly powerful fusion. The newspaper, in Anderson's assessment, is "merely an 'extreme' form of the book": it is "sold on a colossal scale" but ephemeral—the "one-day best-seller." He views the book, on the other

hand, as a durable good with its own hermetic self-sufficiency, characterizing it as a "distinct, self- contained object, exactly reproduced on a large
scale" and "the first modern-style mass-produced industrial commodity."[12]
While analyzing Indonesia's (also serialized) *Semarang Hitam* (1924) as a
later example of national literature, Anderson notes the intradiegetic force
of embedding the image of a young man reading a newspaper within the fictional narrative: "The imagined community is confirmed by the doubleness
of our reading about a young man reading . . . It is fitting that in *Semarang
Hitam* a newspaper appears embedded in fiction."[13] What to say, then, of the
extradiegetic force of embedding of entire novels in the pages of newspapers? Or, as in the particular case of Lizardi's *Periquillo*, the sudden substi-
tution of a biweekly newspaper with a biweekly novel from the same press?

The novel-published-as-pamphlets (serialized) strategy led by the journalist Lizardi breaks through the dichotomy of book and newspaper. Moreover, understanding *El Periquillo*'s original serialization is crucial to our
understanding of its content and importance as a foundational text for the
Mexican nation. Elements present in the novel and in the newspaper as
separate entities become doubly potent in the hybrid form of the serialized novel, which in the Hispanic world became the most popular vehicle
for nation-building fiction.

Yet serialization does not constitute a substantial focus in any existing work on *El Periquillo*—Anderson doesn't mention it at all—perhaps
because of the variations and omissions among its first four editions, and
scant information regarding their conditions of publication and reception.
Carmen Ruiz Barrionuevo provides a useful summary of the textual problems that she attempted to mitigate in her 2008 edition of the novel.[14] The
first book edition (1816), a bound collection of the original pamphlets, is
incomplete, with only the first three volumes successfully issued (and the
fourth volume censored by the Viceroy Apodaca). This first bound edition
of *El Periquillo* consisted of three volumes containing twelve chapters each
(each chapter corresponding to a pamphlet), a total of thirty-six chapters
(pamphlets) altogether, printed by Alejandro Valdés, calle de Zuleta, with
engravings by Mendoza.[15] Of significant interest is an 1817 summary of the
censored material, entitled "El Periquillo Sarniento, tomo IV, extractado
por el Pensador Mexicano, año de 1817."[16] This manuscript was handwritten
by scribes who were contracted by Lizardi and appended to some copies
(of the third volume) to circumvent censorship. The second edition (1825)
was intended to be a corrected and completed version of the first, but—
perhaps because of the author's financial difficulties—only one of the four
volumes was issued, existing now on a defective microfilm, consulted and

FIGURE 1.2. Engraving by Mendoza from the first edition of *El Periquillo Sarniento* (1816), entitled "Periquillo with the trophies from his adventures." Image courtesy of Benson Special Collections, UT-Austin.

elaborated upon by Ernest R. Moore.[17] The third edition (1830–1831), which contained what we think of as the full novel, did not go to press until after the author's death, issued as a five-volume set, with the formerly censored material appearing in Volumes 4 and 5. The fourth edition (1842) was significantly altered by editors using undisclosed "manuscripts" yet came to be the most popular and widely reprinted in subsequent years. Ruiz Barrionuevo's presentation of *El Periquillo Sarniento* leaves aside this popular fourth edition, instead relying on the first "complete" edition of 1830–1831 (in consultation with the incomplete first and second editions).

Lizardi had probably begun to write the novel in 1815: in December of that year he stated in a prospectus that its installments would be released on Tuesdays and Fridays, beginning February, as well as in four bound volumes. The prices, print runs and total sales of the original pamphlets are not known. Each volume would consist of twelve installments (chapters) and twelve lithograph prints, at an anticipated base price of four pesos per volume.[18] It has been estimated that the first edition consisted of some five hundred copies, though Lizardi makes a reference at the end of that first *Periquillo* to the existence of "three hundred copies in Mexico and beyond."[19] The first bound edition contained both a list of 102 subscribers (88 in Mexico City, 14 in the provinces) and a two-page notice addressed to them ("Advertencia a los señores suscritores"). The second edition acknowledges 78 "esteemed subscribers" ("Lista de los señores subscritores [sic] que hay hasta el día de hoy 19 de octubre de 1825, en que sale a luz este tomo primero)."[20] By the fourth edition in 1842 there was talk of three thousand copies of the novel in existence, showing however anecdotally that interest in *El Periquillo* continued to rise.[21] The sheer quantity of references to Lizardi's books in political pamphlets of the day indicates that their circulation went beyond the numbers implied by the scant statistics available.[22]

We have other anecdotal clues that the pamphlets themselves were "immediately popular," in the words of Nancy J. Vogeley: "Mexicans eagerly bought the chapters as they came out and discussed Lizardi's characters, as if they were real people, in the other popular literature permitted at that time (newspapers, pamphletry, and so on)."[23] The little we know of *El Periquillo*'s reception upon first publication—that the *cuadernos* sold well— tells us that Mexicans were not associating the text with past or foreign elements in Mexican culture, but instead with their present-day realities and the recognizably Mexican human beings that populated the pamphlets' pages. Lizardi's popularity indicates that Mexicans claimed the story as made by one of them and as a means by which they could relate to their countrymen. Lizardi's 1817 effort to provide consumers with a summary of the missing fourth volume seemed to arise from significant subscriber interest, not just economic necessity:

> The deadliest danger to befall Periquillo was shrinking in size by his fourth volume. […] Here we have the worst state of affairs, not just for our Periquillo, but also for me, for the printer, for the subscribers, and for the public at large.

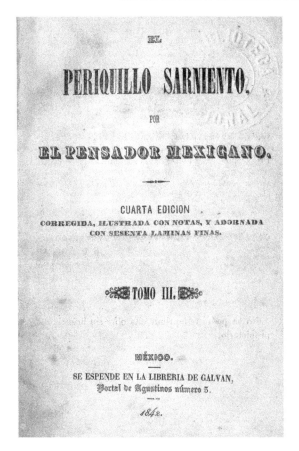

FIGURE 1.3. Title page from the 1842 edition of *El Periquillo Sarniento*, distributed by the Librería de Galván. This edition was known for its many fine quality engravings. Image courtesy of Fondo Reservado, UNAM, Mexico City.

We were all interested in seeing the work completed—in rescuing it from those faraway regions. For Periquillo it meant being able to finish the tale of his misfortune and returning to respectability as I told of his conversion and change in behavior: for me, it meant getting off my back any number of nosy people, inquiring daily about his health instead of mine; for the publisher it meant getting paid; for subscribers it meant having a complete series; and for the public, it meant not getting left hanging with an incomplete ending, wondering about unfortunate Perico's uncertain fate.[24]

From these words and other sources we can glean that installments were not only read by the literate few who subscribed to the work, but shared between readers and listeners in public spaces, extending the novel's reach. Pablo Escalante Gonzalbo notes this growing tendency in early nineteenth-century Mexico: "The political processes that began in 1808 with the establishment of the new State were favorable to the printing of newspapers, pamphlets, and political flyers, preferred among the masses who were eager to inform themselves, who shared them, passing them from person to person, or listened to them read aloud at pulque taverns, cafés, and in the town squares."[25] Lizardi himself records that his novels circulated in much the same way as his newspapers: in announcing his second novel, *La Quijotita* (1818), Lizardi warns subscribers to take good care of their weekly chapters and, if they should lend them, to ensure that the borrowers would likewise take good care of them, since "not everyone knows how to treat a piece of paper."[26] In the same text, Lizardi says that he knows of many readers left with a dirty or incomplete *Periquillo* some two years after its initial publication, a statement indicating that his debut novel was widely available in pamphlet form between 1816 and 1818.

As a serial novel, *El Periquillo Sarniento* combines the nation-building potency of narrative fiction with that of the newspaper (each amply theorized by Anderson, as outlined earlier). It avails itself of all the imaginative resources that helped consumers of novels perceive themselves as part of a community, such as the mimesis of everyday realities and the didactic modeling of desirable and undesirable national traits. At the same time *El Periquillo Sarniento* is even more intimately linked with the newspaper, providing a two-in-one punch toward the reimagining of time and space that Anderson sees as essential to the construction of the nation. A novel published in installments shares a closer relationship with the newspaper than a novel published as a book, both in the mode readers and listeners consume the material and in the heterogeneity of the material itself. For Anderson, both novel and newspaper allow for the collapse of a vertically structured messianic time into a horizontal timeline that is linear, causal, chronological, or successive in nature.[27] The serial novel intensified this effect not only through its narrative content but also through its form—that is, the sequential publication of installments linked by "temporal coincidence" and meted out in calendar time. Sonia Marta Mora has written about the impression of continuity created by *El Periquillo*'s ongoing and at times seemingly endless succession of events, each interlaced with the next. Mora has also discussed how picaresque autobiographies conceptualize time on a line that focuses all events through the final lens of death: the endpoint of the serialized narrative is the endpoint of the *pícaro*-rogue protagonist and his career. *El Periquillo* holds true to this framework—a structure congruent with the horizontal conceptualization of time required for the emergence of the nation and emphasized by the novel's serialization.[28]

Serialized novels emulate the newspaper not just in terms of their periodical delivery, but also in their content. Heterogeneous material is presented under an arbitrary date of publication; editorials, almanacs, current events, discourses, and sermons are all linked within a given edition, if only by the date on which they appear. To Anderson, this imposed linkage is an emblematic characteristic of both novel and newspaper: "If we turn to the newspaper as cultural product, we will be struck by its profound fictiveness." Listing a half-dozen independent events that might together occupy the front page of the *New York Times*, Anderson asserts that "the arbitrariness of their inclusion and juxtaposition [. . .] shows that the link between them is imagined."[29] This heterogeneity is exacerbated in the case of the serialized novel and mirrors the newspaper tradition from which it arose.

The public consumes a serial novel in a similar fashion as the newspaper, and thus experiences dosification and its subsequent building of an imagined community, which are magnified in serialized (versus non-serialized) fiction. The regular and relatively predictable delivery of the serialized narrative emphasizes horizontal time as linear, causal, and progressive in its development, in contrast to the messianic time exemplified in a monolithic text such as the Bible or *Don Quixote*. In such tomes, which are revealed to the consumer in a dense, final form, time is vertical, top-down, understood through epiphany. The novel-published-as-newspaper, on the other hand, arrives as a series of singular pieces, each flowing into the next—as opposed to the hermetic self-sufficiency of the published book—divisible into measurable mathematical quantities.[30]

Like a soap opera or the modern-day sitcom, the serial novel also propels the creation of community by taking mass consumption—initially observed through the daily reading of the newspaper—to a higher level. This ritual is described by Anderson as an "extraordinary mass ceremony: the almost precisely simultaneous consumption ('imagining') of the newspaper-as-fiction." This ceremony becomes even more potent with the simultaneous reading of each new fictional installment. The serialized novel served to unite a larger community whose members partook of the narrative, discussed with one another what happened in the last installment, and speculated about what might happen in the next. To Anderson's rhetorical question regarding the newspaper—"What more vivid figure for the secular, historically clocked, imagined community can be envisioned?"—the most obvious response is "the serialized novel."[31] The serialized presentation of narrative exaggerates the very characteristics that Anderson presents as essential to the newspaper's nation-building properties.

This intimate connection between newspaper and book was certainly not lost on Lizardi, who was, indeed, a master of the inverse version of Anderson's newspaper-as-form-of-novel: he was the inventor of the novel-as-form-of-newspaper in Mexico. Aníbal González explains that in Lizardi's time "newspapers in Mexico and the rest of the Hispanic World made use of genres currently considered 'literary' in presenting their information, since [. . .] journalism up to the late nineteenth century was less concerned with objectively presenting news than with self-expression, opinion, and ideological debate."[32] Lizardi purposefully packed each chapter of *El Periquillo* with as diverse a range of genres and topics—entertainment, morality, erudition, and information—as he could fit in one installment. In this respect, *El Periquillo* is, as described by González, "fundamentally a pamphlet passing itself off as narrative fiction. [. . .] Save for its plot, there is little to distinguish *El Periquillo* from the hundreds of other pamphlets Lizardi had already published and would continue to publish after the restrictions on his journalism were lifted in 1840."[33] When the installments were published together as a book, Lizardi annotated them, referring his public to specific editions of *El Pensador Mexicano* for additional information on some topics. These notes were omitted in subsequent editions as extraneous. Their presence in the first edition, however, highlights the crucial interplay that Lizardi himself perceived between his novel and his newspaper writings.

Within this chronological narrative structure, a newly national identity was gradually assumed over time. Interlocutors incorporated the "reality" of *El Periquillo* into their daily life and got to know the character of Don Pedro de Sarmiento (best known by his nickname Periquillo, the Mangy Parrot) like a close family member as they consumed the book across a prolonged period, in steady doses, twice weekly, over months. The work-in-progress nature of serial publication made it more of a participatory process for consumers, more closely mirroring the experience of national subjects watching their place in the nation-under-construction unfold. As narrative installments are linked together, so are national subjects, woven together into the larger fabric of the novel and the nation in progress.

We no longer have any copies of *El Periquillo* from its initial distribution as pamphlets—only their posterior presentation in the bound volumes of 1816, of which only four copies remain. We must thus look to the narrative for certain indications of and references to its original publication.

These residual signs of serialization are most apparent in the prologues to *El Periquillo*'s various editions, as well as the opening and concluding pages of the work itself. In these narrative spaces, which frame the autobiographical voice of the *pícaro*, the serialized *Periquillo* reconfigures readers' conceptions of space and time through an overarching focus on the family unit as an inclusive allegory for the Mexican nation.

The different prologues of *El Periquillo* stress the importance of this family unit and the past-present-future relationships among a family of readers (Periquillo's putative children and grandchildren) and provide instructions on how the book should be read. Vogeley refers to "family" as the "imperial metaphor that had been used to foster ties between the Spanish king and his two sets of sons (one on the Iberian peninsula and the other in his far-flung colonies)" prior to the narrativization of the new American community that Anderson describes.[34] The autobiographical voice of El Periquillo develops this theme, as he first chronicles the failure of relationships with his now-deceased parents (an allegorical reference to Spain), continues with episodes from his wayward life and the shortcomings of his own generation, and ends with a focus on changing the behavior of future generations. In these prologues, Lizardi and his character El Periquillo effectively appropriate the voice of a new, secular father figure to speak directly to his family (the Mexican nation-to-be) as to how the community might learn from Periquillo's mistakes and evolve toward a more prosperous future. The fatherly voice induces interlocutors, not to wait passively for a rapturous messianic moment to safeguard their future (vertical time), but instead to perceive Mexico's history as an ongoing chain of cause and effect (horizontal time) for which their own actions are ultimately responsible.

The first of the novel's three prologues reminds us of the work's initial serialization and the importance of that innovative format to this text's creation, propagation, and survival. It appears in all of the first three editions (under slightly varying titles and lengths, ranging from six to eight pages).[35] It begins with the authorial voice of a fictionalized Lizardi directly confronting his public with a radically new proposal: the need for a new sponsor (*mecenas*) for the nation, a common metafictional device used by Lizardi throughout the 1820s that popularized his works and made him more accessible to his interlocutors.[36] He pokes fun at the tradition of dedicating the book to a wealthy aristocrat who funds its publication, and then records a conversation with an "unnamed friend" (in a device reminiscent of *Don Quixote*'s famous prologue) regarding the considerable difficulties that *criollo* writers face in their efforts to publish books in the colonies.[37] Cost represents the most formidable obstacle:

"And to whom are you thinking of dedicating your little literary work?"
my friend inquired.

"To whomever I consider might dare pay for its printing."

"And how much might that amount to?" he continued.

"Some four thousand, one hundred and something pesos, give or take a few."

"Saint Barbara!" my friend exclaimed, beside himself. "A little literary work
of four volumes could cost that much?" (90–91)

At one point, Lizardi says that poor people such as himself should not
become writers ("los pobres no debemos ser escritores," 91). The friend
then suggests the Mexican public as Lizardi's new patron. Those who have
supported his newspapers in the past will now finance his novel: "In all
fairness, to whom should you dedicate your works, other than to those
who would pay good money to read them? For they are the ones who pay
for the printing, turning them into your most trusted patrons. So wise up,
don't be a fool" (93).

Lizardi was aware that publishing his novel as a book would reduce the
already small group of potential consumers to those few who could afford
to buy a complete version for their personal libraries. Lizardi had made
direct references to this problem on other occasions, as when stating that
"many poor persons [. . .] who buy the *Pensador* don't have the *Quijote* or
have [n]ever [sic] read it."[38] The first prologue to *El Periquillo* reminds us
that Lizardi chose to distribute his novel initially as pamphlets (indicated by
his use of the word *cuadernos*), which the public could purchase individually or by subscription in the course of subsidizing the work:

> Do deign yourself, then, to give this work a most favorable welcome by buy-
> ing yourself some six or seven chapters each day, and subscribing ahead
> some five or six issues, at the least [...] even if you should end up rolling
> them up into cones or making napkins with them; for should each of you
> fund this printing through small sums, I may never regret having followed
> my friend's advice; so from now on and for henceforth, I declare and select
> you as my only patrons and benefactors [...] asking God to keep you well
> for many years, granting you the money to spend in benefit of the authors,
> printers, papermakers, booksellers, bookbinders, and any others who depend
> on your good taste. (95)

This approach was revolutionary, especially when we study the sociological composition of Lizardi's audience. According to the author himself, it is
a motley crew: "I am very well aware that . . . you are related to fratricidal

Cain, to idolatrous Nabuco, to the prostitute Delilah [...] and to a multitude of other scoundrels, male and female, who have lived and continue
to live in the same world as you do. I know that perhaps you may be, at
least some of you, commoners, Indigenous peoples, mulattos, blacks . . ."
(94).[39] This catalog, while sardonic, speaks directly to a swath of society that
read only minimally, and explains Lizardi's frequent cautions throughout *El
Periquillo* on how to best read the novel. It demonstrates the author's acute
awareness of these new interlocutors'—and soon-to-be citizens'—interpretive limitations.

Considering the range of consumership delineated in the first prologue,
the feat of Lizardi's second prologue—of subsuming all these readers and
listeners under the rubric of one big family—is quite remarkable. This
prologue, written in the paternal voice of the reformed rogue Periquillo,
appears consistently in the first three editions under the title "El prólogo del
Periquillo Sarniento" (occupying approximately 3–4 pages in each version).
In this section, El Periquillo speaks lovingly about his two most important
creations—his *hijos* (children) and his *cuadernos*. Both are under certain
threat. His children are at risk of making the same moral mistakes as their
father, and the purpose of the *cuadernos* is to prevent this downfall, as
articulated in the prologue's opening lines: "As I write about my life, I do it
with the sole and wholesome purpose that my children become educated
in the subjects I speak about" (95). But, in turn, it is the children's responsibility to protect the teachings of their father from unfriendly minds: "I
wouldn't want these notebooks to leave your hands, and so I entrust them
to you" (95).

Serialization optimized a broad diffusion of content to readers and non-
readers, sympathetic and unsympathetic. The immense distributive capacity
of serialized literature was cause for real concern: Lizardi feared the mis-
readings, misuse, and censorship his work might incur from a wider consumership—that is, those outside of El Periquillo's "family." As El Periquillo,
he doubts that his offspring will obey his words; he anticipates them lending these *cuadernos* beyond the family circle.[40] Here we may suspect both
the power of suggestion exercised by the savvy businessman Lizardi, and
a real anxiety about right readings of his work. The mandate to avoid censors is even more adamantly reiterated by El Periquillo at the beginning of
Chapter 1:

> Finally, I charge and command you not to let these notebooks leave your
> hands, that they not become the subject of slanderous talk by fools or
> immoral folk; but that if you should ever fall prey to lending them, I beg

you to not lend them to those kind gentlemen [...] Either keep and read my notebooks for yourself, or if you must lend them, may it be to only the most righteous of men, who though they may err or have erred in their fragility, they realize the strength of truth's lessons without suffering from their wounded ego. (104–5)

The express role of the second prologue is to provide such injunctions and to make clear, once more to all, the nature of his intended audience as reflected in his teachings:

I find myself in need [...] to write for myself some sort of prologue, without trusting anyone else to write it; prologues silence the foolish and the malicious, at the same time serving [. . .] to anticipate some of the problems a book might incur, so for this reason I declare: this little literary work is not intended for the wisemen, since they may not need my humble lessons; it may be of use, however, to some boys who perhaps lack better works from which to learn. (95–96)

El Periquillo repeatedly emphasizes that the *cuadernos* are tied to the fate of his children: "I hardly write for the people at large, but rather, for my children, the ones I most care about and whom I have a responsibility to educate" (97). We also see his fatherly hope that his words will be useful to them. For that reason, he states his intention to use our language ("nuestro idioma") in a natural style (97). Unlike the European novels traditionally imported to the colonies, this new novel is meant to speak directly to his children's needs and unique reality, and the repetition of this concept closes the second prologue: "In the end I find solace in the idea that my writings will bring my children delight, for it is they for whom I created these writings in the first place. If others do not feel similarly, I shall feel that the work does not meet my expectations" (98). Vogeley claims that colonial ambivalence toward colonizers was mirrored in their mistrust of the book as cultural product—that colonials "seem to have come to a consciousness of language's importance through their perception that European books did not match American life." She concludes that "many [colonials] distrusted books, yet they remained powerful symbols of European civilization."[41] This would indicate that a novel distributed in pamphlets could have particular appeal to Lizardi's public on the eve of Independence.

The last of the three prologues appears in each of the first three editions with slight variations to the title of "General Notice(s) to the Readers" (*Advertencia[s] general[es] a los lectores*) and a length of three pages. It is

written in first person, in the voice of a fictionalized Lizardi. In its introduction of Lizardi as the editor of the deceased Periquillo's *cuadernos*, this
final prologue serves as the brief but crucial set-up for a metafictional trope
that will reappear in the book's ending chapters, again highlighting the
novel's serialization. It features Lizardi's assurances as "editor" that he has
followed the desires of his deceased "friend" Periquillo ("in honor of the
friendship I professed to him") in his amendments to the original *cuadernos*
(99). This prologue is connected to the book's penultimate chapter, where
El Periquillo describes the new friend Lizardi who mysteriously appears to
him at his deathbed: "In these days my friends would visit me, and by sheer
coincidence a new one came by, some man called Lizardi [...] an unfortunate writer in your Patria, best known to the public by the epithet that distinguished him when he wrote during these hard times, the epithet of the
Mexican Thinker" (920). The serial nature of the text is also underscored in
one of El Periquillo's final mandates: "Take those notebooks so that my children may benefit from them after I pass" (921). In so saying, the moribund
pícaro bequeaths Lizardi with the installments in which he has recorded his
life story. At this point the fictionalized Lizardi claims complete editorial
authority as Don Pedro Sarmiento's life passes safely into his hands. These
metafictional touches clearly distinguish *El Periquillo* from its European
picaresque antecedents, a genre often functioning as open-ended autobiography, where the first person *pícaro* narrator remains alive and there is
frequently suspense as to whether the rogue will lapse into his former ways,
so that sequels were possible and often published. In *El Periquillo*, the omniscient editor soundly shuts the door on the mistakes of the past, assuring
his public of the authenticity of the *pícaro*'s repentance.

In the "Mexican Thinker's Notes" (*Notas de El Pensador*) that close the
novel's first complete edition (1830–1831), the fictionalized Lizardi directly
addresses El Periquillo's now extended "family" of interlocutors for the first
time. The authoritative journalist Lizardi guides their final interpretations
as well as the future of the text, stepping into the void left by El Periquillo's passing: "As has written my good friend Don Pedro Sarmiento, whom
I loved as much as I love my own self" (921). The fictional Lizardi's role is
not only to annotate, correct, and organize the *cuadernos*, but also to seal
the protagonist's tale—to literally have the last word on the future of Periquillo's text. At the end of this volume, published after the real Lizardi's
death, interlocutors see themselves described as part of the broader future
audience that the fictionalized Lizardi envisions as he persuades El Periquillo's widow to circulate the *cuadernos* beyond the circle of Sarmiento's
now well-instructed children:

Tomo 3.°   EL PERIQUILLO.   Lam 1.

FIGURE 1.4. Engraving from the 1842 edition of *El Periquillo Sarniento*, entitled "Encounter between the author Lizardi and his character Periquillo." This image highlights the strong metafictional bent of Mexico's inaugural serial. Image courtesy of Fondo Reservado, UNAM, Mexico City.

Three years on, once the woman felt less aggrieved, I asked for the notebooks that my friend had written. [. . .]

"Heaven forbid," the woman said, now highly scandalized. "How could I ever allow my husband's silly stories to circulate in the town square?"

"None of that shall come to pass," I responded. [. . .] "These gifts [are] worthy to be read and published . . . It is true that Don Pedro wrote his notebooks with the intention that they only be read by his children; still, they are the ones least in need of reading them, as their temperaments are already well

formed. In Mexico, Madame, and in the entire world over, there are quite
a few Periquillos who may benefit much more from this tale and the moral
lessons it contains. (937–38)

In the novel's closing pages (Ruiz Barrionuevo edition), the fictionalized
Lizardi declares the resounding success of Sarmiento's writings: "I never
expected this silly mess of papers to achieve the success it did. From one
to another the copies so multiplied that today there are surely more than
three hundred in Mexico and beyond" (936–37). This deliberately cultivated confusion between reality and fiction, exacerbated by the metafictional Lizardi's investment in the future of the *cuadernos*—to be turned into
a book such as the one that consumers in 1831 might have held within their
hands—facilitates the material merging of that creation with the consumers'
lives, thus increasing its influence within their realities. This casual progression from the interior space of the novel to the exterior space of the consumers' everyday life grants that "hypnotic confirmation of the solidity of
a single community embracing characters, author and interlocutors, moving ever forward through calendrical time" of which Anderson speaks.[42]
The three nested prologues of the serialized *El Periquillo* ensure—as they
bounce between a fictionalized author and his literary fabrication—that fiction seeps quietly and continuously into consumers' realities, inspiring the
confidence of community in anonymity that for Anderson is a hallmark of
the modern nation. Serial publication, along with the measurable, predictable reading habits it fostered, is the perfect embodiment of a literary practice that fostered this new mentality, or community, in its public.

    The need to create the narrative continuity that characterizes a family
from generation to generation is mirrored and reinforced by connected
episodes among a family of contemporaries with whom the consumer has
become intimate—a community linked through temporal coincidence. By
establishing temporal and causal links between the Mangy Parrot's bad
decisions in the recent past and his endangered present, it becomes possible to predict and even change the future in a way that will best benefit his
"family," in the march toward "progress" that Walter Benjamin describes as
"homogenous, empty time." In Benjamin's critique, this shift in temporality is a product of capitalistic society, governed by clock and calendar, with
time advancing in equal, measurable, and even predictable units toward an
ever-perfectible future.[43] (Benjamin saw such progress as risible, writing in
1940 from the perspective of a Jewish refugee living through the horrors of
World War II, and longed for a return to the prophetic promise of messianic

time—a vertically structured "simultaneity-along-time" that imagined the past and future coexisting in a single rapturous moment.)[44] Though Anderson adopts Benjamin's terminology, he is more keen to establish the origins of "homogenous empty time" at the beginning of the nineteenth century (to comprehend one of the conceptual shifts that made the nation-state possible) than to judge the later outcomes of its emergence.[45] Lizardi's urgent concern, on the other hand, was most visibly the historicization of the present—a "now" that makes the best use of the past and is pregnant with future possibility. It was this specific and explicit linking of Mexico's present moment with a palpable future that produced such immense reader association with the author and his narrative voice. That voice imbues the present moment with a sense of the ripeness that is passed on to El Periquillo's "children": it is only in the present-time of his narrative that El Periquillo's children are capable of change, and only in this recognition is there any hope for their future.

At the end of the century, an anonymous writer calling himself "a disciple of the Mexican Thinker" offered a reformist novel in installments, entitled *Perucho, Grandson of Periquillo* (1895–1896), in a Mexico City newspaper.[46] That publication is but one proof of the intergenerational vitality of *El Periquillo* that Lizardi had aimed for in the careful bequests of the prologues: Periquillo's grandchildren were speaking, showing the influence of his story on the Mexican imagination almost one hundred years after its initial publication. It is precisely through the overlooked serialization of this novel—its creation of a community through the ritual of biweekly reading, its drawing on already extant print media structures to reach the broadest possible readership, and its reinforcement of the calendrical clocking of homogenous empty time—that El Periquillo's final wishes come true: his interlocutors were made into Mexicans, his descendants into reformists. Serialization is one of the key reasons that we continue to read *El Periquillo* as Mexico's first national novel, through successive generations, up to the present moment and into the foreseeable time and space beyond.

Audience investment has kept *El Periquillo* in print since its initial publication, during which time a volume came to be valued at two to three times its original price.[47] *El Periquillo* appeared in a new edition almost every decade until the end of the nineteenth century; in addition to those mentioned earlier, (1825, 1830–1831, and 1842, with two printings of the fourth edition), there were versions produced in 1865, 1884, 1896, and 1897.[48] It has proliferated through sequels and rewrites, almanacs, calendars, lithographs, and stamps. In the twentieth century, El Periquillo's story has been retold through *radionovelas*, *telenovelas*, and comics; in the twenty-first, it

FIGURE 1.5. Front cover of the "Joyas de la Literatura" series from 1987, *El Periquillo Sarniento*. This late 1980s comic book serial offered yet another colorful (if lurid) take on Lizardi's classic. Image courtesy of Christopher Conway.

has been discussed on blogs and social media, such as the *Periquillos del XXI* (Mangy Parrots of the 21st Century) Facebook fanpage.[49] This narrative planted the early seeds of Mexican transmediality, and Lizardi's success with the serial format provided a template for future Mexican novelists.

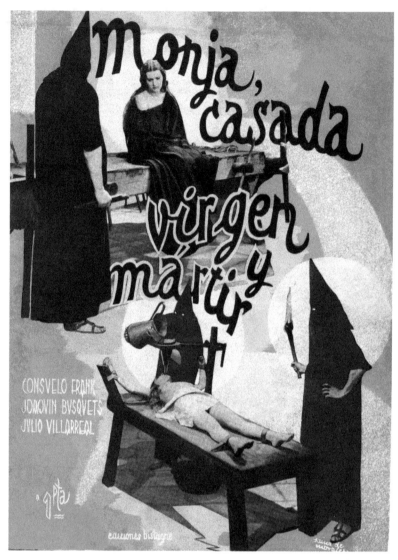

FIGURE 2.1. Book cover from the 1935 edition of *Monja y casada, vírgen y mártir* (Ediciones Bistagne, Spain). This sensational cover design was taken directly from stills of Bustillo Oro's movie and lists the names of the movie stars who appeared in starring roles. Beginning during the silent film era of the twenties, various Spanish editorial houses like Bistagne published illustrated "narrations" of recent movies, some up to seventy-two pages long. Image courtesy of the Agrasánchez Film Archive.

CHAPTER 2

Back to the Future

Mexico as Serial Hero in Riva Palacio's Historical Novels (1868–1872)

In Latin America the *folletín* is the melodramatic universe that allows the *pueblo* to make sense of its history. **Carlos Monsiváis**

Riva Palacio more than meets the primordial duty of a storyteller: to engage and never bore his readers. Once you start to read *Martín Garatuza* you won't put the novel down until its end, and with the start of every new chapter you will be asking the same essential questions: "And what now?" "What happens next?
José Emilio Pacheco

In his 1984 memoir, Golden Age Mexican filmmaker Juan Bustillo Oro remembers how he had decided a half-century earlier to draw on Vicente Riva Palacio's *Monja y casada, vírgen y mártir* for the movie that would make his career. Searching through popular novels to find something with broad appeal, Bustillo Oro came across two phrases—*married nun, martyred virgin*—that proved just as intriguing to audiences in the twentieth century as they had been in the nineteenth. Bustillo Oro recalls a friend's response upon hearing the title: "Damn! This sounds like a real blockbuster!" In 1934, the novel continued to be read —most recently in its mid-1920s re-edition by Mexico City publisher León Sánchez— and Bustillo Oro was attracted to its hold on the Mexican public. *Monja y casada, vírgen y mártir* the movie (1935) was a hit.[1]

Here we will explore the many reasons that a six-hundred-page historical novel and its sequel, both written in 1868 and set in the seventeenth century, retained the public's interest throughout the twentieth century, attracting numerous adaptations and reworkings. Most of these reasons have to do with *Monja*'s part in the serialization of the *pueblo*'s (hi)story as orchestrated by its author.[2] Riva Palacio's vision across multiple works—some

FIGURE 2.2. Movie still from *Monja y casada, vírgen y mártir* (Juan Bustillo Oro, 1935). Consuelo Frank's expression of suffering features prominently in this still, which inspired Bistagne's cover (fig. 2.1), showing Blanca's oppression at the hands of multiple Inquisitors. Image courtesy of Mediateca, Instituto Nacional de Antropología e Historia, Mexico City.

novels, some histories, all published in installments—positioned the *pueblo* as a protagonist in an ongoing story, told using cause and effect on a linear timeline moving from past toward future. As discussed in Chapter 1, these are the hallmarks of a modern nation brought about by novel and newspaper—an audience that has shifted from a vertical to a horizontal sense of time and community. Serialization was the impetus that put history, novel, newspaper, and the *pueblo* on the same page, for readers and listeners alike (referred to as "consumers" going forward).

Serialization is intimately related to proliferation: of characters, of storylines, of spin-offs, of consumers. In the year of its publication, *Monja* generated its own sequel, *Martín Garatuza*, based on a character of the same name whose adventures tie the two novels together.[3] *Martín Garatuza* became the most adapted novel of its time; in a twentieth-century assessment by José Emilio Pacheco, "The highest praise for Riva Palacio is that—even after all the movie series, comics, radio dramas, photo-novels, and soap operas—we still follow his plots with the same intense interest as those first readers in 1868 must have experienced."[4]

If culture is a realm of repetition and variation, the particular dance of repetition and variation that emerges from narrative serialization

FIGURE 2.3. Inside cover and page 3 of *Martín Garatuza* (Novedades Editores, series "Novelas Inmortales"), June 14, 1989, illustrated by Humberto Sandoval. An ad for the serial "Spidey" shares the opening page of *Martín Garatuza* in this comic version from the 1980s. Image from the author's personal collection.

FIGURE 2.4. Pages 4 and 5 of *Martín Garatuza* (Novedades Editores, series "Novelas Inmortales"), 1989. Don Leonel arrives at the ancestral home of his childhood sweetheart. A few pages later matriarch Doña Juana poignantly quips, in words taken directly from the novel (Riva Palacio, *Martín Garatuza*, 1:57): "What does our family's future look like? Don Leonel, have you ever thought about this?" Image from the author's personal collection.

guarantees consumers' engagement. Riva Palacio's primordial objective with *Monja* and *Garatuza* was to invite the Mexican public to engage with one of the darkest moments of national history, the Colony, which he would innovatively depict as the fertile seedbed of the rich culture of modern Mexico. Serialization was the perfect form for teaching the *pueblo* to look at the past with new eyes, through the lens of the present, and rewrite it into an ascendant future, re-envisioning itself as the protagonist in its own never-ending story. The serial novel was essential to Riva Palacio's ideological project.

From the vantage point of Riva Palacio's generation, there was indeed a sense that Mexico was starting anew: the country had emerged victorious in 1867 from what he and his liberal cohort called its Second War of Independence, or the Second French Intervention.[5] The Conservative party was so discredited by its losing alliance with foreign invaders that it became temporarily defunct, leaving the Liberal party to govern unchallenged during the first years (1867–1871) of the restored republic, part of a period known as the Restoration. Yet, even as the country seemed to finally be joining the brotherhood of "civilized" nations, Mexico remained vexed by a difficult colonial past. How to understand its conquest by Spaniards and three centuries of subjugation as part of a path toward progress? How to cast Mexico's colonial origin story—the betrayal of its people, the rape of its women—in a positive light? How to make sense of the long bloody fight for Independence, and the thirty-some years of internecine conflicts—the decades of chaotic infighting—that ensued?

Vicente Riva Palacio was well poised to frame generative answers to these questions, as the well-known grandson of one of Mexico's most popular founding fathers, Vicente Guerrero, who was of humble origin and Afro-Mexican descent.[6] The now-prominent Riva Palacio family came not from the old nobility of New Spain, but from a new Mexican meritocracy being established throughout the nineteenth century. In the period leading up to the Intervention, young Riva Palacio had demonstrated great ability in government and jurisprudence, as well as writerly aspirations.[7] During the liberal *Reforma* period (1861–1867), he had become one of Mexico's most popular and prolific playwrights, co-authoring some fifteen patriotic dramas from 1861 to 1862. Featuring characters and customs from oral tradition, the plays employed vernacular speech in sketches, zarzuelas, *letrillas*, and other forms, satirizing Mexican society's most conservative sectors in an audiovisual genre that did not require literacy.[8]

Riva had also become involved with a new periodical that is now regarded as one of the most impressive satirical publications of the nineteenth century.

During the *Reforma* Riva wrote theater reviews for and published at least one of his dramas in *La Orquesta: Periódico Omniscio, de Buen Humor y con Caricaturas* (1861–1877), a four-page biweekly founded by Carlos R. Casarín and Manuel C. de Villegas (owners) and Constantino Escalante and Hesiquio Iriarte (illustrators), a fraternally progressive cadre united by its dedication to oppositional politics. *La Orquesta's* principal cover image was of a collection of different instruments playing *ensemble*, with the motto "We intend to write for all audiences," an appropriate motto given the paper's broad-based appeal. It dedicated two pages in each issue to editorials, current events, and announcements; one page to political caricatures; and one page to literature. In these four short pages, *La Orquesta* combined copious visuals with verbal satire to encourage free thought and societal critique. The caricature page was distinctly Mexican, drawing from images, proverbs, refrains, and songs that helped the *pueblo* access and engage with its content, which questioned certain Liberal reforms and exposed contradictions in the ruling group's interests.[9] The paper also made a point of promoting national verses, *folletines*, and other popular literature, with contributions by Guillermo Prieto (1818–1897), Francisco Zarco (1829–1869), and Florencio María del Castillo (1828–1863), as well as short serials by the editors themselves, alongside translated works by French authors such as George Sand.[10]

In March 1861, when *La Orquesta's* inaugural issue was printed, President Benito Juárez had authorized Riva Palacio to take possession of the Mexican archbishop's papers on the Inquisition, considered one of the most important and complete archives of its kind—and, at the time, a veritable arsenal with which to discredit conservatives and the clergy.[11] Congress had recently commissioned Riva Palacio and author Pantaleón Tovar (1828–1875) to publish *causes célèbres* from the collection in contemporary newspapers.[12] Despite legal opposition from clergy, *El Monitor Republicano* had announced in a May 1861 prospectus that these documents would soon be published for the public good, citing "a certain avid and insatiable curiosity about the thousand details" that had not previously come to light.[13]

Later that year, however, Riva Palacio was instead requesting the government's permission to form a group to fight French invaders. Riva Palacio's name would become closely tied to the *chinacos*, *guerrilleros* whom he subsequently shepherded into battle through five years of resistance in the mountains of Michoacán.[14] He would be crowned as a champion of these corn growers, coffee sellers, workers, artisans, Indians, and *soldaderas* (female fighters)—referred to by some as the *populacho* or *canalla* (mob, lowlifes)—on his victorious return to Mexico City in 1867, by now widely known as Brigadier General Riva Palacio of the Central Army, following the successful siege of Querétaro and Emperor Maximilian's surrender.

What did elites such as General Riva Palacio mean when they evoked the *pueblo*, a word repeated frequently in Restoration rhetoric? The War of Intervention had mobilized the masses militarily. *Chinaco* forces were considered largely responsible for the Liberals' victory. How would the Liberals now form the *pueblo* as a body of citizens? With what tools?

Riva Palacio chose a bold move: the young hero turned down various immediate opportunities to continue his military career or to ascend in politics.[15] Instead he became editor of *La Orquesta*, which had survived the Intervention to remain one of the most popular periodicals in Mexico at that time.[16] Riva Palacio and other members of the Renacimiento saw journalism as an effective vehicle for moving past the bipartisan politics plaguing Mexico's progress, as well as reaching a broader audience—the *pueblo*—beyond the nation's capital. Riva's decision was ostentatiously published on the front page of *La Orquesta* on June 26, 1867, and he was invited by the Junta Patriótica to speak at a commemoration of the *Grito de Dolores*—the anniversary of Mexican Independence—on September 16.[17]

In his speech to a crowd gathered on the streets surrounding the Alameda, Riva Palacio first articulated a vision of the *pueblo* that would soon resound in his writings: the key to Mexico's future—its destiny as a great republic—is through understanding its complicated past. With the clairvoyance of a historian, he personified the *pueblo* as Prometheus or Christ, moving closer to its ultimate redemption and transfiguration through past trials—a suffering body for whom progress is an essential condition. Riva repeats the words *pueblo*, *progreso*, *camino* (journey), and *adelante* (forward), as well as the refrain of "ni un paso atrás" (not one step back), to emphasize this body's predestined journey toward freedom and civilization, deriving momentum from remembering shared sacrifices together at patriotic occasions such as this one. In his closing exhortation, Riva Palacio spoke of his pride in all that the *pueblo* has accomplished: "I, in your name, my chest swelled with that sacred and noble pride that each of you harbor, my memories rooted firmly in the past, my sight in the present and my faith in our future, would urge you all: 'Defend [our freedom], reestablish it, ensure it.'"[18]

With these words, Riva Palacio assumed his new role as a guide to the nation's origins in its long ascendant march to greater heights. The "second wave" of nineteenth-century liberals to which he belonged would be the first to take on the construction of the imaginary of the modern *pueblo* in Mexico, to present that body as an integrated and central actor, and to exalt and idealize its protagonism within national patriotic history.[19] According to Illades, Riva Palacio's generation was the first to place the nation's moral reserve in the *pueblo*.[20]

At the end of that same year, in December 1867, Riva Palacio began participating in the *veladas literarias* (literary *soirées*) initiated by his friend Ignacio Altamirano.[21] Both Riva Palacio and Altamirano had returned from the fighting with similar visions, which these gatherings were to promote: fostering literature and education during peaceful times, establishing a unified national culture to squelch divisive politics, and engaging and including the *pueblo* in Mexico's cultural identity, an ongoing struggle since Independence.[22] In their view, war and petty partisan politics had stunted Mexico's path toward civilization, with thirty years of near anarchy and fierce ideological polarization impeding progress for several generations.[23] Riva's position at the beginning of the Restoration was of amnesty and forgiveness between liberals and conservatives. In *Revistas Literarias* (1868–1869), itself a series of informal yet in-depth journalistic essays narrating the story of Mexico's literary past and current renaissance, Altamirano summarized the activities of a new generation of *literatos*, with him and Riva Palacio among its founding members.[24] He described the "nueva raza literaria" (new literary breed) as virile, disciplined, and indomitable—ready to serve as the young prophets of Mexican culture.[25] Altamirano was calling for cultural unity through literature, and General Riva Palacio answered by involving himself integrally in the construction of a common national patrimony through narrative. He hosted at least two of the eight impassioned literary summits, during which he read the first installments of a novel based his battle experiences during the French Intervention. The appropriately entitled *Calvario y tabor: Novela histórica y de costumbres* built on the trope from his 1867 speech about the *pueblo*'s heroic path from martyrdom (the road to Calvary) toward Christ-like transfiguration.[26]

Altamirano's real-time reflections in *Revistas Literarias* were already promoting historical novels as the best means of teaching history to the *pueblo*. For Altamirano, the educational opportunities of the genre seemed unparalleled: he saw the novel as a modern vehicle for sharing progressive ideas with the broadest possible audience, placing it "alongside journalism, educational freedom, the theater, and industrial advancements, railways, telegraphs, and steam engine," all "genius inventions meant to improvement our humanity and to bring the different social classes together through education and shared customs."[27] Prior to the invention of the printing press, the *pueblo* had oral traditions, but no sustained narratives: "Only the shortest stories could survive through oral circulation, and even those that scarcely remain in existence were the ones needed by wet nurses to entertain or lull children to sleep."[28] Social doctrine, formerly the exclusive property of lite-rati or intellectuals, could now be available to all through the engaging plot-lines of novels designed to be read aloud to the larger public: "As of today, the story of that great book of human experience is more open than ever before everyone's eyes, its knowledge not limited to one group of privileged men, because now adorned with the trappings of storytelling, the *pueblo* is made to learn its most beneficial lessons."[29]

Altamirano sees the historical novel in particular as nothing less than a new way of writing the *pueblo*'s history. He faces critics who say that the historical novel "distorts and corrupts the sources of truth" by arguing that this could be true of any historical writing, depending on its author's skill and integrity.[30] He suggests that novels produce an exchange of ideas between classes that have been historically isolated from one another, with the potential to integrate Mexican society through increased education of the masses: "Perhaps the novel is meant to open the way for lower classes so that they reach the heights of the privileged circle and better blend with it. Perhaps the novel is nothing more than the *pueblo*'s initiation into the mysteries of modern civilization, its gradual instruction and initiation into a priesthood of the future."[31] He declares that the now-curious *pueblo* is impatiently demanding novels about its past—"wanting to know what has happened in all spheres of the republic"—given its lack of coverage in offi-cial historical publications.[32] For Altamirano, the most important use of the new "philosophical history" is to "encourage the *pueblo*'s masses to orga-nize their memories and inquiries," offering sources where people can go "to look for a historic date, to find a famous person's profile, to confirm one of their recollections."[33] Enrique Anderson-Imbert and José Ortiz Monas-terio emphasize that the nineteenth-century historical novel, as promoted by Altamirano, offered a way of understanding the past as a decisive pro-cess following a predetermined path, allowing for a historicized vision of society.[34] The protagonist in Mexico's myth would become the *pueblo*, a word used by Altamirano in his *Revistas* no less than ninety times in three hundred pages.

Riva Palacio's generation held high Lizardi's model, recognizing his genius in the use of journalism and novels to teach the *pueblo*. Altamirano claims that no Mexican—of any social class—was unfamiliar with *El Periquillo Sar-niento*: "We can assure ourselves, without exaggerating, that there is not one single Mexican who does not know the *Periquillo*, if only because of our *pueblo*'s frequent allusions to it, because of the nicknames it made famous, and because of its stories that everyone still talks about." He emphasizes that

Lizardi accomplished this through his willingness to represent the *pueblo* through their language and their way of life, which formerly had been considered too low for literature but had since appeared in masterpieces by famous European novelists: "The reproach of its style, long expressed by shallow critics, vanishes when we see famed authors of the likes of Victor Hugo and Eugenio Süe, making their characters speak the slang of the lowest Paris commoners; and it is already known that *Los misterios de París* and *Los miserables* are works that take first place in our contemporary literature. Evidently this is, far from a defect, a quality, as it faithfully portrays our way of life."[35]

The Restoration would become a golden age for both novels and journalism. With uncensored possibilities for the press, Mexican journalism would rise to an apex in terms of stability and distribution, fettered only by high publication costs and illiteracy rates.[36] The majority of novels published during the Restoration's Renacimiento were certainly consumed through newspaper installments. Novels published via newspapers continued to break down barriers separating the written word from the general population, and also "broke through the Renaissance divide between the 'discreet reader' and the 'vulgar masses.'"[37] Serial novels were found to be instrumental in promoting literacy, opening access to a broader audience through widened distribution, and stimulating regular collective reading habits and discussion.[38] Their episodic format encouraged group consumption, an activity inciting commentary and impassioned debate, which supported the democratizing and inclusive principles of Mexican liberalism.[39] Riva Palacio's highly dialogued novels would in fact be designed for new readers, the semiliterate, and even the illiterate, who might hear the novel read out loud by others.[40] In Mexico City, public readings were announced not only in newspapers but also guesthouses, coffee shops, and bookstores, while in the provinces folks would gather in the back rooms (*trastiendas*) of a business to hear the news read as the papers arrived by train.[41] Popular reading was a collective act that went beyond readers to include listeners in the discussion and debate. It is no coincidence that Vicente Riva Palacio's most intense period of journalistic activity (1867–1876) dovetailed with his most intense period of novelistic activity (1868–1872), when he wrote seven historical novels. Between 1867 and 1869, he wrote five of those seven.

Calvario y tabor, the historical novel Riva Palacio had begun to share during the *veladas literarias*, was a resounding popular success. Altamirano, in his prologue to the first installment (April 13, 1868), had exhorted the *pueblo* to consume the novel as the story of its own soul, in whose pages its sons could read the history of their sacrifices.[42] Altamirano had also encouraged the *pueblo*'s internalization and propagation of this "family narrative" through reading and reciting "scattered sheets that spoke of pain through fiery tears" to future generations "in the quiet hours of the night, seated by the fire, reading aloud to dearly beloved children . . . telling them that this is not a fable invented to entertain their idle moments, but rather, that it is the truth."[43] Judging from a letter sent to Riva Palacio from a Guadalajara reader, *Calvario y tabor* was indeed being read in collective settings per Altamirano's exhortations: "Given my scarcity of resources, I live with a family in which there are children ranging from ages 9 to 12; well there I was, pleased to see them sitting in a circle, attentively listening and moved by the eldest brother's reading, because with charming simplicity you have known how to touch the most delicate fibers of the heart by writing your novel within reach of all minds." Not only had this reader witnessed children reading *Calvario y tabor* aloud to one another, he relates how he himself had read the story to others, and how it had moved him immeasurably to do so: "In the course of this novel, while reading it aloud at night to a person who listened initially with mere indifference, I still felt that tears were coming in my own eyes and I would have to stop reading in order to wipe them away with a handkerchief."[44]

La Orquesta describes how the first edition's six thousand copies were snatched up, and a second print run undertaken immediately.[45] As the twentieth and final episode of *Calvario* went into circulation, Altamirano attested to the novel's resounding success: "It was natural that the work of such a well-known and beloved man of the *pueblo* should be received with applause. The subscriptions were numerous."[46] A month before *Calvario*'s conclusion was published (on July 8, 1868), *La Orquesta* published a prospectus for Riva's second historical novel, *Monja y casada, vírgen y mártir*; Altamirano reported that the public was "running to subscribe" to this new novel foregrounding Mexican history."[47] The serialization of *Monja* began on June 10, and *La Orquesta* soon announced on July 23 that its first installments had been reprinted due to demand; in an advertising note, the paper compared the public's interest surrounding the novel to that of the publication of Mexico's famed 1857 Constitution.[48] As before, *La Orquesta* announced the imminent arrival of *Monja*'s sequel, *Martín Garatuza*, before the end of *Monja*, "so favorably received by the public."[49] *Martín Garatuza* would engage the public for four months, concluding its twenty installments on January 30, 1869.

The seven illustrated historical novels that Riva Palacio undertook between 1868 and 1872, one after another at a feverish pace, used the same successful format and distribution template. *Calvario* and *Monja* were adorned with lithographs by *La Orquesta*'s Escalante.[50] After the artist's untimely death, *La Orquesta*'s Santiago Hernández and Hesiquio Iriarte illustrated the remainder of Riva Palacio's novels (*Martín Garatuza*, 1868; *Piratas del golfo*, 1869; and *Memorias de un impostor: D. Guillén de Lampart, rey de México*, 1872), as well as other works, such as *El libro rojo* (1869) and *Los ceros* (1872). Visuality, including engraved illustrations of the most crucial scenes, supported multiple ways of accessing a story. The priority Riva placed on illustrations built on Lizardi's template to establish deeper associations between serial narratives and the images that accompanied them.

La Orquesta had the resources to standardize the publication and delivery of Riva's histories *por entregas*, having established since 1861 a reliable system of distribution in the capital as well as the provinces, and proven its resilience through surviving the Intervention.[51] Each novel was first advertised in the newspaper, and then sent to subscribers directly from the printing press of owner Manuel C. de Villegas, who would receive praise within the paper for his timely and formal distribution of the novel: "He distributes installments with a punctuality to which our public is unaccustomed."[52] A single installment of thirty-two quarter-folio pages, with quality printing on good paper, was priced at one real in Mexico City and one and a half *reales* in the provinces, postage prepaid. Each novel consisted of twenty weekly installments, with a guaranteed conclusion. *La Orquesta* also distributed flyers on street corners and sent installments to rival papers as they appeared, as a form of additional publicity.[53]

This steady publishing scheme made Riva Palacio one of Mexico's first "professional" and certainly most prolific serial novelists, providing an ongoing (and sometimes repetitive) history lesson for an ever-expanding audience who consumed his novels from 1868 to 1872. If characterized by some as frivolously fun reading, Riva Palacio's project was highly intentional and labor intensive on the part of the author, taken on at a key time and requiring a profound investment: Riva Palacio wrote three of his seven novels in 1868 alone, totaling some 4,800 pages produced in one year.[54] Given their quick succession upon cessation of his military duties, it is likely that Riva Palacio wrote all three on the fly, penning weekly chapters while simultaneously serving as a supreme court minister and *La Orquesta*'s editor, doggedly following the distribution schedule that he had promised to his followers.[55]

One distinct factor likely influenced his personal dedication to writing historical novels on a deadline and would eventually transform Riva Palacio from novelist into historian: privileged access to Mexico's infamous colonial Inquisition archive.[56] Since 1861, Riva Palacio had received requests to return the archive, including from the director of the Archivo General de la Nación.[57] Yet Riva seems to have kept its papers under lock and key in his home for as long as possible.[58] Though he turned over the majority of its contents in 1869, Riva Palacio held onto some parts until his death.[59] These papers contained the true stories that he would soon novelize, such as the trials of the Thirty-Three Slaves or the Carbajal Family, both of which would serve as significant intertexts in the *Monja-Garatuza* series.

Historia de los tiempos de la Inquisición and *Memorias de la Inquisición*, the respective subtitles of the wildly popular *Monja y casada, vírgen y mártir* and *Martín Garatuza*, both sensationalize their author's exposé of the colonial Inquisition. The two historical novels were set in Mexico City during the colonial period. Both examine a crucial aspect of the lead-up to the War of Independence: popular rebellions taken up against the viceroys in 1612 and 1624. The prospectus for each novel advertised plots taken directly from the Inquisition archives, promising that Riva Palacio would divulge the deepest, darkest secrets of the colonial Inquisition to the public, and advertising his access to historical truths via documents from the controversial archive.

Such claims provoked the ire of prominent clergy, such as the Jesuit father Mariano Dávila, who took umbrage with Riva Palacio's representations of the Spanish colony and its institutions.[60] Dávila's efforts in 1869 to defend the Inquisition give a sense of its continued cultural strength—it had been fully abolished only as recently as 1827—as well as the threat posed to conservative sectors by the popularity of Riva Palacio's historical novels. The novelist's known possession of the archives granted him the authority to write history through fiction—a point not lost on critics such as Dávila, who complained in 1869 that Riva Palacio's public "would swear but on the word of the storytellers, believing with a clenched fist all they were told by them, and more so when novelists claimed to avail themselves of nothing more than the historical facts."[61] The priest famously burned copies of *Monja* and wrote thirty-one extensive articles against it, furious with the public's reception of the novel as historical truth. *La Orquesta* both published and refuted these attacks, using them as publicity. The newspaper's tactics included humoristic verses that made light of Dávila's efforts to discredit Riva Palacio and jocular threats to cancel the clergyman's subscription.[62] The novelist himself responded directly to Dávila from the pages of *La Orquesta*, calling the Jesuit's response "an attack on all of our modern institutions" and alluding to future non-fiction books "that will contain irrefutable data of historical truth, as referred to in this novel."[63] Like Lizardi, Riva Palacio would begin his most controversial truth-telling through the

FIGURE 2.5. Lithograph from the first edition of *Monja y casada, vírgen y mártir* (1868), entitled "A trial in the court of the Inquisition." Constantino Escalante was responsible for the beautifully evocative images in this first edition, an inspiration for subsequent scenes in Bustillo Oro's movie. Image courtesy of Benson Special Collections, UT-Austin.

fictional medium of the novel, and then move to "less fictional" genres such as history. His access to the archive granted Riva a perceived authority and omniscience about Mexico's past that neither Father Dávila nor anyone else in Mexican society could claim. These two novels made the Archive public for the first time—and, as Juárez had hoped, effectively scandalized (and discredited) Mexican society's most conservative sectors.

Riva Palacio's serialization of the Inquisition archive in *Monja* and *Garatuza* transformed the deep past history of Mexico's colonial period into an engagingly accessible origin story, with the *pueblo* featured as the protagonist throughout. In a trope repeated in his speeches, historical writings, and novels alike, Riva portrays Mexico as a chosen nation, predestined for greatness, not in spite of but because of the many setbacks it had faced. In his view, part of the exceptionality of the Mexican *pueblo* was its capacity for martyrdom and transformative suffering, similar to that of the representations of the Jewish Carbajal family from within *Garatuza*. The linear, episodic publication of *Monja* and *Garatuza* mirrored the *pueblo's* slow, seemingly ineluctable march from painful past through palatable present toward promising future. The very idea of the *pueblo's* progress along that ascendant, linear timeline was embodied in historical novels' serial publication, either *in* newspapers or *like* newspapers (reflected in Riva's historiographical writings from this period as well). This story would be delivered directly to the *pueblo* in a form that deployed literature, history, and journalism in nearly equal parts, in the model of Lizardi, as advocated by Altamirano.

In his prologue to *Monja*, Monsiváis declared Riva Palacio's novels, read today in book form, to be practically impossible to summarize (xi).[64] But in their first appearance, as installments, these incredibly complex plots were broken down into successive bits that were not only digestible but desirable, tantalizing readers through compelling cliffhangers. Serialization turned the colonial period—a potentially grim and defeat-filled time in Mexican history (even within contemporary liberal ideology)—into a familiar storyworld, the knowable universe of Mexico, which served a space of great intrigue for consumers. Now offered a place for themselves and their own lives within the narrative, interlocutors became engaged in the storylines' immersive, metafictional qualities. The seventeenth century is presented as the start of the *mestizaje* (racial mixing) that had created the Mexican people and would now redeem them.[65] This was an innovative vision, based on a timeline that began not with the brightness of Independence but the darkness of the Colony, in a period of gestation lasting three long centuries (1521 to 1821), with an independent republic emerging as the unavoidable and predetermined destiny of the Mexican pueblo.

The central story of *Monja* is that of Doña Blanca, a sixteen-year-old *criolla* exploited by her Spanish-born brother don Pedro de Mejía, who tries to confiscate her inheritance by forcing her into a convent. The vulnerable Blanca's greatest ally is a freed slave, Teodoro, who protects her from the Inquisition and saves her life on more than one occasion.[66] Teodoro's best friend is Martín Garatuza, a *pícaro* with surprising connections across the highest and lowest echelons of colonial society, mixing his involvement equally between high and low characters, from the Indigenous witch La Sarmiento, to the all-powerful archbishop. Martín, Teo, and their band of merry rogues support the archbishop in a continuous power struggle with the viceroy, who is backed by a group of greedy Spanish noblemen (such as Blanca's brother). *Garatuza* begins in the same year that *Monja* ends, in spin-off style, opening with a new family melodrama involving the *criollo* sons of a hypocritical Spaniard who married a *criolla* but looks down on his offspring:[67] Father Alfonso de Salazar is involved in a *criollo* plot to take over the government, while his brother don Leonel has just returned from Spain, where he had been sent by his father to serve in the military. Upon his arrival, he visits a distant cousin, Doña Esperanza de Salazar, whom he loved as a child but whose mother, Doña Juana de Salazar, forbids him from marrying unless the *criollo* uprising succeeds. We soon discover that Doña Juana is herself deeply involved in this conspiracy to promote *criollo*

LA CONJURACION.

FIGURE 2.6. Lithograph from the first edition of *Martín Garatuza* (1868), "The conspiracy." After Escalante's untimely death following *Monja y casada*'s publication, *Orquesta* colleague Santiago Hernández took up the illustrations for its sequel, *Martín Garatuza*, in a similar style. Image courtesy of Benson Special Collections, UT-Austin.

dignity (1:34), involving "men from all classes" (1:27) who aspire to "the call for freedom, to raise again the throne of Guatizmotzin and Moctezuma Ilhuicamina . . . to free Tenochtitlán, and the ancient empire of the Aztecs" (1:30). Juana's deceased mother and two aunts are the (in)famous Carbajal sisters, accused by the Spaniards as *judaizantes* (those who were sympathetic to Jewish religious practices, adopted those practices, or influenced others to do so) and burned alive at the stake in 1575 (1:194); these women serve as the emblematic martyrs of the Salazar-led rebellion. Don Leonel soon becomes acquainted with the versatile Martín Garatuza, now undercover for the conspiracy as a servant in the new viceroy's household. When the Carbajals' ancestral home burns to the ground, killing Doña Juana and her grandfather Don Felipe—and fulfilling the family's curse through their immolation—Martín saves the life of the last remaining member of their family, the now orphaned Esperanza, ensuring that she will rightly inherit the fortune of her villainous father, Don Pedro de Mejía (a villain recycled from *Monja*). While Pedro lies dying, Martín enters Mejía's home in his favorite of many disguises, as priest, to convince the villain to bequeath his fortune to Esperanza. As the novel barrels vertiginously toward its open-ended close, Martín and Teo exact complete vengeance on the enemies of first Blanca and now Esperanza. After justice has been served, the remaining bad guys flee to Spain, while Martín temporarily leaves the city to find some fresh tricks for his sleeve.

Quintessential Mexican *pícaro* Martín Garatuza is the clear protagonist of this series, in which he evolves into a leader, or father figure, to the *pueblo*.[68] Martín de Villavicencio y Salazar had existed in real life, so the serialization of his ongoing escapades gives coherency to *Monja* and *Garatuza*'s sprawling plots, as well as aiding their metafictional blur between history and fiction, novel and real life. He was a Houdini and master of disguises, as beloved by the people—a shining example of *ingenio criollo* (creole ingenuity)—as he was hated by the authorities. His presence in popular language and culture of the nineteenth century, propagated through oral legend in refrains and verbs, was legendary. Julio Jiménez Rueda attributes his nickname of "Garatuza" to a Mexicanized verb: "'Engatuzar' has evolved in our creole language into 'en*garatuzar*.'"[69] He also recognizes the *pícaro*'s trickeries as the origins of a popular Mexican refrain "¿En qué pararán estas misas, Martín?," roughly translatable to "How will this all turn out, Martín?"[70] In 1842, *El Mosaico Mexicano* had offered a brief biography of Martín, sourced from a 1648 Inquisition edict (*auto de fe*), indicating his 1601 birth (Puebla) and then his reappearance in prison at age 47:

> The most famous [of the inmates] was Martin de Villavicencio, whom because of his tricks and cheats some called Martín Droga; others, for his evil, Martín Lutero; and everyone, for his cunning deceit, Martín Garatuza. Having stolen credentials from a priest, he took his name to exercise all the priestly rites, using this ruse to earn money. He was sentenced to two hundred lashes and five years in the galleys. He declared in his own confession that when he listened to the penitents, he gave the following absolution: May God protect us both. When he celebrated mass, it is commonly said that he started with the phrase: Martín, where will these masses lead us? How will this all turn out?[71]

An important dictionary (1853–1856) on the Mexican Republic also testifies to Martín's fame, in a lengthy entry under "Garatusa."[72] There he is described as "a good-natured scoundrel, wide-wandering and humorous, who traveled much of the Mexican Republic mocking justice with no shame . . . Never did he shed blood, nor use violence, but earned a living through his creativity paired with shrewdness. His name has now passed from father to son, and he remains proverbial among us."[73] The dictionary cites Martín

as a well-known figure, about whom the *pueblo* had been spinning elaborate yarns for some time:

> The voice of the public on its own provides news of countless entertaining
> escapades, in which a lot of soul and spirit can be seen; a mocking and cre-
> ative flair; a tireless capacity to shift roles, or gears, no matter how difficult;
> and the enormous insight required to get out of compromising and compli-
> cated predicaments; all of this is passed down through oral traditions, while
> the historical story of our most famous trickster is now reduced to an excerpt
> of his trial once published by the Inquisition.[74]

Another contemporary source, likely known and consulted by Riva Palacio
for his 1868 novels, was *Los conventos suprimidos en Méjico: Estudios biográficos, históricos y arqueológicos* (1861–1862), by Manuel Ramírez Aparicio.
There a lengthy dialogue indicates that Martín Garatuza was one of the
most famous victims of the Inquisition, in an account taken almost word
for word from the 1842 entry in *El Mosaico Mexicano*.[75] There are mentions within Riva Palacio's *Martín Garatuza* corroborating this protagonist's
growing fame over the centuries (1: 109, 257).

Riva Palacio's selection of Martín Garatuza as a rogue hero and father
stand-in for the Mexican *pueblo* was without doubt a strong nod to Lizardi's
pícaro Periquillo and that family history. Yet Riva Palacio's choice of this
colorful historical figure also increased the author's store of metafictional
ammunition, as he availed himself of a general porosity between history
and literature that was characteristic of the times, existing prior to the defining of separate disciplines.[76] Riva Palacio's provocative use of Martín de
Villavicencio y Salazar as a protagonist operating among the major historical figures of the Mexican colony (such as viceroys and archbishops) was
not just a ploy to uplift the common man. It was a stroke of verisimilitude,
unsettling for conservatives, that infuriated critics such as Father Dávila,
who watched helplessly as the Mexican public believed that all elements
in Riva Palacio's novels to be equally "true," invented characters alongside
historical figures.[77] The priest was appalled that an honorable archbishop
would be portrayed as "surrounded by the most lying and corrupt people
of the Republic," with a criminal such as Garatuza serving as his right-
hand man.[78]

Martín Garatuza and the omniscient narrator work together to bring
consumers into the mysterious colonial period. Similar to the rhetoric in
his 1867 speech, Riva Palacio wields an authoritative narrative voice to
construct a "we"—a *nosotros*—and a "them."[79] Through invocation and

inclusion of its interlocutors, that voice invites participation in an inclusive community, predicated on "our" history, "our" nation, and "our" identity. The author's known credentials strengthen interlocutors' relationship with that opinionated voice, as well as their suspension of disbelief and willingness to be carried along for a wild narrative ride. Though Martín never narrates the story in first person, the highly dialogued novel offers many theatrical asides in which he speaks aloud, revealing his inner thoughts, with help from an omniscient narrator that privileges Martín's thinking, assisting interlocutors to understand this unlikely hero's motivations.[80]

Martín's omniscience (in showing) and the narrator's omniscience (in telling) collaborate to create explicit comparisons of Mexico City's past politics, customs, and mores with those of the present. In the tradition of Lizardi, Riva Palacio offered the public a map-like specificity that allowed them to recognize the familiar spaces in which his stories were set.[81] Within this well-known urban topography, both authors placed their *pícaros* as witty and necessary *lazarillos* (guides) to a confounding colonial city, which Martín claims to know better than the inside of his own home (68). But Martín the *pícaro* is more than a guide to the colony. For families both inside and outside the book, his narrative journey is about coming home: coming to terms with dubious origins, the colonial beginnings of Mexico's identity. For the mid to late nineteenth-century consumers who "befriended" this character and followed the twists and turns of his journey, Martín was the perfect guide to Mexico's contested past. He, in his very essence, was like the *pueblo—multiforme* and *mestizo*, neither Indigenous, African, or Spanish. Martín uses this hybridity to gain access to all spaces and levels of society.

As a guide and eventual father figure, Martín Garatuza is also morally ambiguous. Though full of ambitious deeds, he is not a traditional hero. At times his relativism is so great as to belie virtue. More like a picaresque anti-hero, Martín depends on deceit to stay alive, wielding disguises and impersonations. His schemes are dosed with healthy irreverence toward authority, which he mocks. In some of his most successful ruses, Martín feigns illiteracy when he in fact "knew how to read perhaps better than the viceroy himself" (1:83).[82] He rubs shoulders with the lowest and the highest classes and serves either, as needed for his cause.[83] It is Martín's capacity for tight-lipped duplicity that grants him the secrets of persecutors as well as persecuted, and a rare level of omniscience (i.e., power) that ensures his survival. Tellingly, his combination of extremes—dark and light, poverty and literacy, high and low—allow for wide-ranging access and success. After all, what makes his tricks any different from the wily ways of the archbishop or viceroy, other than a difference in social status?

Martín Garatuza's eventual canonization through his eponymous novel as the *pueblo*'s hero seems to be a reversal of standard (European) characteristics. Unlike Sue, Dumas, or Soulié, with their clear-cut villains and heroes, Riva Palacio builds on this ambiguity to present a Mexican universe of surprisingly relative morality, where an absence of trustworthy authorities or institutions produces men and women who must look out for themselves. Within this universe, pure evil and pure virtue do exist, but Martín's astute gaze allows few to maintain their hypocritical façade.[84] All levels of society are laid bare and implicated in Mexico City's corruption, from the underworld outside the city limits to the highest echelons of colonial administration.

Riva Palacio adapted the traditional binary morality of the European *folletín* to speak to the cultural circumstances of his audience, encouraging reconciliation throughout society by dispensing with the righteousness of either side.[85] In the restored Republic, Riva Palacio had become a well-known promoter of tolerance toward past enemies, and therefore of reconciliation. This came at a time when Mexico's cultural landscape had been locked for decades between two parties deeply divided between black and white views of the world. *Garatuza*'s content is also inclusionary, representative of the diverse realities surrounding Mexicans in 1868, demonstrating the relativism (as opposed to binarism) that Riva Palacio wished to model politically. In his desire to present new approaches to the *mestizo pueblo*, Riva Palacio subverts the time-honored European code of civilization versus barbarism, in which the latter becomes a *sui generis* heroism, gutsily defiant, built on a different code that questions authority and honors resilience at all costs. This is a new code, embodied in the heretical heroism of Martín Garatuza, champion and incarnation of Mexican *mestizaje*.

The importance of the Carbajal and Salazar family trees and their direct lineage from Cuauhtemoc becomes a veritable obsession in *Martín Garatuza*: the novel concerns itself with ancestors, founders, and martyrs; origins, lineages, and physical genetic markers; inheritances, orphanhood, bastardy, and above all, hybridity.[86] The first half of the novel is entitled "Los Criollos"; the second, "Los descendientes de Guatimoc" (The Descendants of Cuauhtemoc). The solidarity and resilience of the *pueblo mestizo* lies at the crux of the myriad stories novelized in *Martín Garatuza*. Martín's family is diverse in race and class, opening the tale to a wider number of potential consumers who could see themselves reflected in the noble *criollos* suffering as mistreated martyrs for having been born in New Spain, a suffering capable of uniting them in rebellion, regardless of social class, as a proto-national community.[87]

The novel is at its essence a motley *mestizo* melodrama of a family that is rescued and reassembled through the agency of the seemingly orphaned *pícaro* Martín de Villavicencio y Salazar, of enigmatic roots, albeit with a surname that implies a maternal connection to the Salazar brothers.[88] Martín supports his own alternative family of *desheredados* (the disinherited), who are unhindered by tradition while sharing undervalued yet important values. Martín is cast as a friend of the *pueblo* who seeks not to get rich but to gather and protect his loyal tribe of family-friends, which includes poor courageous misfits as well as their wealthy protectors. Who falls under Martín's honorary and honorable protectorate? In addition to including and protecting victimized virginal damsels like Blanca de Mejía (1:147), Martín forms the family around his stalwart friend the now-freed slave Teodoro, as well as the eminently persecuted Carbajal family, represented in this novel as direct descendants of the last Aztec emperor, himself portrayed as Mexico's first patriotic hero (1:159). The survival of Cuauhtemoc's descendants rests on finding answers to the questions "Who are we? Where did we come from? How did we come to be as we are?" The answers to these questions lie within an intertext of *Martín Garatuza*, the family's *Memorias*, which Martín protects and interprets intradiegetically, mirroring Riva's extradiegetical relationship to the Inquisition archive.

This genealogical novel prioritizes the subaltern stories of its protagonist's "chosen" family. Martín's role within these novels as the interlocutor to subaltern voices within Mexican colonial society—as a knower of their landscape and speaker of their language—gives rise to various stories-within-the-story told directly in the voices of his band of alternative (super) heroes, namely Teo's tales of slave rebellions within the larger 1612 uprising of the *pueblo* and Doña Juana's story of *criollos* persecuted as *judaizantes*.[89] These two privileged intertexts were based on true stories from the colonial period, which Riva Palacio mined from the archive, and which comprise significant sections of the series; "El Libro de Doña Juana," for example, forms the entire second half of *Garatuza's* Part 1. Significantly, racial persecution and/or desire for inclusion are frequent themes within these embedded stories, written in the voice of the Other. The alternative perspective they offer on the canonical history of the colony reveals new and urgent truths to the *pueblo* about its identity. Upon receiving her memoirs, Leonel tells Doña Juana of his burning desire to know the stories of his real family, feeling a suspense that makes each instant seem like a year.[90]

In *Martín Garatuza*, the intertext goes back to the very beginning of *mestizaje* in 1521, when the nobly suffering, Christ-like Cuauhtemoc—last emperor of the Aztecs, father-to-be of the *mestizos,* and first Mexican patriot—is tortured by Cortés in the first *hoguera* (Inquisition bonfire) of the colony (1:158–59). The proud but compassionate *española* Isabel de Carbajal, daughter of one of Cortés's soldiers, falls in love with the disgraced emperor (1:159–65) and Felipe, the first *mestizo*, is the fruit of their wholesome love story. In Cuauhtemoc's voice, the narrative states that "the shadow of the eagle covered the dove and hope was born for my lineage and my people; a man of a new race, whose offspring will perhaps break his brothers' bonds, allowing my empire once again to be the one and only, Tenoxtitlán will be free . . . The decaying trunk will make room for a vigorous sapling . . . From my blood and your blood, Isabel, heroes will be born" (1:170).[91] Cuauhtemoc's great-granddaughter's retelling of the family's origins features an important twist to *mestizaje* reversing the traditional nobility of lineage, here belonging to the Indigenous side. Cuauhtemoc and Isabel's love story also softens the violence of the powerful male Spaniards' subjugation of vulnerable Indigenous women, in that Isabel chooses to love Cuauhtemoc of her own free will.

Felipe is the first to bear on his back the birthmark that will curse his family for generations: "The boy was beautiful and showed an extraordinary resemblance to the emperor, revealing nothing that would denounce the Spanish blood running through his veins. He had on his back, however, a red spot similar in the shape to the flame of a fire, of the sparks that a bonfire might give off" (1:171–72). It is presented as a corporal mark on a despised race—"Before the world our family carries a stain that nothing is capable of erasing" (1:14)—that Doña Juana describes as slaves (1:15). The flame-shaped birthmark plagues three daughters, the Carbajal sisters (Isabel, Violante, and Leonor) who suffer endlessly at the hands of the Spanish: raped, tortured, blackmailed, abused, they are finally denounced to the Inquisition as Jews and, in the consummate and tragic Baroque spectacle, burned at the stake (1:198–99). Their offspring are kidnapped and mistreated as well: Juana—born in the same year as the Inquisition, the fruit of her mother Isabel Carbajal's rape by a Spaniard—bears her daughter Esperanza after being raped by Spaniard Don Pedro de Mejía.[92] In addition to negatively marking these women for cyclical generational tragedies, the birthmark produces the novel's most powerfully positive moments of recognition (anagnorisis), as the dispersed family members are able to locate and identify one another by way of their common birthmark.[93]

These stories arrive to the interlocutor via the voice of the Carbajal family's matriarch Doña Juana, penned in first-person memories going back to her fifth year of life. The memoirs' title, *La marca del fuego, Memoria de Doña Juana de Carbajal*, highlights the flame-shaped birthmark,

LA LOCA.

FIGURE 2.7. Lithograph from the first edition of *Martín Garatuza* (1868) by Santiago Hernández, entitled "The madwoman." In this emblematic scene of anagnorisis, the afflicted Isabel and her long-abandoned son Felipe are able to recognize and protect each other from the surrounding crowd (1:182–84). Image courtesy of Benson Special Collections, UT-Austin.

emblematic of the Carbajals' ongoing suffering and as well as courage. In these memoirs, Juana reveals the Carbajals' truths, shedding light on the unjust reasons for the traumas inflicted on their ill-fated family (i.e., persecutors' duplicitous schemes, lust, abuse of power, and desire to get rich).[94] The story is meant to garner the empathy and understanding of those who hear this intertext, listeners both within the novel and outside of it, inspiring them to rebel against injustice.[95]

The formidable Juana, experiencing abandonment and discrimination as a *criolla*, does not give up, becoming living proof that "Patriotism often resides in the female chest" (the title of chapter 2, and a controversial concept in nineteenth-century Mexican society).[96] A scholar and the historian for her tribe, Juana will educate her daughter about their past: "I dedicated myself to that reading, and although it was a lot of work, I was able to find myself a good library, where I would spend the days and evenings confined, studying and endeavoring to cultivate your soul" (1:250). Her memoirs are in fact dedicated to and intended for that only daughter, whose name—Esperanza—signifies hope for the future nation.

The Carbajals' Indigenous-hued ancestral home—"La Casa Colorada [The Red House], as they would call it, for being built entirely of that stone, a kind of lava that comes from igneous foam, called *tezontle* in Mexico" (1:46)—houses a hidden museum-library belonging to the family, as well as its ancient grandfather, Don Felipe de Carbajal. But, like Juana's family, the house appears abandoned and sad (1:5), isolated from the rest of the world (1:13). There the family, as well as its book ("el libro de nuestra familia," 1:92), is protected under lock and key.[97] Martín inadvertently becomes the "keeper" of the family and its archive when the Inquisition threatens both.[98]

In another metafictional stroke, Martín's role vis-à-vis the *pueblo* and the archive within the novel mirrors that of Riva Palacio's in the real world. Martín's interception and protection of the manuscript can be compared to Riva's experience as the long-time keeper of the Inquisition Archive and the first to share its secrets. The interlocutor of Riva's novel reads the memoirs alongside Martín, beginning in the following manner:

> Then [Martín] approached the flame, took Don Leonel's little box, and pulled from inside a handwritten book, exquisitely bound. He began to flip through it; there were unusual letters and scriptures; he read one piece, and then another, at last exclaiming: "This is certainly a curious story that is well worth the work of reading it: I have time to do so before handing it back to its owner . . . Let's see, from the beginning now . . ." (1:155)

The highly literate Martín shows himself to be an excellent reader of the family memoirs, according to the various exclamations and interpretations (1:253) that reveal his engagement: "As for this book, I surely will not give it back" (1:254–55). He finds the book so absorbing that he decides to hold onto it as long as he can, even though he has promised Leonel that he will take it back to La Casa Colorada (1:142). In not doing so, he saves the archive from being destroyed in the flames that will eventually engulf that home and take the lives of Doña Juana and her father.

Like Riva Palacio, access to the archive gives Martín an omniscience over the family story, with a sense of agency and responsibility that we see in his metafictional commentaries to himself. Martín makes light of the book's increasingly difficult plot, which only he can understand, as the temporary keeper and interpreter of Juana's memoirs:

> And now that I have the hang of all this, the rascal Don Baltasar is the grand-father to Don Nuño's daughter, who is the new wife of Don Pedro de Mejía, who has married his niece and is now the father of Doña Esperanza, who is the girlfriend, it seems, of Don Leonel, himself the brother of Catalina de Armijo, who is hiding in Teodoro's house and who . . . Hail Immaculate

> Mary, what a tangled plot! May God protect us, to prevent fathers from marrying their daughters and brothers from marrying their sisters . . . and then, since I hold the secret of all of this, perhaps I can be dutiful in spirit. (1:328)

Finally, with Martín's help, the complicated events of the novel's second half translate into a victory for these underdogs, the formerly defeated descendants of Cuauhtemoc. Martín transforms into a swashbuckling superhero, opening wide his full bag of tricks on the way to victory: feigning illiteracy to his advantage; availing himself fully of his talent for disguise; resolving multiple conflicts simultaneously; morphing into a severe *justiciero*, adjudicating vigilante-style justice to a whole host of villains; watching over Esperanza at all times. Finally, it is Martín who shares Doña Juana's memoirs with Esperanza and Leonel before their marriage. This knowledge allows them to break the family curse and ensure the birth of future generations. Like Riva Palacio, Martín is responsible for the sharing of a manuscript with those who matter most: in his case, Esperanza and Leonel; in Riva's, the *pueblo*.

FIGURE 2.8. Pages 74 and 75 from *Martín Garatuza* (Novedades Editores, series "Novelas Inmortales"), 1989. Sandoval's illustration shows the importance of Doña Juana's retelling of the family story of the long-suffering Carbajals to her daughter Esperanza de Salazar. Image from the author's personal collection.

The significant intertext of Doña Juana's book details the matrimonial alliances between two families with a common oppressor. The tale contains a clear allegorical quality: the union of Esperanza and Leonel stands for the unification of *mestizos* across race and religion. While it is an oversimplification of the complex ethnic panorama of Mexico's colonial period, this revision of Mexico's origin story modulates the seemingly disparate and stratified identities of *criollo*, *mestizo*, Indigenous, and African in play since Mexico's colonization. Interestingly, the novel rarely uses the word *mestizo*.[99] *Criollo* means "mestizo" in the novel, a stand-in that substitutes allusions to miscegenation with a more historical term. The historical term *criollo* was understood over time to be a racial mix, but originally referred to someone born in the Americas, and at the very beginning a Spaniard born in the colonies. Here the *Memorias'* message addressed both past and present realities, serving as a contemporary call for union to nineteenth-century consumers. The double layer of interlocutors (colonial intradiegetic—Esperanza and Leonel—and nineteenth-century extradiegetic) melds into one, creating a metafictional effect for Riva Palacio's interlocutors upon participating in Juana's melodramatic revelation of the "true" origins of Mexico's *pueblo mestizo*.

Pueblo, on the other hand, is used frequently, usually in the context of revolts or in reference to its sons as patriots.[100] Martín becomes an unlikely father figure for this *pueblo*—a prototype of the superhero, complete with a superhero's league. This *pícaro* and his collective community of outcasts mirrors Riva Palacio's fellowship with the *chinacos* during the Intervention. Over the course of the series and its episodes, and through his contact with the written archive, Martín grows in heroism. The novel becomes an improvised bildungsroman in which the *pícaro* and his family serve as a simulacrum of the Mexican *pueblo*, and a realistic model for its hybridity and its progress. *Martín Garatuza* offers an important alternative mythology of how *mestizo* Mexico came into being, and the development of its most distinguishing and distinctive qualities.

Riva's serialization of family in *Monja* provided a recurring cast of characters for consumers to invest in and follow from installment to installment, with a host of new family members appearing in the sequel. The way these characters know each other and interact over the course of the *Monja-Garatuza* series creates an impression of a verifiable universe, particularly in *Monja*'s chapter 17, where the title observes that "even stones can meet while rolling along," and in which all the novel's characters come together, high and low, through their relationship with Martín. Garatuza's new audacities and the question of whether his makeshift family will survive provide

FIGURE 2.9. Lithograph from the first edition of *El libro rojo* (1870), whose startling illustrations were executed by Primitivo Miranda y Hesiquio Iriarte, entitled "Doña Isabel de Caravajal [*sic*]." Here we see yet another rendition of the vulnerable female facing her Inquisitors. Image courtesy of Benson Special Collections, UT-Austin.

suspenseful hooks that sustain the lengthy narrative. Doña Juana's *Memorias* add a new dimension to the narrative by offering the backstory of how various characters—heroes as well as villains—came to be as they are.

In Riva Palacio's hands, Mexico's origin story becomes a source of pride rather than ignominy—no small task in 1868.[101] Riva Palacio converts the traditional story of shame—the conquistadors' violation of concubines such as the emblematic Malinche—into the noble Aztec emperor Cuauhtemoc's selection of a Spanish woman as his one true love. This is one of the many tropes through which Riva Palacio novelizes (and subverts) the vexing ontological binary between Spanish and Indigenous that truncated Mexico's "family tree" through a negation of one (or both) of its principal roots. The author instead constructively affirms *mestizaje* and integration as generative processes. The main message from Riva's 1867 patriotic speech is echoed within the moral of the Carbajal *Memorias* and again through *El libro rojo*: Mexico's dark past must be revisited to gain perspective on the present and achieve a better future. This teleology of progress, with the *pueblo* as the protagonist of rebellions borne out through Independence, can be seen in Riva Palacio's nonfictional works as well as his historical novels.

El libro rojo: Hogueras, horcas, patíbulos, martirios, suicidos y sucesos lúgubres y extraños acaecidos en México durante sus guerras civiles y extranjeras, 1520–1867 was announced through *La Orquesta* and published by Villegas (1869–1871). This deluxe chronicle of civil violence and suffering in Mexico spanned from the events of the Spanish Conquest to the French Intervention. It was a vast, revolutionary serialized project, with contributions from three other major *folletinistas*: Manuel Payno, Juan A. Mateos, and Rafael Martínez de la Torre. Riva Palacio said that its blend of historiography and literature, which included Inquisition *causes célèbres*, was designed to refute allegations that with his novels he had taken too many liberties with the Inquisition archive.[102] Its plates, designed by *La Orquesta* lithographers Hesiquio Iriarte and Santiago Hernández (working from drawings by Primitivo Miranda), included images of plague, torture, and murder, depicting various political and religious martyrs from Mexico's early history. This serial was circulated to a smaller public than Riva Palacio's novels, yet was still profitable for Villegas, as consumers paid more for each installment.[103]

In *México a través de los siglos* (1884–1889), Riva Palacio insists once more that Mexico come to terms with its dark colonial past. *Martín Garatuza* is nothing less than a novelized prewrite of this historical tour de force in which Riva the historian describes the *mestizaje* of the colonial *pueblo*: "That class, already very numerous in society, neither Indigenous nor Spanish, needed to blend together and recognize itself as Mexican; it did not seek that family tree through sets of grandparents from both races, who would not recognize its grouping, but wanted to form its own place for itself in the world, setting an example, in turn, by not ignoring its origins."[104] In *Martín Garatuza* this process is already present in the novelist's exploration of the rise of a new race, seeing in their unrest and uprisings the signs of future Independence. As Riva Palacio turned to history instead of historical novels, he would reprise his representation of modern Mexico as "a society that, through great difficulties, embodies the evolutions that lead it to occupy its worthy position alongside the most enlightened *pueblos*" (Prospectus, *Historia general de México*).[105] As we can see from the title's translation into English, *Mexico through the Centuries* reiterates Riva Palacio's vision of Mexico's history and the role of the *pueblo* within it as "an evolutionary process whose path was to forge a desired national integration and fulfill 'unyielding laws of progress.'" Evolutionary themes dominate the five-volume story of how three hundred years of Spanish domination produced a new *pueblo* that could claim both the Aztec kings and Spanish captains as ancestors, generating a new entity with an entirely new level of protagonism.

The serialized history project *Mexico through the Centuries* would define Riva Palacio's intellectual career. Its installments were written by five different authors, under Riva Palacio's direction and vision. None was exclusively a historian: like the team members for *El libro rojo*, each collaborator was a polymath adept in two or more narrative genres, including journalism. The timeline for *Mexico through the Centuries* is set from 1521 to 1867 (beginning with Cortes's conquest of the Aztecs and ending with the most recent ouster of the French), and the narrative arc is one of suspense and ultimate ascendance—a climactic apotheosis structured very similarly to the denouement of a novel in which the protagonist is the Mexican *pueblo* and the Republic emerges triumphant. In *Mexico through the Centuries* Riva Palacio reestablishes the teleology of progress based on the *pueblo*'s protagonism that was so readily apparent in his use of the serial novel to tell Mexico's never-ending story.

While much has been written about this definitive work, less attention has been paid to the serial format in which it was published. Like Riva Palacio's novels, *Mexico through the Centuries* was serialized in installments (1884–1889).[106] Its title evokes the existence of nation as an entity whose enduring essence remains consistent over centuries, with a story that was impossible to tell in one sitting. Like Riva Palacio's novels, this serial was lavishly illustrated, its text accompanied by some two thousand magnificent images, to an extent never before seen in a history book. At least half of these were specifically commissioned by Riva Palacio and editor Santiago Ballescá for the occasion. Riva Palacio wanted Mexico's new history book to be saturated with images: "Colored prints, engravings, designs, manuscripts, all in abundance and each executed by the best artists using the best models; landscapes, city views, buildings, monuments, portraits, images of collections of weapons, of art objects, of fine art, of coin collections, of ancient hieroglyphs and inscriptions, all that was necessary for a perfect understanding of the text."[107] Attractive illustrations seduced innumerable consumers who would browse the pages in fascination.

Riva's authorial contribution, volume 2, is dedicated entirely to the colonial period and the Inquisition. Written from his prison cell,[108] it embodies the vision of history as process Riva had debuted in *Monja/Martín* with the *pueblo* described in evolutionary terms, as an embryo that contains all the necessary resources for its future development:

Such odd elements came together in the sixteenth century, forming the embryo of a nation that over the years was destined to become an independent Republic . . . A laborious and difficult evolution had to be consummated by that inchoate grouping of families, peoples, races, suddenly and haphazardly united by a violent social and political upheaval, left to be organized . . . in order to build a society in which a *pueblo* would emerge that was neither conquered nor conqueror, but which inherited virtues and vices, glories and traditions, characters and temperaments from both sides . . . identifying its best interests, turning a land of the formerly dispossessed into a Patria that would shape the national soul . . . a *pueblo* whose embryonic formation and development must be scrutinized in its three centuries under Spanish rule, during which, through the mysterious work of the chrysalis and multiple heterogeneous components, a unique socio-political entity, robust and potent, was formed, which would go on to proclaim its emancipation in 1810.[109]

Mexico through the Centuries was Riva's culminating intellectual and historiographical achievement, cementing for posterity Riva's reputation as a serious historian. Its importance is well established, lauded by Enrique Florescano as the first national history to deal thoroughly with each of the various periods of Mexico's past, and still read and referenced to this day.[110]

Like Lizardi, Riva Palacio started with serialized fiction as a more palatable and entertaining way to tell his historical truths. The *Monja-Garatuza* series presents the gradual and historical development of that "class" in addicting episodes, each a fragment of the grand narrative backdrop of the Mexican "we." As Juana explains to her future son-in-law Leonel, "That reading is long, requiring time and seclusion. I will not set a deadline for you to complete it, but do try to hurry; many have written in that book who are no longer here with us" (93).

This effect of slow, gradual world creation (and the consumer's corresponding desire to keep finding out more) was generated through the meting out of bits of narrative over time: most effectively, through the process of serialization.[111] Indeed, the density of a family story such as Mexico's—with its many twists and turns and cliffhangers—could be told only in serial format, emphasizing the cumulative nature of a nation under construction and its never-ending story. Sequels embody the to-be-continued nature of the nation, in continual evolution (and under occasional threat of suspension).

Beginning with the Porfiriato, and with increasing determination on the part of revolutionary intellectuals, the nation would be imagined in metaphorical terms as a *gran familia mexicana*, a body organically unified through a bloodline that required protection and development.[112] Closer

FIGURE 2.10. Pages 8 and 9 from *Martín Garatuza* (Novedades Editores, series "Novelas Inmortales"), 1989. The grand melodrama of this ongoing family narrative enthralled generations of Mexicans who consumed the various versions of *Martín Garatuza* that circulated decade after decade. Image from the author's personal collection.

to the century's end, Justo Sierra (1848–1912) would further develop the concept of the *gran familia mexicana* in relation to *mestizaje*—a national body made ever more homogeneous through biological mixture—in his 1889 essay, "México social y politico": "Given that the social phenomenon of the Mexican family's formation, derived from the races that have populated our country, has led to a nation, to peace, and to progress, our entire future rests in promoting the growth of that family, in activating that mixture, in creating a *pueblo*."[113]

Some twenty years later, on the eve of the Mexican Revolution, the Liberal Party would publish their agenda in their newspaper *Regeneración*, accompanied by Ricardo Flores Magón's "Exposición de motivos" (1906). Flores Magón favored a secularization of education that might "end the focus on divisions and hatred among Mexico's children" by "building on the most solid foundation, for the near future: the complete fraternity of *the great Mexican family*" (emphasis mine). Flores Magón conceived of this family as a serene and harmonious democracy, a "shared community of feelings and aspirations which is the soul of the most robust and advanced nations," consolidating the idea of the nation as an organic body made ever more homogeneous through education and union. The principal purpose of the revolutionary state would then be to protect and develop that family, in which all the hope of the new social pact created between the middle and lower classes would reside.

Riva Palacio's promise of unlocking a grand family narrative that could guide and unite Mexicans to a better future was the feature that made his historical novels immediately relevant in 1868 and beyond. The end of *Martín Garatuza* remains open-ended for this key reason—open for the next installment: by the next author, in the next century, in the next media. In true transmedial fashion, Riva Palacio's novels became movies and comic strips and ultimately, in the 1980s, found their way into a televised soap opera. *Continuará.*

FIGURE 3.1. *El Heraldo de México* (April 17, 1921), Sunday supplement. Don Catarino and company are chased by funhouse mirrors, in images that evoke his family's disorientation vis-à-vis urban entertainment. Image courtesy of Biblioteca Miguel Lerdo de Tejada, Mexico City.

CHAPTER 3

Family Education through Mexico's First Comic

Don Catarino y su apreciable familia
(1920s–1960s)

> The nation is not a comic, of course, but this nation's inhabitants, those who have come before, and those here now, certainly have the comic in their blood.
> **Carlos Monsiváis**

"Real Votes! No Boss-Rule! No Re-Election! Long Live Mexico!" This was the battle cry of Mexico's first national comic strip hero, Don Catarino Rodríguez Rápido, from the pages of *El Heraldo de México*.[1] The strip, *Don Catarino y su apreciable familia*, was not overtly political in its beginnings—making little or no direct remark on contemporary Mexican affairs—yet its rise, and temporary demise, were intimately tied to the issues embedded in Don Catarino's well-known slogan. Like the fun-house mirrors in which the *charro* and his family find themselves distorted in one of the strip's earliest episodes, *Don Catarino y su apreciable familia* exaggerated the strengths and weaknesses of the *gran familia mexicana* during a narrowing window of opportunity for the *pueblo*'s participation in that body.

El Heraldo de México's notable efforts in the early 1920s to create and sustain the first nationally produced comic strip interrupted a marked tendency to import US comic strips for weekend supplements. Veteran caricaturist Salvador Pruneda tells in his memoirs of an important gathering of the editorial staff, circa 1920, while he was serving as director of the Sunday supplement. US proofs had not been arriving in time to satisfy the Mexican public's demand for weekly comics, and *El Heraldo* hoped to replace imports with a strip exclusively dedicated to national characters and themes.

Comics had become popular and influential enough that this was deemed a worthwhile (though more expensive) undertaking.[2]

As the armed phase of Mexico's Revolution drew toward a close, there was a palpable need to design an identity appropriate for a "new" country with a long lineage of (often-opposing) forebears. State-promoted cultural nationalism was the order of the day. Movements such as the one headed by José Vasconcelos, as he ascended in 1921 to become the first secretary of public education, signaled that power was in hands of a new middle class. We can situate educational projects such as *Don Catarino y su apreciable familia* alongside governmentally sponsored murals from the same period, emanating from the private sector, that integrated the country's rich history with its potential future. Newspapers provided a space in which rural and urban, past and future, could be visually and narratively integrated through the modernizing force of journalism for an expanding readership, in preparation for the right to vote.

Journalism had begun to rebound well before fighting ceased, with newspaper founders and editorial teams eager to play a role in the restructuring of the nation. *El Heraldo de México*, from its first edition of 1919 (April), was a groundbreaking example, with strong claims to modernity and a rebellious leader: former general and potential presidential candidate Salvador Alvarado, who used the paper as a platform to discuss progressive ideas. By 1920 it had established a serious and well-articulated program for producing national comics, which served as the launching pad for the more clearly Mexican comics of that decade, boldly initiated with *Don Catarino*.

After its debut in *El Heraldo*, the story of Don Catarino and his family ran for thirty years, entering into an entire generation's Sunday routine and becoming a standard bearer for decades of Mexican family strips to follow.[3] Here we will focus on the foundational features of *Catarino* in its nascent iterations from 1921 to 1923: namely, its presentation of a reformed version of the *charro* as a spokesperson for Mexican modernity through a serialized educational undertaking.[4] Serialization allowed readers to conceive of themselves as part of a community being built on a linear progressive timeline—a timeline on which the national past could be effectively revised, and the national future could be productively imagined. Seriality spawned metafictional connections—alongside a sense of immediacy—often achieved through intermediality, which enhanced and encouraged readers' identification and participation with narrative. Because of built-in features such as routine, dosification, and sequencing (accumulation), seriality was an ideal medium for a long-term project such as *Don Catarino y su apreciable familia*: characters and storyline permeated readers' daily lives

FIGURE 3.2. Photomontage entitled "Caricaturist Salvador Pruneda with his creations," 1927. In this image we feel the proximity of the artist to the characters he created, appearing here as a father to Catarino and his family. Image courtesy of Museo del Estanquillo, Mexico City.

through frequency, repetition, and review, generating a long-running serial *familia* within which forward movement was conceivable.

Though *Don Catarino* was devoid of explicit references to crucial postrevolutionary political dynamics, it was hardly apolitical. To fashion a unique strip for *El Heraldo* featuring *mexicanidad*, journalist and satirical writer Carlos Fernández Benedicto revived a character he had brought into being as the Revolution began: provincial *charro* "Don Catarino Culantro."[5] Fernández Benedicto took on the colorful folk-style pseudonym "Hipólito Zendejas," while his former creation was now dubbed "Catarino Rodríguez Rápido." Pruneda was responsible for freshening up Catarino's look. Don Catarino retained, however, his trademark vernacular, as well as his colloquial call to arms from the 1911 presidential elections: "¡Sufragio eleitivo!

¡No re-elección! ¡Viva México!" It was a distinctive shout that was surely recognizable to readers a full decade later. This series of words had first been wielded by Francisco Madero to bring down Porfirio Díaz's dictatorship, and it now appeared on official government documents such as the letterhead of the newly formed Secretary of Public Education. Questions about the popular vote and presidential succession affected three presidential campaigns from 1917 to 1928.

Madero's slogan was repeated time and again from the pages of *El Heraldo de México*, and its pro-suffrage, anti-reelection position eventually cost its director his life. When Salvador Alvarado founded *El Heraldo* in 1919, he was perceived by then-president Venustiano Carranza as enough of a threat to merit arrest; Alvarado was killed in 1920 by assassins associated with incoming president Álvaro Obregón, who saw him as a viable opposition candidate in the upcoming elections.[6] Though reelection was formally prohibited by the 1917 Constitution, conflicts surrounding the concept of "Real Votes, and No Reelection!" plagued the 1920–1924 period of Obregón's tenure. These led up to an election largely understood, in hindsight, as "the first successful postrevolutionary presidential campaign (1923–1924)" as well as a landmark moment in "the formation of a non-competitive and authoritarian political system."[7]

By 1923, *El Heraldo*'s director, Vito Alessio Robles, was president of the National Anti-Reelection Party (Partido Nacional Antireeleccionista; PNA), opposing Obregón's selection of a successor in Plutarco Calles.[8] By August of that year, the paper officially supported opposition candidate Adolfo de la Huerta, seen as the independent candidate for the 1924 elections because of his rebellion against former allies Obregón and Calles, and his decision to run against the latter.[9] The defeat of that uprising forced *El Heraldo* to close its doors at the end of 1923.

Don Catarino's family story began in *El Heraldo* during a potential broadening of the composition and leadership of the *gran familia mexicana*. One of the least questionable legacies of the Revolution was the increased protagonism of the *pueblo*, particularly of the "common" man from the countryside. Popular groups had acquired significant force during the years of fighting, and upon the cessation of armed conflict in 1920, Francisco "Pancho" Villa and Emiliano Zapata controlled over half of the country. President Carranza's assassination that year seemed to temporarily break the spell of excessive militarization and overt ties to the Porfirian ruling class; with the 1920 Pact of Agua Prieta, power shifted into the hands of a socially and ideologically distinctive group.

De la Huerta's five-month interregnum as president, initiated by that 1920 pact, has been recognized as a brief period of integration between middle and lower socioeconomic tiers. Gestures were made to disassemble Porfirian-era oligarchies with new configurations offering greater access to power (and self-governance) for the popular classes. De la Huerta's concessions to the rural groups led by Zapata and Villa, for example, opened the possibility of greater union to the warring factions of the *familia revolucionaria*, whose leadership—or potential patriarchs, if you will—had been in open dissent since 1914. In a sense, their conflict was related to alternate models of a father figure for the roiled Mexican family—a figure who would unite its divided sons and daughters.

Oligarchs of all stripes had found a formidable enemy in the popular figure of Villa, enemy of the rural landowning monopolies. Villa's prominence had striking peculiarities for 1920s Mexico: he had not held a local office in his base region of Chihuahua, nor come from the upper or even middle class. He was instead a self-made man, with the humblest of beginnings as an outlaw, bandit, and "illiterate." This rebellious, charismatic loose cannon was a hero to the lower and working classes, having surged to recognition through his organic capacity for leadership in those sectors. The State took note of the need to work with, or at least co-opt, Villa's notable strength. In 1920 President de la Huerta was the first to make agreements with Villa and the popular groups he championed, orchestrating Villa's ostensible retirement from anti-state guerilla activities through an "honorarium" of the Canutillo Ranch in Chihuahua. This was given in apparent exchange for other services, beginning a noteworthy alliance with de la Huerta that would extend from 1920 through 1923, the year of Villa's assassination. These efforts by de la Huerta signaled the growing need in the 1920s for the ruling classes to recognize and integrate rural sectors, who now enjoyed greater relevancy as a more visible and vocal part of the *gran familia mexicana*, in order to consolidate power and move forward in the nation's democratic reconstruction.

Pruneda, the caricaturist sharing responsibility for Don Catarino's postrevolutionary rebirth, was well versed in this increasing role of the common man in Mexico's Revolution, perhaps initially through his participation as the illustrator of John Reed's 1914 homage to the lower classes, *México insurgente*, featuring Villa.[10] Pruneda himself came from a family of middle-class revolutionaries personally acquainted with Catarino's rebel yell: in 1911, upon Madero's call to arms, his father and his two brothers—all journalists— had joined the Constitutionalist Army to fight Díaz's "reelection." Pruneda's

philosophy of caricature would later be clearly articulated through extensive writings. In *Caricature as Political Weapon* (*La caricatura como arma
política*, 1958), Pruneda chronicles the history of what he perceived to be
Mexico's most subversive popular genre and its role in societal change from
the nineteenth century through the Revolution. The book is also a tribute
to those who had dedicated or even sacrificed their lives to the art of caricature—including his father, Álvaro Pruneda, who had been repeatedly
imprisoned during the Porfiriato for his opposition to Díaz. For Pruneda,
the job of caricaturist held serious filial responsibilities to the martyrs of
free speech, his family, and ultimately to the *pueblo*.

In the opening pages of *Caricature as Political Weapon*, Pruneda argues
for its distinctive appeal to the common man and its capacity to express *lo
mexicano*. Caricature wields the powerful weapon of effectively exaggerating both positive and negative traits to criticize or exalt the ideals of an
entire *pueblo*:

> The principal purpose of caricature is not always to ridicule. Certain carica-
> tures do not seek to deride, but rather to exalt the ideals or outstanding fea-
> tures of *todo un pueblo*. As an example we see the *charro*—boasting of his
> bravery, clothing and fondness for weapons (a symbol of contempt)—who
> is best brought to life through a caricature that personifies one of the most
> authentic expressions of our national idiosyncrasies.[11]

Here we see how Pruneda's representation of Catarino was no laughing
matter. Pruneda stated early in the strip's evolution that Catarino would
need to be "a great Mexican, patriotic, astute, brave, talkative, rowdy and
rabble-rousing."[12] Yet the figure's success also depended on his reframing.
This was an early chance to redeem the 1911 *charro*—his potential "contempt
for life"—with a more positive, pro-social purpose. For the new Catarino
to successfully represent *mexicanidad*, certain aspects of his lineage would
need reform.

Like other Mexican heroes, the *charro*'s strengths and weaknesses resided
in his very hybridity. The *charro*'s antecedents in Mexican society—both
before and during the Revolution—are as unclear as Pancho Villa's. This
obscurity of origins is highlighted, for example, in the ambiguous historical relationship between the *charro* and bandit archetypes. The murkiness
of this lineage was also emphasized in pre-revolutionary serial novels such
as Ignacio Altamirano's popular *El Zarco* (first published in 1901), starring
the famed historical bandit as a decidedly edgy *charro*. His *plateados* (gilded
bandits) were brutal, as were the federal *rurales* (rural police) who pursued

FIGURE 3.3. Autographed picture of Don Catarino, circa 1954, signed by Pruneda for Monsiváis. Image courtesy of Museo del Estanquillo, Mexico City.

them; both outlaw and lawman, at times heroic, at times ruthless, existed on the borders of society. It could be difficult to distinguish between the two, which was in fact one of *El Zarco*'s messages regarding the difficulty of administering justice in Mexico during the 1860s. Both *plateados* and *rurales* were versions of the nineteenth-century *charro*—two sides of the same masculine coin. These renegade cowboys existed within a rural hierarchy where their positionality was not easy to pin down, and in which their survival, and even heroism, depended on precisely such fluidity: a certain ethical ambiguity of equal parts "bad" to "good."

Similar contradictions were evoked by rural "machos" such as Zapata and Villa as the Revolution became consolidated into governmental structures, and post-revolutionary Mexico established new icons. Which heroes would belong in the *familia revolucionaria*? Which martyrs would rest in the National Pantheon? Villa's remains did not arrive there until the 1970s, delayed by the ongoing questioning of Villa as a suitable national hero.

Martín Luís Guzmán alludes to the interrogations of this period in his *Memorias de Pancho Villa*, serialized by *El Universal* in 1936. In the 1938 preface to the episodes (which would only later be released in book format), Guzmán described the need for Mexicans to better understand the man behind the myth and felt compelled "to make a more eloquent defense of Villa in the face of the iniquity with which the Mexican Counter-Revolution and its allies have unburdened themselves of their sins by setting him up as a target."[13] Villa's figure was of particular concern to those parties in 1921: as one of the few remaining revolutionaries alive (Zapata had been assassinated by President Carranza's men in 1919), he could remain vocal in shaping Mexico's new course, even in light of co-optation by de la Huerta. With valences of both bandit and *charro* in his humble origins, alongside his ties to the land and continual rebellion against the establishment—not to mention his famed connections with Hollywood and capacity for self-promotion—Villa embodied the problems and possibilities of the rural majority class under referendum by a minority urban population. As phrased by Guzmán, in discussing the aesthetics of representing Villa:

> Motives of a didactic *and even satirical nature* required me to bring into greater relief the way a man born of Porfirian illegality, entirely primitive, entirely uncultured and devoid of schooling, entirely illiterate, could rise—an inconceivable fact without the assistance of an entire social order—from the abyss of banditry to which his environment had driven him, to the heights of great victory, of the greatest victory over the system of exalted injustice, which was a regime incompatible to him and to his brothers in grief and misery.[14]

This too was the purview of caricature—to redeem—and we see intriguing parallels in the fictional biography of Don Catarino.

Indeed, 1921 was a very important year for the figure of the *charro* in the Mexican capital: Catarino's debut as a spokesperson for the *pueblo* resonated with a historical moment in which rural and urban Mexico were meeting together in the city for the very first time. Mexico City as an unprecedented melting pot in the years from 1920 to 1930 has been well chronicled: thousands relocated there with their families following the Revolution's ravaging of the countryside, and the cultural combinations that arose were vibrant and intriguing.[15] The matrix of many innovative combinations was the *carpa*, a vaudevillian space where the *charro* appeared regularly, among other beloved national "types," to enthusiastic audiences.[16] Mexicans sought a fresh start, in diversions that both reflected and entertained them. Unlike the *pelado*, another character from the *carpa*, the *charro* was consummately hardworking, and masculine.[17] He represented productive possibilities in terms of both virility and his capacity to assert himself (*imponerse*) and rise above his former social status (*superarse*). His arrival in the city—reflective of historical reality—meant a metaphorical new day for the nation: he stood for tradition at the same time as his presence in the capital signaled the potential for a fresh start. His need to integrate himself into metropolitan life was a lived experience for large numbers of contemporary consumers. Pérez Montfort has noted the explosion of *charro* advertising beginning in 1920, and in 1921 the National Association of *Charrería* was established in Mexico City to promote urban recognition of rural traditions; such commercial efforts would culminate by the 1940s in the highly exportable *comedia ranchera* (light musical films in provincial settings). These point to a reconciliation of the divisions between countryside/capital, provinces/center, past/future that had caused the Revolution and continued to play out on the postrevolutionary stage.

The redemption of the ambiguous *charro* as a productive paterfamilias in *Don Catarino y su apreciable familia* becomes a noteworthy piece of cultural nationalism, at its height from the 1920s through the 1940s.[18] *El Heraldo*'s casting of Catarino as a family man served important political purposes, as the domestication of the provincial *charro*-bandit spoke to the amplification and socialization of an entire sector of readers. For three decades, Don Catarino rarely appeared without his constant sidekicks—wife Ligia and children Tanasia and Ulogio—who serve as his adventuresome partners-in-crime. While in the earliest US family strips, humor often resided in conflict (between husband, wife, and children), intrafamilial strife is notably absent from this first Mexican family strip: moreover, their relationship is modeled for national readers as one of mutual admiration. Even as their zany adventures at times endanger the tribe, Don Catarino learns over time to become less of a rowdy *provocateur* and more of a paternal protector to his offspring.[19]

Offering the *charro* a formidable family (as in the strip's title) was part of *El Heraldo de México*'s modernizing marketing plan. The ongoing storyline with Catarino's wife and kids made the strip attractive to entire families, turning women and children into followers.[20] There is evidence that Sunday

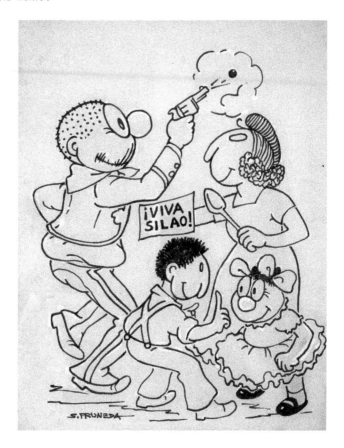

FIGURE 3.4. "Don Catarino's family," by the artist Salvador Pruneda, circa 1954. Image courtesy of Museo del Estanquillo, Mexico City.

supplements across the globe created a family ritual around interacting together via the newspaper, as seen in US cartoonist's Alfred Andriola's childhood recollections of full-color comics being shared among his brothers: "This was the Sunday ritual: comics were passed from person to person" until they were returned to him, who "would carefully cut the best-liked ones to save them in envelopes, stacked on a chair in [his] bedroom.[21] Through comic strips such as *Don Catarino y su apreciable familia*, Sunday newspaper reading could become a family affair in Mexico as well. Strong weekly reading rituals were created around these strips, as seen in slogans from ads of this period such as "Sundays are Boring—Buy Our Supplement to Make them Fun" and "*El Heraldo* Makes Being Home Enjoyable," alongside images depicting families reading the paper together.

FIGURE 3.5. Advertisement in *El Heraldo de México* (March 23, 1922) offering weekend entertainment alongside political blurbs. "Sundays are boring. Buy the Artistic Supplement of *El Heraldo de México* and you will spend your Sundays happy." And in the upper right, "Our editorials are a vigorous scourge against social injustice. Read them every day." Image courtesy of Biblioteca Miguel Lerdo de Tejada, Mexico City.

Through the serialized representation of the Mexican family, urban intellectuals could reach out to and incorporate readers who felt themselves newly reflected in *El Heraldo*'s pages. *Don Catarino*'s earliest episodes feature his country family engaged in a variety of slapstick mishaps with Mexico City modernities that many readers would have encountered in their daily lives, such as skates, bicycles, *espectáculos* (metropolitan circuses and *plazas de toros*), movie sets, and public sewer systems. Their language utilizes the pleasing vernacular of the *carpas*, the provinces, and the *vecindades* (tenement houses where many provincial newcomers were housed). Yet Catarino and Ligia are not savvy in these surroundings, and the strip's humor resides in Catarino's general misguidedness as the family's leader. His misuse of language (similar to the *cantinflear* of the *carpas* from the same period) gets them into trouble, and Catarino is frequently duped thanks to inexperience. He quickly resorts to a .33 pistol to solve difficulties, typically creating more problems by doing so. In many trials he comes across as ignorant or credulous, rebellious with authorities, and obsessed with family honor.

While there may have been a thrill to be found in representation, how were rural consumers to feel that this joke was not on them? Catarino's creators show their hapless country hero from Silao, Guanajuanto, as having solid *materia prima*: with an essential compassion and good heartedness that is rarely deceptive or self-serving, Catarino's passions are simply misplaced. Over the strip's first three years, the rural *charro* is redirected and transformed into a modern family man. The initial means of Catarino's

FIGURE 3.6. Advertisement in *El Heraldo de México* (January 3, 1923) offering to make consumers' domestic life more pleasant. We see the entire family reading their respective sections of the paper, including the children, and in the background, the maid. Image courtesy of Biblioteca Miguel Lerdo de Tejada, Mexico City.

education is international travel. By 1923, the rancher, who in an early episode did not know the names of the letters on the ophthalmologist's chart, becomes a reader and finally a writer. These two traits definitively aid him on the road to accessing modern citizenship, culminating in his bid for presidency as *El Heraldo's* official candidate in March 1923. Catarino's nuclear family members likewise gradually educate themselves through traveling the world. Meanwhile, Don Catarino's larger family also evolves, expanding its circle to include Mexican households regularly following the storyline, a larger narrative encircling those who identified with and learned from characters' mishaps as they read along.

Seriality—with its frequent companions of metafiction and intermediality—was essential to the involvement of new readers in this educational family narrative. Hybrid Catarino's growth (as a stand-in for Mexico) depended on successive episodes of exposure to modernity, and education was the key to movement away from a troubled past. The comic strips themselves were a form of hybrid consumption that encouraged emergent readers to participate in the narratives of nation being written, via a regularized reading habit or routine. The essential pedagogical features of serialization— repetition and review—augmented *Don Catarino's* odds of succeeding in 1920s Mexico, where more than 65 percent of the population (of ten years of age and older) was illiterate according to the 1921 census. Those who followed *Don Catarino* through the years began to imagine themselves as part of a broader community developing over time.

Metafiction has been theorized since the 1990s as a device that blurs boundaries between reality and fiction, and the recurrent metafictional scenarios generated by seriality allowed readers to imagine their own place within a fictional universe whose boundaries with readers' realities were continually confused.[22] A typical feature of metafiction, for example, is an author's direct conversation with their characters; another is characters' direct interaction with the world outside of the work. While some such interactions convey the power of an author over their creation, metafiction appearing in serial narratives often demonstrates the opposite, where the character and their world transcend the author's control.[23] Seriality, metafiction, and related forms of intermediality functioned together in these ways during the essential first years of *Don Catarino* to cultivate higher levels of participation in the narrative, resulting in new sectors of readers in 1920s Mexico, as indicated by *Don Catarino*'s commercial success and continuous regeneration.

Serialization's metafiction is additionally articulated through repeated intermedialities that blur the lines between reality and fiction. The world of Don Catarino, for example, was not circumscribed to the weekly strip, but spilled over into simultaneous iterations in numerous other media, such as advertising (including classifieds), memoirs, columns, publicity pieces, sheet music and manifestos, as well as in live acts such as musical performances, comic skits, circus sketches, puppet shows, and bullfights. The effect of this spontaneous expansion of Catarino's family into multiple spaces merits attention: it promoted the sensation that the family did exist and in fact was everywhere, permeating daily life not just through regular episodes with repeated metafictional nods, but also through the family's penetration into other spaces, both inside the newspaper and outside of it—a proliferation that confirmed the family's real-time presence in the consumers' world.

The strip was initially announced to the public through metafictional publicity sketches, such as Pruneda's drawing of Ligia, with a text directly addressed to the reader. It begins with "Here we have Dona Ligia, the legitimate wife of Don Catarino Rodríguez, mother of two beautiful youngsters whom, dear reader, you will soon meet" and closes with a reminder that readers would soon see Doña Ligia for themselves, perhaps out for a walk in their very own neighborhoods: "Doña Ligia will come to Mexico City. You will see her there, dear reader . . . walking about our blessed streets."[24] Less than one month later, the reader *had* met Ligia, in episodes

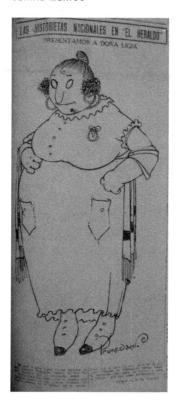

FIGURE 3.7. *El Heraldo de México* (March 2, 1921). Ligia arrives in Mexico City. This image introduces readers to the earliest, most primitive version of Don Catarino's wife, described here as having a speech defect and prohibited by her husband from speaking in public (due to her "Bolshevist ideology"). Image courtesy of Biblioteca Miguel Lerdo de Tejada, Mexico City.

En la Alameda y en "El Heraldo"
Estuvo Ayer Don Catarino

DE LA PENINSULA HA
LLEGADO SIN FIN
DE PROTESTAS

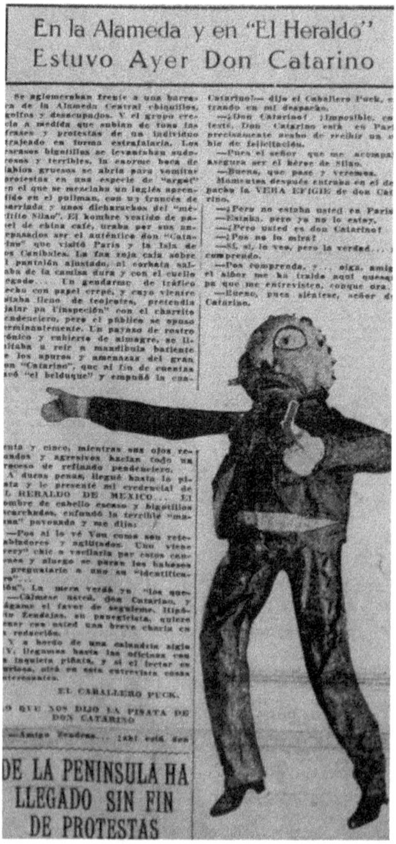

FIGURE 3.8. *El Heraldo de México* (December 25, 1921). Caption reads "Yesterday Don Catarino was in La Alameda Park and *El Heraldo*'s offices." Here we see the image of Don Catarino's piñata as it appeared for a gathering of his fans on Christmas Eve 1921. These real-life events that were staged with characters reached fans in a way that textuality alone could not. Image courtesy of Biblioteca Miguel Lerdo de Tejada, Mexico City.

showing the family's arrival from Guanajuato and initial encounters with the overwhelming modernity of Mexico City. In an outdoor skating episode in Mexico's capital, for example, the reader witnessed the family being taken for a ride, both literally and figuratively, by urban hooligans—one of many instantiations of Catarino's lack of experience with city culture. Yet these initial episodes have no explicit linkage among themselves to hook the reader—no overarching storyline to help them make sense of the disjointed *costumbrista* sketches.

Sequentiality, however, is the ideal medium for education—for it is mostly through sequential episodes that progress is imagined—and the author himself appears to be learning this concept over time. By May of 1921, Fernández Benedicto seems to have realized the need for scaffolding to maintain readers' attention over successive episodes. The first indication of this can be seen in a storyline that begins with the May 22 episode, when Don Catarino and the children fall through a manhole into Mexico City's newly constructed sewer system ("¡Cómo apestan los de Silao!") during their first bicycle outing. The next episode (May 29) follows up with a metafictional moment: Doña Ligia arrives at *El Heraldo*'s offices to submit a classified in search of her lost family. The strip's third frame publishes Ligia's nearly illegible handwritten note in the newspaper-within-the-newspaper, signaling the character's proximity to readers' real-life Mexico City.[25]

Catarino's momentous first year ended with more metafictional moments that catapulted its fictional family members out of the paper's pages and into the world. On Christmas Eve, *El Heraldo* sponsored a piñata party in Mexico City's central Alameda Park, featuring a humorous skit between *tejocote*-stuffed effigies of Catarino and a city policeman. Through such happenings, *El Heraldo* promoted readers' sense of a character so real that he was breaking through the text into recognizable city spaces.

A Christmas Day headline further fostered a sense of Don Catarino's real existence: "Yesterday Don Catarino was in Alamenda Park and the *Heraldo*'s Headquarters."[26] In *El Heraldo*'s coverage of the event, a motley crowd of "youngsters, hooligans, and the unemployed" supported their hero in his ongoing conflict with urban authority, while a journalist presented his credentials directly to the Catarino piñata, coaxing it into an interview with an astonished "Amigo Zendejas" back at *El Heraldo*'s headquarters: "Calm yourself down, Don Catarino, and please do follow me. Hipólito Zendejas, singer of your praises, wants to have a quick chat with you in the newsroom." His author is reported as visibly surprised, having just received Catarino's holiday telegram from the City of Lights. Zendejas goes on to interview his creation in the pages of the Christmas Day *Heraldo* (1921).[27]

Through such intermediality (events and interviews) and metafictional gestures (authorial interactions with characters), *El Heraldo* played with consumers' sensibilities, helping them to penetrate ever more deeply into Don Catarino's world, and to welcome the "hero of Silao" into theirs. By then, readers may have wanted to know more about the figure who entered their homes on a weekly basis: Who *was* Don Catarino? What was his background? Why had he decided to sell his ranch and move to Mexico City, and then to take his family to Paris? The interview was in a format that let Don Catarino speak about himself and express his pride in his ancestors, his patriotism ("I am Mexican and I don't let anyone speak poorly of Mexico"), and his interest in landmark moments and men from Mexican history—Hidalgo, Juárez, Maximilian—however mangled his recollection of specific dates and facts.

These elements of Catarino's personality (*pirsonalidad*) would be further developed in his memoirs, which were serialized for three months, beginning in December 1922, for a total of ninety installments. The daily pace significantly increased Don Catarino's cumulative presence in readers' lives, and the complementary intermedial space of the *Memorias* emphasized Catarino's interiority, allowing him to expound on his lineage, his evolution, and his subjectivities and positioning him in a better light as a redeemable hero for the redeemable Mexican story-in-progress. Their metafictional aspect was writ large by a daily headline claiming that they were being dictated by Catarino to Zendejas.[28] This headline also regularly advertised that these memoirs were fact, not fiction, and that their publication was an *El Heraldo* exclusive, further indication of the special relationship between Catarino and Zendejas.[29] In keeping with the Christmas Day interview from the year before, Don Catarino's *Memorias* were a privileged space for *El Heraldo* readers to get to know their hero, as well as the backstory to more cryptic elements of his wild adventures.

Memoirs, in general, were a revelatory genre, intended to *reveal* the private side of public men in relation to profound collective events. It is not surprising that the genre experienced a revival in the early twentieth century, given the need to explore the motivations and intentions of the Revolution.[30] These memoirs, now appearing on the front page of *El Heraldo*'s second section, implied that Don Catarino belonged to the category of "public man"—someone who had a vital story to share with the Mexican people.

Don Catarino's exaggerated vernacular language and comic foibles were part of a linguistic and situational humor that proved as entertaining in the memoirs as in the simultaneously running strip. The regularity, density, and

FIGURE 3.9. *El Heraldo de México* (January 3, 1923). *Memorias de Don Catarino* by artist Salvador Pruneda and writer Carlos Fernández Benedicto. This headline proclaims that the daily memoirs were dictated by Don Catarino to his scribe Hipolito Zendejas, showing the *Memorias*' strong metafictional bent. At the bottom of the page we see an illustration of Catarino surrounded by his long line of relatives. Image courtesy of Biblioteca Miguel Lerdo de Tejada, Mexico City.

arc of the memoirs' narrative were all quite ambitious, for beneath the façade of caricature lay an increasingly serious purpose. While the weekly comic strip continued to advance Don Catarino's escapades into the future, daily memoirs delved deep into his past, communicating the *charro*'s profoundly Mexican roots through the story of his efforts to establish and educate a nuclear family. The first month of the memoirs was dedicated to linking the character's ambiguous hybrid origins among picaresque bandits to a more illustrious line of father figures that began with Father Hidalgo. The inaugural installment was accompanied by Catarino's self-denominated *ahuehuete genealógico*, an illustrated family tree in which the *charro* is shown as the product of a *mestizaje* that can be traced back to the initial contact between Spanish conquistadors and Aztec princesses.[31] (These roots were regularly illustrated on the lower-page border of the memoirs, where Catarino appears surrounded by a motley ancestral crew.) His earliest male antecedents are represented as *aventureros-ladrónes* (adventurer-thieves) whose ethical ambiguity is echoed in Catarino's evoked literary lineage: both the visual portrayal of Catarino's antiheroic forebears and the memoirs' colloquial narrative, verbal satire, and caustic humor were highly reminiscent of *El Periquillo Sarniento*.

The initial installments set about to vindicate this paternal lineage by having Catarino wax poetic on Padre Miguel Hidalgo y Costilla as Mexico's "Father of Independence," and Guanajuato State, part of El Bajío region, as Mexico's cradle of national independence ("cuna de la independencia nacional"). Catarino's attachment to these people and places had already been suggested in the 1921 "interview" with Zendejas, when Catarino insisted that Hidalgo had been born not in the Hacienda de Corralejo but in his hometown of Silao. His zeal for perpetuating historical inaccuracies notwithstanding, Catarino's pride in connection to Hidalgo and to Mexico's heartland is underscored by the family tree's visual and verbal depictions of Catarino's paternal ancestors, including the "grandfather of none other than Dolores [*sic*] Hidalgo y Costilla himself" whose wife hailed from the Bajío. The memoirs further reinforce an association between Catarino's patriotism and Guanajuato, through a first-person account of his birth, which he dates to Christmas Day 1872. Humorously referring to the Mexican republic in his characteristic word salad as the "homeland of my spiritual and aromatic loves," Catarino describes the time when he first "felt in [his] lungs the telepathy of the national winds that whisper, melancholy and pleasing, the colors of our national flag and its three guarantees."[32]

Catarino's more honorable origins are further established through the story of his father, Teniente (Lieutenant) Catarino, the original patriarch of the family's rural ranch, El Rancho del Buey on the outskirts of Silao.[33] In a device common to serialized narrative—the embedding of one text within another, allowing for a temporal flashback—Catarino discovers his deceased father's own memoirs in a desk drawer while settling the family estate.[34] They reveal his father's loyal service in the Second War of Intervention (1862–1867) under General Porfirio Díaz, who awarded him a medallion for his bravery. The war hero's participation in the "liberal forces"—the "right" side of fighting against foreign invaders—is intended to correct any possible misconceptions regarding the rural man's loyalties to *patria*. Detailed battle scenes invite readers to process the recent Revolution, as well as Porfirio Díaz's shift in national standing over time. This segment of the story-within-a-story ends with Catarino questioning General Díaz's official version of events, which omitted the role of the common man in the victories of the nation:

> The preceding lines anticipate that in the Memoirs of General Díaz, there are many things left unsaid; who the heck knows why. But through the lines that my father wrote, it can be deduced, if one wanted to, that my old man participated directly in quite a lot of combat; and that he fought like men fight; and General Díaz says nothing about this in his aforementioned writings. Who's to know, by the time he wrote that Memoir, maybe he had lost his memory? But I, as the one and only son of the late Lieutenant Catarino, I avidly protest and demand action, so that all Mexicans may know that my father was a true hero.

While his customary malapropisms lighten the tone, young Catarino is serious about questioning Díaz's legacy as he exalts his own, dedicating the memory of his beloved father to each and every Mexican ("toditos los mexicanos").[35]

The memoirs then elaborate on Catarino's foundation of a new family after his father's death, and his explicit decision to eschew local politics, which he articulates as corrupt, by rejecting the offer of a leadership position in the county government. Instead, Catarino focuses on managing his inherited property (El Rancho del Buey) and on caring for his mother, Tanasia, and their lifelong family servant Tonchi.[36] The juxtaposition of these two priorities emphasizes Catarino's desire to establish his own clan or tribe, perhaps as an unspoken alternative to participation in a regional version of the politically corrupt *familia revolucionaria*.

Patriotism and love are shown as redemptive for Catarino. In this *bildungsroman*, the soon-to-be orphaned Catarino struggles with his emotions during the period after his father's death, with thoughts of suicide followed

by bohemian excursions to the capital. This recklessness is initially miti-
gated through activity on his father's ranch, and courtship of his wife-to-be
(a relationship that will sustain him through the deaths of their firstborn
and his mother). Catarino's sincerity throughout these difficult life episodes
is perhaps best encapsulated in the *costumbrista* wedding scene where his
romantic and patriotic passions are joined to perfection. His recollections
first highlight his deep love for Ligia: "Everyone there ate like starving cats,
with the exception of Ligia and I, who could only look deep into each other's
eyes, and ate nothing, as we had no appetite other than for love, for gazing,
quietly and lovingly, with grave longing. That was when they began to make
the toasts for our soon-to-come honeymoon." Catarino then recounts the
toast in which he evoked his filial responsibilities to both his own father
and a national one, Benito Juárez: "I swore, with my open hand placed on
my heart, to fulfill my constitutional and civil duties through marriage, just
as my papa had done, an unforgettable patriot, who had watered the flowerpots [*sic*] of the country, fomenting respect for the words of the great Mr.
Juarez, who proudly preached: Respect for the Rights of Others is Peace."
That is followed by Catarino breaking into song, celebrating his love for his
newly formed family, in what is perhaps the debut of Mexican mass media's
singing *charro*:

> "If ever in your life you should drink / from the cup of pleasure with crazed
> frenzy . . ." No sooner had I finished my song, everyone started to applaud,
> and so I shouted cheers to Mexico, and to my late father, and to San Miguel
> Allende and Costilla [*sic*]. The entire crowd answered back with their own
> cheers, and by standing on the tops of the tables.

The romantic ballad is spontaneously echoed by the assembled crowd's
emotional version of the national anthem, in a scene during which the language and rituals of Catarino's *patria chica* are consecrated through colorful
description:" 'Mexicans, yell your battle cries! / Prepare your swords and
bridles!' Tears rolled freely down our cheeks, and our hearts pumped with
passionate patriotism, with our hands we grabbed our bandannas, blow-
ing stalactites our from noses. We finished singing, and we calmed down,
and then we went to the living room, where tepache and hot punches were
served and the dancing soon began."[37]

The memoirs' country scenes go beyond merely depicting rural speech.
In chronicling rural customs, they fostered familiarity and understanding—and even integration—among hybrid urban readerships in postrevolutionary Mexico City. In keeping with *costumbrismo*'s classic purpose of

documenting ways of life perceived at risk of disappearing, these *costumbrista* scenes reinforce the idea that these memoirs were not just a portrayal of Catarino's own education, but also part of the modernizing education directed at *El Heraldo*'s consumers. Fernández Benedicto's insistence on recording rural speech encouraged urbanites' closer examination of the conversational vernacular they were now hearing regularly on city streets.[38] New rural readers would find some pleasure in recognizing their traditional customs in urban papers—customs that would prove difficult to preserve in city contexts.

Catarino articulates exposure to cosmopolitan cultures (albeit humorously) as something he wants for his children:

> I told Ligia that we should leave the ranch behind and go to Mexico City, where we could enroll the kids in a school where they could learn foreign languages; that this was good; what if in the future our children could stick their tongues out to everyone else by earning their livings as decent and highly educated persons? Ligia reminded me that the children already attended school in Silado, and that they already knew a lot; still I insisted that it would be better if they received their schooling in Mexico City.[39]

The format of the memoirs allows Catarino to share his pedagogical motivations for moving his family from the countryside to the city. These are motivations that were missing from the telegraphic comic strip, now elaborated in a more expansive format, the memoir, that privileged subjectivity and reflection.

Catarino's departure from Silao signals an overall shift: the memoirs now model an intensified educational focus through an increase in repetition, a common feature of serials. Repetition was attractive to new readers—not only those arriving to the pages of *El Heraldo* for the first time, but also those who like the fictional Ligia or Catarino were becoming initiated in reading and writing. They were assisted by the memoirs' consistent, predictable placement within the paper—each day, in the same spot—as well as their location on the page, accompanied by the familiar headline, bottom border, and so forth, enabling easy reader orientation. The stable format catered to readers with varying amounts of time or reading capacities. Each installment contained four different iterations of that day's plot (fig. 3.9).[40] The heart of the page featured the quickest and most basic entry point via four illustrations, to be read left to right, up to down.[41] Below that was a set of numbered captions, offering the simplest explanation of each image—a potential pedagogical aid for emerging readers. There was also a verbally telegraphic (though content detailed) synopsis at the top of the page, in the form of a list that summarized the entire installment (while omitting conjugated verbs).[42] This short-list functioned as a pedagogical aid for new and experienced readers alike, as it could be digested by less advanced readers as a pre-reading device or a stand-alone text; for others, it could be consulted as a quick review option, a roadmap, or even a translation of the dense and difficult vernacular prose occupying the majority of the page.

Serving up narrative in a serialized format consistently increased overall readership for newspapers. Those who had been enticed to get to know their hero better through the comic were now challenged to undertake a much harder project, that of reading up to seven dense chapters per week, as well as potentially delving into other pages and sections of the paper as items caught their attention. As demonstrated by the successes of Mexican *folletines* throughout the nineteenth century, dosified narrative in regularly episodic installments systematically helped to sell newspapers and build readerships, maximizing the number of people who interacted with newspapers on a routine basis, bringing in new daily readers through (repeating) captivating storylines, as well as drawing them into the news stories that surrounded the fictional narrative. Catarino's memoirs appeared predictably on the first page of the second section, surrounded by announcements and articles relating real news events that encouraged readers to dip into the stories surrounding the memoirs on the page, grazing on readily available content. (This permeation of fiction into the pages of the news at times encouraged confusions between reality and fiction.)

During the same period, Fernández Benedicto attached an additional layer of repetition: the rerun. Repetition through rerun served a pedagogical function necessitated by the sheer duration of these long-running projects. On January 23, 1923, the *Memorias* told of the family's arrival in Mexico City, and from then until February 26, they recounted particular scenes from the family's travels that had originally appeared in the 1921–1922 strips. Here the *Memorias* went beyond Catarino's backstory to revisit and add information to select episodes in which family education was the focus. In this deliberate backtracking, the family's adventures in Mexico City, New York City, and Europe were reviewed, along with a couple of island shipwrecks between these crucial cosmopolitan sites of learning and expansion for modernizing Mexicans.

Temporal overlap in the form of reruns was both helpful and pleasing to existing readers. They needed a plot review after two years, and the repetition of older stories gave them time with a familiar character whose personality and antics were now well known. These reruns were doubly enjoyable now, as they occurred after readers had become acquainted with Catarino's past and antecedents through the previous month of memoirs, and they allowed Fernández Benedicto to continue that process by elaborating on memorable moments from the strips.[43] Rerunning stories from the beginning of the comic strip at the point of its established success was an excellent means of bringing new readers to *Don Catarino* and *El Heraldo* and involving them in the ongoing storyline. Lastly, the repetition of episodes from earlier strips in expanded narrative versions was pedagogically helpful to individuals just learning to read. As they advanced from the abbreviated narrative of comic strips to denser serialized narratives, the element of recognition and review would have promoted a feeling of mastery and improvement. Emerging readers who had followed the strip since the first episodes could feel pleasure in graduating to a more advanced narrative version of the same story. Above all they would enjoy following the progress of Don Catarino's education as one would a family member's, with his successes mirroring their own.

In the campaign period leading up to the crucial 1924 elections, *El Heraldo* used the beloved comic *charro* and his family to appeal to Mexican readers about the importance of the ballot, with respect to the common man's inclusion as a voter and even candidate.[44] In the final stretch of the serialized *Memorias*, *El Heraldo* pays particular attention to certain traits through (episodic) remediation that position Don Catarino as potential *padre de la patria* (a patriotic patriarch in the lineage of Hidalgo and Juárez), as well as commending his and his family's sequential education. Through subsequent episodes, Don Catarino and his family become educated—and through them, vicariously, their readers—in questions involving Mexico's history and image abroad, as well as in the reading and writing of modern newspapers and other texts. In the months before March 1923, as Don Catarino's "children" become the Mexican family itself, *El Heraldo de México* fictionally grooms Don Catarino for the Mexican presidency through the *Memorias*, thereby highlighting, as well, the most desirable qualities for the father of the Mexican nation.

The reiterative space of the *Memorias* reworks and reshapes key episodes from the strip that presented Catarino with the necessary lineage and now education to lead his larger family, the nation. His pedigree, however, remains hybrid, as shown by the definitive ups-and-downs in his learning curve. This remedial explanatory quality is first evident in Catarino's own expanding role as teacher and learner, as he guides his family through their initial days in Mexico City. The *Memorias* elaborate on Don Catarino's teachings about the nation-as-family as he leads his tribe on a tour of some the city's most distinctive sites.⁴⁵ He uses, for example, a visit to the remains of the Niños Héroes (the child heroes of the 1847 US invasion) to entertainingly explain the importance of the entire Mexican "family"— men, women, children, and elderly—when defending the beloved *patria* from ruthless foreign invaders:

> I talked to them about how all Mexicans know how to die fighting for their most glorious flag; and that they could all die wearing a helmet: men as well as women; women as well as children; children as well as elderly; old men as well as women, and elderly women the same as fiery volcanoes! If ever there were a dangerous foreign invasion, the adobe would fall from our walls to whack the invaders on the head; the thorns of our prickly pears would stick into their sickly flesh; and the Mexican volcanoes would erupt like pimples, throwing out stones at the most disgraceful, disgusting, filthy, starving witches and traitors, unhappy infidels, who would strive to steal the smallest of sums from our Mexican lands. Well, that land is ours, and ours alone, belonging solely to us Mexicans who have watered it with our blood.⁴⁶

Our rural *charro*'s heartfelt and hyperbolic hymn to the land climaxes with an inspired cry for national sovereignty and the inclusion of all Mexicans in the *gran familia*:

> Fierce foreigners who arrive here with the intention to do us harm, you already know how this will turn out! Just remember Maximiliano and what happened to him for getting involved with us over here! Long live Silado! Long live the Mexican Republic, our Indigenous boss of a mother who rocks us on her loving lap, and no sooner do we suffer, she wipes away our tears with her huipil; and if we should laugh, she hugs us tight with patriotic satisfaction! Well, she is our dear mother, the mother of all our Mexican brothers! Is she not, my wretched men?⁴⁷

Catarino's "lessons" to his family embellish scenes from the strip in ways that demonstrate his ignorance as well as his exuberance, while also highlighting the patriotic values he attempts to inculcate in his children.

Their family tour concludes after a visit to the final resting place of Benito Juárez. Here Don Catarino reinforces once more the (spurious) geographical connection between his birthplace of Silao and that of founding father Juárez, claiming him as "the Indigenous man from Silado, as he is called." The episode ends humorously after Catarino attempts to buy a button off of

Juárez's frockcoat from the shrine's caretaker, with dreams of assembling a proper altar in his new living room in Mexico City.[48]

Through the *Memorias'* elaboration on the sincere motivations behind Don Catarino's slapstick behavior, the readers' understanding of the rural figure continues to develop: clearly Don Catarino still has a lot to learn, but the reader is increasingly on his side, rooting for his advancement. After selling his ranch and winning the lottery, Catarino decides to take his family on the road, with a first stop in New York City. The episode's summary encapsulates Catarino's educational theories: "Don Catarino dismisses his people's patriotic enthusiasm and encourages them to return to Mexico once thy have studied the customs and conventions of other countries. Travel is enlightening."[49] His family's nostalgic desire to return to Silao prompts Catarino to expound on his theory of travel as a tool of enlightenment for both his own group and their larger Mexican family. *El Heraldo* depicts Catarino on his subsequent journeys as an exporter of Mexican culture and its hallmarks of history, republic, and revolution as he assumes the role of fathering foundling republics abroad.

The expansion of the storyline through these remedial episodes of the memoirs spotlights Catarino's markedly hybrid leadership (as president of an island republic) as a mirror of Mexico's own hybrid modernization. In five episodes from February 1923, the shipwrecked patriarch is captured by locals who choose him as their new king because his superior use of arms (his preferred .33 pistol).[50] Don Catarino sets about instructing them on presidential republics, proposing that instead of selecting a monarch they write a constitution, and insisting on fair elections, without which he will not assume office.[51] Upon being duly elected, Catarino models proper state formation "with great tenderness and energy"—assembling his cabinet and ministers, writing a constitution, forming the judicial system, and creating a necessary (albeit makeshift) Mexican flag for the new "Ripublica de Silado" as an "annex" of Mexico.[52] The process culminates in a request to other nations for recognition via letters intermedially published in the memoirs in Catarino's version of five different languages.[53] Catarino's rule as head of state is humorously displayed: he values knowing other cultures and languages as a sign of civilization, while his own mastery of those languages remains laughable.[54]

Still, there is no question that Catarino recognizes the importance of education within the successful state, and mastery of language as key to citizenry. One of his very first acts as leader is to set up schools, stating that he needs to get things done in a way that is not possible without sharing a common language. As president, he establishes "Schools for Elementary Instruction" where locals are taught to read and write Spanish, soon declaring that "the Indigenous were making real progress." As usual, these educational ideals are ironic given his own demonstrated difficulties with standardized spelling, but Don Catarino forges forward with his vision of "Nuebo Silao."[55]

Neither does his own hybrid historical knowledge keep Catarino from instructing citizens on the importance of knowing national history in order to be "civilized."[56] This he makes clear in the episode's close as he unveils a monument to his own version of Juárez as the "hindígena de Silao" (the Indigenous one from Silao), just prior to authoring the laws of the new republic in Juárez's name. A passionately patriotic Catarino declares his allegiance to the figure who protected Mexico from "pernicious" foreigners, evoking his own presidential lineage as a son of Juárez in this narrative retelling for this new *pueblo*-under-formation: "In this way, as I unveiled the monument, I tore out a fistful of hair as I was hatless, and I shouted with all the strength of my pulmonary powers: 'Long Live Mexico! Love Live the Free Republic of Silado, Free of Any Chains or Bonds! Long Live Juárez, the Irrepressible Indigenous Man from Silado!' And all the citizens assembled there who heard me answered back, absorbed by the very patriotism I had instilled in them: 'May They Live Long!'" (February 13, 1923).[57] Catarino cuts a ridiculous figure on the podium, dressed (as the natives) in a toga with his belly exposed, reeling from recent mishaps with inadequately domesticated tigers and his .33 pistol. Readers see him as a lovingly laughable leader of this "branch of the Mexican Republic," and might forgive his presumptions, thanks to this explanation from his memoirs:

> Well, that moment will never be removed from the place in which my very heart dearly holds it; even as many years may pass, and I may be dazed by the ups-and-downs of this ungratefully difficult life, I will not forget when, far away from Mexico, in a savage country (and I do not say this to offend anyone), I established, on a deserted island in the seas of that far-away part of the world, a branch of Mexico itself, which I and I alone conquered, upon which I placed the Mexican flag and made everyone there sing the Patriotic Anthem of Mexico.[58]

Catarino's nostalgic and patriotic motivations for establishing this community are entirely missing from the 1921 strip, but the *Memorias* have room for them to be voiced.

This is not the end of Catarino being groomed in *El Heraldo* for greater things. Although Don Catarino's First Republic ends badly, the *Memorias* end with a second, more successful island Republic, where the entire family valiantly and successfully fend off mutual attacks. and the "savages" again try to adopt them as kings.[59] Catarino immediately begins his educating responsibilities, this time with his wife and children as instructors.[60] Meanwhile, Catarino's good governance takes the form of efficient use of local resources and even repartition of local lands.

The Second Republic concludes as Don Catarino remembers his patriotic responsibilities in Mexico, rushing back just in time to give the *Grito de Dolores* in an equally rushed (and extra-long) series of antics that never appeared in the original strip. The nature of these add-ons bear comment, as they foreshadow Catarino's upcoming bid for presidency through his interaction in international political events: each of Catarino's whirlwind stops establishes him (with the now essential help of his family) as the creator and exporter of the (Mexican) Revolution abroad, first by fomenting a rebellion in Ireland, then stopping in Russia to help a sick Lenin support his hungry revolutionaries by importing Mexican tamales. The family even makes a stop in China, where they head a mini-uprising against the mandarins, leading to an imprisonment from which they are rescued by Chinese revolutionaries. In this adventure, both Ligia and children support the revolution by donating arms and money to the rebels and entering in combat against the mandarins.[61] The grateful revolutionaries give them a dirigible that takes them home to Silao, where they are given a heroes' welcome for their success as ambassadors of Mexico. Catarino himself has earned the patriotic honor, typically reserved for those in office, of tolling the local liberty bell.

This last episode links to future ones by showing Catarino's everexpanding community as clamoring for his story, beginning with Cholita, the local corner *estanquillo* vendor in Mexico City, who anticipates how well these episodes will sell in her stand. This episode speaks of itself as being the very installment that readers held in their hands.[62] The following day, Catarino is to begin his next trip, by request of the Mexican government, as a researcher (in agriculture and natural resources) and Mexican ambassador abroad; the installment thus sets the stage for the comic strip that on February 27 places Catarino and his illustrious family in India.

Of course, this is not the end, but merely a suspension, of Catarino's ongoing story. In March 1923, some two weeks after Catarino had dictated his "Fin de las Memorias" to Zendejas, a full-page spread in the same space features Pruneda's portrait of *El Heraldo*'s bashful candidate for the upcoming elections. This momentous culmination of Catarino's *Memorias* exemplifies each of seriality's accompanying traits: metafiction, intermediality,

FIGURE 3.10. *El Heraldo de México* (March 17, 1923) devoted a full page to their announcement of Don Catarino's candidacy, by artist Salvador Pruneda and writer Carlos Fernández Benedicto, offering their metafictional candidate for the nation's upcoming elections. Image courtesy of Biblioteca Miguel Lerdo de Tejada, Mexico City.

and repetition as key to the overall success of Catarino's story. It is the maximum metafictional coup, as it plays with the thin boundaries that had existed all along in *El Heraldo* between fiction and the "realities" that surrounded it on the newspaper's page. At the same time, it is the ultimate text for inclusion of Don Catarino's readers, as it both asks them to discern regarding his candidacy and prepares them to become mental participants in their nation's future: imagining themselves as voters. As Don Catarino and his family became educated enough to become presidential, his readers became sufficiently educated for suffrage. Through this mid-March spread, *El Heraldo* achieves a desideratum for a certain kind of candidate—a candidate for the common man—in the upcoming elections, which it has modeled through the *Memorias* and made real to readers through a heightened, enhanced serialized textuality, used to affect and even create reality through intermediality, intertextuality, metafiction, and repetition. *El Heraldo* also establishes itself here as the singular voice of Mexican public opinion—in contact with all Mexicans, of all classes—a role that it has been advertising and establishing for itself over the same stretch of time.

El Heraldo—now speaking for the entire republic—proposes Don Catarino as the only viable candidate for Mexico's president in the next set of elections, which *El Heraldo* introduces as of the highest urgency to the nation: "If the most prominent figures of our national political scene consider it premature to talk about who will be our next president, the Mexican Republic is of a different opinion." To accomplish this metafictional turn, *El Heraldo* depends on intertextuality, publishing a fictional news story in which citizens arrive at the newspaper's headquarters demanding Catarino's candidacy.[63] As in December 1921, Hipólito Zendejas's role remains key, as he communicates directly with Catarino, presently traveling with his family in Calcutta: "90 percent Mexico's population offers you candidacy for President of the Republic in next election. Send telegram if you accept. *Heraldo* unites with popular opinion. Hipólito ZENDEJAS."[64] The intertextual cablegram, dated March 14, 1923, is published "verbatim" on the same page of *El Heraldo* to prove its authenticity, and presented as further textual proof of interactions between the public and their preferred candidate. Catarino's acceptance is also published as an intertext, again simulating authenticity through the many reproduced misspellings and deep vernacular of Catarino's now-familiar first-person voice.

In his response, Catarino is deeply emotional about being nominated—he attributes his selection to his fitting "pirsonalidad," which Mexicans have come to know and trust, and which resonates with Mexico and its people. He states his acceptance out of respect for the will of the sovereign *pueblo*. He closes with the revelation that he is about to complete his first piece of solo writing: *México a través de los días suconscientes* [sic], a clear pun on the titles of Riva Palacio's historical tomes.[65] With fresh gestures of intermediality, Catarino claims to have already sent *El Heraldo* the first few chapters so that they can publish them "just like they did with his Memoirs," and only then will he start his presidential manifesto. He closes by evoking the brotherhood of all Mexicans, in recognition that *El Heraldo* is accessible to everyone.[66]

The entire spread engages readers-as-voters in the upcoming elections, inciting their participation through fiction, creating hoped-for future realities through the power of suggestion. Fictionally "reader-created" textuality, for example, is cited as proof of the nation having spoken, ready to fight for the right to vote. *El Heraldo* claims to have received telegrams, letters, and messages in which citizens from across the nation, in both city and

FIGURE 3.11. *El Heraldo de México* (March 18, 1923) offers Don Catarino's manifesto, a running list of his unique plans and attributes, in support of this candidate as the "Messiah of the Mexican Nation!" Image courtesy of Biblioteca Miguel Lerdo de Tejada, Mexico City.

countryside, are talking about only one candidate, Don Catarino.[67] It supplies reporting on events that these fictional witnesses say have occurred and parties that they say have been hosted to support this candidate since early March. Once again, fictive textuality is cited as proof. Each of these documents is reproduced intertextually in the form of special reports from regional correspondents dated in real time, showing Don Catarino's "99% representation" from various regions.[68]

The metafictional connections drawn between real and fictional time stand out, culminating in a prophecy of Catarino's unstoppable success: "We predict an electoral triumph that is without precedent, overwhelming, unexpected." *El Heraldo* had in fact created this candidate and his special viability during the three months of his *Memorias*, in which his lineage had been carefully burnished, along with a record of his patriotic deeds.[69] In *El Heraldo*'s explanation of Catarino's fourteen unique attributes, half in particular stand out as having been essentially cultivated and elaborated through the *Memorias*: his heroism; his multilingualism; his ability to write; the practical education and enlightenment he acquired through travel; his solid finances; his ultimate love of what is Mexican over what is foreign.[70] Having improved himself, Catarino can now save his country: "The entire Republic turns its eyes toward Calcutta and from there awaits the presidential Messiah, who shall redeem the Mexican Nation . . . Mexicans! Vote for Don Catarino! He is this country's salvation!"

As an author, Catarino makes good on his promises: his intermedial, metafictional *Manifesto*, addressed to the "Siudadanos mexicanos," is soon published in the same space his *Memorias* had occupied. His "Manifiesto a la Nación y Programa de Gobierno del C. Don Catarino" is "received" by Zendejas via cable in a special delivery to *El Heraldo*.[71] This acceptance speech appears in bombastic patriotic prose, in which Catarino declares that his selfless motive as the people's candidate is to avoid more bloodshed for the nation.[72] Catarino repeats many of the ideals he had expressed in the *Memorias* as to what constitutes good governance, including adherence to the laws of the Constitution (which he humoristically refers to as *las Leyes del Paseo de la Reforma*) and to the lessons of his forefather Juárez.[73] He also reiterates his belief in foreign travel and cultural exposure beyond national confines, as they have helped him in his preparation to become a future head-of-state.[74] He evokes his lineage from Guanajuato as an essential component of his patriotism, while also proclaiming that when he becomes president, Mexico will enter the ranks of civilized nations.[75] He stresses the importance of the candidate knowing the country and his constituency, and of the constituency knowing the person for whom they are voting.[76] The manifesto closes with a flurry of platforms on education, public works, and the like.[77] A promise of further intermediality appears in the announcement of Catarino's *Historia de México*, set to begin publication on May 6, 1923.[78]

The lead-up to the 1924 elections was a crucial moment in the formation of Mexico's fledgling democracy, in which serialized space continued to provide a forum for the public "referendum" on the common man's participation. We can imagine how *El Heraldo*'s representation of the redeemed *charro* Catarino as the protagonist of Mexico's first national comic was, again, no laughing matter: if the nation was in fact not a comic, a comic could indeed speak for at least one large and disenfranchised piece of it. Don Catarino's space had expanded both metafictionally and intermedially

FIGURE 3.12. *El Heraldo de México* (May 12, 1923). The byline of Don Catarino's *Historia de México*, "written by Don Catarino and sent to Hipolito Zendejas," promotes the formerly illiterate Catarino to author, with Zendejas now serving as emissary of his writings. Image courtesy of Biblioteca Miguel Lerdo de Tejada, Mexico City.

over the course of 1923 to encompass "real politics" and "real suffrage" around the still unresolved issue of "Real Votes, No Re-Election." Even as Don Catarino's adventures became zanier than ever—celebrating his continued efforts to export the Mexican versions of Revolution and Republic to faraway climes such as India and Egypt—his mouthpiece *El Heraldo* became increasingly embroiled in the 1923 upheaval surrounding the the de la Huerta Rebellion.

Only three short months after Catarino's *Manifiesto* was published (and while his *Historias* were still being written), Pancho Villa's assassination stopped Mexico cold. (As a long-lived mass-media legend, Villa was second only in duration to Chucho el Roto, whose legendary exploits began during the early Porfiriato.[79]) Villa's elimination was a decisive moment in

FIGURE 3.13. *El Heraldo de México* (August 10, 1923). Front page announcement of the *"Memorias del General Francisco Villa (Archivo del General Felipe Ángeles)"* and photograph of Villa on horseback, mirroring the front-page memoirs of Catarino from the same year. Image courtesy of Biblioteca Miguel Lerdo de Tejada, Mexico City.

the lead-up to the contentious 1924 elections, in which Obregón hoped to maintain his own power through direct selection of a successor. With Villa's death, a unique window for the *gran familia mexicana* seemed to close, and with it the opportunity for the middle (and by extension the lower) classes' relevancy in the consolidating *familia revolucionaria*. Though the connections between Obregón and Villa's assassination have never been proven, it was a fact that Villa posed a huge obstacle to Obregón's aspirations to name Plutarco Calles as the next president. Villa openly supported Adolfo de la Huerta and had been currying favor for de la Huerta among governors of the northern states. Villa had enjoyed substantial popular support and was himself considered by some as a contender for the Mexican presidency. What is known for certain is that under de la Huerta's term as Secretary of

Hacienda (overseeing the borders and customs), Villa had stockpiled a considerable quantity of weapons at his Canutillo (Chihuahua) border ranch, some said in promotion of an armed uprising against Obregón and Calles.

With Villa's July assassination, *El Heraldo* immediately employed Don Catarino's customary space to serialize Villa's *Memorias*. While other papers such as *El Demócrata* were also running Villa's serialized story by August 1923, *El Heraldo*'s efforts to tell Villa's story "in his own words" was distinctive due to its connection to Catarino's *Memorias* (and later Catarino's serialized *Historia de México*). In occupying the same habitual space in the minds of the readers, Villa's *Memorias* inserted itself into the same family of readings and created a new link of lineage between the redeemable national *charro* Catarino and the redeemable national hero Pancho Villa. And, in occupying the same space and format, Villa's *Memorias* offered a new perspective on Catarino's, and vice versa.

Like Catarino's, Villa's memoirs are first advertised as "dictated directly to a scribe"—in this case, Villa's confidant Ramón Puente.[80] They feature a serialized first-person revelation of the personal side of a public figure: his inner thoughts, preoccupations, and passions. As with Catarino's, the purpose seems to be providing the public with the opportunity to get to know Pancho Villa's motivations, making him more understood and beloved over time. Villa's installments also highlight images (first photographs, later drawings) as well as captions and summaries to attract all levels of readership. They continued in a "Continuará mañana" format over some three months, with embedded documents (akin to Catarino's father's "found" papers). And like Catarino's, certain aspects of Villa's serialization were portrayed to the public as exclusives: *Las memorias de un dorado*, "serialized only in *El Heraldo*" (August 1923) were touted to the public as a chance to get to know the members of Villa's special forces—the rural common men from Chihuahua (*los dorados*)—as never before, and were advertised as a continuation of Villa's own memoirs, embedding the reproduction of Revolutionary documents from the library of Felipe Ángeles with these texts. Last, and most importantly, these *Memorias*, like Catarino's, focused on the redemption of a self-taught, self-made *charro* in the figure of Villa, bringing attention to his efforts to learn to read, to establish a family, and to rule his forces. The memoirs featured many images of Villa with his nuclear family (Luz Corral and children) or with his broader group of loyal and legendary "sons," *los dorados,* already immortalized in the popular *corridos* of that time.

In hosting Villa's voice, as if speaking from the grave to the Mexican people, as well as the voice of the common Revolutionary soldier from the

FIGURE 3.14. *El Heraldo de México* (August 17, 1923). Front page photograph of Villa with his children, echoing the campesino Catarino's recent front-page images with his own brood. Image courtesy of Biblioteca Miguel Lerdo de Tejada, Mexico City.

FIGURE 3.15. *El Heraldo de México* (August 18, 1923). Front page photograph of Villa's wife, Luz Corral, evoking a resemblance to Catarino's frequently featured wife, Ligia (shown in Figure 3.7). Image courtesy of Biblioteca Miguel Lerdo de Tejada, Mexico City.

Ángeles archive, *El Heraldo*'s space for serialization kept getting more "real," making the potential political uses of the serial space ever more evident—not just in the repetition of episodes, but also in the type of hero being reiteratively proposed.[81] This project became more urgent and more explicit as opinion-makers scrambled to secure Villa's place in the heroic pantheon as the newest martyr for the popular cause. *El Heraldo*'s coverage of the assassination and subsequent trials was extensive. There were serialized stories published on the confession of the killer, the exhumation of Villa's body, and responses to controversial films about his life.

By August 1923, Obregón had signed the Tratado de Bucareli into law, provoking de la Huerta's open rebellion and the subsequent closure of *El Heraldo*, which in turn, temporarily "killed off" Catarino. With Villa's assassination, dreams for the new cultural identity under formation—the space of the *carpa*, the circus, the hybrid mélange of the city—seemed to be dashed as well. The moment of possibility from 1921 to 1923 had been fragile, yet Don Catarino entered it wholeheartedly helter-skelter, as was his "pirsonalidad." The paper had vocally supported free elections and free suffrage, and paid a price for its rejection of Obregón's selection of a successor. After Obregón's assassination in 1926, the Partido Nacional Revolucionario (PNR) was created. It would be an antecedent of the Partido Revolucionario Institucional (PRI), Plutarco Elias Calles's 1929 version of the consolidated *familia mexicana*.

But like Villa's inextinguishable legacy in popular memory, Catarino would come back in successive iterations of his story throughout the coming decades. Episodification itself had become fundamental to the essential educational "family" narrative: *Don Catarino y su apreciable familia* had become believable to its followers as its characters erupted into their daily lives and recognizable world, seeming to exist on a plane equal to that of the *gran familia*. By 1926, his story had jumped to *El Demócrata*, and other newspapers were attempting to imitate the formula of *El Heraldo*'s success. *El Universal*, for instance, initiated a 1927 contest for the creation of its own national strip. The winning comic was another *charro* with a family ("Mamerto y sus conociencias"), which shows *Don Catarino*'s foundational influence from the 1920s going forward.[82] After *El Demócrata*, the strip jumped to *El Nacional*, to appear until the mid-1950s, as well as into Mexico's first known animated film, executed by Pruneda circa 1935. The tradition was continued some thirty years into the future, with Catarino resurfacing in the serialized *Pepines* (1950s) and a popular film figure named Don Catarino (Eusebio Pirrín), loosely related in origins (the *carpa*) to our *charro*. Still, nothing approximated those heady rebellious years from 1921 to 1923, when Don Catarino had first reigned supreme: not as king, but president—the president of Mexico's Republic of the Common Man.

FIGURE 4.1. Title page from 1922–23 novel *La verdadera y única historia de Chucho el Roto*, "compiled according to the memoirs of his adviser and secretary Enrique Villena" [Registrado]. This first serialized version of Chucho's story appeared in Mexico City's *El Mundo*, representing itself as a de facto memoir, faithfully transcribed by Chucho's secretary. Image courtesy of Hemeroteca Nacional, UNAM, Mexico City.

CHAPTER 4

Mexican *Radionovelas'* Serial "Stay Tuned"

Announcing . . . *¡Chucho el Roto!* (ca. 1965–1975)

In a highly illiterate country like Mexico, it was not newspapers but radio that allowed citizens to identify with the new state that emerged from the revolution.
Rubén Gallo

Culture became the most important arena for political struggle in the postrevolution-ary era. **Anne Rubenstein**

In the mid-1960s, *Chucho el Roto* began its run as one of XEW's last and greatest radio dramas, entrancing listeners with more than three thousand episodes for over a decade, without a single rerun, "to please an audience that is not content with small quantities, and is always demanding more."[1] Mexican radio producer Jaime Almeida Pérez (1949–2015) considered the *radionovela* legendary because of its longevity, its high quality, and the sus-tained level of interest it generated in the public.[2] *Chucho el Roto* hit the air-waves at a time when radio was connecting with the maximum number of Mexican listeners in an industry that had experienced robust development over the prior two decades.[3] Because it did not require literacy to follow sto-rylines, radio served as a national form of education, both emotional and cultural, for those who tuned in, from rural as well as urban areas. Addi-tionally, by the 1960s an extremely refined ratings system allowed produc-ers to gauge the tastes of the public and provide programming accordingly. XEW producer Carlos González Cardozo saw *Chucho el Roto* as exem-plary of the entire Mexican *radionovela* genre.[4] Chucho's story had already seen the 1880s newspaper, the 1900s theatre stage, and most likely that era's *carpa*. It had appeared on Mexico's earliest silver screens (1919/1921) as well as in 1930s comic strips: generations of Mexicans were already familiar with Chucho's story. The obsessive reissuing of that story forms a pattern of transmedial macroseriality (i.e., repeated series of serializations) that lasted nearly a century, with the most popular of these iterations appearing as serials themselves.[5] So what accounted for the *radionovela* becoming Chucho el Roto's most successful revival among various media formats?

Mexico's fascination with urban bandit Jesús Arriaga (1835–1885), alias "Chucho el Roto," is indeed unique in its intensity and duration. We can piece together a few facts about the historical Arriaga from the newspaper articles and legal documents that proliferated during the last four years of his life. Arriaga was said to have been born circa 1835 in Chalchicomula (Puebla), trained as a carpenter, and for undocumented reasons became a bandit, traversing the cities on the developing rail route (1873–1882) from Mexico City to Veracruz.[6]

The public evidently felt a growing interest toward this intriguing character, as Arriaga's career was distinguished from that of other contemporary bandits by his nickname and his capacity for category crossing.[7] Arriaga's hybrid flow between Mexico's highly stratified classes was a source of his great notoriety in the years just before Benito Juárez's death (1872) and the earliest years of the Porfiriato (1876–1911). A master of disguises, Jesús Arriaga was able to insinuate himself into the humblest group of street vendors as easily as into society's créme-de-la-créme: 1884 newspaper articles report that he was apprehended under the guise of a Querétaro coffee peddler who also attended operas in that city's Teatro Iturbide.[8] Even the question of his ethnic origins reveals a degree of shape-shifting uncertainty. Arriaga's arrest report from that same year classifies him as dark-skinned (*color moreno*), while the accompanying mug shot shows a seemingly pale-skinned light-eyed bearded man.[9]

The same arrest reports and newspaper articles stress Arriaga's attributes as a literate, well-read person, with a pleasantly urbane countenance and a love of culture as well as finery: in one capture, his suit is adorned with solid gold buttons.[10] By the later years, his use of polished manners, learning, and wit to infiltrate and subvert the elite classes had become legendary. In fact, Arriaga's general likeability, personal charisma, and leadership qualities were sufficient for at least one newspaper to nominate him as a worthy 1884 congressional candidate; poet Manuel Gutiérrez Nájera (1859–1895) used his example to advocate for prison reform, proposing Jesús Arriaga as a suitable minister of the interior, and Arriaga found another defender in Veracruz's politicized poet Rafael de Zayas Enríquez (1848–1932), who

FIGURE 4.2A. *El Mundo* (April 1, 1923). Advertisement from an ongoing campaign for *Chucho el Roto* the serial novel, Part II. The text provides a visual suggestion of Chucho's infinity, and an advertising hook to any new consumers who might not have seen Part I to start now with Part II. Image courtesy of Hemeroteca Nacional, UNAM, Mexico City.

FIGURE 4.2B. *El Mundo* (April 8, 1923). Another advertisement from the ongoing campaign for *Chucho el Roto* the serial novel, Part II. Image courtesy of Hemeroteca Nacional, UNAM, Mexico City.

FIGURE 4.3. Advertisement in *El Mundo* (Tuesday, April 17, 1923) for the serial novel *Chucho el Roto*, scheduled to appear on Friday, April 21. Note the centrality of this campaign to editor Martín Guzmán's front page, where it appears centered above the newspaper's masthead and the day's headlines. Image courtesy of Hemeroteca Nacional, UNAM, Mexico City.

publicly castigated authorities for their unjust treatment of Mexico's most celebrated bandit after his final capture in 1884.[11]

Arriaga's own ability to eloquently argue the case for his robberies to government officials, even citing penal code in self-defense, was part of his famous philosophy of stealing for noble causes and abstaining from physical violence.[12] This ideology, along with his humble roots and sophisticated bearing, was a source of much admiration in popular lore as well as newspapers, as indicated by this obituary published in *El Monitor Republicano*:

> THE DEATH OF JESÚS ARRIAGA
> Veracruz, October 29, 1885 . . .
>
> Jesús Arriaga (a.k.a.) "Chucho the Urban Bandit," who was serving out his sentence in the Ulúa Fortress, died this morning of acute dysentery. Famous for his audacious robberies, "Chucho el Roto" always stood out because he took no-one's life. His misdeeds were aimed at acquiring money through robberies, without shedding a drop of blood; and according to what he said in justification of his behavior, were in order to find the resources to bring up and educate his daughter. May the earth of his grave rest lightly upon him.

While his obituary offers scant details regarding Arriaga's origins or home life, this mention of a daughter is a key seedling for the future legend of Chucho el Roto's family tree.[13]

Newspaper coverage from the early Porfiriato points to a crescendo in Arriaga's fame at the time of his relatively young death (near age fifty), indicating that his story spoke to contemporary Mexicans who could not seem to hear enough about the unusual story of Jesús Arriaga. Newspaper articles from 1881 to 1885 themselves show a certain serialized, "to be continued" quality, particularly the brief notes published in the *Gacetilla* (news roundup) of *El Monitor Republicano*. Other updates, like those of *El Tiempo*, were regularly published to satisfy Jesús Arriaga's obvious readerly appeal. Such *folletín*-style news stories were aided by oral testimonies, by word-of-mouth sightings and, above all, by how Arriaga's legendary imprisonments and amazing escapes confounded (and disgraced) authorities. Newspapers also engaged in correcting "errors" such as the rumors swirling around his true cause of death—which some were already depicting as that of a victimized and unfairly abused martyr—at the infamous political prison San Juan de Ulúa.[14]

It is not surprising, then, that the initial literary homages to this intriguing figure bore the marks of oral traditions, such as the first documented dramas of Jesús Arriaga's life, which appeared on stage just three years after his death.[15] Arriaga's story incited contemporary questioning of social injustice, as indicated by protests surrounding one play's initial performance (*La Voz de España*, 1899).[16] His continued rise to popularity in the years leading up to the Mexican Revolution is evidenced by various plays written between 1888 and 1911 and performed from the capital (1888–89), Querétaro (1891), and Chihuahua (1903/1910) to San Antonio, Texas (1911).

Arriaga's name surged posthumously in these reenactments of his unique class-crossing qualities and often humorous capacity to sophisticatedly outwit the unjust authorities in his pursuit. The most noteworthy plot development in these early works, however, is Jesús Arriaga's gradual acquisition of a fictional family. The first play (1888) posits Chucho's family life as a sacred antidote to his life of crime, and explains his banditry in terms of avenging a family offense.[17] At its close, a repentant Chucho begs both God and his deceased mother for forgiveness, before attempting to escape Mexico with wife (Isabel) and daughter (Angela) for a fresh start in Europe.[18] The centrality of Chucho's family story continues in the 1911 play *Chucho el Roto, o La nobleza de un bandido*.[19] This drama was the first to add the tale of two families that would be featured to greatest effect in the 1960s *radionovela*. Here the wealthy *afrancesado* (francophile) Don Diego de Frizac and his family first appear as principal foils to Chucho's honor. Frizac's seductive niece Matilde replaces humble Isabel as Chucho's love interest; their daughter is now named Dolores "Lolita" de Frizac.[20]

Most striking of all is the bandit's strong emergence from the Mexican Revolution—in a first novel, from 1916, that served as the principal source from which most subsequent versions of Chucho's story would be drawn—with an elaborate cross-caste family and an increasingly articulate social vision. *Chucho el Roto, o La nobleza de un bandido mexicano* (1916), of anonymous authorship, also features the Frizac family as Arriaga's principal adversary.[21] The novel's omniscient narrator offers an account of Arriaga's interior trials and tribulations that increased public empathy for the distinctive bandit, with a prologue feigning initial objectivity but at the same time revealing Chucho's immense Revolutionary appeal (in its paradoxical use of an anti-establishment anti-hero to promote new normativities): "It is not our intention in this work to write an apology for the man who has been shrouded with a luminous aura of charm and admiration by popular fantasy, which considers the feats he accomplished as extraordinary and praise-worthy deeds, even to this day (2)."[22] The author closes this first volume of the novel with a teaser for the sequel, featuring Chucho's next generation: *Dolores, o La hermana de la caridad: Continuación de Chucho el Roto*, setting up readers with cliffhanger inquiries typical of the *folletín*: "Did Dolores Arriaga keep the oath she had sworn to her father? Did she dedicate her entire life to doing good for others? Did she sacrifice herself for the humble? Readers who want to know about the life of Jesús Arriaga's daughter can read on . . . in the sequel to this true story."[23] But it is the first volume's powerful allegorical cliffhanger—not the sequel—that serves as the principal source from which the numerous subsequent versions of *Chucho el Roto* were drawn. Since 1916 the transmedial reiterations of that novel have become nearly too numerous to list, issuing forth in new editions, movies, *radionovelas*, comic books, and television. The first of these included two films from 1919 and 1921, in which the worthy *mestizo* workingman's seduction by wealthy, willful Matilde de Frizac, member of society's Europeanized elite, is further canonized as a pseudohistorical twentieth-century foundational fiction for postrevolutionary Mexico.[24] (Mexico was "starting over" again, after the long internecine conflict, in its efforts to reimagine and rebuild the nation.) The allegory was potent, and effective, at a time when Mexico was winding up a revolution based on unresolved class issues. Just as potent, however, was the hint of seriality in Chucho's cliffhanger ending. As long as Mexico's class issues remained unresolved, so would Chucho's story.

The gradual mass mediatization of Chucho's historical legend and fictionalized family drama included a highly successful 1934 film and accompanying reissue of the 1916 novel.[25] These were followed by a *novela de aventuras* that appeared weekly on Thursdays during 1935, and a second reprint of the 1916 novel by Imprenta Tricolor in 1937.[26] An abundantly illustrated black-and-white comic strip ran in the magazine *Pepín* from 1939 to 1941.[27] Two elements of these versions from the postrevolutionary period stand out. First is Chucho's perceived *mexicanidad* and faithfulness to national traditions. The prologue to *Cinematográfica Mexicana*'s deluxe reissue (1934) of the novel, replete with movie stills, emphasizes the enduring quality of this inherently Mexican figure as the basis for the film:

> Chucho el Roto! Who, among Mexicans thirty or older, doesn't remember having heard from the lips of their own grandmother, from among the juiciest tales, the legendary story of this character? . . . True or made up by the common folks, Chucho's adventures would require volumes of pages were they to be published in their entirety . . . Surely each little old woman who talked about the life of this mysterious personage, would add an episode of her own . . . that never took place; this didn't take a thing away from the character of this generous hero who, like all who have earned a long life in a country's oral tradition, always awakes the interest and affinity of his public,

who never sees with indifference the works that portray and promote those legends they once heard in childhood. (3)

The legend's other standout quality is its radical social message, perceived by the 1930s in terms of "socialism," and the incipient censorship that message provoked. The 1934 film, entitled *Chucho el Roto: El bandido generoso; Una vida de nobles hazañas*, was barred from the United States because it contained "radical" social content that supposedly "praised" robbery, as well as "sacrilegious scenes and a likelihood to contribute to class warfare."[28] In the 1935 *novela de aventuras* (adventure novel), Chucho represents Mexico among a cast of international crime-mystery figures such as Raffles, Sherlock Holmes, and Nick Carter, in a version focused less on Chucho's story and more on the ideological feats of Chucho and his band.[29] Unabashedly declaring the Revolution's limitations, the series criticizes the failure to create a Mexico less polarized along class lines, thanks to the unfair enrichment of corrupt authorities.[30]

By 1940 young readers of *Pepín* had not missed the message, demonstrating a clear-eyed understanding of both Chucho's Mexican qualities and his idealism, judging from candid responses to a magazine contest prompt, "Why I Read *Chucho el Roto*":

He was no vulgar bandit, he shared his spoils with the poor who live under the scourge of vile capitalism . . .

Although it takes place in a bygone era, the theme portrays the social doctrine of the present day very well; really, Chucho el Roto was a selfless defender of the oppressed . . .

It is the story of a noble, audacious and very Mexican man who struggles against injustice, aiding the social class he came from . . .[31]

In a context where many 1930s series were of foreign origin, the inherently Mexican and radical quality of Chucho's story stood out, bringing the Chucho el Roto family of narratives squarely into the 1940s.[32] A first *radionovela* of this ongoing Mexican family melodrama may have appeared around this time.[33] XEW producer Cardozo, for example, recalls hearing of a live version of *Chucho* made during the 1940s of which there is currently no written record.[34]

Unfortunately this is true of much *radionovela* production in Mexico's so-called Golden Age (1940–1960).[35] *Radionovelas* were not taped until the late 1950s, and much of their early history survives only in the memory of

FIGURE 4.4. Movie still from *Chucho el Roto* (1934). Ill-fated lovers Chucho and Matilde de Frizac are captured in a dramatic embrace in this still from Gabriel Soria's 1934 super-production, perfectly timed to a re-release of the 1916 novel. Image courtesy of the Agrasán-chez Film Archive.

the few remaining individuals who lived through that era.[36] Such is the case with the first *radionovela* of *Chucho el Roto*, dating from the period when "radio dramas were definitively the most important production in the most important media of that moment, which was radio."[37]

Mexico's foray into the world of *radionovelas*, like Chucho's, is also a family story—that of radio station XEW's gradual establishment as a public institution intimately connected to the private space of the Mexican family. In the 1920s and 1930s radio had slowly centered itself as the medium of the home: in contrast to other contemporary novelties such as cinema and the automobile, radio brought Mexican families' entertainment back into the domestic space.[38] It therefore comes as no surprise that radio's heyday in the 1940s produced the Golden Age of *radionovela*, with serialized melodramas focused largely around the themes of families and family formation.[39] The growth of Mexico's radio industry over the course of the 1920s–1930s was itself a decidedly family enterprise.[40] Formidable patriarch Emilio Azcárraga Vidaurreta (*El León*) built his radio empire around paternal relationships with employees, as well as grooming his son (and later grandson) to perpetuate a media dynasty in which various members of that family had been consolidating power since the early 1920s.[41]

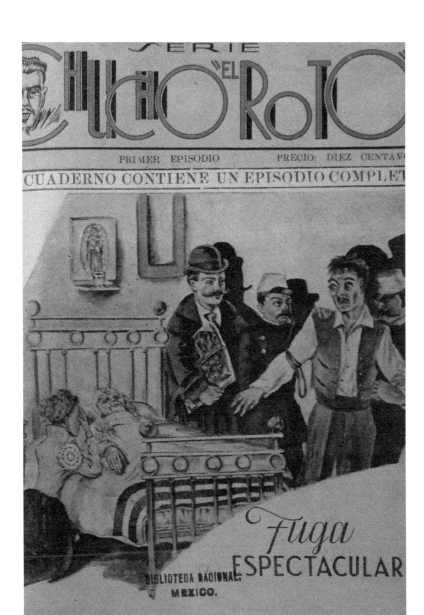

FIGURE 4.5. Cover of first episode ("Fuga espectacular") of the colorfully illustrated series *Chucho el Roto, la novela de aventuras*, by Fernando Ferrari, Editorial Tolteca (1935). This episode featured one of many spectacular escapes by the Houdini-like Chucho. Image courtesy of Hemeroteca Nacional, UNAM, Mexico City.

FIGURE 4.6A & 4.6B. Pages 44 and 45, *Pepín II*, Series *Chucho El Roto* (no. 233, 1939). This expressive black-and-white comic strip ran in the magazine *Pepín* from 1939 to 1941; each episode featured two double-page spreads of eight large frames each, for a total of sixteen frames per episode. Image courtesy of Hemeroteca Nacional, UNAM, Mexico City.

Azcárraga took strict care of his employees as he would children, often demonstrating a concern for their well-being that went beyond the strictly professional.[42] Azcárraga's paternalism extended, in a sense, to the Mexican people as well. Early radio was a close signifier of modernity, and Azcárraga launched his historic "factory of dreams" (*fábrica de sueños*) for Mexicans— flagship radio station XEW—on the evening of September 18, 1930.[43] The next day, one of the country's most important newspapers, *El Excélsior*,

FIGURE 4.7. Movie poster for *Chucho el remendado* (1952), featuring comedian Tin Tin (Germán Valdés) and exotic dancer Tongolele (Yolanda Yvonne Montes Farrington). This comic knockoff was but one of a spate of Chucho movies made in the 1950s. Image courtesy of the Agrasánchez Film Archive.

crowed about XEW becoming the most powerful station in the Western Hemisphere, with listeners as far away as Havana, Cuba: "We must emphasize the importance of the new radio station. Its power is 5,000 watts, with 100% modulation. It boasts the best equipment intended for use toward high cultural purposes."[44] As "La Voz de América Latina desde México," it was also a conveyor of ideas at a time when national education, and literacy rates, had not caught up with the utopian rhetoric of men such as Education Minister José Vasconcelos, who in 1923 had broadcast, via *El Mundo*'s radio station (under the aegis of Martín Luis Guzmán), a speech on the medium's possibilities in educating the Mexican masses, constituting a form of public education in a country where the vast majority had no access to schools, and could not access written texts.[45] Scholar Anne Rubenstein notes the improvement that took place during the Golden Age: "Unreliable census figures indicated that in 1930, about 33 percent of the population over the age of six was at least minimally literate; by 1950 that statistic had reached 56 percent."[46] Still, in 1935, Mexico had only

600,000 radio sets in a population of over 10 million, and some 80 stations total.[47] Yet radio's potential—its possibilities for synchronizing the national family—was an ideal not lost on Azcárraga, who for commercial motivations aimed to continuously expand the reach of his broadcasting powers from Mexico's urban center into the provinces and beyond.[48] Through the gradual success of the blended public/private model cultivated by this patriarchal figure, Mexican radio reached into an ever-increasing number of family spaces, at the same time that the industry itself was coming to be associated with Mexico's public good, and the modernity and progress of the nation itself.[49]

Radio's capacity to culturally synchronize Mexico increased after the outbreak of World War II, with media's growing connection to national security through official news broadcasts.[50] This period also showcased XEW's ability to strengthen the Mexican "family" in difficult times. XEW's cultural programming was a crucial component, transmitting specifically Mexican content and demonstrating the unifying potential of sound (through the power of inspiring voices and music, as well as uplifting content).[51] Though unabashed in his adoption of foreign business models, Azcárraga and his media family privileged nearly exclusively national language and content, contributing to the cultural unification of Mexico's vast geographical spaces and regional diversities throughout the 1940s.[52] With Azcárraga's 1943 creation of Radiópolis—his ambitious consolidation of XEW/XEWW into a farther-reaching radio conglomerate—the medium's literal and symbolic reach to the broadest possible swath of the national family was achieved.[53] If Radiópolis was a stand-in for Mexico City as its national headquarters, and Mexico City a synecdoche for Mexico itself, then Radiópolis was Azcárraga's founding of his National Republic of Radio.[54] XEW's broad transmission of a canon of national culture is again conceived in terms of uniting the collective Mexican Family:

> XEW is the station that managed to bring the Mexican family together . . . that with its power covered the entire territory of the nation and was able to spread Mexican musical, literary, and critical talents, its quest for knowledge far and wide. As Marshall McLuhan said: the medium is the message, that is, the very existence of the medium is in itself a message causing social changes, and the appearance of radio, particularly [XE]W, united Mexico, bringing us together. Values, principles, emotions and illusions were shared for the first time by all Mexicans; the regional borders that isolated us started to disappear . . . The W is just that, one of the most powerful drivers of social union that we have ever had.[55]

FIGURE 4.8. Movie poster for *Chucho el Roto, el bandido generoso* (1954). This evocative image foregrounds the well-known disguises of Chucho el Roto. Reforma Films, starring Luis Aguilar. Image courtesy of the Agrasánchez Film Archive.

FIGURE 4.9. Movie still from *Chucho el Roto, el bandido generoso* (1954), showing another impassioned embrace from ill-fated lovers Chucho and Matilde de Frizac. Reforma Films, starring Luis Aguilar. Image courtesy of Hemeroteca Nacional, UNAM, Mexico City.

Radiópolis was an entrepreneurial arrangement that would endure formally until the 1990s. XEW, like other cultural producers in Mexico, took full advantage of US involvement in World War II (1939–1945) to develop facets of national production that would have otherwise experienced fierce competition from the United States. In the words of Almeida, during the boom period of the 1940s, the *radionovela* began to constitute a crucial piece of Mexican cultural production itself associated with progress and modernity:

> It should be noted that . . . the '40s are the most important years, in which radio dramas stood out as a genre, because the world was at war. . . and that is when the Golden Age arrived . . . of everything! People here in Mexico could create international content. . . The demand for Mexican products rose abroad, bringing economic well-being. There were political concerns, but Mexico was headed toward modernity. . . It was a glorious period for Mexico, the '40s, and . . . I tell you this, the radio drama is one of the highest manifestations of art from that time, at one of its greatest moments.[56]

During the period surrounding World War II, Mexican *radionovelas* became a staple of XEW's family programming; these increasingly successful serialized sound-based melodramas both reflected and shaped Mexican family culture on a plane parallel to Mexico's famed cinema throughout the Golden Age.[57]

While it is said that *radionovela*'s earliest Mexican appearance was due to Cuban imports of the early 1940s, even earlier associations between sound and spoken word had been built by Azcárraga's XEW and associate XEQ's work with Mexican *radioteatros* (a combination of popular theatre and *folletín*), founded in the 1930s in the XEQ's Teatro Alameda.[58] During the same period, XEW sponsored *radioteatro* to an enthusiastic audience in its premier salon spaces:

> When radio was still completely live on the air, radio dramas were broadcast live as well; the actors were obviously very experienced, the special effects were made live, and the music, as everything, had to be created in the moment. They were able to do things as they had been done in some *radioteatros* . . . even on stages within the radio station, like at the XEW: there were shows like *Verde y oro*, and *Azul y plata*, and they created a sort of dramatized show. The actors . . . were there reading, but . . . the imagination of the listeners took them toward what they heard and not what they saw . . . because ultimately, that is the purpose and the means through which radio communicates.[59]

The roots of Mexican *radioteatro* reached deep into the nineteenth century—to the serialized *folletines* formerly published in newspapers (and
then read aloud in public spaces as a way to increase readership: see Chapters 1 and 2), as well as to *carpa* and more formal theater traditions.[60] Sometimes (but not always) featuring serialized works, these 1930s *radioteatros*
professionalized public reading traditions through enhanced production in
sound as well as in the use of practiced readers.[61] By the end of the decade,
XEQ was transmitting *radioteatros* live over the airwaves, and here Mexican *radioteatro* lay some of the local groundwork for sound-based storytelling, soon to be exploited by the *radionovelas* initially imported from Cuba.

The history we have of these early Cuban sound serials is largely anecdotal (and at times contradictory), but in this version of the story from
radionovelas insider Luis di Lauro we find some of the essential contours:

> All these shorter stories transmitted over the radio come out of the *folletines*,
> though they did not yet have the structure of a radio drama. In the early
> '40s a man by the last name Rabasa, international supervisor for Colgate-
> Palmolive, went to Cuba and heard . . . a broadcast of the radio drama titled
> *Anita de Montemar, o Ave sin nido* . . . There Rabasa records a reel with some
> of *Anita*'s chapters . . . and comes to Mexico to meet with José Luis Lemus,
> Colgate's manager, and José Manuel Delgado, deputy manager, to propose
> the broadcast of these radio dramas in Mexico. An adaptation was made . . .
> and an actress was found: the Cuban Emma Thelmo. When it was about to
> end and due to its enormous success, they quickly booked a second radio
> drama . . . Caignet's *El derecho de nacer*. After that, the number of live radio
> dramas increased and began to be recorded for broadcast to the rest of the
> country, to the provinces.[62]

In essence, international corporations such as Colgate-Palmolive and
Procter & Gamble stumbled across the most successful formula for selling their wares: sound-based serialized storytelling to ensure an avid and
regular listenership.[63] Serialization with sound captivated and enthralled
listeners, who then absorbed the sponsoring company's catchy advertising
along the way. Higher production budgets allowed for extensive development of the element of the genre that made it most successful—the emotive
qualities of sound. Corporations had the resources to further professionalize readers' voices, as well as cultivate a production corps providing sound
effects and music at a level not possible in earlier *radioteatros*. At the out-
set *radionovelas* in Mexico were produced entirely by these sponsoring
corporations, in partnership with XEW for their broadcasting needs, yet

remaining initially independent in the development of their own scripts and casts.[64]

Though the storylines of these first imported *radionovelas* were set in Cuba, Mexican producers began to realize that national actors and stories held a special draw for local audiences.[65] From the beginning the venture's commercial aspect ensured a tight feedback loop with listeners, whose tastes and interests were gauged through an increasingly sophisticated system of ratings: if the *radionovela* was not popular with its public, it was immediately pulled and replaced with another storyline. Listeners' tastes thus began to drive cultural production in the radio industry with a greater immediacy and to a greater degree than ever before. By the end of the 1940s, the two principal broadcasters of *radionovelas*, XEW and its competitor XEQ, found themselves in a healthy ratings rivalry.[66] Some of the savviest and most creative participants in the Mexican entertainment industry began to make their careers in radio. Almeida recalls:

> Radio soap operas are from the best of times . . . the time when talented, intelligent, sharp people—to summarize—went into radio and accomplished glorious things. There were writers who wrote fabulous screenplays . . . their use of language, their ability to describe, their way of communicating feelings and emotions that moved us so . . . At that time there was status, there was visibility and outreach . . . That was the best place to be in media at that time, they were in it, and they accomplished amazing things![67]

By the late 1950s, the entire production process of *radionovelas* was being profitably taken over by Mexico's XEW, and a robust local industry had grown up around the creation and broadcast of serialized Mexican storytelling.[68]

Much of XEW's Golden Age storytelling was directed toward Mexican families who, gathered around their kitchen tables, were a principal target (as well as source) of the era's radio programming. In the words of Juan Pablo O'Farrill, it was an exceptional feeling to know that entire families across generations "eagerly awaited the soap opera."[69] Cardozo remembers the excitement: "The family would gather together around the radio to listen . . . During that period, people would sit down to listen to the radio to relax, to be moved, to find out what had happened, to catch up on the storyline."[70]

Radio's increasingly routine presence in society's public as well as private spaces was mirrored by its tendency to broadcast "public" as well as "private" stories. Radio's blended discourse consisted of important news mixed with personal stories, of fictional mixed with nonfictional narratives, while radio's continued connection with important government interests, and even national security, gave the medium a register of "authority" that occasionally caused confusion for listeners. There are numerous anecdotes of that nature, such as *radionovela* veteran Rita Rey's recollection of public reaction to one of Mexico's first homegrown melodramas:

> Radio dramas began at Colgate-Palmolive in January 1941 with *The Life of Pancha Velasco* . . . This poor woman was supposed to come from the provinces, a widow with two children and nothing else to speak of . . . It was a tragedy. People were very moved by it. We were in the middle of a world war. Then so many letters began to arrive, offering help to the poor woman . . . their homes, their food, their money. They asked where to send it . . . [71]

When listening to fictional storylines based in the heavy realism of local *tipos* (types) and topographies—from the same source that delivered their daily news—some listeners came to believe that the stories and characters they heard were real.

The intrusive immediacy of radio's medley of live daily programming amplified this irruption into the everyday "realities" of its family of listeners, further diffusing boundaries between fictional and nonfictional narratives. The earliest Mexican *radionovelas* of the 1940s—such as *La dramática historia de Francisca (Pancha) Velasco* and *La vida de Gloria*—were popular serialized family melodramas that convincingly mirrored, and "dialogued" with, real Mexicans' family lives. In a period in which the home radio set was marketed worldwide as a new vehicle for family togetherness, radio programming was increasingly geared toward the construct of the family at a time when that unit was at the center of the nation's perceived progress: "The programming was created with families in mind. And for XEW to reach them, it was necessary that families existed and were considered as such, at least theoretically . . . In reality (and here the reality is the social discourse of the '40s), little by little the family achieves a national mystique, the only one conceivable: Family becomes . . . part of an ideological landscape, which helps explain the great generalizations that were created around it."[72] Having replaced the parlor piano and the *tertulia* at the center of Mexican domestic life, radio's family melodramas invaded listeners' private spaces like no other medium, punctuating routines and structuring daily life through a predictable presence in the emotional intimacies of the home: "Radio dramas penetrated the structure of how folks lived their everyday lives: they interrupted all kinds of tasks, anything in the name of following the exciting plots. Sociologists continue to try to understand the impact of these stories on listeners in the '40s and '50s."[73] By the 1950s, *radionovelas* were a constant companion in the homes of those who had a set: XEW began its broadcasts of its popular *radionovelas* at 9 a.m., Monday through Friday; since the 1940s, that station had been airing up to five 20-minute *radionovelas* per day.[74] A greater number and diversity of Mexicans were able to tune in simultaneously to these storylines, intensifying the ritualized consumption of narrative that had begun with the *folletines* in Mexico's nineteenth-century newspapers. But whereas the newspapers' narrative dosing had come on a weekly (or at most daily) basis, radio finetuned simultaneity, allowing for routine reception of second-by-second storytelling synchronized across multiple regions of Mexico's vast expanses.

Because not all Mexican families had a home set in the 1940s–1950s, however, the radio brought "families of listeners" together in public spaces to listen collectively, in an "illusion of intimacy."[75] Radio broke down habitual barriers of high and low, public versus private, as the shared spaces of plazas, local bars, tenement houses—even street corners and eventually public transportation—became sites of communal listening.[76] Radio brought together wider cross-class communities as neighbors, servants, and various family members gathered regularly to share cross-class storylines. Almeida paints this vivid scene from his own 1950s childhood:

> Just imagine, I remember coming back from school . . . to eat at home at midday . . . everything was still, and voices could be heard coming from the radio, and it seemed that there was no one in the house, and then I would leave my backpack and my things there, and I would go straight to the kitchen to see if I could get something from the fridge . . . There I found the girls who helped with domestic service, my mother and my sister and sometimes an aunt, all silent, silent just like that, listening . . . yet there were many people there! and you could otherwise hear a pin drop, you could only hear the voices [from the radio], and I remember perfectly what you heard was a radio soap opera . . . *Corona de lágrimas* . . . some story about an ungrateful son who goes off with a rich girl and starts looking down on his mother and his brother.[77]

The feeling of unification during Mexico's Golden Age of Radio, though poorly documented on paper, lives most vividly in the minds of those who experienced it: Cardozo says that radio was an "eraser of social classes" and that "everyone listened to the radio" at a time when "society was smaller, more united, more based in community."[78]

By the 1960s, radio's availability had reached its heights, bringing Azcá-rraga's dream of a united Mexican Republic of Radio to fruition. Radio dispensed with a need for literacy as a prerequisite, making participation vastly more immediate and accessible than print for a population in which literacy rates still hovered around 50 percent.[79] Radio transmission of a serialized storyline provided immediate nearness to anyone who had ears to hear, at a time when access to education was still limited and public school systems still developing. Radio was establishing itself as a national source of education and culture, particularly in rural areas; for many, the radio was their first exposure to literature.[80] A home radio set began to be seen as a relatively lasting investment in terms of family entertainment as well as education, "the center of family life and learning."[81] Availability had gradually increased, not just through efforts to extend broadcasting, but also through the gradually decreasing price of home radios and rising purchasing power during the so-called Mexican Miracle of the 1940s–1960s.

Industry critic Fernando Mejía Barquera describes the first half of the 1960s as a time when radio producers enjoyed a relatively unfettered freedom as influencers:

> During the '60s . . . franchises [such as XEW] found themselves in a completely favorable situation, not only to disseminate their concept of the world and their ethical values to the masses . . . but also their political ideas, with the sole limitation of not attacking the State's policies head on . . . through a medium that was listened to by practically all Mexicans, influencing decisively the thoughts and actions of millions of fellow countrymen.[82]

Investment in radio continued to increase, alongside an increase in the industry's overall profits, still exceeding that of television.[83] Radio's net profits in 1961 were over 207 million *pesos*, increasing to almost 289 million by 1968. The number of Mexican radio stations was still growing, from 377 in 1960, to 438 in 1963, to 529 in 1968.[84] XEW's growth continued as well, now as part of the thriving conglomerate of Radio Programas de México (RPM).[85]

Within this context of growth and competition, *Chucho el Roto* was XEW's most successful *radionovela* of all time, resulting in not just a decade of episodes, but a series of transmedial spin-offs in print, film, and television that lasted well into the 1970s. *Chucho el Roto* successfully capitalized on a mood: 1960s nostalgia for the 1940s Golden Age, the period in which a foundation was laid for radio-based storytelling intimately connected with national family. *Chucho el Roto* embodied the perfect conjunction of nostalgia for a wishful "do-over" of another key era in Mexico's history, itself replete with "unfinished business": the Porfiriato leading up to the Mexican Revolution. The macroseriality of Jesús Arriaga's never-ending story exacerbated an ongoing postponement of closure to a Mexican family melodrama that had captivated the attention of multiple Mexican generations. This lack of resolution dovetailed with *Chucho el Roto*'s plot—a storyline of an irresolvable divide between two families and of injustice toward a maligned father, the entire allegory resonating anew with Mexico's current social context. Chucho's private sufferings were emblematic of society's public injustices, his unfinished family business an allegory for Mexico's unresolved class issues and still-incomplete quest for social justice, percolating since the Porfiriato and rising again to a head during *Chucho el Roto*'s time on the air.

The mid-1960s marked the beginning-of-the-end of the Golden Age, when commercial radio had consolidated itself as an extremely profitable industry—the end of an era in which the industry's capital could remain concentrated in a small "family" of businessmen. The RPM conglomerate had allowed Emilio Azcárraga Vidaurreta, Rómulo O'Farrill, Clemente Serna Martínez, and their families to exercise inordinate economic as well as cultural influence over Mexican society.[86] Development strategies begun in the mid-1950s had advanced monopolies such as Azcárraga's while creating strong social tensions thanks to simultaneously declining standards of living among the popular classes. These forces dovetailed to generate socioeconomic conditions that by the beginning of the 1970s would lead Mexico into a profound political and economic crisis.

As XEW was developing *Chucho el Roto*, Oscar Lewis's now iconic *The Children of Sánchez: Autobiography of a Mexican Family* was first published in Spanish, to great scandal, at once declared "obscene, defamatory, subversive and anti-revolutionary" in a lawsuit that eventually ousted its editor.[87] The book chronicled a single Mexico City family from the late 1950s to the early 1960s as representative of Mexico's urban "culture of poverty"— a culture whose story, said Lewis, was very seldom told.[88] Jesús Sánchez (a pseudonym) and his four children related their own family tale of suffering and deprivation, as well as that of a class excluded from society's institutional protections.[89] Lewis's conclusions showcased the contradictions of the Mexican Miracle: despite growing up with "cars, movies, radios . . . TV . . . free universal education . . . free elections . . . and the hope of upward mobility," Sánchez's children (unlike their father, born in 1910 at the start of the Revolution) had not been able to move out of the systemic poverty into which they were born. In 1960, about one and a half out of Mexico's four

FIGURE 4.10. A 1959 poster announcing a four-film series (1960–1962) featuring Carlos Baena in the role of Chucho. Image courtesy of the Agrasánchez Film Archive.

FIGURE 4.11. Movie still from *El tesoro de Chucho el Roto* (1960), with Gilberto Martínez Solares as producer, starring Joaquín Cordero. Chucho's love of disguise produces an unusual screen moment for Mexican film in the 1960s. Image courtesy of the Agrasánchez Film Archive.

FIGURE 4.12. A 1960 movie poster for *Chucho el Roto* featuring images from the film. Películas Nacionales, starring Carlos Baena, and co-starring Aurora Alvarado as Matilde de Frizac. Image courtesy of Hemeroteca Nacional, UNAM, Mexico City.

FIGURE 4.13. Movie still from *Chucho el Roto* (1960) showing Carlos Baena on set as Chucho the prisoner. Películas Nacionales, starring Carlos Baena. Image courtesy of Hemeroteca Nacional, UNAM, Mexico City.

million inhabitants lived in a scarcity that persisted despite the overall rise in Mexicans' standard of living.[90] In 1956, over 60 percent of the population remained "ill-fed, ill-housed, and ill-clothed," 40 percent remained illiterate, and 46 percent of children did not attend school.[91]

Mexico's seemingly miraculous transformation into an industrial state unraveled from the late 1960s to early 1980s, a tumultuous period revealing deep fissures within the established system. While Lewis's work had confirmed popular classes' sense of family as potentially sustaining in the face of a neglectful state, a belief in male authority and authoritarianism within the family was tested by the abuse of those same models on the national level.[92] For at least fifteen years the Mexican government had resorted to authoritarian tactics to contain popular movements demanding democratic representation.[93] In the fall of 1968, the state responded to those movements with extreme use of power, when government troops massacred hundreds of protesting students and workers on the eve of the Olympics to be hosted in Mexico City. With the Tlatelolco Massacre, "taken-for-granted pillars of the old order, patriarchy and machismo, were rocked to their foundations," as was the symbiotic and mutually reinforcing relationship between individual males and the state.[94] Within this political zeitgeist there was rejection of the patriarchal authoritarian figures entrusted with the *gran familia mexicana*, and perhaps even a sense that traditional family dynamics themselves might need rethinking.[95]

Chucho el Roto offers a timely exploration of Mexico's family models, virtually unchanged in their essence since Chucho gained his fictional postrevolutionary family in 1916. Desire is heightened out of continual postponement—a formal trait of serialization—and the desire fueled by the injustice in Chucho's family story had proven more powerful than its resolution, creating Mexico's first mass-media historical legend since the end of the 1930s. Chucho's heroic genealogy had become overdetermined, combining forces with multiple popular sources: Jesus Christ, Robin Hood, Martín Garatuza, even Houdini. Everyone knew the predestined end to Jesús Arriaga's life in San Juan de Ulúa, but as with the martyred Christ, Jesús's message lived on, yet to reach its proper conclusion. (If only the story could be told enough times for the ending to change!) In the meantime, Jesús's tragic family story would be told and retold to an ever-increasing body of listeners. In that 1916 "nation-building" fiction, Matilde falls in love with Jesús, and their union begets the illegitimate child named for the "dolores de la nación" (national sorrows and sufferings). Dramatic tension increases as both families (i.e., classes) vie for possession of Dolores, in a protracted rendering of two family models (one humble and sincere, the other corrupt and hypocritical) pitted violently one against the other. Jesús's greatest desire is for an honorable cross-class family, while Matilde's strict upbringing—based in her weak uncle's hypocritical concern for honor, status (*apellido*), and reputation (*el qué dirán*)—poses endless obstacles to their revolutionary love. Jesús's honorable desire to successfully found the new Mexican family, and to serve as its responsible father, is repeatedly thwarted by societal prejudice against this vision.

What factors in 1964 enhanced this familiar storyline, essentially unchanged since 1916? *Chucho el Roto*'s treatment of nostalgia combined fortuitously with the high point of radio as a medium, at the pinnacle of its art form, embodied in the *radionovela* as a potent exploitation of serialized aurality. Professionals in the creation of suspense-based melodrama manipulated the structural lack of resolution that was essential to serialization. The *radionovela* now amped up this decades-old message by introducing the serialized sounds of potent *melos*-drama and a powerful punch of nostalgia to the original (postponed) allegory.

At the beginning of the 1960s, the industry itself was changing rapidly: corporate sponsorships such as those of Colgate-Palmolive and Procter & Gamble were coming to an end, *radionovelas* began to feature commercials as opposed to sponsors, and it was around this time that *radionovelas* first began to be recorded.[96] This would be the last great era of the Mexican *radionovela*, with intense competition between XEW and newcomer RCN. Cardozo gives us some idea of the rivalry:

> It appeared in 1963 . . . RadioRed (at that time, RCN) had begun producing radio dramas, and the competition was once again strong, very strong, and they were fighting for rating points, and television was already present... already competing to have audiences, so the aim was to do things better each and every time, to come up with more interesting things that would move people so that they would follow them, and let's say, that was the *ultimate* goal.[97]

Both stations began to feature original twenty-minute *radionovelas* in prime time (evening) slots, intended for the maximum number of listeners, every Monday through Friday. According to Cardozo, in 1963 XEW settled on *Chucho el Roto* as their most competitive offering to attract and maintain the largest possible audience, using all the resources at its disposal in that moment "to create what would be a mega-hit for the W": "They wanted to bring together the best of the best, and they achieved that, in terms of the script, for which they brought in people with extraordinary experience, like . . . Carlos Chacón Junior, a very professional writer, with an extraordinary vision."[98] He was highly experienced in the genre, having cut his teeth on successful serialized stories of popular saints for XEW radio.[99] Chacón cultivated deeply subjective parallels between the Catholic paradigm of the *sagrada familia* (the holy family of Jesus) and Jesús Arriaga's family, both past and future. While these touches were present in the original novel, the *radionovela* exploits these connections through sound.[100] Jesús's humble family is cast as the force exhorting him to tradition, evoking the model of his hard-working father, his saintly sacrificing mother, his pious sister Guadalupe (a reference to Mexico's patriotic virgin, Lupe appears under the image of the Virgin in Chucho's movie versions), and his own honorable career as a carpenter. Like the biblical Jesus's story in the international hit *radionovela* "The Greatest Story Ever Told," the message of Chucho was far from new, but rather had grown more insistent through the cumulative effect of five decades of serial/transmedial repetition in a serially

FIGURE 4.14. XEW-2 advertisement in the magazine *Radiolandia TV* (no. 986, August 5, 1966). This ad powerfully links the international symbol of the torch of the upcoming Olympics, held in Mexico City in 1968, with XEW's legacy—"symbol of trust, resilience, and service"—as Mexico's undying flame, through past, present, and into the future. Image courtesy of Hemeroteca Nacional, UNAM, Mexico City.

cliff-hanging story, as well as Chacón's masterful use of suspense within the *radionovela* itself. Chacón's considerable skills in this area are emphasized by experienced XEW producer Cardozo:

> Because it is not just writing . . . Even literary people . . . acknowledge the genre of the radio drama, the radio script . . . as a very special writerly skill-set. Why? Because the structure of the plot has to maintain constant interest . . . constant suspense, so that people are left wondering about what is going to happen next . . . so, tomorrow they have to come back to watch more . . . Well, this is not something that an ordinary novelist has to deal with.[101]

An equally important touchstone of *Chucho*'s success was Chacón's recreation of earlier times. Specifically, *Chucho el Roto* evoked two past moments of great possibility for the Mexican Nation: the beginnings of the Mexican Revolution, and the more recent Golden Age. Chacón invokes these two historical palimpsests so skillfully that for posterity there remains confusion as to when *Chucho el Roto* was actually on the airwaves. In his 2012 listening session (*sesión de escucha*) on *Chucho el Roto* as Mexico's most legendary *radionovela*, Jaime Almeida enthusiastically reminisced about the 1940s:

> It was another time! It was a different Mexico! It was a smaller Mexico. Radio dramas belong to the '40s, let's say, their golden age! So the whole country— and I'm talking about all of Mexico!—had fewer inhabitants . . . In other words, the population here in the Valley of Mexico today, was the entire country. So here in Mexico City there was a bit of everything: Indigenous people . . . not the huarache [*sandals*]-wearing kind, but yes, there was popular culture. People listened to the radio, regardless of social class. They were informed, right? We weren't so full, as we are now, of a social class that is— well, I wouldn't say uneducated—but *miseducated* . . . Things were different then. Quality was appreciated. Those were the days.

Almeida immediately had to clarify that "*Chucho el Roto* is *not* from the '40s. He comes a *little* later."[102] Though partly caused by the lack of available documentation, these temporal confusions may also be related to the successful use of nostalgia on the part of Chacón to evoke not just the Porfiriato in which *Chucho el Roto* was set, but also the Golden Age of *radionovelas* whose enchantment and community *Chucho* so satisfyingly evoked.[103] The associations between radio narratives and nostalgia were inescapable: the 1940s was a simpler time, Radio's Golden Age of Family, when communities were smaller and families were more intimate. The evocation of this time through a 1960s *radionovela* made for a wonderfully "familiar" entertainment and a reenactment of the community's gathering together to hear a story that united them.

Moreover, *Chucho el Roto* relied on specifically Mexican forms of storytelling that can even be seen as a revisiting of the nineteenth-century oral traditions from which Jesús Arriaga's story arose. These traditions were often experienced from within the bosom of the family, and so hearing legendary Mexican stories such as *Chucho el Roto* triggered intimate recollections, such as memories of listening to relatives tell family tales during childhood. In the Fonoteca listening session dedicated to *Chucho el Roto*, a young journalism student attests to these associations in his own experience, which he believes to be representative for many young people, even in 2012:

> We have said that listening to a radio drama is like listening to a story told by . . . our parents or grandparents, who are telling us a story . . . It is thought that we young people or kids are not very interested in that genre, right? Yet we really are . . . I who grew up . . . with this type of story, it takes me back to my childhood, right? And so I think that it reminds many people of those kinds of things.[104]

Chacón's *Chucho el Roto* was undoubtedly intended as a nostalgic period piece that, like earlier iterations of Chucho's storyline, reflected its specific chronological and geographical settings—of the late Porfiriato leading into the Mexican Revolution, and of the heartland's urban centers from Mexico City to Veracruz.[105] The story mirrored the style of the *folletines* of that same period in their use of heavy description, strong narrative voice, and intense serial suspense. In addition, Chacón's *radionovela* contains numerous references to the newspapers in which the story of the historical Chucho el Roto originally appeared. The nineteenth-century newspaper plays a featured transmedial role, in fact, at several key moments of the *radionovela*'s storyline, further accentuating *Chucho el Roto*'s deep roots in nineteenth-century narrative.

In the *radionovela*'s charming revisiting of the Porfirian past, replete with *musicalizadores*' (sound technicians') selection of period pieces such as Ricardo Castro's waltzes, the listener is regaled with extensive, realistic descriptions of local customs, city streets, contrasting urban topographies, and period dress.[106] The reenactment of nineteenth-century family-style oral traditions begins with the pleasantly soothing voice of an omniscient narrator whose job, according to Cardozo, was to verbally "paint the scene" to "cause folks to *see it*" (*hacer que la gente la viera*), as with these words that open the series: "The story that we are going to tell happened in Mexico, in what is currently our country's beautiful capital city, when its population barely reached 250 or 300 thousand inhabitants, when automobiles and electric trains were not yet known, when the city limits to the west were found at Bucareli Street."[107]

Chucho el Roto's most important strategy was its return to nineteenth-century melodrama—or, quite literally, *melos*-drama: sound-drama. The origins of that term in *sensu stricto*, lie even earlier, in eighteenth-century stage productions' use of sounds—mostly music—to heighten spectators' emotional responses. In the nineteenth century, widely disseminated newspaper texts such as the *folletines* adapted these "melodramatic" tones into prose fiction, converting sound into verbiage through exaggerated emotional descriptions functioning as written "sound effects."[108] 1940s *radionovelas* were able to re-introduce the dimension of aurality to stories once told by the *folletines*. By the 1960s advanced production teams included one or more *musicalizadores* whose sole responsibility was to punctuate the script with sounds and music.[109] This staple feature of *radionovelas* not only elicited impassioned responses, but also enhanced realism.[110]

Part of sonoric serialization's particular intensity is the visceral effect that sound has on listeners. Listening, unlike reading, has the capacity to provide a corporal experience. This becomes evident when we perceive physical reactions to sounds, such as jumps, jolts, or the gasps of surprise we can hear from the audience during the re-transmissions of *radionovelas* in the listening sessions at the Fonoteca Nacional.[111] This visceral effect is true of music and speech as well: the power of associative emotion is different when we hear someone speak the word "grandmother" as opposed to reading that word on the page. The effect is again different depending on the nature of the voice enunciating the word (e.g., the recognizable voice of a loved one versus an unfamiliar voice, or a soft versus strident one). The effect may be magnified even further if we add tones or music. Each layer of sound potentially deepens a sensation that can also be exaggerated through serialization: that is, if familiarities or affinities to sound are developed over time through regular replay, they acquire the capacity to instantly stimulate a specific effect. Listeners' emotions upon hearing the opening narration of *Chucho el Roto* each day at the same time for ten years, as opposed to hearing it once or twice, could become more intense. Listeners develop relationships—embodied connections, intimate to each individual—based on repetitive experience with certain sounds.

Sounds actively engaged listeners as co-creators in Chucho's storyworld through privileging their singular sense of sound—an advantage well understood by veteran producers such as Cardozo, who worked on hundreds of Mexican *radionovelas* during the 1950s–1960s:

> This is the magic of radio . . . Relying on a single sense, which is not entirely an objective one, leads us to use our imagination, where we can plot and believe anything we want. We can create *everything* in the mind . . . With a good actor, good music, and a good script, we can make people go to any place that we want, and basically transmit to them what we want. We believe that this is a common denominator for everything done through radio, for all that can be achieved . . . The truth is that the world of radio dramas is a fantastic world.[112]

The special powers of sound, as knowingly manipulated by radio professionals to captivate and maintain audiences, triggered listeners' active involvement in the creation of personalized images based on individual interpretation of sounds—an exercise that demanded intensely imaginative activity. The use of disembodied sound to provoke embodied experience increased individual investment in a private version of the serialized narrative—a creative process occurring on each individual's internal "screen" through their visualization of the characters, landscapes, and events that they were aurally imbibing. Each person was charged with the creative freedom to picture their unique version of the hero (or villain), an asset elaborated on by Almeida:

> I have to insist that radio is an audiovisual media . . . Radio has *video*, but what happens on the screen is inside people's minds, the screen is their imagination, people see things, they do *see* them. I'm not talking about you having a vague notion of what something might be . . . no, no, no! When radio is done well, the listeners *see* the girl's dress, its color, how it moves. Sometimes one can even . . . perceive scents, like when we hear, "He opened the door and there she was, making a spot of coffee like every other morning, putting the pot on the fire and the aromas reached the door, and he went toward them because he already knew that she was next to the cup and". . . one is there, experiencing those smells too . . . Radio in its essence is an audiovisual media . . . Its essence is to lead the listener into the world of images, through sounds.[113]

Actors such as Manuel López Ochoa were carefully cast based on the quality of their voices and the connections they were capable of producing.[114] Indeed, over time, the hearing of a particular voice such as López Ochoa's would become coupled with an entity (a character) that seemed to exist outside of the narrative—living in the listener's very mind, the most potent site of all—facilitating the lack of boundary between text and reality already being promoted by sound plus serialization.[115] A specific voice (even out of context) would be tied to the fictional character it represented, making the textual character come alive in a striking simulacrum of realism-through-sound, potent in its metafictional capacity.[116]

The direct nature of aural interaction between listener and character, unmediated through the printed page, enhanced listeners' connections with characters over long periods of time. Emotion was palpable, comedy immediate, and realism facilitated by a variety of accents and registers that pleasurably mirrored listeners' daily experience.[117] In the case of *Chucho el Roto*, the maximization of sound and music commenced with the opening credits, in which the combination of Chucho's signature lonesome whistle and the musical themes associated with his character began to operate on an emotive level beyond the textual. Chucho's motto was also repeated at the start of each episode—"Chucho el Roto! The tale of a man who protected the poor, and fought against injustice!"—following a prelude of dramatic, suspenseful chords, the music playing a definitive role. Afterward a flowing waltz-like segue whisked listeners into the world of the past.

The narrator habitually introduced the actors at the beginning of each episode. "With the performance of singing cinema's leading man, Manuel López Ochoa" would be paired with the actor resonantly repeating "A poor man will be less sad if he knows the smile and the support of a friend." A distinctive waltz then swept the listener into the announcement of "lead actress Ámparo Garrido, in the role of Matilde Frizac," layered with the sounds of a delicate minuet-like arrangement. Over the course of the *radionovela*'s run, listeners developed firm sound-based associations between Matilde and her waltz, and Chucho and his whistle, as well as a recognition of and emotional responses to Chucho's comforting voice, Matilde's breathless whisper, Don Diego's annoying whine, and Carolina's shrill reprimands. Such sound cues were difficult to measure or articulate, yet palpable in their triggering of associations. The *radionovela* genre's privileging of the experiential sense of sound was the perfect means of delivery, heightening the *melos*-drama of Chucho's narrative to an urgent pitch.

The sounds of suffering underscoring the unjust persecution of Chucho intensified readers' experience of his plight. Through the serialized *melos* of his struggles, the drama of *Chucho el Roto*'s very familiar and ever-postponed family story entered indelibly into the felt sense of the national

FIGURE 4.15. Cover of *Radiolandia* (no. 984, July 22, 1966). Manuel López Ochoa as Chucho el Roto. The charismatic actor from Tabasco began his career as a model in live television commercials, before landing the role of a lifetime as Chucho, the figure with whom he was closely associated until his death in 2011. Image courtesy of Hemeroteca Nacional, UNAM, Mexico City.

body through the ear. This habitual activation of sound-based intimacy and imagination proved habit-forming for *Chucho*'s listeners. Their daily involvement with *Chucho* over an entire decade fostered connection with more co-creators than had ever before been possible in the history of Mexican serialized literature, synchronizing them with the same storyline across a vast expanse of geography and class. The fact that so many individuals were listening to Chucho's family drama amplified the sense of community among those who wanted to discuss the hero's sufferings or the societal injustices portrayed by the *radionovela*, as a cathartic form of group therapy in a progressively troubled time. In the words of Almeida, this serialized contact with *Chucho*—living out his episodes on par with one's own days—also consisted of Chucho's "family of listeners" regularly checking in to see what had happened with their old friend since the last episode: "Just imagine! People here in Mexico City, who are listening every day, and suddenly, Don Diego de Frizac was a name they heard more than their husbands' at home, right? People were closer to Chucho from the radio drama than to their relatives. Let me tell you—that story is based on a real character. He did exist!"[118] Indeed, Chucho's sorrows were those of Mexico's common man.

Despite the nostalgia of the genre and mode in which it was delivered, *Chucho el Roto* the *radionovela* was not a simple escape to the good old days—to a past portrayed as an unequivocally better and more wholesome time. Rather, Chacón's version of *Chucho el Roto* emphasizes exactly what *had not* changed in Mexico's past: namely, the striking persistence of poverty, injustice, and inequality in the urban centers of the nation, almost a full fifty years after the Mexican Revolution. John Mraz notes how the Golden Age is indivisible from nostalgia for a national family that seems lost, now unrecoverable:

> We use the phrase Golden Age as a metonym for a nostalgically depicted bygone era, a period when *lo mexicano* still invoked a series of roughly shared assumptions about cultural belonging and political stability under a unifying patriarchy. That patriarchy . . . was anchored by "the untouchable core of the nation," *El Señor Presidente* himself. He presided over a formidable cultural state in which "the wealthy and powerful were to be emulated, the underdogs made picturesque or ignored completely or demonized if they did not follow the rules, [and] the nation was one, indivisible and homogeneous.[119]

Indeed, Pável Granados memorably defines nostalgia as an "encounter with that which is irreplaceable."[120] Earlier times were called forth in contrast to a present in which values such as the commitment to family, patriarchy, and a tight sense of national community seemed to be slipping away. Yet *Chucho* slightly adjusts this nostalgia, its storyline a vehicle for remembering key moments in Mexico's history when an alternative national community seemed possible. Its serially postponed ending, above all, provided a space for imagining how the patriarchy might still turn out differently. Its political message is not effective in spite of but *because of* the love story that unites Chucho's private sorrow with Mexico's public suffering, in a serial format that repeatedly reminded listeners of all that remained to be done. Chucho's role as Romantic hero did not incapacitate his message; it only made it stronger.

Chucho's idealistic message was at the front and center of the story. The *radionovela*'s opening lines, repeated on a daily basis, drove home the element of social justice inherent in this historical Mexican figure:

> This [is] the story of a bold, brave, invincible thief with a heart of gold, a man: Jesús Arriaga. He never stained his hands with blood, and dedicated the proceeds from his robberies to alleviating the hunger and grief of the poorest people. Wherever there were tears, he was there to comfort. Wherever there were orphaned children, he always extended his kind hand to protect them. And wherever there was injustice, he was there to destroy it. Chucho el Roto, that's what they called him, and that is the name by which we now remember him.

In Chucho's family story, the intertwined elements of family (private) suffering and ideological (public) suffering are foregrounded. In a twist to the usual melodrama plot, Matilde is the blue-blooded seductress who abandons Chucho once their love has been consummated.[121] A heartbroken Chucho reveals to his mother (as well as to listeners) his sense of impotence, which intensifies with the realization that Matilde is pregnant with their child.[122] Matilde insists that the child will never need to know the father—the Frizacs will see that she receives the rights and protections that come with their family name—leading Chucho to show his first signs of (righteous) indignation.[123]

Throughout his story, Chucho el Roto repeatedly refuses to accept and remain within the place that society has allotted to him, dispensing with the belief that his situation will "turn out for the best" through sacrifice, self-abnegation, and acceptance of God's will.[124] His proclamations of injustice to his mother are initially plaintive and sentimental, coming from a passive place of victimhood.[125] But, ultimately, Chucho is not swayed by his mother's religious platitudes, and his demands become more insistent against an old social order that prevents his new family from forming.[126] After Chucho writes a letter of protest to the head of the Frizac family in which he claims his rights as a father, he begins to understand the collusion of the authorities with the elite; by episode 17, Chucho has stolen his child, Dolores, from the Frizacs out of desperation.[127]

Chucho's mother's death is the emotional turning point through which his movement from despairing victim to decisive actor begins. Chucho's listeners are catapulted into involvement through the combination of universally potent family content (a mother's death), sounds, and music.

In episode 24, Jesús's mother implores her son to change his rebellious behavior, weakly whispering that he is no longer the man she raised him to be.[128] Her dying words, punctuated by mournful violins, will form Jesús's ethical creed: "Do not stain your hands, my dear son, with another's blood . . . never cease to help the most destitute . . . with your own hand, invite the poor to accompany you . . . and whenever you are able, whenever you can, offer encouraging counsel to your fellow men . . . with that I die in peace." In episode 25, upon his mother's death, against a backdrop of melodic melancholy, Jesús concludes to his sister that rebellion is now inevitable:

> You see what life is, Lupe . . . I have been an honest man, a good worker, and now that I have to bury my dear mother, I don't have what I need to do so with dignity. I, who try to be a loving father to my daughter, am threatened by police and by hate from the Frizacs' millions. I have my youth and my strength, I am a hard worker, yet today I was fired from my job. While some have millions to spare on luxuries, we lack enough *pesos* to fulfill a sacred duty. Those are the rich, and we, we are the poor. They have justice on their side, bought with money, while I don't even have the right to defend myself . . . I rebel against this. What sin have I committed . . . ? Why do they chase me as if I were a rabid dog?

As he speaks, the police burst into the humble home to take him away for his theft of Dolores. Over his mother's dead body (which he cannot afford to bury), Jesús makes his vow: "As I promised her, I will protect the weak and I will never stain my hands with the blood of a neighbor, but I do swear that I will avenge these blows that life has dealt me." Chucho then disappears into prison for years, thanks to the Frizacs' abuse of their privileged status, as the radionovela exposes institutionalized corruption within Mexico's legal system.[129]

López Ochoa's monologues became the mouthpiece of what Oscar Lewis claims was missing from Mexican culture when *The Children of Sánchez* was published: the poetics of an urban poor who had remained voiceless for too long.[130] (Perhaps giving voice to that sector was part of the national love affair with López Ochoa's portrayal of Chucho.) Based on the purportedly massive ratings, it seems that all classes were listening to *Chucho el Roto*, yet the 1964 *radionovela* must have been especially appealing to the impoverished majority who recognized the same lack of justice in their own lives. The testimonies collected by Lewis shows that the radio set was a ubiquitous accompaniment to tenement daily life, making regular appearances in family stories and occupying a privileged place in the home—"As long as I can remember, we had a radio, a little RCA Victor, that stood on a shelf made especially for it" (94).[131] Lewis discovered that in 1956, 79 percent of the tenement families where Jesús Sánchez lived had radios (while only 21 percent had televisions).[132]

In its portrayal of Jesús's imprisonment, *Chucho el Roto* describes inhumane conditions and police brutality in vivid, sonorous detail, while the hero's diatribes against corruption become increasingly fierce. In episode 28, a now-familiar stormy music swirls around the narrator's description of Jesús's new situation.[133] After a lingering thirty-second prelude, Jesús prays to his deceased mother, his breathing labored, in a monologue climaxing in angry resistance as the dramatic music insistently rises: "Get me out of here! Get me out of here! I am innocent. I am innocent. My God, Most Holy Virgin, why? Why does this have to happen to me? Is it because I am lowly? Is it because I am poor? Don't allow this, do not allow it! Get me out of here! Get me out of here!"[134] Audible echoes resound from the prison depths, as if to underscore how low Jesús's spirits have sunk.

But prison is where Chucho comes up with a plan to convert private pain into public action. One of his cellmates explains that "all of these jails are full of political prisoners," and Jesús begins to speak truth to power, confronting corrupt officials.[135] A heroic anthem plays as Jesús directs his invective at a man who denied him due process:

> I will go against the motley crew of civilians that makes up the courts . . .
> against you and the millionaires like Don Diego de Frizac . . . against you and
> the policemen who blindly follow your orders in exchange for a miserable
> bone or crust of bread to gnaw on. Against you, yes . . . and against all those
> who abuse the power of the people! Against you, and against the whole world
> if necessary . . . They are going to know who Jesús Arriaga is, or Chucho el
> Roto, as they call me, because I will go forth to avenge all injustice!

The other prisoners, becoming his compatriots, recognize that his speech and presentation are more distinguished than theirs. Jesús often shares his developing philosophies with them, as in episode 30: "I have been thinking that there are so many poor people in the world! And that they are the ones who suffer the most. We are poor because if we weren't, we would be in a palace instead of this pigsty. We lack money . . . money that opens all doors, and creates all the channels . . . Money is what we don't have. We're going to form a society of friends, founded through misfortune. We have to help each other."

FIGURE 4.16. Movie still from *Chucho el Roto* (1934) showing Chucho and his hard-scrabble gang of social outcasts. Image courtesy of the Agrasánchez Film Archive.

In the next episode, Chucho begins to organize these *descamisados* (marginalized classes) and plant the seeds of a more action-based ideology: "I do not advise wrongdoing and much less toward our fellow man, but when wrongdoing to one may help many, we have to think about it and wonder if maybe that is best . . . One day I'll be understood." This brotherhood of men is bound by true friendship and respect, as opposed to hypocrisy.

Chucho's story, far from rejecting the patriarchy, becomes its reenvisioning: a presentation of an alternate model of fatherhood for a more diverse and inclusive national family, led by a father figure ready to rebel against societal injustice. In episode 37, upon escaping from prison (and helping others to escape), Jesús eloquently declares his new plan to his sister Guadalupe:

> Well, I do feel anger toward all of them, toward the Frizacs, toward those millionaires who exploit and put down the *pueblo*, against all those mothers who, in order to cover up their age, deny their children's existence or get rid of them, against the greedy authorities who punish us without rhyme or reason, with no other purpose than to frighten the defenseless. I do not forget the oath that I made over my mother's lifeless body . . . I will never stain

my hands with blood, but I will do justice . . . I will fight for the poor and the helpless and I will show the rich how unjust they are.

By episode 39, Lupe (who until this time had carried a traditional maternal philosophy) supports Jesús's nontraditional mixed-class family. It is composed of Dolores and three escapees—Changa, Rorro, and Fiera—adopted brothers to whom Jesús explains, "I learned that you are not bad people, that life circumstances brought you to commit crimes."[136] The three men Jesús has rescued from prison life will now help him challenge the system, with the narrator noting that "the ideas of nobleness and human nature flying around in Jesús Arriaga's mind were slowly taking form . . . Everything would depend on the amount of money they could get to put them into practice." The *radionovela* portrays this unorthodox group as a blended "family": Chucho is a new kind of patriarch, serving as a thoughtful teacher and reliable head-of-household to his crew whenever their faith begins to wane.[137] XEW broadcast *Chucho el Roto* during prime evening hours, not during morning hours of the domestic soaps, primarily directed at housewives—*Chucho* was a melodramatic narrative included in evening prime time (*el horario estelar*) that broke down gender boundaries by portraying a sensitive and suffering but strong male. This message was not limited to domestic female listeners.

Jesús's revolutionary message had been hitting the airwaves daily (since 1964) when the events of 1968 erupted. Against the backdrop of the Tlatelolco Massacre, which would become known as Mexico's most infamous act of state-sponsored violence, Chucho's story now read as a fresh allegory—an expression of a need for new patriarchal models. It was a tale of two families, one put forth by *Chucho el Roto* and the other by the Mexican government, which was clearly taking initiatives to develop its influence in radio (and TV), couched in a paternalistic discourse of protecting Mexican families. In 1968, the PRI's future president (and then secretary of the interior) Luis Echeverría directly addressed the broadcasting industry with these concerns: "When faced with these means that you wield, *youth, children and young people find themselves vulnerable, unprepared . . .* It is your obligation to ensure that no other interest is placed before the vital interests of the community. The State, radio broadcasters, parents, the entire society, we are all obliged to make ourselves aware, collectively, of the problem . . . by realizing that there can be no interest superior to that of the correct molding of future generations" (emphasis mine).[138] The PRI presidencies of Díaz Ordaz and Echeverría would recognize the vast influence of the media as they attempted to reestablish paternal rights over "childlike" Mexican citizens, openly acknowledging their need to distribute propaganda without interference from commercial radio interests.[139] In December 1968 the government began a series of campaigns to command more influence (via increased taxes), but by 1969 the broadcasting monopoly had closed ranks, demonstrating the high level of influence they enjoyed within the state.[140] The broadcasting industry, for its part, was not accustomed to being questioned, but after 1968, their monopoly over information and its transmission was being disputed, not just by the government but also by intellectuals and civil society.[141] Azcárraga's Radio Programas de México (RPM) and Telesistema Mexicano found themselves under unusually high pressure to promote a positive image of themselves as motors of national progress and development.[142]

Meanwhile, incoming president Luis Echeverría continued to acknowledge radio's broad reach and influence. In another direct address to the industry upon taking office in 1970, he spoke about its important educational role across Mexico's vast regions and social divides:

> Thanks to the technical development of the media that you all manage, we are now reaching Mexicans who live in the most remote parts of the country, in the mountains and in the deserts. It is truly moving and highly promising at the same time to see a symbolically small radio receiver hanging from a plow, the handlebars of a bicycle or a worker's cart out in the field. And I also think that, when we walk through the popular neighborhoods of our big cities and see antennas . . . we shall come—in a revolutionary sense—to create change, an improvement in the preparation of more nutritious food in homes, in civic outreach among those who most lack culture . . . so you all will help us to make inroads into broader educational viewpoints outside of the schools, in the many modest homes where traditional programs can alternate with specific social programs that contribute, when properly thought out, to raising the pedagogical, moral, and economic standards of our fellow citizens who are most in need.[143]

Despite an uneasy relationship with Echeverría throughout his *sexenio*, the media industry's initial response to the president's educational charge seemed favorable, revealing an understanding of its own power and reach in 1970: "From now on there will be no village outpost, communal Indigenous land or desert . . . in which our radio stations cannot be found . . . making you a permanent guide and counselor in each Mexican home and in the mind of each of our compatriots. We aspire to be the invisible but permanent link between you and the *pueblo* and the best vehicle for our national unity."[144] It is within this environment of radio influence that *Chucho el Roto*'s radical message persisted in its prime-time spot on Mexico's premier station airwaves up until 1974. Chucho's unorthodox behavior rubbed against the grain of orthodox social norms: in the name of combating injustice against his family, Chucho broke laws. When the system did not provide reasonable alternatives, Chucho made his own path. This was a deceptively simple but powerful message in 1968, when the political patriarchy was in transition and Mexico's vulnerable populations had risen up in protest of mistreatment. Chucho's family story highlighted certain issues as left unresolved over time. As Mexicans tuned in together for twenty minutes each evening, the *radionovela* served as comfort to the poor, but also an inspiration to action, delivered by voices that seemed to understand and acknowledge their plight. Chucho's private (melo)drama had become a publicly aired and processed affair. Through the sacrifice of Chucho's individual suffering, public questions of justice were made urgent, and personal matters (*lo personal*) became a collective matter (*un asunto colectivo*).

Mexicans responded by faithfully following *Chucho el Roto*'s storyline. Almeida stresses this factor when discussing Chucho's unusual longevity: "When radio dramas were being made, believe me, one did not last long if it wasn't good, because if it didn't have an audience, if it didn't have strong ratings, just wow, out it went, let's bring in the next one . . . and to last as long as [*Chucho el Roto*] . . . it had to be extraordinary, a real phenomenon."[145] Cardozo describes the impossibility of ignoring public feedback via the *radionovela* ratings in the 1960s–1970s, as XEW had refined various methods of ascertaining their approval:

> They depended a lot . . . on their ratings, on the public's preferences. There are ways to know what the public thinks and wants, quantitatively measuring that through ratings, and qualitatively by keeping the telephone lines open for people to call in and write . . . These were the efforts made for radio dramas . . . at the time when they existed . . . They were the highest production cost for a radio station.[146]

XEW's investment in its signature programming of the late 1960s bore lucrative fruit, as suddenly, from 1968 to 1970, *Chucho el Roto* was everywhere.

A unifying figure for the masses, *Chucho el Roto* spawned multiple transmedial adaptations in the wake of 1968, with a new burst of celebrity for its star, the rest of the cast, and the scriptwriter. The success of the *radionovela*

FIGURE 4.17. A behind-the-scenes photo (1969) of Manuel López Ochoa during filming of *Los amores de Chucho el Roto* (1970), directed by Alfredo Zacarías. This movie was part of a series based on the successful *telenovela* and was released serially from 1970 to 1971: *La vida de Chucho el Roto, Yo soy Chucho el Roto, Los amores de Chucho el Roto*, and *El inolvidable Chucho el Roto*. Image courtesy of the Agrasánchez Film Archive.

had generated Chucho's serial presence in other media forms, mostly through initiatives pursued Manuel López Ochoa in conjunction with Carlos Chacón Jr. As explained by Cardozo, López Ochoa "had, in a way, his own vision about Chucho el Roto . . . He was a character very, very dear to his heart."[147] First out of the gate was a folksy *corrido* made popular in the voice of Manuel López Ochoa himself.[148] Then in 1968 came the beginning of the transmedial flurry spearheaded by Chacón and López Ochoa working together to adapt the *radionovela* to *telenovela*, which was released by Telesistema Mexicano under the aegis of producer Valentín Pimstein and director Fernando Wagner.[149] The *telenovela*, again starring López Ochoa, was so successful that production began on four films shot that were shot over the course of 1969–1970 and released serially from 1970 to 1971: *La vida de Chucho el Roto, Yo soy Chucho el Roto, Los amores de Chucho el Roto*, and *El inolvidable Chucho el Roto*.[150] The films, though heavier in action and lighter on character analysis, were often based on recognizable scenes first narrated by the *radionovela*, particularly with regard to the first two of the series. 1976 saw a dubiously kitschy comic book version advertising sex and politics, and in 1981 we have the last known major adaptation of the legend by playwright Emilio Carballido.

Macroseriality and the transmediality it spawns creates cultural repetitions that drive home certain points—in this case, the continued postponement of an acceptable ending to the story of Chucho's (and Mexico's) suffering. Mexico's emblematic radio drama *Chucho el Roto* entranced XEW listeners with over three thousand episodes for nearly thirteen years beginning in the early 1960s, its success predicated on the perfect confluence of medium, form, content, and context—a historical moment in which its serialized message was arriving to the maximum number of Mexican listeners through a potent radio industry that had arrived at its peak over the course of the prior two decades. The story of the historical Jesús Arriaga, the figure on whom Chucho's legend had been based, became popular in the 1880s during the bandit's lifetime, but after close to a century of increasingly mass-media retellings Chucho had become Everyman. Through his protracted family melodrama, Chucho had assumed the role of the fatherly leader for a long-disenfranchised branch of the Mexican family that might now begin to demand justice. A Christ-like figure who championed the poor and chose wits over violence, Arriaga met an unjust death at San Juan de Ulúa (historically reserved for political prisoners), ensuring his name would live on. Ultimately Chucho's tragic story had become that of a different kind of martyred leader—a deferred patriarch who might one day come back to take his rightful place as the father that Mexican society had not properly modeled or accepted. Indeed, the sheer number of tellings and retellings of his story prompted critic Jorge Ruffinelli to use a different family metaphor to describe the phenomenon of Chucho el Roto, calling him Mexico's "collective son."[151]

Likewise, in an epilogue to one of Chucho's most recent literary manifestations *Tiempo de ladrones: La historia de Chucho el Roto* (1983)—playwright Emilio Carballido describes him as the "legitimate son of the Mexican *pueblo*'s dreams." Carballido first wrote the work as a television series featuring the colorful renegade figure in his search for ways to express a Mexican reality deeply rooted in tradition. When Televisa network decided it would not produce a piece that political at that time, the artist deftly morphed it into a unique work written for two settings (*dos tandas*) with a decidedly episodic structure that reflects the playwright's original series. *A Time for Thieves* is now considered to be one of his most

FIGURE 4.18. Cover of the comic *Chucho el Roto, el nieto* (año 1, no. 13, July 6, 1976). This titillating 1970s spin-off featured Chucho's grandson as protagonist. It offered James Bond–like plots, foregrounding sex and political ideology, in its successful bid for a broader audience for Chucho's modernized family story. Image courtesy of Hemeroteca Nacional, UNAM, Mexico City.

experimental plays, with a large cast representing what has been described as a complex dramatic *folletín*. Carballido, like Ruffinelli, notes the capacity of Chucho's world, and its place in Mexico's collective memory, to generate never-ending stories: "I cohabited one short year within the world of Chucho . . . and I regretted that the deadlines of my contract prevented me from continuing to add episodes indefinitely. Others will do so, after me . . . Chucho el Roto, the legitimate son of the Mexican *pueblo*'s dreams, has a guaranteed long-term place in our collective memory, for as long as it lives on."[152] Even now the name of Chucho el Roto has not been forgotten. In some sense we are simply waiting for the next installment.

CHAPTER 5

History's Eternal Return in Televisa's *Telenovelas*

Martín Garatuza (1986) and *El extraño retorno de Diana Salazar* (1988–1989)

Mexican soap operas replicate themselves using an admirable genetic pattern repeated from generation to generation. They are cyclical and repetitive enough to provide certainty to those who watch them. In a country where you don't know what is going to happen the next day, whether prices will rise, whether peace will return, there's nothing as rewarding as watching a serial melodrama . . . Isn't it wonderful that in a context of violence and economic upheaval there is a means of entertainment that allows the inhabitants of a country to feel safe? Isn't it fantastic that people who don't hold the reins to their own lives can experience a certain authority and even knowledge in the face of a soap opera's eternally predictable plot?

Álvaro Cueva

Right now [1986] the main problem in Mexico is the economy. Real income is falling and there are all kinds of problems. People are angry. There is social unrest, latent social unrest. What you are going to find is that Televisa is one of the most important elements keeping the country peaceful. People are going to sit down and watch the soap operas.   **Rubén Jara**

The full story of Mexican soap operas, as a legitimate form of contemporary storytelling, is yet to be told. A key feature of these series is the intense recycling of past elements, also known as *remediality*, and the refashioning of prior elements to present needs, termed *remediation*, which can occur both in form and content.[1] One of the important functions of remediation is to demand viewers' understanding of the present by way of the past— a very specific quality of the two soaps that we will examine in this chapter. Here we come full circle, with themes from Riva Palacio's historical novels (Chapter 2) entering Mexican television through a 1980s neobaroque revival. We investigate the rebirth of the colonial baroque aesthetic

FIGURE 5.1. Sensationalist front cover of a 1980s comic book version of *Martín Garatuza*, illustrated by Humberto Sandoval (Novedades Editores, series "Novelas Inmortales," año XII, no. 604, junio 14 de 1989: Precio pacto 390 pesos). Foundational serial novels live on in nostalgic reproductions from the late twentieth and early twenty-first centuries. Image from the author's personal collection.

and its remixing and rebooting through TV series, demonstrating how foundational serial novels live on in nostalgic content, form, and aesthetics through transmedial productions from the late twentieth and early twenty-first centuries.

Many have observed a return of the baroque in global culture. It has been noted in terms of themes and topoi, as well as of form, such as the accumulation of stylistic features and special effects. Indeed, in the twenty-first century, some say "baroque" best describes the style assumed by contemporary entertainment in a fragmented modern culture, "as if the entertainment industry had exploited the potential of the historic baroque and, through modern technology, brought it up to its full realization."[2] This resurgence began toward the end of the twentieth century and, in the case of Mexico, was emblematic of a return of the repressed: a period of colonial origins in Mexican culture that needed reexamination and reprocessing thanks

FIGURE 5.2. Front cover in color (1981) of the SEP comic *Martín Garatuza*, illustrated by M.I.C. and Ulises Mora. This cover shows how episodes from *Martín Garatuza* were grouped with *El Periquillo Sarniento* under a single cover. Image courtesy of Christopher Conway.

FIGURE 5.3. Inside back cover (1981) of the SEP comic *Martín Garatuza*, illustrated by M.I.C. and Ulises Mora. "Don't miss next week's episode of *Martín Garatuza* and another riveting chapter of *Periquillo!*" Image courtesy of Christopher Conway.

to current societal crises. As it turns out, one of the best ways to reexamine and reprocess was through soap operas. There, the return of Mexico's colonial baroque was palpable: *telenovelas* revisited the aesthetics of the seventeenth century through serial logic, polycentric storytelling, and the incorporation of new media and spectacle, as well as through the creation of specific contextual conditions such as intense viewer engagement and mass consumerism.[3] Two innovative and interrelated soap operas that illustrate the relevance of the neobaroque—its stories and its style—to Mexican audiences of the late 1980s are *Martín Garatuza* (1986) and *El extraño retorno de Diana Salazar* (1988–1989).

Soap operas inherently demonstrate a "serial logic" that defines contemporary culture.[4] In this logic, repetition provides pleasure, and pleasure through repetition—as opposed to originality—attracts viewers.[5] Defying reliance on a textual center, or urtext, as these narratives cannot be found within a single text or static structure such as a book, the storytelling of soap operas is instead polycentric, exhibiting diverse centers and drawing from many sources across multiple media platforms—a form of remediation that further reinforces an aesthetics of repetition.

Serial narratives have a long history of tending toward new media environments to engulf and engage spectators in ever stronger and more intense "experiences." Soap operas, the quintessential melodramatic spectacle, rely on ongoing enthrallment and involvement of viewers for their survival. As in any spectacle, viewer experience is key, and new technologies are essential to enhancing the thrill of that experience.[6] Through their heightened emotions and reactions, soap opera viewers are continually invited to return, participate in, and shape the spectacles that they consume.

The connection of narrative to mass media and consumerism originated in the seventeenth century as a baroque quality, with novels such as *Don Quixote* (1605/1615) exhibiting an early serial logic and textual concern with the aesthetic value of repetition, the value of originals versus copies, metafiction, and intense reader involvement (as modeled by the protagonist himself).[7] Certain historical configurations, if repeated, generate recognizable forms of cultural production and exhibit affinities with certain cultural expressions. According to Angela Ndalianis, the triggering historical configuration for the baroque's resurgence is crisis, with the main difference between the seventeenth century (early-stage capitalism with an emerging mass audience) and the twentieth (late-stage capitalism with a consolidated mass audience) being essentially one of intensification, as seriality becomes ever more integral to mass entertainment and our conceptions of popular storytelling.[8]

In 1980s Mexico, we see these elements in play with a recycled Hispanic Baroque by way of the televised soap opera, at a time when the transformative potential of neobaroque national storytelling was particularly ripe. The power of television as a medium had risen, there was a developed infrastructure for creating soap operas, and according to Rubén Jara, director of Televisa's Institute of Communication Studies, a latent social crisis was underway. The Azcárraga family empire, as pioneer investors in radio and *radionovelas* (see Chapter 4), had erected sound scaffolding for their future control of television.[9] Throughout the 1960s, ailing scion Emilio Azcárraga Vidaurreta had set the stage for the transition from radio to television, to be carried out by his son Emilio Azcárraga Milmo in the 1970s.[10] Azcárraga Vidaurreta's Telesistema Mexicano (TSM) orchestrated an early monopoly that remained intact until 1968: by that year, the national system of electromagnetic waves was complete, and with that technological achievement, television established its dominance over radio.[11] Like Mexican radio, Mexican television would be indebted to serialized narratives, looking to soap operas to build and maintain their audiences, as well as sell products and promote consumerism. This symbiotic relationship between commercial success and serials guaranteed seriality a central spot, front and center, in the new media landscape.

Daily televised soap opera programming had existed in Mexico since 1958, when TSM aired its first soap, *Senda prohibida*, in the 6:30 p.m. slot for Channel 4.[12] At this point, Mexican soap storytelling served an essentially conservative function.[13] Television stories in the 1960s reinforced a survival-of-the-fittest mentality, racial determinism, and elitism that encouraged spectators to accept their preordained place in the world. Under the 1960 law enacted in response to its power (*Ley Federal de Radio y TV*), TSM practiced self-censorship as well as allowing the Secretaría de Gobernación to habitually review its scripts.[14] During this honeymoon period, lasting until 1968, Mexican soap opera programming promoted economic development and socio-political stability—goals in convenient correspondence with the needs of the government.[15]

Though they were not all repeats of literary works or prior *radionovelas*, early soap operas were a veritable hotbed for remediality and the emergence of linked narrative scenarios across media. Many were remakes of *radionovelas* such as *El derecho de nacer*, whose first soap opera version in 1966, in the capable hands of producer Ernesto Alonso, mesmerized Mexico City at 9:30 p.m. on Mondays, Wednesdays, and Fridays.[16] Cubans had been adapting their own favorite *radionovelas* for TV since the 1950s. By the time of the Revolution, numerous writers had left Havana for Mexico

City, and by the 1960s a real boom in Mexican *telenovelas* had begun, as soaps ceased live transmission in favor of prerecording in studios. During this period of transition, "it was common to use narrators, so that that audiences would understand the audiovisual language that previously they could only hear on the radio, and the credits were read aloud so that the illiterate could understand the words."[17] Mexican television was realizing a level of impact, importance, and reach—with concomitant possibilities for commercialization, education and entertainment—that was infinitely superior to any print or electronic medium that had come before. As television sets became more affordable, more Mexicans tuned in, and television became a pervasive power in society. TSM turned into a veritable assembly line of production, cranking out programs for three thriving channels.

The government was coming to grips with television's growing influence when the watershed year of 1968 arrived. Some speculated that TSM held inordinate power over the government after the Tlatelolco Massacre (see Chapter 4), as the channel purportedly possessed footage of the events. TSM promptly canceled contracts with local newspapers and started its own news department, fortifying its hold on televised reporting in Mexico and causing some government officials to question the extent of Azcárraga's loyalty. TSM was in a strong position vis-à-vis the PRI, a party that had enjoyed its own monopoly since 1929. The PRI wanted tighter control over national media, and over time it became clear that granting TSM even more exclusive privileges through the consolidation of its media powers was desirable for governmental purposes.

The *sexenio* (six-year presidency) of Luis Echeverría (1970–1976) was a turning point in the relationship between TSM and PRI, during which the government's threat of nationalization loomed over the television industry like a sword of Damocles. TSM's most popular productions were daily *telenovelas*, which had migrated in 1970 to TSM's oldest, leading channel, Channel 2. Admittedly, however, content was subordinate to the industry's advertising needs: "We were not being very creative," admits Romulo O'Farrill Jr., a TSM owner.[18] Television's commercialism garnered much negative attention from vocal intellectuals, who denounced the medium's lack of culture and the Mexican people's limited access to alternative avenues of entertainment, information, and education. President Echeverría began to promote national culture through television and encourage cultural initiatives that might stave off US media influences.[19] Televisa emerged from these crucibles in 1972, when President Echeverría formed a task force to chart a new path for commercial television. One result was the January 1973 merger of national network Televisión Independiente de México with TSM.[20] Azcárraga Milmo's monopoly was vastly strengthened by this move, but he was simultaneously forced to compromise with Echeverría's demands for Mexican-themed television for the Mexican people, reflecting the president's concern for the "stories" that were (or were not) being told through the increasingly powerful medium of television.[21]

Televisa's birth in the early 1970s, and its subsequent investment in the soap opera "factory" that would define its success, is the birth of contemporary Mexican media culture. Until that point, the Azcárraga ideal of entertainment had not explicitly included education; both Vidaurreta and Milmo had envisioned an empire of commercially viable offerings built largely around viewer escapism. They nonetheless were aware of serial storytelling as a long-proven method for connecting with audiences, heightening their engagement, building community, and, of course, increasing consumerism. Serial narratives had demonstrated that they could be lucrative in any medium. With television as his family's most profitable market thus far, Azcárraga Milmo was banking heavily on the soap opera genre as one of his most viable moneymakers. In Televisa's earliest days, Azcárraga Milmo equipped San Ángel studios to become the epicenter of *telenovela* production in Latin America, with TSM's *telenovela* stockpile ready to form the backbone of a future export business. Among Azcárraga's preferred producers was Chilean emigré Valentín Pimstein, who upon arriving at San Ángel became known for his formulaic Cinderella-style stories, later called the plague of "Marías" for their indistinguishable naming of heroines.[22] Pimstein's *telenovelas* elicited intense approval from the mass audience he was famous for courting and regularly tracking. With the debate about television's potential in full swing, fresh tensions emerged between television's growing commercial fortunes and its possibilities as a Mexican cultural force.[23] What positive role might this potent storytelling form exert on national culture?

A cohort already existed within Televisa that understood Mexico's long tradition of serialized storytelling (and had set high-quality precedents going back to the 1960s with TSM): Ernesto Alonso (1917–2007), Miguel Alemán Velasco (b. 1932), and José Miguel Sabido Ruisánchez (b. 1937) shared an intellectual interest in the intersection of didactic theater, radio, and television. Both Alemán and Sabido had become well versed in literary traditions through their studies at UNAM (Alemán with a degree in law, and Sabido in literature) and together with the experienced actor Alonso formed a triumvirate that recognized the cultural importance of popular storytelling in Mexico, by way of nineteenth-century foundational texts and the oral traditions in which they were based. Their work tapped into a non-elitist, participatory repository of entertainment that drew from a reservoir of national identity and culture. Alonso—"an important young film actor who abandoned his career to devote his life to serial melodrama"— was one of the first producers of Mexican soap operas and a key member of the Azcárragas' team throughout the 1960s, producing innovative work that contrasted with Pimstein's formulas.[24] Alonso's earliest efforts shared a distinctive focus on Mexican history, featuring an ostentatious, baroque style. His in-color series *Leyendas de México*, with many segments set in the colonial period, appealed both to the middle class and to some intellectuals generally averse to the television medium.[25]

In the first half of the 1960s, Alonso teamed up with Alemán Velasco to develop Mexico's first historical soap operas, as commissioned by the Mexican government.[26] Alemán Velasco was named TSM's general director in 1966, while working for former UNAM law professor and future president Luis Echeverría, then serving as secretary of the interior (1963–1969) under President Gustavo Díaz Ordaz (in office from 1964 to 1970).[27] From that privileged position, Alemán Velasco became one of the earliest promoters of educational television in Mexico, believing it an apt vehicle for a *pueblo* in need of knowledge of its history.[28] His initiatives in the 1960s produced a wave of expensive yet successful *novelas* that served as valuable precedents for the cultural expenditures that would be required of Televisa in the 1970s. The *telenovelas* processed themes originating in nineteenth-century serialized historical novels.[29]

Throughout the 1960s, the Mexican government showed keen interest in soap operas' potential for teaching history.[30] The historical series *Maximiliano y Carlota* (1965), one of Mexico's first *telenovelas*, was itself a reprise of one of Mexico's first *radionovelas*.[31] As the story goes, upon watching it, Díaz Ordaz paid particular attention to its "negative" depiction of President Juárez.[32] Díaz Ordaz called in Alemán and Alonso to request a superproduction that would emphasize Juárez's positive legacy. Using *Gone with the Wind* as their model, Alemán and Alonso co-produced with the government one of TSM's greatest hits: *La tormenta* (July–September 1967) was "a fictional love story at the center of a period drama that took important historical forces into account. Entertaining while educating was the challenge."[33]

La tormenta was the biggest domestic television production of that time: filmed on location, consisting of ninety-one thirty-minute episodes, this epic covered over fifty years of Mexican history (1857–1917), with a 800,000-*peso* budget and co-sponsorship from the Instituto Mexicano de Seguro Social (IMSS).[34] Historian Daniel Cosío Villegas, who initially scoffed at the soap opera as a means to teach history, would see in *La tormenta* a brilliant example of "democratic television that gives people an awareness of themselves through the evolution of national history."[35] To entertain while educating viewers, Alemán and Alonso assembled a brilliant intellectual team that included historians (who researched the plot's accuracy), the poet Eduardo Lizalde (who drew up the historical characters), and Sabido (who wrote the purely fictional scenes).[36] Years later, Sabido would remember that the aim was "to allow a space to present various opposing points of view . . . letting viewers decide where to best place their sympathies. *La tormenta* broke the canons of communication for the PRI and opened doors to a truly democratic soap opera."[37] Viewed by more than half the nation—an estimated twenty-six million Mexicans—*La tormenta* elevated the reputation of Mexican *telenovelas*.

Sabido would go on to become the key advocate of educational entertainment within Televisa for the next twenty years. He used his experience with the groundbreaking *La tormenta* "to propose the form of narrative discourse that he would later fine-tune for a series of educational soap operas."[38] He had arrived at TSM at the beginning of the decade as a writer recruited for Alonso's *Las momias de Guanajuato* (1962). Still in his twenties, Sabido already had an extensive background in drama and playwriting, having studied privately with Salvador Novo and with Luisa Josefa Hernández at UNAM, where he had earned his bachelor's degree with a thesis focused on Baroque theater, followed by further study with Hernández and Emilio Carballido.[39] Alonso quickly recognized Sabido's talent, and introduced him to many opportunities at TSM. Sabido's profound knowledge of colonial didactic theater and the history of Mexico's cultural movements meshed especially well with Alonso's baroque aesthetics and interests.[40]

Once TSM morphed into Televisa, Sabido would shift the predominant conservative tone to potent storytelling for social change.[41] He was to become a powerful middleman between Azcárraga and Echeverría, pressuring the newly formed Televisa to create educational initiatives. In 1972, Sabido shone in a series of meetings with President Echeverría, where he successfully argued that Mexican TV could be simultaneously educational, entertaining, and commercially profitable.[42] This formula—dubbed the "Mexican Model," for its viable ratio of education to entertainment—was a hybrid of the US (commercial) and European (government) models, freeing Televisa from competition and dividing profits between the private and public sectors. Each channel was designated for a specific socioeconomic segment, with "the popular classes" as Channel 2's target audience.[43] Sabido articulated Televisa's social uses to Echeverría, who then exercised a very forceful intervention toward this "project of sustained social benefit" that influenced the company throughout the 1970s.[44] Sabido would orchestrate Televisa's new social and cultural programming; Alemán Velasco, serving as Televisa's executive vice president, would handle public relations with Echeverría's government.[45] Sabido describes his job as setting the tone for daytime and evening programming and helping Azcárraga "to make dignified television for the Mexican *pueblo*."[46] Until the early 1990s, Sabido's ideas would be essential to Televisa's successful synthesis of business and exportation possibilities with its educational and cultural responsibilities.

During his years as Televisa's vice president of research and evaluation, Sabido redefined the soap opera as one of Televisa's most substantial cultural contributions, after convincing Azcárraga that Televisa should experiment with didactic melodrama.[47] In 1974, Sabido formed the Instituto Mexicano de Estudios de la Comunicación (IMEC), which hosted the inaugural Worldwide Communications Conference (*Encuentro Mundial de la Comunicación*). With a second edition in 1979, the *Encuentros* were international summits held in Mexico in which TV's role in culture and society was debated by theoreticians such as Marshall McLuhan and Umberto Eco, alongside national politicians such as Luis Echeverría, one of several efforts sponsored by Televisa to research how best to combine social themes with popular entertainment. Though Azcárraga supposedly referred to Sabido's educative projects at times as "bullshit" (*pendejadas*), he was nonetheless willing (or persuaded) to designate resources to charting viewer response to didactic soap operas.[48]

Sabido's *novelas educativas* began in 1975 as part of Televisa's "necessary social programming," at a time when television's ever-growing influence in society had been clearly borne out by statistics. When President José López Portillo arrived in office in 1976, he lauded Televisa's *novelas educativas* and soon contracted Azcárraga to serve as his public relations consultant (*asesor de imagen*) in 1977. Throughout the López Portillo *sexenio* (1976–1982), Televisa flourished—generating social prestige, profit, industry wealth, and publicity markets—at a time when the rest of the Mexican economy was floundering. During this period, Sabido directed and produced his first series of didactic *telenovelas*, engineering four successful titles in five years with the financial support of the Secretaría de Educación Pública (SEP) and additional support from the IMSS. Beginning with *Ven conmigo* (1975), which dealt with the importance of vaccinations, Sabido assembled all-star production teams—including his sister Irene and future dream-duo Carlos Olmos and Carlos Téllez—alongside powerhouse casts, with particularly strong women characters played by newcomer

Alma Muriel and veteran Silvia Derbez (who went on to work with Sabido again in 1977, 1979, and 1997).[49] Soaps such as *Ven conmigo* found a potent equilibrium between melodramatic and didactic content. Their success with the public, and their study by IMEC and through Sabido's *Encuentros Mundiales,* constituted a full-fledged social experiment far exceeding Echeverría's original demands.[50] At IMEC's second summit, communications luminaries were asked to articulate an international model for what Sabido had accomplished in Mexico.[51] A new era of Televisa soap operas had begun, espousing progressive values such as personal improvement, family integration, national pride, and community unity. Sabido became known as a "protagonist of that genre's evolutionary take-off" and a "development of its own language, with its own national accent," by relating soap operas' twentieth-century pedagogical possibilities to those of the seventeenth-century festive morality plays or popular pageants, known as *pastorelas.*[52] In Cueva's words, "Educational soap operas started from the assumption that the viewer was seeing a reflection of his own existence on the screen, and had to learn through the characters so as not to make their same mistakes, much like a large scale morality play (*pastorela*)." Cueva adds that the programs affect viewers by employing "images accepted by the group since time immemorial."[53] In the 1980s, on the shoulders of giants such as Sabido, the national storytelling showcased in Mexican soap operas would truly come into its own. In the crisis-ridden Mexico of that decade, the transformative potential of neobaroque stories—narrated serially through *telenovelas*—was particularly vital.[54]

As the government's credibility dwindled during the severe socioeconomic crises of the 1980s, Televisa became a stronger cultural force than ever. Soon Azcárraga would be considered the most powerful man in Mexico after the president.[55] 1978–1982 had been a period of galloping inflation, followed by heavy recession. When the government devalued its currency in 1982, deep economic chaos ensued; on the heels of devaluation came a devastating 1985 earthquake, rocking Mexico City to its core. The rest of the 1980s saw further deterioration of the economy, continued inflation, and increased unemployment. Between 1982 and 1987, Mexicans' personal purchasing power plummeted some 40 percent.[56] In the midst of these crises, however, television's influence kept rising. Heidi Nariman quotes Rubén Jara's observations: "More and more people don't have the money to go out to the movies, to the theater, or to take trips . . . What you will find is a real need to give people entertainment. Television is becoming the sole source of entertainment."[57] By the arrival of the Miguel de la Madrid *sexenio* (1982–1988), Azcárraga had fully consolidated his national television empire, with

Televisa as "the nearly absolute owner of the images that reached Mexicans through their television sets. Many programs arrived at their maximum splendor through these means."[58]

By 1985, journalist Alan Riding referred to television as Mexico's ministry of culture, education, and information: "The government's traditional responsibility for transforming society is being challenged by Televisa." [59] During this moment of great anxiety and possibility, the equilibrium required by the Mexican Model ceased to function. As entertainment imports were no longer viable, Televisa had to accelerate its domestic production schedule to a rate that compromised quality, and generalized economic uncertainty soon led to layoffs in production staff.[60] Azcárraga struggled to expand Televisa's cultural and educational programming during this precarious *sexenio*. Sabido collaborated with UNAM on a channel dedicated specifically to national culture (Channel 9, 1982–1983; Channel 8, 1985).[61] Televisa also cultivated relationships with intellectuals such as Octavio Paz to provide on-air commentary and assumed administration of some museums and other cultural institutions, as well as establishing a foundation that offered creative grants to academics and artists.

However short-lived, this period of cultural crisis would foster unexpected experimentation and innovation in Televisa, which met increased governmental demands for cultural programming with new national soap operas, strengthening the Mexican economy in turn through their exportation.[62] Mexico's economic woes had ironically created a climate favorable to domestic production. As more middle-class viewers tuned in, *telenovelas* became a bigger industry than ever, providing the public with a refuge in the form of "grand productions, to avoid great problems."[63] During this *sexenio*, the *novelas vanguardistas* of Victor Hugo O'Farrill began to take off, infusing a wonderfully dark neobaroque quality into the storytelling of national soaps.[64] O'Farrill had taken over operations at the San Ángel studios in 1976, working to attract more middle-class viewers by promoting significant innovation in the genre from 1976 to 1986.[65] Cueva describes Alonso, now reporting to O'Farrill, as specializing "in promoting the landscapes of a good part of the country, nearly at the level of touristic advertising."[66] Under O'Farrill's leadership, Pimstein produced *Rina* (1977), a terror *novela* inspired by *The Exorcist*, with a gothic-influenced script by Luis Reyes de la Maza (1932–2014), adapted from a radio serial by Cuban *radionovelista* Inés Rodena.[67] Once the Center for Radio and Television (RTC) relaxed censorship (1983), the O'Farrill era of experimentation accelerated, attracting new creative talent for the *telenovelas vanguardistas*.[68]

Since *Rina*, nearly all of Channel 2's featured evening programming was dedicated to national soap operas.[69] Within this robust environment, Televisa began airing *Martín Garatuza* on Channel 2 in June 1986.

Martín Garatuza and *El extraño retorno de Diana Salazar*, both broadcast on Channel 2, exemplified the strong neobaroque aesthetics of this highly creative period. Cueva describes the climate of the de la Madrid *sexenio*: "Serial melodramas, which had already reached a peak during the previous presidential period, now allowed themselves greater license, progressing from enclosed theatrical spaces, to grand locations. Torrid storylines indulged in experimentation with surprising open endings or mysterious last-minute revelations, and a new generation of younger producers began to sneak into the scene creating a movement toward renewal during that decade."[70] When back in the early 1970s Televisa executive Luis de Llano Palmer commissioned Reyes to select a Mexican classic—attractive to a broad national audience, young and old—for adaptation as a historical soap opera, he intuitively gravitated toward the works of Vicente Riva Palacio, like filmmaker Bustillo Oro before him (see Chapter 2). With a degree in Hispanic literature from UNAM, Reyes was well acquainted with the entertaining dramas and novels of "Don Chente," which he re-read for this occasion, in his search for a full expression of *lo mexicano*.[71] Like Sabido, Reyes had a rich background in didactic theater. He was recognized as an expert on theater's role in Mexican culture, and his memoirs indicate a vast familiarity with nineteenth-century Mexican letters.[72]

Reyes successfully straddled a career between literature and television, partially through leading a double life professionally, and using more than ten pen names over the course of his time at Televisa.[73] His entry into soaps coincided with the rise of Victor Hugo O'Farrill and the period of intense growth for Televisa (1976–1986), with soap operas at its center. From 1972 until 1980, Reyes directed Televisa's Department of Literary Supervision, which dealt with censorship and the correction of scripts.[74] Soon he began converting literary works into *telenovelas* that stood out for their sharp wit and darkly irreverent humor. First Pimstein invited Reyes to adapt the classic Mexican film *Nosotros los pobres* to television (1973); Reyes then worked with Pimstein on *Rina*, which he reworked directly from serial radio scripts written by Cuban *radionovelista* Inés Rodena.[75] He continued their collaboration with the successful *Viviana* (1978–1979).[76]

Following in the footsteps of his colleague Sabido, Reyes's intervention at Televisa in the 1970s and 1980s was marked by progressive soap operas centered on Mexican culture, and he soon came to be seen as an innovator of the genre.[77] He was recognized for his pioneering selection of surprising storylines; the broad diversity he cultivated in authors, styles, and themes; his use of social commentary to denounce hypocrisy; and his general interest in soap operas' artistic and social possibilities. By the 1980s, Reyes had filled several executive leadership positions in Televisa that allowed him to influence the way soap operas were being made.[78]

In 1985, Reyes used that standing to resuscitate his 1971 adaptation of Riva Palacio, and *Martín Garatuza* the soap opera was born, listed as a "free adaptation" under the pseudonym J. M. Rubio. Televisa director Fernando Moret, known for his eye for distinctive projects, reassembled his team from the long-running educational hit *Plaza Sésamo*.[79] *Martín Garatuza* aired in the daily slot of 7:00–7:30 p.m., Monday through Friday, on Channel 2, which by this point was known both as "El Canal de Las Estrellas" and "El Gran Canal de la Familia Mexicana," with the largest national viewership among Televisa's properties.[80] Its ninety episodes aired from June 30 until October 31, 1986, a four-month period covering approximately fifteen years in New Spain (1615–1630). *Martín Garatuza* was conceived to promote Mexican culture in a co-viewing package appealing to both young people and their families. The series highlighted Mexico's unique landscapes, ranging from Mexico City's recognizable urban streetscapes to sweeping panoramas (mostly shot on location in Guanajuato, Hidalgo), in an expansion of Riva's original plots. The son of *Martín* and *Plaza Sésamo*'s cinematographer Federico "Fritz" Weingartshofer, C'Cañak Weingartshofer (himself now a film editor and scriptwriter) would often accompany his father during filming. He remembers that taking technical crews out of their San Ángel comfort zone to shoot in natural settings raised *Martín*'s artistic credentials. The budget for the show provided for this luxury, as well as the expensive sets and extravagant period costumes that made historical soap operas so costly to produce (and displeasing to Azcárraga). Cast member Surya Mac-Grégor—nominated in 1986 for best supporting actress for her role as the villainess Luisa—recalls how the concept, cast, costumes, and filming on location proved a hit with audiences, and *Martín Garatuza* enjoyed reruns through the 1990s.[81]

As Reyes explains in his *Memorias*, his was no straightforward adaptation of Riva's classic novel. Reyes's retelling for a twentieth-century audience defies reliance on any one text, exposing a network of interrelated story sources all relating to the seventeenth-century baroque. He describes his process of adaptation as free form, drawing from other serial works of similar tone and storyline. Reyes intuited *Garatuza*'s compatibility with French journalist Michel Zevaco's anticlerical *Les Pardaillan*, a novel that daily newspapers had begun publishing in 1900 (and which was first translated to Spanish in the 1950s).[82] *Les Pardaillan*, like *Garatuza*, was a family melo-drama—a cloak-and-dagger historical novel also set in the seventeenth cen-tury, with a protagonist who was a rolling stone, enemy of the nobility, and ally of the common man.

To make matters more complex, *Martín Garatuza* the *telenovela* oper-ates under a serial logic much larger than the original storyline of its name. Reyes's main source was not its namesake novel, but rather its predecessor, *Monja y casada, vírgen y mártir*. By way of Riva's works, *Martín* the soap opera draws on oral tradition, the Inquisition Archive, and nineteenth-century novels published by newspapers. For Reyes, this was pure polycen-trism at play: "Since not even those five novels together gave me enough material for sufficient nonsense, I calmly mixed together with that the seven volumes of *Los Pardaillán*, by Zévaco, and made myself an extraordinarily beautiful cocktail."[83] This intertextual playfulness is typical of the neoba-roque, bursting the boundaries of a seemingly closed story to expose its belonging to multiple networks. Through shifting allusions to multiple texts, Reyes's adaptation decenters and opens the storyline to endlessly expand-ing narrative scenarios as needed, featuring numerous plot twists (*enredos*) that allow him to extend the work to ninety episodes.[84] These add-ons, par-ticularly to the last third of the soap opera, either come from *Les Pardaillan* or were inventions with no link to Riva's novels. (This chapter's summaries omit many of Reyes's most chaotic embellishments.)

Reyes's neobaroque "cocktail," with nineteenth-century historical nov-els set in the seventeenth century as its base ingredient, centered its inno-vations on irreverent social heroes and unexpected popular uprisings. As Walter Moser puts it, neobaroque protagonists tend to embody the "com-plex cultural paradigm changes" that "crystallize into anthropomorphic figures . . . They are usually figures from the cultural past who, through processes of re-use and re-interpretation, take on new meanings and are put to new uses."[85] Reyes's mash-up showcases Garatuza as a swashbuckling urban trickster circulating freely through Mexico's spaces and classes—a Riva Palacio redux. Its exuberant storyline required spectators to put their own order to the labyrinthine narrative chaos, with some essential take-aways: Garatuza's loyalty to his cross-class family and friends is never in question, and his determination to take care of his inner circle at all costs is a trait that cemented his reputation as New Spain's most fearless swords-man, most loyal friend, and superlative father.[86] The soap opera opens with a dramatic scene of his house in flames, with his wife dying in his arms and Martín (played by leading man Miguel Landeta) swearing to his child: "Son, will you help me avenge your mother? There will be no peace in New Spain until the Garatuzas cleanse this stain from our family's honor!" The soap opera is based on a sensational story of family vengeance, with allies arriving from all classes. Martín vows to protect the poor, the disenfranchised, the weak, and the oppressed, including but not limited to New Spain's most virtuous women. Despite his cynicism, our hero is a believer in true love, in bringing worthy individuals together in spite of the massive social forces pushing them apart. The widower Martín has no love interest himself but finds an unexpected confidant and valuable companion in like-minded swordsman Antonio, who joins his fight against New Spain's injustice and hypocrisy, embodied in the institution of the Inquisition.

The plot of the soap opera's first half follows Riva's *Monja* rather closely, with the exception of Antonio's story, which is based on the legends surrounding the intriguing historical figure of Catalina de Erauso, "La Monja Alférez," a seventeenth-century cross-dressing female who called herself Antonio, known to kill men and sleep with women. Antonio appears on the scene in *Martín Garatuza* in "that low-life dive, the Zambo's tavern," declaring himself from Lima, now working the dangerous mule route between Mexico City and Veracruz, where he fights *bandidos* in hand-to-hand combat and never loses a duel. He has arrived in Mexico City in search of Garatuza, whose fame had reached from Peru to the Philippines. He and Martín over time become fast friends (episode 44, 8/28/1986). Alongside Martín Garatuza (and later La Princesa Éboli), La Monja Alférez is an example of Reyes's choice to incorporate characters lauded in folklore for the sake of pleasing his audience. He was aware of viewers' familiarity with these oral traditions and knew that the incorporation of recognizable folk figures into *Martín Garatuza* would be a source of enjoyment for his viewing public.

True to Riva's novel, Martín's principal enemy is the Spaniard Don de Mejía, "the richest and most powerful man in New Spain," who is also close friends with the viceroy Marqués de Gelves and King Felipe II. In this soap opera, self-interest separates the good from the evil characters: with no intrinsic moral code or firm loyalties, villains are out for themselves and can easily be bought, quickly dismissing their debts: "let's forget about the past, and think only about the future" (episode 57, 9/16/1986), in the words of Pedro's villainous sidekick, Alonso.

In a storyline recycled from *Monja y casada*, Martín endeavors to protect lovestruck couple Fernando and Beatriz from her brother Alonso, who wants Beatriz to marry Pedro, his partner in crime. In the soap opera, Martín helps the couple overcome many obstacles until they finally marry and have a daughter, Lucía. Similarly, Martín defends Pedro's wealthy eighteen-year-old niece, Blanca (Mariana Levy), against her power-ful uncle. But Blanca finds a formidable enemy in the jealous femme fatale Luisa, who frames Blanca to be imprisoned and tortured by the Inquisition.

In the second half of the soap opera (beginning with episode 46), some elements of Riva's *Monja* and *Garatuza* remain, but the plot jumps ahead some years to focus on the aging Martín's sixteen-year-old son, Román, now following in his famous father's footsteps as an iconoclastic swords-man, and continuing the long family legacy as a staunch defender of virtu-ous women. When Román meets the noble Lucía, they fall in love in spite of their difference in social class. Father and son fight the growing injus-tices of the Spanish viceroy and his lowly local mercenary El Ahuizote. The Garatuzas eventually become fugitives in a fight for family and *pueblo* against the Inquisition. This second half features many winding side-plots involving female villains such as the enigmatic witch La Sarmiento (taken from Riva's *Monja*), and the aristocratic *criolla* princess La Éboli, a Reyes-constructed Mexican pastiche of the irreverent historical Spanish courte-san and powerful woman of intrigue from the Court of Felipe II.[87] In the denouement, Martín, Román, and Antonio escort Fernando, Beatriz, Lucía, and Blanca to Querétaro, where Román and Lucía are to be married. Pedro and Ahuizote ambush the group, and Antonio is mortally wounded in the crossfire. Martín discovers that his loyal swordsman Antonio is actually a woman—a former lady of society who abandoned her life of luxury to become a mercenary. "Antonio" declares her love for Martín while dying in his arms. Martín rides off into the sunset alone, having saved the lives of Blanca and Román once again.[88] This ending, like Riva's in 1868, is left open-ended to encourage further continuations, sequels, and remakes.[89]

On the surface, after decades of distance, *Martín* the soap opera might seem like an average escapist period piece with a swashbuckling hero. But a very specific quality (and function) of remediation is the call to under-stand one's present by way of the past. The formal strategies used to contest the "truths" of a dominant ideology, originally present in Riva's novel, are transposed into the twentieth century via Reyes. Viewer engagement inten-sifies when metafictional strategies blur fiction with reality, providing veiled commentary on controversial societal crises of the present. The challenges of Mexico's colonial baroque return to make their presence known in con-temporary crucibles, presenting a magnification by accumulation. This rep-etition reverberates in viewers' understanding, intensifying the urgency of these issues through repetition. Reyes's *Martín* refracted critical twentieth-century issues of class, gender, and sometimes race through the lens of Mexico's seventeenth-century past—as Riva once encouraged nine-teenth-century reflection on the colonial past through the historical novel. At a time when socioeconomic divisions in Mexican society had never seemed greater, *Martín*'s representation of the disenfranchised poor and subjugated women, oppressed by society's most powerful sectors, resonated fully with the public, highlighting complex relationships dating back to the colony and continuing to the present day. Such enduring inequalities are channeled through the neobaroque trope of existential illusion repeated in the original *Monja-Garatuza* series and then threaded all the way forward to this twentieth-century iteration. Offering a mirror by way of the baroque to a contemporary urban society in which similar social and gender-based oppression was recognizably present, Reyes's *Martín* offers its take on the question of women's liberation in Mexico's twentieth century.[90] In the soap opera's melodramatic spectacle of good versus evil, the archetypal bad guys are abusive to women, starting in the first episode, when Alonso threatens to punish his sister for refusing to marry his villainous buddy. These men conspire to marry off women against their will, exert physical force when dis-obeyed, and refuse to recognize females' intellectual capacity and free will.[91] They work together with the Church to oppress via the Inquisition or con-vent.[92] Pedro explains to Blanca, for example, that women's marriages should be planned by fathers or male guardians such as himself, and that a woman must marry who is prescribed for her or receive punishment from the Inqui-sition. The scene then cuts to Beatriz and her forbidden lover Fernando, kiss-ing each other passionately in Mexico City's open air. Virtuous women are shown to be motivated in their relationships by love; they are also kind and respectful to the disenfranchised, as seen in their treatment of servants.[93] Yet nearly all of Reyes's female figures rebel against the patriarchy in their own way: by episode 21 (7/28/1987), it has been established that both the arche-typal good women (e.g., Beatriz and Blanca) and archetypal bad women (e.g., La Sarmiento and Luisa) act unequivocally as powerful agents of resistance, regardless of their positive or negative coding within the storyline.

Although there are stereotypical catfights between female rivals over a male suitor, women are also seen helping each other to defy the patriarchy: the viceroy's clever wife, for example, endeavors to assist the victimized Blanca behind her husband's back (episode 16, 7/21/1986), and Blanca and Beatriz remain close allies in spite of men's attempts to divide them (episode 5, 7/4/1986).[94] "Bad women" such as La Sarmiento and Luisa are perhaps the most liberated of the women depicted, but will ultimately be punished for their transgressions (e.g., mercenary attitudes, lack of principles, and incursions into witchcraft and the occult).[95] There is an ongoing contrast in the first half of the soap opera between the oppression of good women and the freedom of bad ones, in which scenes with the prototypically good Beatriz are juxtaposed against those with the seductive La Sarmiento (episodes 4–6, 7/3–8/1986).

Reyes disrupts this pattern through his addition of La Monja Alférez. Playing further into the neobaroque trope of "things are not as they seem," Antonio/Catalina appears exactly halfway through *Martín Garatuza*, highlighting the questionable nature of socially accepted realities and breaking the typical melodramatic binary with which women were represented through the 1980s. Reyes positions the hybrid figure of Catalina de Erauso as an arbiter in the battle of good versus evil. Up until the midway point, the soap's plot was wound tightly around the contrast between two feminine opposites—Blanca (angel) and Luisa (devil)—both brutally punished by cohorts of powerful men during the climactic episodes 30 (8/8/1986) and 31 (8/11/1986), whose broadcasts were suspensefully separated by a weekend.[96] The forces of evil seem to have won, but then Antonio/Catalina arrives in episode 40 to turn the tide, and the virtuous finally begin to receive their just rewards.

In the neobaroque aesthetic, spectacles of illusion involving gender and identity are potent. Those who should be most honorable are not; those who seem men might be women. Casting a woman in the role of Antonio is a gesture of female power, as well as a cultural nod to the baroque's Monja Alférez. Additionally, it was a twentieth-century reversal of seventeenth-century baroque theater in which male actors frequently performed female roles while dressed as women. The Mexican public would have recognized actress Cecilia Toussaint playing the role of Antonio; she had already appeared in eight films (1978–1985) and one television series prior to *Martín Garatuza*. Presenting as a man throughout the soap opera, this character kills evil Alonso in hand-to-hand combat in the grand finale, but not before she has already won the respect and trust of the highly guarded Martín. In fact, the motor for Martín's ultimate vengeance against Pedro is his love for Antonio, appearing last but not least in his list of dearly beloveds—"For Blanca, for Beatriz, for Román . . . for Antonio: die, you filthy dog!"—as he thrusts a final blow into the murderer's chest. In the finale, Martín and Antonio (now revealed as Catalina), kiss and declare undying love for one another before Antonio expires.[97]

Martín's connections to all layers of colonial society replays the quintessentially neobaroque theme of illusion and disillusion. Martín and his motley cross-class alliance despise the corruption of the wealthy ("crooks and scoundrels of the lowest ilk. . ."; episode 3, 7/2/1986), while respecting the ethical essence of society's weakest members.[98] It is notable that the only unique story from Riva's *Martín Garatuza* that makes it into the soap is that of the defiant Carbajal family, fitting with Reyes's repeated theme of popular

rebellion, and showing his familiarity with the plot of Riva's original novels, which he had read many times over. Descendants of the Carbajal family, featured in Riva's melodramatic account of origins, appear in Reyes's
chaotic second half, with Ana de Carbajal y Arau serving as best friend
to the kindly elite Beatriz. The bad guys speak ill of the family while the
good guys embrace Ana and her relatives, in spite of their legacy as outcasts whose infamous ancestors were ignominiously burned at the stake.[99]

Meanwhile, Riva's fascinating tale of Teo as a noble African slave is left out
of Reyes's soap opera entirely, while in Riva's original *Monja* and *Garatuza*,
Teo is a principal figure whose heroic backstory is boldly told in his own
voice. In Reyes's *Martín*, Teo is a secondary figure—Blanca's servant. He is
played by a white man (filmmaker José Antonio Serrano Argüelles), and
Teo's voice in the soap opera is limited. Likewise, the wily tavern owner El
Zambo, whose name indicates a mixed racial category and who plays a significant role in the novel, never appears in *Martín Garatuza* (1986), even as
his tavern is a recurrent setting. These casting choices, and the line in which
the supposedly progressive character Román Garatuza refers to El Zambo's
mestizaje as a defect, indicate the soap opera's limits in terms of depicting
or discussing race.[100] Most important, the strange incident of Luisa being
shamefully "blackened" (though relatively faithful to the 1868 novel) and
her representation by a light-skinned actress in blackface are uncritical in
nature and go unquestioned. Blackness is presented as a punishment, albeit
at the hands of bad men, without any narrative commentary or context to
problematize it. The twentieth-century version of *Martín Garatuza* is nearly
whitewashed of racial referents.

The closest the soap opera comes to proactively and progressively
addressing race is through the supposed *mestizaje* of its central character
(in spite of the fact that the actor selected to play him, like nearly all the
actors in this soap opera, looks distinctly European—even the Indigenous
Ahuizote, played by Alonso Echánove). From the beginning of the soap
opera, Martín is declared *criollo* and *mestizo*, son of an Aztec princess and
a conquistador—a hybridity that, as in the novel, grants him access to all
social classes, as we glimpse in this early conversation between the elites
Beatriz and Fernando, who is a a close friend of Martín's:

> Beatriz: I have never heard so many adjectives used for one man . . . Where
> is he from? Is he a Spaniard?
> Fernando: No, he was born here in Mexico, apparently the grandson of a
> man who arrived with Cortés . . . They say his grandmother was an Aztec
> princess.
> Beatriz: Be that as it may, he is a good man.[101]

Martín's diverse networks model a meritocracy in which the difference between good and bad is not based in class but in principle; he participates in a brotherhood of trust, as opposed to the friendships of convenience generally modeled by the elite. Bad guys, in contrast, insist on preserving rigid hierarchies and the traditional patriarchy, displaying prejudice toward mixed castes and Indigenous people.[102] They abuse the oppressed, such as their servants (episode 16, 7/21/1986) and most women, whom Pedro describes to Blanca as highly submissive: "Life in this Colony is very quiet for the females, women spend their days at home embroidering or making sweets in the kitchen, and from time to time a lady or a priest visit, offering wholesome conversations that are good for the spirit." He tells her, "You must submit to the customs of this Colony . . . You will have no contact with the outside world and will avoid the temptations this city offers for a young woman such as yourself" (episode 7, 7/8/1986).[103]

Martín paints a contentious relationship among elites ruthlessly competing for colonial power. Kings and noblemen, Spanish or *criollo*, are generally portrayed as corrupt and classist, taking advantage of the disenfranchised who might otherwise benefit from their leadership. While the *pueblo* suffers on in the background, the Real Audiencia pits itself against a powerhouse alliance between Spain's King Felipe II and Viceroy Gelves.[104] In return for being overlooked, members of the lower classes express an overall ambivalence toward government: "Viceroys come and go like waves on the sea," says the character Anselmo (episode 40, 8/22/1986). Some become mercenaries out of lack of leadership and opportunity. "The world upside down" trope is also visible in the potentially benevolent institution of the Church, which is shown to be unequivocally evil as the source of Inquisition horrors and elite society's most conservative elements, intent on destroying the lives of mixed caste and Indigenous peoples and their allies.[105] Martín subverts these colonial stratifications to produce change, using rebellion, subterfuge, and disguise to buck the rigid structures imposed on the weak by a repressive society.

Related to this dynamic of social tension are the popular uprisings that advance Reyes's script. They were more influential in Riva's *Martín Garatuza* (than in *Monja*), whose central plot features a conspiracy led by Garatuza and his band of *criollos*, Africans, and Jews. Reyes times his relatively race-neutral rebellions to intensify his portrayal of a colonial class structure based in disparity that produces unrest. Popular uprisings punctuate the plot at its most climactic moments, placing the *pueblo* center stage as the soap opera's protagonist.

These chaotic rebellions are shown to be moments of extreme possibility, both for good and bad, and a paradigmatic neobaroque example

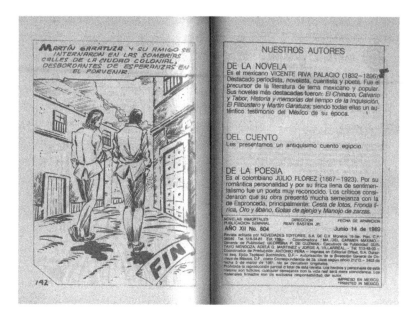

FIGURE 5.4. Page 142 and the back inside cover of *Martín Garatuza* (Novedades Editores, series "Novelas Inmortales," 1989), poignantly captioning the comic's end: "Martin Garatuza and his friend faded into the somber streets of the colonial city, overflowing with hopes for the future." Image courtesy of Christopher Conway.

of "the world upside down," in which a swashbuckling trickster is more honorable than a king's servant.[106] The plot of *Martín Garatuza*'s more topsy-turvy second half formally mirrors the popular unrest portrayed throughout, thus meshing with the soap opera's larger theme of rebellion. The first uprising, which takes some eight to ten episodes to represent, is incited when Don Pedro conspires with the viceroy to monopolize the *pueblo*'s lifeline crop, its corn. He raises prices to cause an uproar so that he might become viceroy as a result of this exploitation (episode 23, 7/30/1986).

The theme of the *pueblo* as protagonist is introduced as early as episode 2 (7/1/1986), when Pedro declares that he has discovered a mine much richer than Potosí: he who controls the corn controls the *pueblo*, setting the stage for a turbulent popular uprising to be used to his advantage. Other villainous characters exploit the perceived lawlessness of these popular rebellions to commit evil acts against weaker populations. In this first rebellion, for example, bad women such as Luisa take advantage of the chaos to manipulate the lower classes, while bad men take advantage of the chaos to abuse women.[107]

The second uprising of the *pueblo* foregrounds the impending execution of good woman Blanca and bad woman La Sarmiento. Here Martín speaks directly about the power of these rebellions to create change, allowing for a neobaroque world-upside-down (*mundo al revés*), which he sees as an opportunity to take rightful possession of a city whose privileges have been denied to certain classes for far too long: "We will be thousands. I am sure that if I focus on enlisting help from all the wretches of this Colony, all the beggars, thieves, murderers, robbers, all those living in the worst neighborhoods of this great Capital, we will succeed" (episode 35, 8/15/1986). A villager (*pueblerino*) confirms: "You're right, none of us will refuse to help you: we are thousands, Martín . . . The disinherited, those of us who have been abandoned by good luck and all fortune." The all-class crew of Martín, Fernando, and César participate fully in this second uprising in the name of good governance and the power of the people: "The crowd will not hesitate to take the viceregal palace in blood and fire . . . All of this colony's inhabitants will come together, it is the only way for our colony to move forward" (episode 26, 8/4/1986). They show themselves as willing to sacrifice their lives, as the close-knit gang will be arrested by the authorities for its participation.

The soap opera ends with the most important uprising of all, coinciding with Blanca's forced union with Alonso. On this occasion, Garatuza's involvement is decisive. While Blanca is being married off to the villain, Garatuza leads a crowd of beggars to storm the evil Princess Éboli's palace, where his son, Román, is being held captive. The guard tells Román that "the *pueblo* outside is rising up. Their wretched voices can be heard: 'Save Garatuza!' It is those friends of yours, the riffraff, the beggars, the wastrels who now come to save you." He then informs the princess that there is a "multitude of armed men and beggar women . . . who want to speak with you . . . more than a hundred . . . they want to take over the palace . . . the leader of this tattered army wants to consult on a life and death matter . . . the situation of Román Garatuza" (episode 87, 10/28/1986). The *pueblo* helps Martín to rescue his son and reunite the family, furthering the soap opera's depiction of Martín's close alliance with the masses.

Through the 1980s, Reyes became more daring in the social messages of his scripts, as well as in his executive proposals. Ironically, his earlier position as a government censor gave him the power and knowledge to envision more progressive uses for television in Mexican society. His desire to professionalize the soap opera industry and open it to more writers led Reyes and the Sociedad General de Escritores de México (SOGEM) to sponsor Televisa's first contest for writerly innovation in 1986, while *Martín Garatuza* was still on the air. In Reyes's 2014 obituary, Cueva writes that without Reyes, some of the most creative Mexican soap operas of the 1980s, citing *El extraño retorno de Diana Salazar* and *Cuna de lobos*, would never have been made.[108]

One of the 1986 contest's most notable submissions, the short story "Hasta que muera la eternidad" ["Until Eternity Dies"] had been penned by a mysterious young veterinarian from Mexico City, Mario Cruz García González (b. 1962).[109] Although no versions of this story are now available, we can infer from Cruz's other works that it was a gothic tale about a figure transported from the past and thrust into current times, with original elements of witchcraft and the occult. This unusual tale of reincarnation caught the experienced eye of Televisa producer Carlos Téllez (1925–1994), who was in search of a new hit. With the help of scriptwriter Carlos Olmos (1947–2003) and intellectual powerhouse María Margarita Villaseñor Sanabria (1934–2011), Téllez fleshed out the story into *El extraño retorno de Diana Salazar*.[110] Reyes was still at the helm of literary administration at Televisa, and it would have been evident to a writer with his experience that *El extraño retorno* was a clever gem.[111] Emblematic of Olmos's later style, this neobaroque bijou featured melodramatic irreverence, black humor, tragic farce, psychological games, complex psychologies, and dark relationships, as well as an acerbic critique of religion, fully fitting for the crisis-filled epoch in which Mexico found itself.[112]

El extraño retorno de Diana Salazar became a multimedia extravaganza, presenting (neo)baroque *bizarrería* at its best. Its production crew shared many of the characteristics of Televisa's more intellectual teams—those brought together by Sabido and Reyes and closely connected to UNAM's Literature Department. Téllez had begun his directing career on Sabido's didactic soap *Vamos juntos* (1979–1980), but his fame as a producer had taken off by the mid-1980s, thanks to a string of hits with Olmos.[113] The two had met in the late 1970s while working with Sabido, for whom Olmos had written the didactic works *Acompáñame* (1977) and *Caminemos* (1980), prize-winning social dramas on family planning and sex education that were lauded for their entertainment as well as commercial value.[114] In the 1980s Téllez invited Olmos to work on a period piece about 1940s cabaret life in Mexico City, *La pasión de Isabela* (1984–1985), starring acclaimed stage actor Héctor Bonilla. From that point on, the Téllez-Olmos duo enjoyed a reputation for quality production values, a strong sense of timing, and innovative endings. These *vanguardistas* stood far above the crowd in Televisa's "factory" of formalistic, Manichaean soap operas à la Pimstein.[115] They completely finished their scripts before beginning production, giving

FIGURE 5.5. Still from the opening sequence of *El extraño retorno de Diana Salazar* (1989). A tearful Lucía Méndez appears in profile during the show's dramatic opening credits. Image from the author's personal collection.

FIGURE 5.6. Still from the opening credits of *El extraño retorno de Diana Salazar* (1989). Professor and critic Margarita Villaseñor Sanabria brought considerable literary and historical knowledge to bear on the script of *El extraño retorno*. Image from the author's personal collection.

their soap operas a distinctive, stylistic coherence. As a producer, Téllez made inspired casting choices, using established, classically trained actors (like Bonilla or Alejandro Camacho) and daringly discovering new talent (such as Diana Bracho, María Rubio, and Rebecca Jones) rather than relying on the *vedettes* and singers for which Pimstein's soaps were known.[116]

Because of his excellent eye for talent, Téllez was soon seen as a star-maker and a team-builder in his own right. Téllez-Olmos had created the highest-rated *telenovela* in Mexican history, *Cuna de lobos* (1986–1987), the work that "enlivened the economic collapse of '87."[117] Olmos had written its script based on strong female protagonists obsessed with their family lineage ("Family First!" / *¡La casta es primero!*]), and a dark villainess styled on Bette Davis's iconic character in *The Anniversary* (1968).[118] Téllez created a finale so definitive that the episode "paralyzed" Mexico City for a day, with millions glued to their TV sets. The *Cuna* phenomenon launched villainess Catalina Creel (played by Reyes's then-wife, María Rubio) into meta-fictional fame, as folks claimed kinship to the Creel family and clamored for Catalina's presidential candidacy, from Ciudad Nezahualcóyotl to Chihuahua.[119] *Cuna de lobos* ended on June 5, 1987, to record audiences, with a nearly 50 percent viewership rating for the finale, becoming one of the most emblematic and most viewed Mexican soap operas of all time.[120] This creative jewel was produced during a rare period known as the "Spring of Televisa": Alemán Velasco was left in charge of Televisa for almost a year, as Azcárraga Milmo had left for Los Angeles in August 1986 to set up UNIVISA/Univisión.[121] Alemán had retained his strong belief in television's educational potential: still, in 1985, fifteen percent of adults remained illiterate and the average span of a citizen's education was five years.[122] Alemán used this brief but important moment to spearhead Televisa's innovation with *Cuna de lobos* and a revival of Alonso's historic soap operas, featuring the Sabido-scripted *Senda de gloria* (1987), a series focusing on the rise of Lázaro Cárdenas in the period from 1917 to 1939. The curtain fell quickly on such experimentation once Azcárraga returned in June 1987, resuming his former leadership style and sharply staunching the flow of money to cultural and educational programming.[123]

But there was one exception. As the story goes, Azcárraga had promised to grant a whim to his favored actress, Lucía Méndez, Televisa's biggest female star at that time. Méndez's wish—to star in a Téllez-Olmos script titled *El extraño retorno de Diana Salazar*—generated one last experimental hit for that team, following the stunning success of *Cuna*.[124] The dynamic duo produced *El extraño retorno de Diana Salazar* with Méndez in the innovative title role. This was a super-production of epic proportions, with a high budget, sophisticated scenes, showy locations, expensive costumes, and a stellar cast. The opening episode was a spectacularly baroque hourlong extravaganza. With Téllez working production and direction, and Téllez-Olmos-Villaseñor on script, *El extraño retorno* consisted of 196 episodes painstakingly filmed over approximately nine months—considerably

FIGURE 5.7. Cover, *Revista Tele Guía* (año 37, no. 1906, February 18–24, 1989). *Tele Guía* was published weekly by Televisa from 1952 to 2007. This 1989 headline features some so-called "White Magic from Miss Lucía Méndez and Carlos Monsiváis, in the most commented-upon encounter of the year, brought to you by *Tele Guía*." Image from the author's personal collection.

longer than the average Mexican soap opera.[125] The 30- to 45-minute episodes were transmitted during prime time (9:30–10:00 p.m.) Monday–Friday, from April 11, 1988, until January 13, 1989. They aired, like *Martín Garatuza*, on Televisa's Channel 2. By the late 1980s Televisa had so much power as a commercial monopoly that it was considered the most important media conglomerate of Latin America.[126]

El extraño retorno de Diana Salazar is an allegory driving at the very essence of Mexico's (neo)baroque remediations of the 1980s: an understanding of one's present achieved by deep investigation of one's past. A young woman (Lucía Méndez), accused by the Inquisition of being a witch and burned at the stake in 1640, is reincarnated in 1988 and subsequently struggles with nightmares of bonfires and an obsession with death. The series begins in seventeenth-century Zacatecas with the young, beautiful, wealthy, and clairvoyant Doña

Leonor de Santiago, happily awaiting her betrothal to local gentleman Don Eduardo de Carbajal (Jorge Martínez). Leonor's family is cautious, fearing that her psychic powers will be discovered by the Inquisition. In addition to hearing and seeing things that others do not, Leonor occasionally enters altered states: her eyes change to deep amber, and she causes damage with a strength that she doesn't comprehend.[127] Lucrecia Treviño (Alma Muriel) curses Leonor, with the assistance of the African witch Casilda (Ella Laboriel), for winning the handsome Eduardo. At Leonor's engagement to Eduardo, before the most powerful members of Zacatecan society, Lucrecia denounces her rival to the Inquisition, a declaration that ignites Leonor's fury, shattering the palace chandelier in front of the astonished guests. Leonor and Eduardo are taken away and burned at the stake as they swear eternal love. Lucrecia hangs herself while grasping Leonor's *relicario* (a tiny locket containing a miniature portrait), dying simultaneously with the ill-fated couple.

Fast-forward three hundred years to the urban megapolis of Mexico City: Diana Salazar, a stressed out and insecure student of business administration, finds a beautiful locket whose hinges pinch her finger, drawing blood—a dark omen. The locket triggers Diana telekinetic powers, and she begins to suffer nightmares in which she sees herself accused of witchcraft and burned at the stake at a handsome gentleman's side. From episode 2 on, we see the theme of history's eternal return, despite the fact that Diana wants nothing to do with the past (4/11/1988). An underlying family drama is that Diana's mother has rejected her, believing that she unwittingly caused the death of Diana's father. Only her sister, the aspiring author Malena (Rosa María Bianchi) keeps believing in Diana. Eventually her nightmares and feelings of guilt lead Diana to seek the help of prestigious parapsychologist Irene del Conde, who uses hypnosis to discover that Diana is Leonor reincarnate. When a newspaper announces the arrival of young Argentine engineer Mario Villarreal at SanTelmo Digital, a Mexico City company interested in Mario's micro-computers, Diana clips his photograph. She "remembers" him as the man who appears in her nightmares, dreams in which her accuser has the face of her psychologist, who dismisses these strange similarities as projections of Diana's subconscious onto the present. Meanwhile, Irene's lover Omar (Alejandro Camacho) has become dangerously attracted to his girlfriend's beautiful client, Diana. Around the same time, Malena attends an antiques auction with her boyfriend Gonzalo and SanTelmo's Mario, where she is amazed to find a seventeenth-century portrait of a woman who looks identical to her sister.

FIGURE 5.8. Doña Leonor de Santiago longs for her wedding to the noble Eduardo de Carbajal in this still from *El extraño retorno de Diana Salazar* (1989). Image from the author's personal collection.

Mario claims that Diana's face exists in his memory, and when Malena tells that story to her sister, Diana inadvertently sets off a music box with her entranced gaze. Gonzalo begins to investigate Leonor de Santiago in historical documents, and when he finally introduces his friend Mario to Diana, she faints with the force of recognition. Mario and Diana fall deeply in love.

Irene travels to Zacatecas, where she purchases Leonor's *relicario* and realizes that she herself is a reincarnation of Leonor's rival. After a serious car accident and the appearance of a strange "servant," Jordana (Patricia Reyes Spíndola), who intends to help her recuperate, Irene sets out to conquer Mario with Jordana's diabolical assistance. Mario and Diana do not yet realize the grave threat that Irene and Omar pose to their lives, although Mario encourages Diana to stop visiting the psychologist, who makes her feel guilty about her powers and has offered her "vitamins" that worsen her mental state. When Mario proposes, he gives Diana a reproduction of Leonor's locket, as worn in her portrait. Mario loves Diana deeply in spite of medical concerns: Irene has told Diana that if she has children, they will be chronically ill. Diana postpones the wedding, afraid that anyone who gets close to her will die. When Irene successfully seduces Mario, Diana marries Omar in revenge. On her wedding day she signs the license with the name "Leonor," as if in a trance, and her mysteriously damaged portrait falls off Gonzalo's wall.

FIGURE 5.9. This still from *El extraño retorno de Diana Salazar* (1989) illuminates modern star-crossed lovers Diana and Mario against the dark backdrop of Doña Leonor's haunting seventeenth-century portrait. Image from the author's personal collection.

As Diana doggedly sleuths the hidden connections between her now-husband Omar and Irene, she realizes that the enigmatic portrait from her past, seemingly alive, holds the key to her present, as she grows in confidence and in the use of her powers (episode 123, 9/27/1988). Gonzalo discovers a similar portrait of a different woman dressed in black, her face concealed by dark paint, with the name "Lucrecia T." As he tries to restore the face in the portrait, it is stolen by Irene, who covers the portrait's surface with a mirror. Gonzalo also discovers in his historical investigations that Don Eduardo de Carbajal had a birthmark considered diabolical by the Inquisition; he knows his friend Mario has the same birthmark, confirming a three-way reincarnation involving Diana, Irene, and Mario.

Taking matters fully into her own hands, the suffering Diana tells Mario about the triple reincarnation. He annuls his marriage to Irene, who has declared she prefers him dead than with Diana. After several tragedies, murders, and suicides, Mario and Diana move in together in spite of continued threats from Irene, whose voice Diana is now able to recognize in the voicemails. At the end, Irene lures the couple to Zacatecas, to the very spot where they had publicly declared their love some three hundred years before. In this final episode, Irene fires at Diana but Mario takes the bullet, as Diana cries out: "Mario will love me always, he will love me for eternity, Lucrecia!" Upon hearing those words, Irene shoots Diana, who is holding

FIGURE 5.10. Cover, *Revista TV y Novelas* (año x, no. 10, May 11, 1988). Diana's fearsome amber-eyed transformations enthralled 1980s viewers, forming part of this movie's dazzling special effects, some executed by young on-set intern Guillermo del Toro. Méndez's expensive contact lenses were state of the art for that time, and this cover caption reads, "Lucía Méndez is giving away Diana Salazar's contact lenses. . . what an amazing gift!" Image from the author's personal collection.

the dying Mario. Diana is transformed, eyes amber, and lifts Irene with her gaze to fatally impale her mortal enemy on the Salazar family's coat of arms.

In another shockingly creative finale devised by Téllez, a terrified Leonor awakes at Eduardo's side, back in the seventeenth century.[128] Leonor and Eduardo, who have been together for six years of complete happiness, console each other while Leonor tells Eduardo about the strangest dream, of a future where their doppelgängers—a young woman named Diana and a young man named Mario—could not be together because of an evil woman named Irene. The dream also contained their past—a terrible night of being accused by the Inquisition, Lucrecia's suicide, their reprieve, and Casilda the witch being burned in their place as her diabolical schemes were discovered. The dream leads the couple to ask, "What price will we have paid for this happiness . . . or maybe we haven't paid it yet?" (episode 196, 1/13/1989). Had it been nothing more than a dream? With this thought-provoking flourish—the neobaroque trope of "Life is a Dream" (*la vida es sueño*) made modern—*El extraño retorno* was guaranteed to persist in viewers' minds long after the TV set went dark. This metafictional finale was brilliantly open-ended. Already longer than the average Mexican *telenovela*, with nearly two hundred episodes, *El extraño retorno* had copious material and a rabid fandom—a promising base for narrative accumulation and proliferation.[129] The reincarnation theme left room for potential remakes to start with the happy life of Diana and Mario and a tragedy that never happened, until another reincarnation emerged from their dark Colonial past.

Sadly, however, the innovation of Televisa's neobaroque period was short-lived. Televisa's creative investment in *telenovelas* died with political and cultural changes in the 1990s: Azcárraga fired Sabido in a rapid return to business-as-usual, and Téllez died of AIDS, his creative value relatively unrecognized at the time of his death.[130] Composer Plascencia Salinas died two months after Téllez. When 55-year-old Olmos died of respiratory failure in 2003, he was purportedly writing a remake of *Cuna de lobos*. (A new version of the series was reissued by Televisa in 2019.) The importance of the period has since been acknowledged and emulated (see Epilogue), in spite of Alfredo Gudinni's melodramatic declaration that "These avant-garde days will never again return!"[131] They have now come back as nostalgia: *El extraño retorno* has become a cult classic, with a very active Facebook page where fans persistently clamor for remakes and reissues, about which there continue to be rumors.

Within this aesthetics of repetition, we see an ongoing recycling of past elements and a notable return of the repressed. First and foremost, Reyes recycles Riva's efforts to bring history to the people—to process critical issues such as gender and class. It is interesting that in the nineteenth century Riva was more ready than Reyes to examine the most repressed elements of the colony such as *mestizaje*: in fact, Mexico's racial mixing during the colonial era is the centerpiece of his novelistic initiatives. During her induction into the Academia Mexicana de la Lengua in 1985, UNAM's Clementina Díaz de Ovando—a great fan of Reyes, having written the prologue to one of his academic works from that same year—spoke directly to Riva's daring engagement with race in Mexico's formative baroque period through historical novels, which like Reyes's soap opera were all serialized:

> The probe into our national identity . . . has been conducted through . . . the historical novel; through this novel [Riva] has endeavored to write the history of our Colonial period; to critique and examine [it], . . . not rejecting it but, rather, making it our own, incorporating it into Mexico's historical

consciousness. Also in these historical novels with colonial themes, Riva Palacio affirms our Indigenous past. These two legacies are united in his novel as essential elements of Mexican development. He speaks loudly in favor of biological and cultural *mestizaje*e . . . Mexican people's independence . . . unlike in other nations, had the peculiarity of resulting from the creation of a new nation, the *mestizo* nation that, for centuries, had been in conflict with itself and its ancestors . . . The *mestizo*, the Mexican, once he was completely and without hesitation master of his biological and historical reality, of his *mestizo* being . . . turns his gaze to his Indigenous ancestry to recover its values . . . and, at the same time, with a clean and no longer tarnished view, rests in the Spanish colonial world, where he accepts it, adorns himself with it, sustains himself with pride in that splendid era that reached, at some point, the glory of including everyone, encompassing everything.[132]

In the reincarnation of such works as contemporary neobaroque soap operas, the *mestizaje* so essential to Riva Palacio's nineteenth-century formulations are largely left out of the equation. Díaz de Ovando delivered this address just one year before *Martín Garatuza* aired. Her message would not have been lost on a scholar such as Reyes, who also knew Díaz. He nonetheless made a clear choice to minimize racial difference in his 1986 re-working of Riva.

The Mexican protagonist Diana Salazar, however, *is* forced through present suffering to examine her historic past—a process that indeed produces some strange "returns" from the colonial baroque. This cycle, at its deepest level, manifests as a baroque-style questioning of one's true identity and the nature of truth itself. The soap's main theme was reincarnation, and Diana's return from the seventeenth-century provinces into twentieth-century Mexico City was a metaphor for something more: a refashioning of past forms for present purposes.

Diana's modern torment is best explained by the return of unresolved issues. The only way to alleviate her suffering was to delve deep into a process through which the neobaroque tropes of a networked aesthetic of complexity—creating a hallucinatory quality by liberating plot from linear time—and of illusion—"things are not as they seem" and "the world upside down"—are foregrounded. These recurrent themes unite Téllez's *Extraño retorno* with Riva's *Monja-Garatuza* by way of Reyes's *Martín Garatuza* in concentric ripples and polycentric circles that reflect a serial logic much larger than a single soap opera. By way of Reyes and Riva Palacio, *El extraño retorno de Diana Salazar* draws on oral tradition, the Inquisition archive, and novels published by newspapers, a network of interrelated sources all

relating to the seventeenth-century baroque, and encompassing the maca-
bre through Mario Cruz's short story. These intertextual evocations are typical of the neobaroque, in which a seemingly closed story in fact belongs to
multiple networks through shifting allusions to multiple texts.

In another strange return from this family of texts, Diana's last name is
Salazar, and her seventeenth-century avatar is Leonor, the name of a *crip-
tojudía* (hidden jew) of the Carbajal family, Leonor de Carbajal, processed
by the Inquisition in 1595,[133] and represented in Riva's *Martín Garatuza*
as the youngest of the three Carbajal sisters. In the 1986 soap opera, the
last name of Leonor de Santiago's seventeenth-century lover is Carbajal.
Salazar is the surname of the historical Martín Garatuza, né Martín de
Villavicencio Salazar, as well as one of the most prominent families featured in Riva's *Martín Garatuza*, where his relationship to them by maternal lineage is implied. The surname of the historic Carbajal family plays a
prominent role both in the Inquisition archive and in Mexican oral tradition. The historical family was notoriously persecuted by those authorities for their supposed Judaism and burned at the stake toward the end of
the sixteenth century. In Riva's *Garatuza*, the Carbajals were portrayed as
heroic underdogs, conspiring to save *criollo* Mexico from the Spaniards
and creating the new *mestizo* race.

El extraño retorno both underscores and intensifies the relationship of the 1868 and the 1986 *Martín Garatuza* to the bizarre and spectacular, and to witchcraft and the occult, associated in all cases with
females. In *Monja*, La Sarmiento is a completely marginalized figure living outside of the city and society. In the soap, she becomes a beautiful and exotic enchantress nearly capable of bewitching the stoic Martín.
Witchcraft and the occult are seen in Reyes's soap as a space of liberation for powerful women operating outside of societal norms, in occult
spheres, privy to baroque realms of alternate realities, of fortune-telling
and spell-casting, all shown as potential spaces for power that eventually end in their punishment. In *El extraño retorno*, however, witchcraft
and the occult are redeemed through the figure of Diana. Although she
suffers in the process of coming to terms with her talents and is mis-
understood by her family members for possessing them, the heroine
uses her superpowers organically—out of self-defense—to defeat injustice. Diana's powers embody rebellion and resistance as opposed to
evil. (It should be noted that true punishment is reserved for the African slave Casilda, who uses her "black" magic to help Lucrecia destroy
Leonor, as well as for the diabolical Lucrecia and the twentieth-century
religious fanatic Jordana.) The binaries of dark and light sorceresses are

FIGURE 5.11. Domestic scene from El *extraño retorno de Diana Salazar* (1989) depicting upper-class customs in seventeenth-century Zacatecas. Image from the author's personal collection.

FIGURE 5.12. Doña Leonor and Don Eduardo face the Inquisition authorities in *El extraño retorno de Diana Salazar* (1989). Image from the author's personal collection.

FIGURE 5.13. Doña Leonor and Don Eduardo are sentenced to their fate by the Inquisition in *El extraño retorno de Diana Salazar* (1989). Image from the author's personal collection.

FIGURE 5.14. An isolated Leonor awaits execution in *El extraño retorno de Diana Salazar* (1989). Image from the author's personal collection.

emphasized through the black and white dresses of the women in episode 1 (4/8/1988). All these women are punished by death, whereas the exceptional Diana is shown to be immortal—the survival of a modern woman who overcomes her past through integration with her present.

Martín Garatuza and *El extraño retorno* each provided links between Mexico's seventeenth- and twentieth-century cultures. These linkages emphasized newfound modernity while highlighting the continuation of the national past into the present, depicting a society in crisis and suggesting ways to break the cycle.[134] As a 1988 production, *El extraño retorno* also referenced *Martín Garatuza* from two years before, playing off its success and building on its themes, reinforcing an aesthetic of repetition that increases recognition while pushing traditional Mexican stories and their retellings into ever more modern contexts.

The seventeenth-century past in *El extraño retorno*, like the twentieth-century present, is full of hypocritical authorities, who must be navigated similarly by both Leonor and Diana. In the seventeenth century, Leonor is surrounded by corrupt authorities (the clergy and wealthy members of her conservative social class) who manipulate and betray her. The vulnerable Diana is likewise surroundedby deceitful authorities (psychiatrists, businessmen, parents) who aggravate her suffering instead of alleviating it. It is only through the protagonist's independent quest—her "heroine's journey" through the convoluted baroque labyrinth—that she uncovers her true origins and breaks the cycle of repetition, empowering herself in the process. This journey and her experience of multiple realities also leads to an existential questioning of reality itself, to the discrediting of voices of authority, and to a revindication of the persecuted that changes the status quo.

The spectacle of *El extraño retorno* in the 1980s was so simultaneously avant-garde and baroque as to bewilder and at times disorient its viewers. The plotline featured an ongoing fixation with the serial, the sequel, the facsimile, and the reproduction in both centuries represented. To reproduce a work of art, in the Benjaminian sense, was a means of renewing it, of making it useful again in the present. We see this in *El extraño retorno*'s repeated motif of original versus copy, in the characters' obsessions with representations and reproductions of the self: Diana's newspaper clipping featuring Mario's photo; Doña Leonor's seventeenth-century portrait where she wears her own image in a baroque locket as mise en abîme; Lucrecia's original seventeenth-century portrait, which is painted over in the antique shop; original versions of the "real" (seventeenth-century) Leonor and Lucrecia versus their twentieth-century "reproductions" (in Diana and Irene);

FIGURE 5.15. The witch Casilda casting a spell in *El extraño retorno de Diana Salazar* (1989). Image from the author's personal collection.

and the appreciation and restoration of antiquities (with expert restorer of antiquities Luis Juárez murdered by the evil Irene in episode 138, 10/18/1988). There is an intradiegetic obsession with portraiture not respecting its limits, as various frames from the past spill their contents into the present (such as when Mario dreams obsessively of the seventeenth-century portrait, with its canvas split wide open), in a chaotic, exuberant dismissal of formal boundaries. The past is alive in the present, and within this context, its eternal return is not necessarily welcomed. At the same time, the technique of reproduction presents itself as a possible instrument for renewal—not just of the work of art but of Diana's understanding of reality. *El extraño retorno* rolls out a preponderance of 1980s technologies of replication: print photographs, microfilm, microfiche, PC micro-discs, voicemails, and altered tape recordings that reveal past truths (episodes 125–26, 9/29–10/3/1988). The duplications and mirrorings that are typical of neobaroque aesthetics play a prominent and pivotal role in *El extraño retorno*'s plot. The focus in episode 6 (4/15/1988) between the lost seventeenth-century portrait and a lost twentieth-century diskette are metonymic objects for the periods they represent, used here to highlight the soap opera's deliberate temporal contrasts.

Likewise, the themes of *El extraño retorno* foreground modernity and tradition concomitantly, entrancing viewers with their eclectic and at times exotic combinations: reincarnation, telekinesis, hypnosis, and parapsychology; international industrial espionage involving Mexico as well as Argentina, Japan, and Russia; a critique of religious fanaticism; and a promotion of women's rebellion. *El extraño retorno* emphasized these topoi through a host of baroque-themed special effects: disguises, visions, levitations, optical illusions (tromp l'oeil), and tricks with portraits and mirrors, not to mention the spectacular conflagrations so relished by the seventeenth-century Inquisition.[135] The multimedia experience intensified viewers' experience of Mexico's past and present through new combinations of textual, visual, and auditory stimulation—a past re-created and reinforced through sounds and images, elaborate costuming, and filming on location. Toggling back and forth between 1640 and 1988, episodes were shot on location in Zacatecas and Mexico City with sophisticated sets, amazing historical costumes and dazzling special effects (such as Diana's expensive amber eyes) that were state-of-the-art and cutting-edge for the 1980s.[136] The music was also spot-on: Téllez favored composer Pedro Plascencia Salinas, renowned for soundtracks that accentuated and complemented Olmos's melodramas to perfection.[137] For *El extraño retorno*, he scored the emotional entanglements of the protagonists and unending struggles between good and evil, drawing spectators into an intense experience manifesting across multiple media. Lucía Méndez sang many of the songs herself, including Juan Gabriel's opening and closing theme songs, which went on to become hits

FIGURE 5.16. *El extraño retorno* foregrounds its obsession with print seriality and original versus copy, such as in Diana's newspaper clipping of Mario's photo (depicted here in a movie still) or in Doña Leonor's seventeenth-century portrait where she wears her own image in a baroque locket as mise en abîme.

FIGURE 5.17A & 5.17B. Pages 32 & 33, *Revista TV y Novelas* (1988). Fans are drawn in by magazines' interactive games and gifts related to their favorite soap opera: "Lucía [Méndez]'s eyes can be yours . . . if only her eyes" and "A mask of Diana's face, just for you." These particular offers play on *El extraño retorno*'s baroque-themed tricks of tromp l'oeil: disguises, visions, levitations, and optical illusions with portraits and mirrors, not to mention spectacular conflagrations and effects at once old and new, baroque and contemporary. Image from the author's personal collection.

on Azcárraga's radio station in true transmedial fashion.[138] These multimedial effects were enthralling, linking old and new, baroque and contemporary, in unexpected combinations that highlighted Mexico's modernity in ostentatious ways.

El extraño retorno de Diana Salazar placed familiar elements of traditional Mexican storytelling into its most modern context to date. In spite of its risks and expenses, or perhaps because of them, *El extraño retorno* was one of Televisa's biggest soap opera wins. *El extraño retorno* lived up to its promise as a Téllez-Olmos star-making vehicle: diva Lucía Méndez consolidated her status, as did Argentine star Jorge Martínez, throughout the Spanish-speaking world; Alma Muriel and Alejandro Camacho also rose to stardom. The series' popularity was breathtaking, its stars accosted by fans throughout its filming and occasionally forced into isolation. During the height of its popularity, it was said that competing shows and channels tried to blackmail *El extraño retorno*'s stars for secrets in order to leak the plotline to reduce viewer interest. A huge hit in Europe, *El extraño retorno* was exported by Televisa International and shown during prime time in more than thirty-five countries. It collected numerous award nominations throughout 1988 and 1989 (including the prestigious Association of Latin Entertainment Critics of New York [ACE] Awards for Best Director and Best Show, 1989). This *telenovela* was memorably innovative and wonderfully creative, inciting dark collective passions both at home and abroad.

This exploration of *Martín Garatuza* and *El extraño retorno de Diana Salazar* reveals the uses of a revival neobaroque seriality in times of national crisis: "Soap operas became an object of collective passion. In other words, serial melodramas are passion-filled stories that likewise generate overflowing and irrepressible passions in their public."[139] Through them we can see these twentieth-century soap opera spectacles as quintessentially neobaroque phenomena, exhibiting many of the qualities theorized through the neobaroque "aesthetic": serial logic, polycentric storytelling, the incorporation of new media and spectacle, inducing contextual conditions such as intense viewer engagement and mass consumerism. The seventeenth-century baroque returns to make its presence felt in the storytelling of the present, both in form as well as content.

As Ndalianis explains, the contemporary neobaroque best "finds its voice within a mainstream market."[140] As we have seen throughout this book, in Mexico these stories' roots go far deeper than the beginning of the twentieth century and mass culture. From *El Periquillo* onward, Mexican serial narratives tended toward ever new forms of technology in ways that consistently enhanced consumers' experiences and involvement. Through the rise of Mexican television from the 1960s to 1980s, we see serial narratives' tendency to gravitate toward "the newest media environment." This connection of narrative to mass media and consumerism originated in the seventeenth century in novels such as *Don Quixote* that exhibited their own serial logic and concern with aesthetic repetition, metafiction, and readerly involvement. According to Ndalianis, the main difference between the seventeenth century and the contemporary era is essentially one of intensification, as seriality has become ever more integral to mass entertainment in the twenty-first century. The highly professionalized environment of Televisa's 1980s soap operas provided a new vehicle for national stories to morph beyond their formal limits, foregrounding intersecting characters and storylines that moved across multiple media. These televised series highlight the neobaroque through their chaotic and exuberant (lack of) form, demanding that consumers participate to make meaning out of their excess. Perhaps most important, this meaning-making process required remediation—an understanding of the present by way of the past. Televised soap opera expressed neobaroque qualities as no other form. Beginning with the rise of the prime-time television in the 1980s, repetitive serialized narratives within televised soap operas enjoyed an increased power to engage and transform national mass cultures across the globe. Foundational Mexican serial novels could live on in nostalgic content, form, and aesthetics through transmedial productions from the late twentieth and early twenty-first centuries, in an eternal return of their own.

FIGURE 5.18. The passionate and shocking conclusion to the now-famous final episode of *El extraño retorno de Diana Salazar* (1989). Serial soap operas of the 1980s were intensely emotional personal stories that could provoke fervent group passions that smoldered long after the series finale. Image from the author's personal collection.

Continuará

To Be Continued

Soap operas are anthropophagous, gobbling up and incorporating other formats, genres, aesthetics, ideas. That is why to understand our [Latin American] reality you have to watch our soap operas and not our news shows.   **Omar Rincón**

Any musings in book format with "now" in the title are doomed to date themselves immediately. It would be remiss nonetheless to end this investigation of serialization in Mexico without speaking of the twenty-first century, now nearing the end of its first quarter. We began this century across the globe with the rise of wireless broadband technology, of smartphones, and of social media. There were related concerns about the death of literature, of the novel, and of print culture, sometimes with finger-pointing as to why: "Print people drive their hordes toward nonprint media."[1]

There has been an unquestionable worldwide decline of traditional "literary reading" (particularly among younger adults), leading some demographic cultural analysts to drastically conclude that "literary reading as a meaningful leisure activity will virtually disappear in half a century," particularly outside of academic environments.[2] Overall print reading has indeed decreased. The rise of interactive media and hybridized audiovisual tendencies, however, has actually increased leisure reading time, not to mention cultural participation in new forms, through the expansion and ubiquity of access.[3]

The questions we ask of serial narratives have also morphed, even as the narratives themselves adapt to new formats: Which writings are we accessing and reading more across the globe, and in what formats? How have podcasts, streaming series, digital graphic novels, and other formats transformed the process of serial consumption?[4] The answers to these questions are evolving. What is certain is that serial production fits twenty-first century modes of consumption: sporadic, episodic, nearly always fragmented, and likely increasingly so.

Among Japan's top ten novels of 2008, five were originally *written* in installments via cell phone. The phenomenon of cellphone novels and novelists (the latter often recognized by one-name monikers, similar to the pseudonyms that were in vogue during the nineteenth-century) began receiving commercial support in 2000 from a provider (*Maho no i-rando*) who discovered that some of their users were sharing installment novels through their blogs. Its popularity in Japan speaks to a segmented leisure time that suits serial production and consumption. Some of these new novelists write while commuting to jobs or whenever they find spare time, typing an episode while in transit, then uploading it to a platform for consumers' instant download. The highest-ranking authors on such sites may then turn their novels into print books based on reader demand, frequently resulting in best-sellers—a cycle that would have been an unimaginable dream for Vicente Riva Palacio: a dream of the future.[5]

There has been another crucial change in this century: serial consumption is less linked than ever to the family, or the nation. Gone are the days when the television screen structured family lives.[6] Everywhere, in nearly every country, consumption has become more individual (versus shared screens), shifting the locus of influence away from the family unit and more toward the single subject. Likewise, myriad choices for viewing content have shifted consumption away from the national, as global producers and platforms such as Netflix and YouTube abound. Nationally produced Mexican series no longer have the power to shape an entire generation of consumers, as Televisa did in the 1980s.[7]

Despite bleak assessments worldwide of reading's declining cultural role, in Mexico we may look to the next narrative installment in a country that is well accustomed to serial consumption through varied media formats. Given the foundational primacy of *la ciudad letrada* in Latin America, it is worth emphasizing that the book has been decentered or displaced in Mexico from the very beginning, with a *pueblo* open to alternative forms of narrative consumption. We have witnessed how serialized storytelling functioned and developed over time, and some of the reasons for seriality's pervasiveness in the development of national narratives, delving into the specific relationships between seriality to transmediality through our case studies. We have seen how serial form has shaped storytelling, allowing for the repeated circulation of certain stories (characters, themes, storylines, and storyworlds). In the twenty-first century the cultural specificity and historical hierarchies of storytelling practices have collapsed, but as always with serial narratives, the stories do not die, but rather morph into their next form.

Given these seismic changes, it is more important than ever to study the shift of serials toward new media forms as part of the long continuum examined in this book. As a dynamic giant among media markets, Mexico boasts the second-largest national economy in Latin America, after Brazil. Most importantly, Mexico has a general habit of narrative consumption, cultivated since the nation's first novel. A national poll through the Instituto Federal de Telecomunicaciones reveals that Mexico has not lost its taste for forbidden romance, demonic possessions, and twins separated at birth. In 2016, serial *telenovelas* persisted as the third most-consumed genre (at 42 percent, just behind news at 49 percent and movies at 47 percent), with television series coming in at 32 percent.[8] National free-to-air (broadcast) Spanish-language products remained entertaining to mass audiences: among the estimated 96 percent of Mexicans owning a television set, 74 percent continued to watch free-to-air programming. Notably, however, among consumers streaming from the Internet, only 26 percent continued to watch free-to-air. The principal sources of online alternatives are global providers Netflix and YouTube, both based in the United States and rivals to national free-to-air products across the globe. Yet traditional television remains a topic of conversation in Mexico, given its prevalence in daily life, even as new options for entertainment proliferate through an intensified twenty-first century cultural and technological convergence. Television's role at society's center may be displaced, but as with the nineteenth-century serial novel, its narratives readapt themselves into other formats.

Mexicans watching Netflix continue to consume serialized *novelas*, but they are no longer limited to local offerings such as those from Televisa, TV Azteca, or Epigimenio Ibarra's Argos Television, taking their once national pasttime into international waters.[9] Yet even as we speak of a decline of broadcast television in the face of online competition, would it be accurate to say that the *telenovela* tradition is simultaneously declining? Hardly. Mexicans continue their centuries-long habit of consuming stories in episodes, as participants in a culture well versed in transmedial storytelling (now known as multi-platform media entertainment) and the play of serialized stories across multiple entertainment channels. Rather than witnessing the simple decline of the Mexican *telenovela*, we are witnessing the proliferation of serial narratives and increased competition within a global market. We are also in an age in which fusions among formats give rise to new ways to tell the old national stories, alongside new international stories on the horizon.

Argos's contributions to quality Spanish-language content began in the 1990s, extending the transgressive tones of 1980s heritage soap operas such as *El extraño retorno de Diana Salazar*. In the groundbreaking series *Las Aparicio* (2010), we see the rise of a matriarchy (reminiscent of Riva Palacio's Doña Juana, or the strong-though-conflicted heroine Diana Salazar) and a death of the patriarchy—rebellious themes that challenged the view of women and their family roles espoused by more traditional *telenovela* storylines. A 2017 report documented *Las Aparicio* as Mexico's most searched for Netflix show from within Mexico.[10] Its continued popularity shows that innovations to social conventions associated with the traditional family— highlighting failed or absent patriarchs and fluid gender identities—resonate with twenty-first-century Mexican audiences. This all-female family melodrama draws from Televisa's style as its counterpoint, availing itself of distinctive visual, aural, temporal, and discursive elements. Though marketed as a *teleseries, Las Aparicio* exhibits the formal hallmarks of a *telenovela*. Its 120 episodes were originally distributed by Grupo Imagen, on Cadena Tres. The show later became available on Netflix (2015–2017); at the same time (2015) it was made into film that, as of late 2021, can be accessed internationally on Amazon Prime and Vudu. In other words, Mexican television continues to evolve in terms of content and business models. While some cultural critics might have hoped for the passing of the *telenovela* in the twenty-first century, the genre has resurfaced in the shape of *webnovelas*, a format initiated by tireless serial creator Miguel Sabido and studied in detail by Raquel Guerrero Viguri.[11]

Given the richness and variety of serialized cultural productions in new formats, it is incumbent upon us to study these emergent forms as well as to ask probing questions of them. As media convergence is increasingly recognized as an opportunity as opposed to a threat, what are the current key movements in screen media consumed by Mexicans? Which new audiovisual trends appeal most to a country that remains one of the world's largest producers of media and culture? What are the newest iterations of stories, and what innovations have been brought to them by the immense changes of intensified convergence? The interconnections between television and transmedia invite us to examine the rich potential of multicultural media in Mexico, encouraging us to combine close readings of significant texts with analyses of contemporary audiovisual industries.[12] Based on the most recent and successful innovations, we can speak confidently of the following new tendencies at this moment: a rise in the modern relevance and human quotient of characters to generate maximum audience identification; a refocus on the storylines' relationship to everyday life and its realities; a welcoming of the global alongside the local; increased formal experiments with narrative points of view, rhythm, and duration, while remaining true to the defining serialized formula and melodramatic mood. In sum, there is a shift afoot in the way in which stories are told and marketed: their intensity, setting, and about whom they are told.

The soap opera in the twenty-first century is an international genre, open to the most original proposals and influences from every corner of the globe. Televisa is still reinventing itself and its traditional *telenovela* in the face of innovative narrative paradigms (such as working with Univision and entirely different business modelsl), even as Turkish, Korean, Argentine, or Colombian soap operas garner success with the Mexican population via online streaming sites, generating global conversations via social media. In this time of cultural convergence and increased international competition, streaming companies (such as Netflix and YouTube) and international networks (such as Telemundo and Univision) both collide and collaborate in a crowded and highly globalized market.

Twenty-first-century on-demand serial viewing practices allow for new formats and new pastiches of old stories, and Mexicans' consumption of series is far from limited to *telenovelas*, encompassing *teleseries* (such as Paco Ignacio Taibo's historical series *Patria*, which in bringing his book trilogy to life shows once again that serial narrative serves as a potent way to work through national histories).[13] And just as *Radio Roma* pays homage to the 1940s radionovela (2015–2016; see Introduction), more recent stage productions such *Los hijos también lloran* ("Even Sons Cry," active between 2018 and 2020) pay homage to the 1980s in a "montage that breaks the limits between realities and fictions generated by the plays, movies and television" so avidly consumed in the creators' and actors' youth.[14] Author Andy Zuno (b. 1982), along with his cast and creative crew, attest that *telenovelas* shaped their entire generation culturally and sentimentally, making the 1980s a sort of "second golden age" of soaps.[15] It was a nostalgic time for the nation when Televisa owned the airwaves, placing Mexico at the forefront of the Latin American media industries as a leader in the creation and manufacture of serial stories that defined an entire generation. Its title is a clear reference both to the emotional 1985 childhood loss of the writer's father, and to the internationally famous Pimstein soap so popular at the time, *Los ricos también lloran* ("Even the Rich Cry," 1979–1980).[16] Zuno's melodramatic *tragicomedia* was not serialized but is full of references to soap operas and other pop culture icons in an autobiographical effort—very *salazariano*—to reconstruct the past in order to understand his present. In the author's words, this is "a Mexican work that talks about us and about our ideological and emotional essence."[17] The live production (which included three musical numbers) even generated its own parody, a spin-off cabaret titled *Los niños también lloran* ("Even Children Cry"), which during the 2020 quarantine was available to stream via eticket on YouTube in an initiative to promote pandemic-era theater.[18]

Since 2013, the expansion of wireless connection and smartphone use has further revolutionized consumption and reception in Mexico.[19] Viewing platforms such as YouTube, TikTok or Periscope, used to promote viewing in conjunction with seductive social media such as Facebook or Instagram, are vast and powerful, providing the interactivity, instantaneity, interconnectedness, and increased visual intensity that we have come to expect from a fully hypertextual multimedia experience. Social networks have long threatened the hegemony of information, allowing for the emergence of digital native media, and more horizontality in communication than ever before. In 2016 the Internet marketing research company Comscore revealed that 98.2 percent of the 63 million Mexicans using Internet are active on *at least* one social network (e.g., Facebook, WhatsApp, Google+, YouTube), confirming that "Mexican audiovisual culture, previously dependent on the television duopoly of Televisa and TV Azteca, has not changed, but has migrated instead to social networks."[20]

It remains to be seen, however, *why* certain serialized practices of democratized creation—interactive user-generated serialized media such as blogs and podcasts—have limited reception in Mexico at this time. In 2016, even though 62.4 million Mexicans had Internet access (70.7 percent of those through smartphones), one could estimate that only 2 percent of the 172 million-plus blogs worldwide (2014; grown from 34 million in 2006) were edited in Mexico by Mexicans.[21] Similarly podcasts made in Mexico have been relatively scarce, given the number of people with Internet access. As one media source has put it, this "seems incredible . . . in a country with such a long oral tradition as Mexico."[22] This may be starting to change. Guerrero Viguri's site *Ratona de TV* (a play on the term in Spanish for "bookworm," cleverly altered to "tv-worm": www.ratonadetv.com) includes a podcast series about television fiction and *telenovelas* that is also available on SoundCloud, Spotify, and Audible.

In the twenty-first century, the cultural specificity and historical hierarchies of storytelling practices collapse, but with serial narrative, the stories do not die but rather morph into their next form. The market for serial stories is now more alive than ever, ready for products that reveal new angles, characters, landscapes, styles. The essential formulas remain, and one of the most successful has been serialized melodrama, featuring intrigue, emotion, sentiment, and certain elements of right versus wrong, good versus bad, that lead to a moral told through the storyline. Installment episodes are the essence, and the key is evolution. Evolution is embodied in the figure of Miguel Sabido, master storyteller and principal proponent of the serialized melodrama as national education. For more than fifty years, Sabido has been one of Mexico's greatest storytellers, working tirelessly behind the scenes to produce narratives that promote Mexican culture. Now in his late eighties, he is eager to carry his legacy forward via streaming, rebroadcasting his baroque *Pastorela* Project (1962–1964) as installments.[23] This is his first project to come full circle, to be transmitted to Mexican twenty-first-century families as unifying national entertainment. *Continuará.*

Notes

INTRODUCTION

1. *Intermediality* is a term used to describe a narrative being porous to other texts, appearing in other texts in the same medium, or cross-pollinating with other texts. *Transmediality* is the crossing of a narrative from one medium to another.

2. In 2001 Debra Ann Castillo and Edmundo Paz-Soldán's edited volume explored the relationship between Latin American literature and mass media, with at least one essay (Fernando Unzueta) interrogating nineteenth-century serial novels as a form of mass media. The collection examines the impact of mass media such as photography, film, and the Internet on Latin American literature, while assessing Latin American media theories by thinkers such as Martín Barbero and Néstor García Canclini. Seriality comes into play, particularly in the essays by Unzueta and by Adriana Estill, who examines *telenovelas* in the context of Doris Sommer's *Foundational Fictions*. Together these essays affirm, at the start of the twenty-first century, that literary works maintain their visibility and the authority of *la ciudad letrada* (the lettered city), while accommodating themselves to mass culture and the highly competitive media ecology.

3. Kelleter, *Media of Serial Narrative*, 1. He lists five interconnected ways to look at popular seriality: as evolving narratives, recursive progressions, narratives of proliferation, self-observing systems of actor-networks, and agents of capitalist self-reflexivity.

4. Kelleter, *Media of Serial Narrative*, 7.

5. The *pícaro* is a traditional roguish trickster whose escapades are typically used as a vehicle for social satire, beginning with the literature of the Spanish Golden Age.

6. The nickname "roto" here means a dandified (urban) bandit: Chucho was well known for "dressing up" as part of his trickster repertoire. Doing so allowed him to shift classes and foil authorities.

7. For a more complete history, see Wright, "Serialization and the Novel."

8. We can distinguish the term *novela por entregas*—the serialized delivery of a fictional narrative at intervals through separate pamphlets/installments sold in public spaces, bookstores or later on through subscription and delivery to individual residences, in which the author/editor usually availed himself of subscriber lists and distribution of local newspapers—from the *novela-folletín*—the serialized delivery of a fictional narrative at intervals through its publication in a newspaper, usually on its front-bottom page, often to attract new readership. See Wright, "Subscribing Identities," 2n1.

9. See Suárez de la Torre, *Constructores*.

10. Spanish novelists Manuel Fernández y González, Juan Martínez Villergas, Enrique Pérez Escrich, and Wenceslao Ayguals de Izco began publishing serials in the mid-1840s. The first full-length Mexican serial novels after Lizardi appeared in 1845. These dates suggest that Mexican serialization's popularity was not initiated by Spain, but rather came in a direct line from France, practically simultaneously, to both Spain and her colonies.

11. Others who tried their hand at popular fiction during this early period include Niceto de Zamacois (1820–1885), Pantaleón Tovar (1828–1876), Florencio María del Castillo (1828–1863), Nicolás Pizarro y Suárez (1830–1895), and Juan Diáz Covarrubias (1837–1859).

12. Mexico boasts a long lineage of *costumbrismo* dating back to Lizardi, whose highly costumbrista *Periquillo* (1816) appeared at the same time that the tendency was beginning in Spain, consisting in the representation of local mannerisms and customs, whether literary or pictorial, with an emphasis on everyday life and people.

13. Representative novelists from this period include José Tomás de Cuéllar (1830–1894), Enrique de Olavarría y Ferrari (1844–1919), Ireneo Paz (1836–1924), and Eligio Ancona (1835–1893).

14. Altamirano, *Revistas literarias*, 40.

15. Altamirano's most famous novel, *El Zarco: Episodios de la vida mexicana en 1861–1863*, did not initially appear in installments—even though its title evokes "episodes"—perhaps because it was published posthumously, in 1901.

16. The artists working with Riva Palacio to illustrate his novels included Constantino Escalante, Hesiquio Iriarte, and Santiago Hernández.

17. See Schmitt, "El folletinista."

18. Olea Franco, *La lengua literaria mexicana*, 102–3 and 106.

19. Over the course of the five-series set, some four hundred of these lithographs were created by José Guadalupe Posada.

20. Ortiz Gaitán posits, "Undoubtedly, abundant use of images was the factor leading to turn-of-the-century periodicals' vast popularity" (*Imágenes del deseo*, 40).

21. *El Universal Ilustrado* dedicated entire sections, and even whole editions, to national novels. For a thorough study, see Hadatty Mora, *Prensa y literatura*.

22. In *Cien años de novela mexicana* (1947), Azuela's highest praise is for two nov-
    elists publishing nearly exclusively in installments (Inclán and Frías). Azuela
    himself confessed to countless readings of Dumas's *Three Musketeers*. *Feui-
    lletonist* Eugene Sue gets a nod in *Los de abajo*, when semi-educated barber
    Venancio entertains fellow revolutionaries by recounting several episodes by
    memory from *Le juif errant* (*The Wandering Jew*).

23. See Quintanilla, "El águila y la serpiente."

24. Hadatty Mora, *Prensa y literatura*, 99–102 and 160.

25. See Rubenstein, *Bad Language*.

26. This part-nostalgic, part-parodic work was produced in Mexico City's *Teatro
    Shakespeare*. Its creators, Camila Brett and Jerónimo Best, drew from XEX and
    XETU broadcasts to evoke Mexican radio's Golden Age. It showcased three
    radionovela plots, interspersed with live "spots," guest appearances, and com-
    mercials, mimicking the original context and requiring audience participation.
    The first part (2015) was seen by more than three thousand spectators in four
    different venues; the second part was performed in 2016.

27. See Wright, "Closest Layer."

28. Trujillo Muñoz, "La literatura," 38.

29. This seeming contradiction can be partially explained through the well-
    documented Zeigarnik effect. As examined and reported by Russian psychol-
    ogist Bluma Zeigarnik in the 1920s, people tend to remember unfinished, in-
    complete themes or tasks better than ones that have been resolved, as thoughts
    of the remaining tasks tend to plague the mind, urging us to return to finish
    what we have already begun. The implications of this effect, for narrative, are
    striking.

30. Vladimir Propp (1895–1970) analyzed many of Russia's folk tales to identify
    common themes, finding thirty-one elements (narrative units that he termed
    "narratemes") comprising the structure of most stories, many of which can eas-
    ily be found in contemporary narratives as well.

31. At the highest level of consumer engagement, we find twenty-first-century
    "prosumers" who expand serial narratives on their own terms, creating paro-
    dies, alternative endings, and spin-offs in rebootings or rewritings of the origi-
    nal content. These strategies of proliferation and consumer engagement, how-
    ever, were already being employed as early as the nineteenth century, though
    under different circumstances and at a different level. At that time, a "snowball"
    effect was more likely: a certain story would become so popular within society
    and culture that it spontaneously generated same- or cross-media prequels, se-
    quels, and adaptations (Ryan, "Transmedial Storytelling," 363). In the twentieth
    century, we began to see more systematic, intentional cases of transmediality,
    in which a certain story was conceived from its beginning as a project or fran-
    chise to be developed across many media platforms, with a central "origin" text
    functioning as a common reference point.

32. Martín Barbero, *De los medios*, 226–27.

33. Monsiváis stated as late as 1999 that family remained at the center of Mexican thought, in spite of modernizing and globalizing influences bearing down throughout the twentieth century (Thelen, "Mexico's Cultural Landscapes," 619). In another instance, Monsiváis attests to the predominance of family over nation in Mexico: "Since the nineteenth century, our most basic element ... has not been the Nation but rather the unit that contains and allows the Nation to exist: the Family, the ultimate bastion of our values" ("Identidad nacional," 37).

34. See Rodríguez for a study of how archetypal Mexican values such as kinship and brotherhood have played out within stereotypically patriarchal families (as a counterpoint to the alternative Chicano family structures on which he focuses).

CHAPTER 1

An earlier version of this chapter was published in 2016 in the *Bulletin of Spanish Studies* (93, no. 5: 839–57). It is included here with their gracious permission.

1. This association was true across Latin America with other early national novels in their associations with revolutionary journalism. *El Periquillo Sarniento*, in addition to being Mexico's first novel, is widely considered Latin America's first novel.

2. *Periquillo* scholar Nancy J. Vogeley writes aptly about this matter of whom, exactly, constituted Lizardi's *pueblo* at that time: "The 'people' is a particularly nettlesome usage, which especially in works of the early nineteenth century written at a time of Independence struggle, reveals the changing political and social relationships. Deciding who belonged in such a category and indeed assigning values proper to it were a problem of the emerging nations' leaders, one which continued to trouble many into the twentieth century" ("Concept" 69).

3. See Martí-López, *Borrowed Words*, chapter 1.

4. Spell, *Life and Works*, 92–93; Wold, "*El Diario de México*," 10–17.

5. Radin, *Annotated Bibliography*, 4–5.

6. Spell, *Life and Works*, 92.

7. Spell, 31.

8. Roberts, "Origins of the Novel," 57–58.

9. Ochoa, *Uses of Failure*, 59–62.

10. González, "Journalism and (Dis)Simulation," 37–38.

11. Anderson, *Imagined Communities*, 30.

12. Anderson, 34–35.

13. Anderson, 33–34. Mas Marco Kartodikromo's *Semarang Hitam* was serialized in *Sinar Hindia* between March 29 and April 8, 1924.

14. "It is precisely *El Periquillo Sarniento*, among all the nineteenth-century works of América, which presents the greatest obstacles to establishing a text." Ruiz Barrionuevo, "*El Periquillo Sarniento*," 151. All citations for Lizardi's *El Periquillo Sarniento* in this book are from the 2008 publication edited by Carmen Ruiz Barrionuevo.

15. According to Rea Spell ("Genesis," 145), the first volume would have appeared from February to March, the second from April to May, and the third from June to July. *El Periquillo*'s first edition included thirty-seven engravings signed by "Mendoza": Each chapter of this three-volume edition featured an engraving, offering subscribers a total of two engravings per week. Among *El Periquillo*'s many editions of the nineteenth century, the 1842 edition distributed by Librería de Mariano Galván Rivera ("adorned with sixty fine engravings") and the 1845 edition by Cumplido have distinguished themselves for the quality of their illustrations, as well as for being the first (1842) to include a dictionary of mexicanismos at the end of the volume.

16. Moore, "Un manuscrito inédito," 6–7.

17. Moore, "Una bibliografía descriptiva," 387; Ruiz Barrionuevo, "*El Periquillo Sarniento*," 153–54.

18. Per the prospectus, each volume would cost four pesos for residents of Mexico City, and an additional four reales for residents of the provinces.

19. Lizardi, *Obras*, 8:xl; Lizardi, *Periquillo*, 937.

20. Unlike the first edition, in the second there is no particular announcement to the subscribers, only "an up-to-date list of esteemed subscribers as of October 19, 1825, upon publication of this first issue" (cited in Moore, "Una bibliografía descriptiva," 386–88).

21. In a note added to the fourth edition (1842), the editor surmises that Lizardi is indeed referring to the quantity of bound editions ordered for the initial print run; the same editor avows that by 1842 the number should exceed three thousand: "It is to be believed that the copies of which the Pensador speaks are the copies of this exact volume, of which three hundred were printed for the first edition. In this regard, the number of copies today exceeds three thousand" (Ruiz Barrionuevo Edition, 937).

22. Vogeley, *Lizardi*, 70. See also an excerpt from an 1820 political pamphlet transcribed by Vogeley, in which various characters from Lizardi's novels appear (*Lizardi*, 59).

23. Vogeley, 59, 70.

24. Moore, "Un manuscrito inédito," 5. In 1938 Ernest R. Moore discovered a copy of the first edition's third volume, to which, alongside the printed material, a handwritten manuscript was appended: *El Periquillo Sarniento, tomo VI, extractado por el Pensador Mexicano, año de 1817*. Thanks to Moore's discovery we now know that Lizardi hired several scribes, evading censorship through the printing presses, to manually disseminate the end of the novel so that his readers could find out what happened to their dear Periquillo.

25. Escalante Gonzalbo, *Nueva historia mínima*, 187.

26. Quoted in Vogeley, *Lizardi*, 36.

27. See the section titled "Apprehensions of Time," in Anderson, *Imagined Communities*, 24–26.

28. See Mora, *De la sujeción colonial*.

29. Anderson, *Imagined Communities*, 33.
30. Anderson, 30.
31. Anderson, 35.
32. González, "Journalism and (Dis)Simulation," 37–38.
33. González, 37.
34. Vogeley, *Lizardi*, 2.
35. Across the three editions, the title appears as variations of "Prólogo, dedicatoria y advertencia(s a los lectores)."
36. By the 1820s Lizardi had become a well-known public persona, partially due to this tendency to talk about himself in his literary writings, as well as in his pamphlets and letters. See Vogeley, 59 and 277n5, for examples.
37. A term referring, at the beginning of the Colony, to Spaniards born in New Spain.
38. Cited in Vogeley, 76; Lizardi, *Obras*, 3:171.
39. In 1803, according to Humboldt, New Spain's approximate population of 5,760,000 included 2,385,000 mixed-race people (a mix of "Indigenous, American, European, Asiatic, [and] African" that was "very different than what has been believed up until now"); 2,300,000 Indians; 1,000,000 Spaniards; and 75,000 Europeans (*Diario de México*, May 18–20, 1807).
40. "I don't know if they will obey me, or if they will go around, lending them to this person or the other on a whim" (96).
41. Vogeley, *Lizardi*, 55.
42. Anderson, *Imagined Communities*, 27.
43. See Benjamin, "Theses," 79.
44. Benjamin, *Illuminations*, 265.
45. Anderson, *Imagined Communities*, 24.
46. *Perucho, nieto del Periquillo, por un devoto del pensador mexicano* (anonymous authorship) was illustrated by Jesús Martínez Carrión and others (Leandro Izaguirre, Carlos Alcalde) and appeared in *El Mundo Ilustrado* (1894–1914), the first illustrated weekly paper produced during the Porfiriato, also featuring illustrated novels in installments (Alfaro Cuevas, "Revisión histórica," 98) under the aegis of Rafael Reyes Spíndola.
47. Lizardi himself reported it at three times more, while Vogeley has stated that it was at two times the original price by the time of Lizardi's death in 1827 (*Lizardi*, 278n12).
48. Vogeley, *Lizardi*, 59, 70–71, and 278n12. In a keynote lecture (*Primer Coloquio Internacional de Cultura Literaria Virreinal*, 2015), Vogeley reports: "Lizardi's memory survived robustly among the members of the *pueblo*. If nothing else remember the numerous editions of *El Periquillo Sarmiento* published throughout the nineteenth and beginnings of the twentieth century; the many calendars that evoke his figure as the Mexican Thinker and others of his works (seven between 1865 and 1866 alone); an 1879 newspaper called *The Shadow of Lizardi*;

and novel published by a "disciple of the Mexican Thinker" between 1895 and 1896, entitled *Perucho, grandson of El Periquillo.*"

49. The student-sourced fanpage, replete with Periquillo-based memes and the express mission to "find fans like *nosotr@s* [us]," was still active as of late 2020. It came out of a 2017 literature course with UNAM professor Mariana Ozuna Castañeda.

CHAPTER 2

Epigraphs. Monsiváis, *Las herencias ocultas*, 41. Pacheco, *La novela histórica*, 122.

1. Bustillo Oro remarks that the novel *Monja y casada* was reissued, read, and frequently circulated during the early twentieth century (*Vida cinematográfica*, 131). Once the movie was released, to the praise of both viewers and critics, he recalls stampedes to enter the theaters for viewings (139–40).

2. Carlos Illades refers to the Romantic conception of the *pueblo* as an *entelequia*, translating as an entity that is not real but imagined (i.e., an abstract notion or empty referent), complementing Anderson's perception of the imagined community as more aspirational than realized.

3. Bustillo Oro considered *Martín Garatuza* the better novel and a true classic of Mexican picaresque literature ("the most fun because of the protagonist's clever tricks, a monument to Mexican literature of the picaresque"), but had commenced with *Monja* instead, to respect the original order of Riva Palacio's series. As a result, director Gabriel Soria beat him to *Martín*, according to Bustillo: "He started filming his *Martín* on the sly, just one month before I started my *Monja*" (141).

4. Pacheco, *La novela histórica*, 122.

5. Based on the timeline of 1520 to 1867 that Riva establishes in *El libro rojo* and *México a través de los siglos*, it is clear that he saw 1867 as a watershed moment in Mexico's history.

6. Guerrero was considered by some as "the moral leader of the Independence movement" (Pacheco, *La novela histórica*, xii) for his conciliatory pact with Agustín de Iturbide. Riva, generally known as a "man of character," inherited to some extent this moral tradition of reconciliation of extremes, observed first in his military efforts—when his motto became known as "Ni rencores por el pasado ni temores por el porvenir" (Neither resentments toward the past nor fears for the future)—and then in his literary career during the Restoration period.

7. By 1861, Riva, formally trained as a lawyer, had already served as a *guerrillero* (guerrilla fighter) in the North American Invasion, governor of the State of Mexico, and governor of the State of Michoacán.

8. His coauthor was his close friend Juan A. Mateos, who had collaborated with him earlier on his first patriotic written project. The two were credited with reviving and mexicanizing what had been a dying theater scene.

9. María Solórzano Ponce observes that "the image of caricature, as bearer of

critical content, united with elements of popular tradition, gradually created a recognizable code, an implicit dialogue, between author and consumer, thus overcoming the difficulties that illiteracy presented to newspapers' circulation" ("Una voz recuperada," 18).

10. See Leal, "El contenido literario," 330–31. Casarín tried his hand at a couple of *folletines*; Frías y Soto later published his *novelita* (little novel) "El vulcano" in installments.

11. Ortiz Monasterio, *México eternamente*, 91 and 376. Had Riva not been in possession of the Inquisition archive during the Intervention, it might have met the same fate as Manila's: destruction at the hands of invaders (Ortiz Monasterio, "Avatares del archivo," 108–9).

12. Ortiz Monasterio suggests that Riva himself requested the commission (*México eternamente*, 71), and José Barragán states that Mateos, favoring separation of church and state, was a congressional supporter of Riva's proposal to publish documents from the archive (26).

13. Mateos affirmed that "the clergy have emissaries all over" (quoted in Ortiz Monasterio, *México eternamente*, 72) and that "everything indicates that the Church intervened to stop the publication of the notorious texts selected by Riva Palacio and Tovar" (quoted in Ortiz Monasterio, 372–73). In words now thought to be written by Riva himself, "There is a certain avid and insatiable curiosity for knowing all the details those trials contained, which no one before had managed to uncover" (*El Monitor Republicano*, May 31, 1861).

14. The designation *chinaco* had been used since the times of Riva Palacio's grandfather Guerrero, during the Independence Wars, to designate a man of the *pueblo* who, though lacking in formal military training, made up for it in courage and natural ability in arms. These seasoned horsemen had an established role in Mexican military tradition, often doubling as patriots and bandits. Riva Palacio had already led *guerrillero* troops once, against the North American invasion (1846–1847). Some *chinacos*, such as General Carlos Salazar, referred to Riva Palacio as "mi muy querido chinaco" (my very dear *chinaco*; quoted in Ortiz Monasterio, *México eternamente*, 74n12). Elites used the phrase, however, to insult those who demonstrated Indigenous or African roots. Riva for his part saw the *chinaco* as a bravely patriotic *mestizo ranchero* (mixed-race rancher) and he "reclaimed" this nickname for posterity, praising how "with little instruction but shrewd intelligence, good health and a vigorous constitution, extraordinary horsemen accustomed to withstanding the elements and living simply, those men formed the core of volunteer soldiers who throughout the ages have selflessly fought for their Patria's independence and the triumph of freedom; from them have emerged the heroes of modern Mexican society, a class that is still today the source of true patriotism, an imperishable bastion of Mexican independence" (quoted in Ortiz Monasterio, 733).

15. President Benito Juárez first offered Riva Palacio an important place in the

reestablished judicial branch, which would have catapulted him easily into a long political career. Riva Palacio did not want to serve under Juárez, but he did not stay away from politics for long (Ortiz Monasterio, *Historia y ficción*, 146-47).

16. Ortiz Monasterio, 187.

17. *La Orquesta* remained affordable and accessible throughout the Restoration: it was sold by the Imprenta de la Paz at the low rate of a half *real* in Mexico City, and a whole real in the provinces (Leal, "El contenido literario," 330). For a history of Independence commemoration speeches, see Plasencia, *Independencia y nacionalismo*.

18. The speech was first published in *El Monitor Republicano*, September 20, 1867 (Riva Palacio, *Periodismo*, 146).

19. For a discussion of the construction of the imaginary of the modern *pueblo* in Mexico, see Guerra, *México*, 1:33.

20. Ilades, 19.

21. The *veladas*, which took place between December 1867 and June 1868, embraced participants of all political stripes. The evenings were based in fraternity and open-mindedness and famed for lasting into the wee hours. For a detailed trajectory of the Riva-Altamirano friendship, see Giron, "Ignacio Manuel Altamirano."

22. Altamirano's creeds were of unity and reconciliation—the creation of a new Republic through literature and culture. He dreamed of a "a small republic that does not concede our command to force, nor to intrigue, nor to money, but instead to talent, to the greatness of the soul, to honesty," where citizens could flourish in "that free, independent and sublime asylum, in which neither thought nor word are spied upon by henchman, nor threatened by power, nor slandered through hatred" (*Revistas*, 6–7). He hoped that his fellow writers would remain "attentive to their literary mission, embracing their brothers in the Republic with open arms, regardless of political belief, in order to help one another in the formidable task for which the intelligence of all Mexicans is needed" (8).

23. Altamirano, 4–5.

24. Altamirano, 7. Altamirano published his *Revistas literarias de México* in installments in *La Iberia* from June 30 to August 4 of 1868, as well as one installment in *El Renacimiento* on January 2, 1869, in which he continued to spotlight the rebirth of literature in Mexico in relation to its newfound place and influence among progressive modern nations.

25. In Altamirano's words, this was a generation "born in the midst of war and well taught by what it had witnessed, not intending to re-submit to silence. This generation has the firm intention to work constantly until it can carry out the creation and development of a national literature, whatever the ups and downs that come with it" (*Revistas*, 7). For these reasons, "the participants who attend

these literary gatherings are the apostles of our future." Altamirano asserts that "Mexican literature cannot die now. From that sanctuary will rise again new prophets of civilization and progress" (16).

26. See Ortiz Monasterio's review of Edmundo O'Gorman's notes on the novel ("Rescate"), particularly page 141.

27. Altamirano, *Revistas*, 30. The doctrines and opinions Altamirano hoped to promote would not have been accessible to the masses had novels not served as "the artifice with which thinking men of our day and age used to bring doctrines and opinions to the masses that would otherwise have been difficult for them to accept." Progress is equally associated with the printing press: "Certainly [it] has been the true mother of journalism and the novel, and there is no difficulty in believing this, if one reflects that, without this wonderful invention, there could be no newspapers, nor could the consumption of these ingenious tales be promoted, to the delight of all social classes, as nourishment to our imaginations" (19).

28. Altamirano, *Revistas*, 20. Pacheco later associates the birth of the historical novel to the ascent of a new class, a liberal ideology, nationalism, technological advances, and a key increase in the reading population (*La novela histórica*, vi).

29. Altamirano, *Revistas*, 80.

30. Altamirano, 30.

31. Altamirano, 40.

32. Altamirano, 60–61.

33. Altamirano, 61–62.

34. Anderson-Imbert, *El telar*, 213–14; Ortiz Monasterio, *La obra historiográfica*, 132.

35. Altamirano, *Revistas*, 41–43. Altamirano rightly describes Lizardi's *Periquillo Sarniento* as a precocious Mexican antecedent to the works of Sue and Hugo. Like the two European novelists, Lizardi had a gift "of examining examining virtues and vices, painting them as they were at the beginning of this century." His was a "pulsating portrait, complete and full of truth, to the extent that there are few who can match him" (43). Altamirano praises Lizardi's dissection of life before the Revolution, revealing "the wounds of the lower as well as the privileged classes, the clergy's vices with extraordinary courage, the dangers of religious fanaticism and the nonsense of colonial administrations; he caricatures that day's false wisemen, and attacks the petty teachings then being offered." Altamirano also states that the author "takes himself to the level of the *pueblo*'s unfortunate masses, sympathizes with their misery and comforts them in their sorrows, offering them a glimpse of hope for better luck, identifying with their pain and weeping with them in their abject sorrows!" (This language brings to mind Riva's speech personifying the *pueblo* as a suffering Christ-like figure. [42]) Altamirano extends the reference by characterizing Lizardi as a saint and martyr: "The Mexican Thinker is the *pueblo*'s apostle, which is why they still tenderly love him, and revere his memory as that of a dear friend . . . He

suffered greatly, ate the bread of the people watered with the tears of their misery, and went to his poor grave in obscurity, yet with the holy halo of freedom's martyrs for progress, and the understanding of one who has fulfilled a blessed mission on earth. The *pueblo* does not visit his unknown tomb to lay crowns of votives, and nary a sad cypress marks the veneration of visiting mourners; yet they consecrate for him an altar in their hearts, and the innocent joy that his precious book brings them, even now, is a tribute that is offered, mixed with sighs, to the memory of his kindness" (42).

36. Writing in 1973, Daniel Cosío Villegas asserted that the press of the Restoration period was "absolutely free, as it had not been before nor has been until our time" (*Historia moderna*, 492). An opposition newspaper such as *La Orquesta*, for example, suffered little or no censorship during the Restoration. See Solórzano Ponce ("Una voz recuperada," 15) and Acevedo Valdés (*Constantino Escalante*, 22), on obstacles other than censorship.

37. Pacheco, *La novela histórica*, vi.

38. Monsiváis, "Vicente Riva Palacio," xiii.

39. Ortiz Monasterio, *México eternamente*, 97-98; Esquivel Obregón, *Recordatorios públicos y privados*, 80.

40. Pacheco, *La novela histórica*, 121. Ortiz Monasterio estimates that there were some five hundred thousand potential readers in 1868 (*México eternamente*, 98). The first scientific census (1895) registered 17.9 percent of the population as literate (1,843,292 people above the age of 19) toward the turn of the century. The habit of reading novels aloud persisted well into the Porfiriato and likely beyond; see, for example, Acevedo Valdés, *Constantino Escalante*, 16–19, which cites anecdotes regarding Emilio Rabasa's *El cuarto poder* (1888).

41. Solórzano Ponce, "Una voz recuperada," 15–16.

42. "Soldier of the Republic, brave son of the *pueblo*, who fought tirelessly defending the land of your parents! . . . You, man of great heart who knows the great sacrifices of the Patria: open this book and read. Here you will find your own story; here you will find the story of your soul" (Altamirano, "Dos palabras," 5).

43. Altamirano, "Dos palabras," 5–6.

44. This letter from Jorge de Manjarrez (July 17, 1868) was found among Riva's personal papers by Ortiz Monasterio (INAH CAOS, foja 28, doc 76) and is cited in *Historia y ficción*, 187.

45. *La Orquesta*, May 9, 1868.

46. Altamirano, *Revistas*, 64–65.

47. The prospectus was published on June 18, 1868. According to Altamirano, "The public rushes to subscribe, and Mexican storytelling substitutes our compatriots' preference for novels by the Spaniard Fernández and González" (*Revistas*, 65). Altamirano had described earlier in his *Revistas* how the well-known serial storyteller Fernández y González was popularizing Spanish history through "serial tales published in almost all the Mexican newspapers, with editions arriving from Spain all sold out upon arrival" (33–34).

48. *La Orquesta*, July 29, 1868.

49. *La Orquesta*'s announcement about *Martín Garatuza* was made on September 3, 1868. The last installment of *Monja y casada* came out at the end of that month.

50. Escalante had become famous for the more than five hundred caricatures he published in *La Orquesta* (Leal, "El contenido literario," 332–33), and for his visual chronicles of the *pueblo*'s battles against the French in weekly lithographs from July to November 1862.

51. Regarding the reliability of delivery, see Solórzano Ponce, "Una voz recuperada," 15.

52. *La Orquesta*, September 9, 1868.

53. *La Orquesta* makes reference to these publicity posters, as does the Jesuit priest Mariano Dávila, discussed later in this chapter (Ortiz Monasterio, *Historia y ficción*, 217). The custom was for rival newspapers to publicly acknowledge receipt, occasionally recommending that their readers pick up an installment (Ortiz Monasterio, *México eternamente*, 94).

54. Pacheco claims that Riva Palacio wrote his serialized novels to "entertain others as well as himself" (*La novela histórica*, xiv).

55. By February 1868, Riva Palacio had accepted a different nomination to the Supreme Court, this time as "tercer magistrado propietario" (Ortiz Monasterio, *Historia y ficción*, 148–49).

56. Ortiz Monasterio, *México eternamente*, 370.

57. Ortiz Monasterio, 372. As early as 1861, Riva Palacio had received requests from Juárez's government, which he seems to have ignored. Ortiz Monasterio has also hypothesized that perhaps there was some sort of collusive pact between Juárez and Riva, allowing the author to keep sole possession of the archive in spite of any official correspondence stating the contrary (374).

58. Ortiz Monasterio, 374. Ironically, by then, the requests had ceased.

59. Ortiz Monasterio, "Avatares," 106. The archive was also his source for less fictional works such as *El libro rojo* and the two volumes on the colonial period that he authored for *México a través de los siglos*.

60. In his refutation, Dávila cited contrasting details such as the supposed benevolence of the Inquisitors and the comfort of the cells provided (Ortiz Monasterio, *Historia y ficción*, 223–28).

61. Dávila, *Breves observaciones*, 79.

62. *La Orquesta*, January 23, 1869. It was obvious that the priest was a subscriber himself, for when he complained that the historical novel presented false history, he used elements of its plot to prove his point (*La Orquesta*, January 2, 1869).

63. *La Orquesta*, January 23, 1869.

64. Monsiváis, "Vicente Riva Palacio," xi. Bustillo Oro also encountered that difficulty when condensing *Monja* for the silver screen (*Vida cinematográfica*, 133).

65. "Throughout his work, *mestizos* are the physical and moral representation of Mexicans, the social product that evolved through the fusion of Indigenous groups with Europeans" (Florescano, *Historia de las historias*, 345).

66. Noble and brave, intelligent and trustworthy, Teo is characterized in stark contrast with the other *negros* or *mulatos* represented throughout the *Monja-Garatuza* series.

67. All references in this chapter to *Martín Garatuza* are to the 2001 Porrúa edition. In this storyline of persecution, *criollos* experience racism from even their own family members (*Martín Garatuza*, 1:133, 246).

68. Ortiz Monasterio alleges that the Inquisition is the protagonist. See *Historia y ficción*, 202.

69. Jiménez Rueda, *Vidas reales*, 126.

70. Jiménez Rueda, 125. He rescues the anecdote surrounding this refrain from the *Boletín del Archivo General de la Nación* (4, nos. 2–4)—the same archive used by Riva Palacio for his novels. Jiménez Rueda includes Garatuza in his gallery of Mexican popular characters of humble origins, focusing on the "lives of the outcasts . . . the illuminated, the astrologers, the Jewish Christians, the scoundrels," stating that "lowly characters have also contributed to our history" (5–6).

71. *El Mosaico Mexicano*, 7:229.

72. Orozco y Berra, *Diccionario universal*, 3:410–12. Father Dávila appears in the same tome as the author of an entry on "Inquisition."

73. Orozco y Berra, 3:412. This dictionary was curated by Orozco and Berra and paid for by subscribers, constituting "the most ambitious editorial project carried out in the Mexican Republic after separating from Spain," according to Nicole Giron, who provides some details regarding its distribution: "The publication was made in generally weekly installments, each one consisting of ten to twelve pages. Subscriptions were the basis of the edition's financing, as was common at the time. Once the installments were all collected, the ten volumes were edited one by one, noting on the covers the names of the collaborators" (232–33). Orozco y Berra's entry on "Garatusa" was republished verbatim in García Cubas's *Diccionario geográfico, histórico y biográfico de los Estados Unidos Mexicanos* (127–28), first in 1888 and then again in 1900.

74. Orozco y Berra, *Diccionario universal*, 3:412.

75. Ramírez Aparicio, 143. The protagonist of *Martín Garatuza* uses similar wording to describe his own irreverences within the novel (1:271).

76. As Ortiz Monasterio has described it, "History, in the nineteenth century, was a branch of the vigorous trunk of Literature, although with its own objectives and laws; hence the authors of *Mexico Through the Centuries* are presented as 'renowned literati'" (*México eternamente*, 20).

77. A common feature of historical novels à la Walter Scott was the use of a minor fictionalized figure among major historical figures to make the story more realistic.

78. Dávila, *Breves observaciones*, 111–12. See also pages 8 and 14.

79. An example of Riva Palacio's use of "they" can be seen in this statement: "The great city of Mexico, as they the Spaniards called it, had fallen into the hands of Hernán Cortés, and the noble emperor Guatimotzín or Guatimoc, as they called him, was taken prisoner" (1:157).

80. Examples of this can be seen on pages 101, 102, 133, and 142 of the novel (vol. 1).

81. See, for example, the mentions of the Calle de las Canoas on pages 3 and 45 (vol. 1).

82. For more examples, see 107 and 132 in the novel (vol. 1).

83. Garatuza enters as easily into the palace of the viceroy (1:154–55) as into the shack of the Zambo (1:145–46), where he makes and hides his disguises.

84. The unequivocal villains in *Martín Garatuza* are the Inquisitors and promiscuous women. True evil is encoded as those who work for the Inquisition and implement its terror within society.

85. In *Periquillo*, there is a greater binarism between the *pícaro*'s good versus bad friends.

86. Cuauhtemoc came to embody indigenist nationalism in Mexico, as the only Aztec emperor who survived the Spanish Conquest.

87. Here is the idea of Chasteen's *americanos*, used interchangeably with *mestizos* and *castas* (Afro-Mexican descendants): a new hybrid race historically interested in the achievement of independence for New Spain, embodying many positive *mestizo* traits.

88. At one point, Martín introduces himself as "Martín de Villavicencio Salazar, fighting name Garatuza, and your relative, which I have deduced based on my last name from my mother's side" (1:32).

89. Teo's account of the rebellions appears in *Monja* (chapters 13–15, beginning as "La historia del esclavo"). Doña Juana's narrative of persecution takes up one hundred pages of *Garatuza* (between chapters 20 and 21, vol. 1). Ortiz Monasterio has asserted that while Blackness is mentioned here and there in the novels, it does not form part of the recipe of *mestizaje* or constitute a great preoccupation of Riva Palacio (*México eternamente*, 169); noble Teo's lengthy important intertext could be viewed as a departure from this, although Teo himself presents an unusual exception to other portrayals of *negritud* within these novels.

90. "I burn with a desire to know this story that is of such great interest to me, such that every moment seems like a year of waiting" (1:93).

91. Felipe's embodiment of both his parents is described thus: "That young man seemed to belong to the pure Indigenous race, and yet the wisemen of that time realized that there was also Spanish blood in his veins, because his hair would curl up and his black mustache was somewhat thicker than what would correspond to a pure-blooded Indian" (1:176).

92. The novel portrays Doña Juana's birth as coinciding with the year that the Inquisition began (1:186, 1:190–91).

93. This occurs, for example, in the scene when the maddened Isabel and abandoned Felipe, separated for years, are able to recognize one other as mother-son, and share the stories of their family history (still not written down) before her death (1:182–84).

94. The ironical assumption here is that the Jewish element of the Carbajal bloodline, so persecuted by the Spanish, originated in their Spanish roots (a theme of hypocrisy prominently exhibited in Sierra O'Reilly's *La hija del judío* as well).

95. The intertext of Teo the slave's origins in *Monja* serves a similar function, revealing his true identity as nobleman and the reasons for his indomitable strength.

96. "El patriotismo suele andar en femeniles pechos" constitutes the title of *Garatuza*'s chapter 2.

97. See Wright, "Genaro García's *Leona Vicario*," for an assessment of nineteenth-century attitudes toward female patriots in the period from Independence to Revolution.

98. These memoirs were "locked with a key hanging from a tiny chain" (1:129).

99. Did Riva Palacio fancy himself a Garatuza of sorts, thumbing his nose at authority (and specifically Juárez)? This would not be the first time he would have identified with one of his creations. While serving as editor of *La Orquesta* he had adopted the name of *Calvario*'s humble protagonist, *pueblerino* Juan de Jarras, as his pseudonym: "At that time in Acapulco there was a poor man whom we called Juan de Jarras, a nickname whose origin I could never decipher . . . who lived peacefully from the produce of his small orchard . . . married to a very hard-working mulatto woman" (*Calvario y tabor*, 16).

100. *Mestizo* appears once to indicate how Spanish used the term to refer to a vile mysterious animal (and by extension, to *criollos* as well): "There was a sort of basement full of foul black mud, where you could observe some of the most disgusting animals to grow in such places in Mexico and which Spaniards would call *mestizos* out of sheer hatred toward the *criollos*" (1:104).

101. The pages that mention *pueblo* include 1:53–54 and 250–51.

102. The historian José María Vigil (1829–1909), a contemporary of Riva Palacio and the author of volume 5 of *México a través de los siglos*, described standard attitudes in 1878 in an essay entitled "Need and Utility of Studying Our Nation's History": "A feeling of disgust passed down to us by the *conquistadores* toward the defeated Indigenous races has caused us to view the pre-Hispanic civilizations of the New World with supreme disdain, without taking into account that, in order to explain the situation of those peoples, in order to deeply understand their nature and resolve their future, it is necessary to go farther back than the colonial period, to study the savagery, which, even though we would like to look down on it, lives and persists among us, creating the most formidable obstacles to establishing peace and the development of the elements that will benefit our society. [. . .] A *pueblo* cannot reject its past" (quoted in Ortega y Medina, *Polémicas y ensayos mexicanos*, 268–69).

103. Ortiz Monasterio, *Historia y ficción*, 219–20.
104. Ortiz Monasterio *México eternamente*, 102.
105. Riva Palacio, *México*, 905.
106. Prospectus, *Historia general de México*; cited in Ortiz Monasterio, *México eternamente*, 202.
107. The five-volume publication was undertaken by Spanish editor Santiago Ballescá, of Casa Ballescá in Mexico and Espasa y Compañía in Spain.
108. Quoted in Florescano, *Historia de las historias*, 338–39.
109. Ortiz Monasterio *México eternamente*, 220. In 1883, with the arrival in power of the conservative government of Manuel González, Riva Palacio's critiques earned him detention and imprisonment in Santiago Tlatelolco.
110. Riva Palacio, *México*, 2:viii.
111. Florescano, *Historia de las historias*, 336–37.
112. This is a theory amply explored by Otsuka Eiji and Marc Steinberg in their 2010 article "World and Variation" (on the "addictive" effects of popular manga in 1980s Japan).
113. See Quintana Navarrete, "Eugenesia y sinofobia."
114. Sierra, *Evolución política*, 313.

CHAPTER 3

Epigraph. Monsiváis, "Gabriel Vargas."
1. "¡Sufragio eleitivo! ¡No re-elección! ¡Viva México!"
2. Cited by Aurrecoechea, *Puros cuentos*, 213.
3. *La Familia Burrón* was the creation of Gabriel Vargas Bernal circa 1937 and is considered one of Mexico's most iconic strips. This story of the life of a working-class family and the characters in their Mexico City neighborhood ran for six decades. *Don Catarino* was its clear forerunner in use of language, idiomatic popular expressions, portrayal of urban life, and a metafictional mix of fiction with reality, and humor with absurdity.
4. I consulted copies of *El Heraldo* from 1921 to 1923, found mostly in the collection of the Biblioteca Lerdo de Tejada. Not all editions or supplements containing *Don Catarino* were available. I was able to find some of the missing strips and supplements in the archive at Academia San Carlos, where there was a file on *Don Catarino* (submitted by Carlos Fernández Benedicto to the SEP in 1921–22 for copyright purposes).
5. That project began in 1911; it is possible that it was still appearing as late as 1919 (see Aurrecoechea 212, illustration). Fernández wrote satirical articles (*crónica satírica*) featuring Culantro. The character was illustrated by a different artist, Spaniard Rafael Lillo, and appeared in the right-leaning anti-Madero magazine *La Risa*.
6. Upon de la Huerta's release in 1920, Alvarado was exiled to Los Angeles. Another of the Sonorenses and soon-to-be-president Obregón was suspicious of Alvarado's journalistic endeavors (seeing potential competition for

a presidential bid). After Carranza's assassination, Alvarado supported de la Huerta (over Obregón/Calles). Obregón's men killed Alvarado between Tabasco and Chiapas.

7. Valenzuela, "Campaña," 22.

8. The PNA's candidate, Arnulfo R. Gómez, was assassinated. When Obregón was assassinated in 1926, the PNR (Partido Nacional Revolucionario) was created. An antecedent of the PRI, it was manipulated by Calles until Cárdenas. In continued opposition, the PNA supported Vasconcelos in 1929.

9. The 1920 Pact of Agua Prieta originally established the "Sonoran Triumvirate" of de la Huerta, Obregón, and Calles.

10. Reed had followed Villa to write the book; Pruneda's direct connection to Villa, if any, remains to be excavated.

11. Pruneda, *La caricatura como arma*, 11.

12. Aurrecoechea, *Puros cuentos*, 213.

13. Guzmán, *Memorias*, xi–xii.

14. Guzmán, *Memorias*, xii; emphasis mine.

15. On Mexico as a melting pot, see Aurrecoechea, *Puros cuentos*, 184–86.

16. In the *carpa*, new identities were acted out freely, while "old" identities were preserved: a distinctive *costumbrista* humor was cultivated that, like caricature, exaggerated, exalted, and criticized certain types of the *pueblo*, including the *pícaro*, the *pelado*, and the *charro*, among others.

17. This term was coined in Mexico City of the 1920s to describe a stereotypical male of the new urban lower class. By 1934, in his *Profile of Man and Culture in Mexico*, philosopher Samuel Ramos would refer to the *pelado* as the most clearly defined expression of the Mexican national character.

18. On the 1920s, see Carreño King, *El charro*.

19. Initial strips (May–April 1921) veered more toward comedic insult, but this detail was ironed out by 1922. It is true that family strips were generally popular at this time, via North American models such as *The Katzenjammer Kids* or *Bringing Up Baby*, and certainly this had some role to play in Fernández and Pruneda's choices. But Catarino was no copy of these strips, from the language used to essential features of character and plot.

20. *El Heraldo* had started with children's strips, but with nonserialized content (such as Aesop's Fables, with Santiago R. de La Vega). While popular, these did not take off as hoped, perhaps in part because of an absence of narrative serialization. In their stead, *El Heraldo* courted young readers to *Don Catarino* through coloring contests.

21. J. Robinson, *Comics*, 142.

22. The novel of the Hispanic world was inaugurated through the quintessentially metafictional *Don Quixote*; its author's prologue, as discussed in Chapter 1, was a model for *El Periquillo*.

23. The classic case of the author who remains in charge is Miguel de Unamuno,

in *Niebla* (1914).

24. "Las Historietas Nacionales en 'El Heraldo': Presentamos a Doña Ligia," *El Heraldo*, March 2, 1921. Ligia is incidentally described as dissatisfied with her husband's overall level of culture, even as her own is called into question. This teaser is extremely critical of Ligia, but her characterization will change once the strip begins to appear.

25. A transcription of Doña Ligia's ad:

    Dende el otor dia ce ah eztarbia-do mi marrido Katarino, Ulogio i Tanacia. Zalieron en vesigleta y ai tienen nomas que[?] no an guelto. ¿Pos onde ce abran metido, mader zantisima de Huadalupe? Dare beinte pezos y un revozo de puritita ceda y un poimeable[?] a la presona que me de la razon.

    [The other day my hubby Catarino, Eulogio, and Tanasia flew the coop. They left on bicycle and, well, they haven't shown their faces since. Where might they have gone, Holy Mother Guadalupe? I will give twenty pesos, my silk shawl and raincoat to anyone who can offer me any info.]

26. "En la Alameda y en 'El Heraldo' Estuvo Ayer Don Catarino": "Youngsters, hooligans, and the unemployed were all gathered together in front of a wooden stand in Alameda Park, the group growing with the crescendo of sentences and protests coming from one individual there, who was quite oddly dressed."

27. Before December 1921, the author's name did not appear in the credits, either as Carlos Fernández Benedicto or Hipólito Zendejas.

28. "Dictadas a Hipólito Zendejas, exclusivas para *El Heraldo*" (Dictated to Zendejas, exclusively for the *Herald*). This conceit is reminiscent of El Periquillo Sarniento bequeathing his manuscript to Lizardi, and its deeper Hispanic lineage as an echo of *Don Quixote*.

29. We have not come across the framing device (potentially metafictional) that was used to introduce these memoirs to a public already familiar with Catarino and his current family.

30. World War I (1914–1918) had overlapped with the Mexican Revolution (1910–1920), and notable European memoirs published between 1915 and 1922 had become popular in the Americas.

31. Catarino's tree, created by Pruneda, is paired with a narrative about the baptism of his paternal great-grandfather, Íñigo Rápido de San Ángel, circa 1577, within the first century of the Spaniards' arrival and conquest. Catarino asserts that his "antepasado de las ramas antiguas" (ancestor from the oldest lineages) was born of an Aztec princess and namesake Spanish adventurer, and that his baptism was attended by Aztec emperor Moctezuma and wife.

32. Fernández Benedicto, *Memorias*, in *El Heraldo*, December 3, 1922; inaugural edition cited by Aurrecoechea, *Puros cuentos*, 219.

33. We suspect that the Teniente was adept at *charrería*, given the January 3 (1923) episode's depiction of his relationship with his horse Prieto upon his death, a trademark sign in popular lore surrounding the *charro*.

34. In the December 18 (1922) installment, Teniente Catarino is also shown penning letters from the 1866 Battle of La Carbonera.

35. Fernández Benedicto, *Memorias*, in *El Heraldo*, January 8, 1923. The memoirs of Catarino's father end with a strangely prophetic dream of fighting wars on elephant-back in foreign lands—something Catarino himself will accomplish in future installments.

36. " '¡Mexicanos al grito de Gue-e-rraa! / ¡el acero aprestad y el bri-i-doo-on!' Las lágrimas no más nos rodaban por los cachetes, y los corazones iscarlatos le brincaban di amorosa conjunción, y las manos li agarraban los paliacates y le sonaban las estalatitas de las narices. Li acabamos de cantarle, y que nos tranquilizamos, y que entonces, li pasamos a la sala, onde se sirvió un tépache y ponches calientitos y comienzó el baile" (Fernández Benedicto, *Memorias*, in *El Heraldo*, January 8, 15, and 20, 1923).

37. Fernández Benedicto, *Memorias*, in *El Heraldo*, January 16, 1923.

38. Even after traveling the world, Don Catarino never loses his signature speech.

39. Fernández Benedicto, *Memorias*, in *El Heraldo*, January 20, 1923.

40. This layout is reminiscent of Mexico's first known illustrated narrative, published prior to the Revolution, in the *Potosina Ilustrada* (1869–71) by Cuéllar and company: *Rosa y Federico* (1869).

41. Similar to their four-panel predecessors from the 1870s, these sets of images accompanied by text do not consist of dialogue like in more modern strips but hearken back to the earlier period of caricaturistic production in which text and image were not yet integrated, as in the older *aleluyas* tradition.

42. It is important to note, however, that the story summarized in the four images did not always correspond to the full narrative arc of the accompanying text; it was almost as if the author and illustrator were not always in close contact over the course of production.

43. In its early years, *El Demócrata* also reran initial strips alongside new ones (and not because they were lacking in new installments).

44. The reader had already been introduced to inclusive community building through *El Heraldo*'s pages via numerous contests to encourage participation. Pancho Villa was thought to be a potential candidate for president

45. The sites include Moctezuma's Bath and the Monument to the Niños Heroes in Chapultepec Forest; the Virgin of Guadalupe's villa; the Aztec Calendar; the Monument to Mexico's Independence; and, finally, the burial site of Benito Juárez (Fernández Benedicto, *Memorias*, January 24–25, 1923).

46. Fernández Benedicto, in *El Heraldo*, January 24, 1923.

47. Fernández Benedicto, in *El Heraldo*, January 24, 1923.

48. Fernández Benedicto, in *El Heraldo*, January 25, 1923.

49. Fernández Benedicto, in *El Heraldo*, February 2, 1923.

50. The initial episode from December 4, 1921, was expanded into five episodes of the *Memorias*, which ran from February 11 through 17, 1923.

51. Fernández Benedicto, in *El Heraldo*, February 12, 1923.

52. "The patriotic emblem that we needed to have, in order for foreign nations to recognize us" (Fernández Benedicto, in *El Heraldo*, February 12, 1923).

53. His letters are to France; to the US (addressed to President Warren Harding); to England's king; to Russia's Lennon [*sic*]; and to Turkey's sultan.

54. He insults his ministers as savages for not knowing other languages, calling them "illiterate slobs" ("unos babosos analfabeitos"; Fernández Benedicto, in *El Heraldo*, February 13, 1923).

55. In a poorly written decree shown in the opening image of the source strip but not in the memoirs, Catarino indicates that Spanish literacy will be key. The decree is posted at the entrypoint into the simulacra of Mexico that he is happily replicating on the island: "'El que no avle ezpañol sera ezpulsado del pais por estrangero pernisosio.'—El precidente Catarino" ("'Anyone who does not speak Spanish will be expelled from the country as a dangerous foreigner.'— President Catarino," Fernández Benedicto, in *El Heraldo*, December 4, 1921).

56. In the 1921 strip, he offers this simplified history lesson riddled with errors: "As you are savages, you may not know who the great Juarez was; his name was Benito Patricio Benemeritus [*sic*]. Juarez was a president just like me, and he wrote the laws of Mexico and they say, though we do not know if this is true, that he separated the church from the state of Tabasco [*sic*]. Well, there you have it, Patricio Juarez [*sic*] took on Maximilian of Hamburg [*sic*] and Mama Carlota and then shot Maximilian in Queretaro, where there are many opal mines. Later he became president and then died, so we built him this monument. Long live Mexico! Long live Silao!!"

57. Fernández Benedicto, in *El Heraldo*, February 13, 1923.

58. Another passage in the same episode humorously juxtaposes the importance of family and patriotism with Catarino's heartache from being without his family at that moment: "After I had finished the ceremony, I grabbed the flag with my trembling hands, and I made all the citizens of the island of Silado swear that they would spill up to the second-to-last drop of their very blood defending the flag of the Mexican army of the three guarantees. All of them swore on their mothers, and one of them swore on his sister, as he was an orphan with no mother to speak of" (Fernández Benedicto, in *El Heraldo*, February 13, 1923).

59. In the First Republic, Catarino is ousted by the natives in a coup (Fernández Benedicto, in *El Heraldo*, February 26, 1923).

60. Ligia, having made great strides since her barely legible classified ad in *El Heraldo*, now teaches urbanity and other subjects to the natives, as related by her husband: "We fixed and oiled their hair, and then we began to instruct those illiterate peoples. Ligia taught them decorum and good manners; Tanasia, arithmetic and verb conjugations; Eulogio taught Spanish and the topography of Mexico; and I taught about copper, which we had collected from the mines on that island" (Fernández Benedicto, in *El Heraldo*, February 26, 1923).

61. Tanasia and Ulogio refrain from killing their enemies with the famous quote from Juárez: "Respect for the Rights of Others is Peace."

62. "Later we returned to Mexico City, and there, at the behest of friends and of Cholita, the lady who owns the bookstand, I began to write these Memoirs of mine, that I will finish now, and then tomorrow I'm off on a trip around the world, commissioned by my country's government, who sends me to other countries to study their agricultural systems" (in *El Heraldo*, February 26, 1923).

63. "Last Wednesday we had the pleasure of receiving in this very newsroom a commission made up of the most distinguished union members, begging us to send a telegram to Don Catarino, requesting his acceptance by telegram of our nomination to the Presidency of the Republic" (Fernández Benedicto, in *El Heraldo*, March 17, 1923).

64. "At the request of the referenced commission, our colleague, Hipólito Zende-jas, sent the telegram to Don Catarino."

65. See Chapter 2 on Riva Palacio for a discussion of *México a través de los siglos*.

66. "Extend your hand to each and every Mexican with the message that I am their brother and I am at their service, and that if they make me president . . . They will soon see for themselves!"

67. "There is talk about only one candidate, in the capital and the provinces. There is only one candidate who is viable and unique: the heroic son of Silao."

68. Morelia's headline proclaimed that "99 Percent of Michoacán is Catarinista." The candidate's supporters identify themselves by hanging from their neck an enamel locket with the portrait of Don Catarino, which reads "Long Live Si-lao!" There was also purportedly the creation of a Catarinista political club in Toluca, the animation of all of Tamaulipas through Tampico's creation of the "Sons of Tamaulipas" party, and a splendid showing of support ("manifestación imponentísima") in Guanajuato, Catarino's home state, where a statue of Ca-tarino had been erected.

69. "Only one candidate is being discussed . . . that patriotic and honorable Mexi-can, who knew how in foreign lands to lift our Patria's flag on high; the un-surpassed Don Catarino; the enlightened legitimate son of Don Catarino and Doña Tanasia (RIP)."

70. "*El Heraldo*, upon making this statement, is considering all of the qualities that adorn our great candidate: Don Catarino is honest. Don Catarino is the most patriotic of Mexicans. Don Catarino is brave to the point of heroism. Don Ca-tarino is a polyglot. Don Catarino is a writer. Don Catarino is a man of great natural talent. Don Catarino has a practical education, acquired through travel. Don Catarino is energetic and generous. Don Catarino is a millionaire. Don Catarino loves the *pueblo* . . . Don Catarino is popular. Don Catarino does not compromise with foreign-ness. Don Catarino is Truly Mexican. Taking into ac-count these undeniable qualities, who will dare to run against this wonderful son of Silao?" (Fernández Benedicto, in *El Heraldo*, March 17, 1923).

71. "Remitido por cable a Hipólito Zendejas. - Especial para El Heraldo" (Fernán-dez Benedicto, in *El Heraldo*, March 17, 1923).

72. "And so I thought things over, and saw, with the clearest of lights (that they call Meridian: meaning, of course, that it hails from Yucatan) that if I did not accept the candidacy, then there could be . . . who knows what, but a true internal digestive revolution [*sic*] in this country; and there could also be bloodshed among my Mexican brothers! So, in order to avoid the bloodshed, I thought I might go ahead and accept the candidacy for president. So I grabbed a pencil, sharpening it with my very own fingernails, to write the telegram that I sent back to Mexico City, and thus I accepted my candidacy."

73. "To govern a country, you do not need anything more than political tact, integrity, patriotism, love for other citizens, and to rule with one hand placed on your heart and the other on the robust Constitution of our Patria, another on the Law, another on honesty, and another on the Laws of Reforma Avenue [*sic*]. Long live Benito Juárez!"

74. "Well, it did not seem a bad thing to have been appointed as a presidential candidate; and well, I do not pretend to have the credentials but I do know the world, and I also know how all countries are governed, because I have been in those countries and I have seen how it is done, and I am full of patriotism, and I have never allowed my country to be diminished in any place where I have lived, and my worldly aspirations are summarized in these subconscious [*sic*] words: Long live México!"

75. "As soon as I am president, I shall look after my magnificent, shining, and compassionate Homeland, and I shall proceed so that the Republic of Mexico enters properly into the hall of civilized nations and that all countries, among the career diplomats of those nations that have been anointed with civilization, will want to be what our Mexico will become as the months and half-decades go by."

76. "Citizens, I hereby send you this manifesto, and no sooner than the days just before the elections arrive, I will return to the Patria, and I will tour the entire Republic, so that everyone gets to know me personally and see my character, to know for whom you are casting your vote. Long live the Liberty Bell of Dolores!"

77. Catarino's full *Programa de Gobierno del Ciudadano Don Catarino* stressed the importance of free public instruction for all (in homage to Vasconcelos), and popular ideas for implementation, such as decreasing illiteracy by teaching reading in public spaces, replete with satirical Lizardi-like criticism that *maestros* don't get paid enough to eat.

78. The *Historia*'s byline—"Escrita por Don Catarino y Remitida a Hipolito Zendejas"—continues the promotion of Catarino as author (and the demotion of Zendejas, from a scribe taking dictation to a mere emissary).

79. See Chapter 4 for an exploration of Chucho el Roto as mass media legend. For the immortalization of Pancho Villa through mass media, see Macías, "Imagining Villa."

80. "The only true account, made by the guerrilla fighter to his confidante and friend, Doctor Ramón Puente" (*El Heraldo*, August 1, 1923).

81. Unlike Catarino's, Villa's memoirs are not transcribed in the vernacular, but

instead feature a highly standardized Spanish. Martín Luís Guzmán hoped to rectify that over-styling in his 1938 version of Villa's memoirs, upon their release in book format (according to the author's preface to that volume).

82. *El Universal*'s quest for a weekly series included guidelines with this stipulation: "The comic's main character or characters, as well as its subject matter, are entirely open, but preference will be given to comics that feature national topics" (January 2, 1927).

CHAPTER 4

Epigraphs. Rubén Gallo, *Mexican Modernity*, 126. Anne Rubenstein, "Mass Media," 637.

1. Precise information on dates and titles in the world of radio dramas can be difficult to come by. *Chucho el Roto*'s episodes are now housed in the Fonoteca Nacional—"so that there is testimony of those who worked on the show, of something glorious" (Fonoteca Nacional, *Radionovelas legendarias*, 6/28/2012, 13:10)—but the 3,149 episodes remain undated. As head of the national audio archives, Fonoteca director Pável Granados presents this as a generalized problem in the study of *radionovelas*: "On this topic, like no other at XEW, opinions remain contradictory: on which stations the radio dramas were broadcast, during what years, their names. We take down the opinion of each person who offers their account" (*XEW*, 248). In the case of *Chucho el Roto*, longtime technical engineer and *musicalizador* (sound technician) Juan Pablo O'Farrill, one of the last surviving staff members to have worked on all of *Chucho*'s episodes, recalls that *Chucho el Roto* ran thirteen years (conversation with the author, August 2016). Other accounts mention ten or eleven, placing *Chucho*'s run, at minimum, at a decade. Both O'Farrill and Carlos "Charly" González Cardozo (head of production at XEW for a decade beginning in the late 1950s) date *Chucho*'s initial production to 1963 (Fonoteca Nacional, 6/28/2012, 44:45–47:00), which would put its run around 1964–1975 or 1964–1977. In 1973 Rodríguez Familiar refers to the Mexican public's generally insatiable curiosity about this character: "If there is a single individual to be considered the most popular, the most legendary in Mexico, it would be Jesús Arriaga, aka 'Chucho el Roto,' whose heroic deeds were being told in yesteryear by the family hearth or being represented on stage, while nowadays the radio, the silver screen and the television relay his adventure-filled stories . . . all to please an audience that is not content with small quantities, and is always demanding more . . . and authors find themselves obliged to create ever-new exciting tales for the telling" (*Efemérides queretanas*, 1:201).

2. Almeida Peréz dedicates an entire *Radionovelas legendarias* listening session to *Chucho el Roto* as the most emblematic Mexican *radionovela* (Fonoteca Nacional, 6/28/2012, 3:00).

3. According to Cardozo, it was an era some forty years long: "This period of radio drama rises in Mexico toward the beginning of the 1940s, and the last radio soap operas aired with XEW around 1982" (6/28/2012, 48:00–52:30).

4. 6/28/2012, 47:00–47:45. *Chucho el Roto* is more "Mexican" in its storyline than *Kalimán*, although *Kalimán* is in a similar league in terms of length. Almeida clarifies that *Chucho el Roto* is "the longest radio soap opera of which we still have copies; some 3000 episodes; by that I want to tell you that this radio drama was on the air for more than ten years" (5/25/2012, 5:30; emphasis mine). *Kalimán*—produced by XEW rival RCN/RadioRed—may be the only *radionovela* to have lasted longer than *Chucho el Roto* (5/12/2012, 20:08:42–20:09:30; 6/28/2012, 1:00), having begun in 1962, according to Cardozo, and running up to 1973, with reruns continuing in the provinces through at least 2012, and generating the famed comic in its wake: in the case of *Kalimán*, however, the *radionovela* was its first known iteration.

5. The first *serialized* version of Chucho's story appeared in 1922–23 in Mexico City's *El Mundo*, under the direction of Martín Luis Guzmán, and constituted its most ideological treatment at that date. The work, of anonymous authorship, was the second novel to be published about Chucho's life and featured a significantly more ideological plot (and completely different love story) that drew very little if any content from the first 1916 novel. The newspaper *folletín* presented strong claims to serving as a truthful, *de facto* memoir—"compiled according to the memoirs of his adviser and secretary Enrique Villena"—and entitled *La verdadera y única historia de Chucho el Roto*. Chucho's urban edge is highlighted (he is no rural social bandit à la Hobsbawm), appearing as a figure of unification, and sharing some resonances with the contemporary escape artist Harry Houdini (1874–1926). This unique treatment bears separate attention as a well-written and widely disseminated social treatise; it was not, however, picked up by any subsequent version. Its unexpected ending in 1923 may be attributed to Guzmán's sudden resignation from the paper's helm (and exile) because of his involvement with the failed de la Huerta Rebellion (see Chapter 3).

6. The newspapers with articles about Arriaga included *El Monitor Republicano*, *El Tiempo*, *El Siglo XIX*, and *El Correo de los Lunes* (Vanderwood, *Disorder and Progress*; A. Robinson, "Mexican Banditry").

7. "Roto" was a nineteenth-century moniker used to describe an individual of humble origins who dressed in an deceptively elegant fashion, thereby "passing" socially from one class into another.

8. *El Siglo XIX*, June 2, 1884; Rodríguez Familiar, *Efemérides queretanas*, 1:202–3.

9. A. Robinson, "Mexican Banditry," 11.

10. *El Monitor Republicano*, June 21, 1884.

11. On Gutiérrez Nájera, see Vanderwood, *Disorder and Progress*, 97. On de Zayas Enríquez, see Rodríguez Familiar, *Efemérides queretanas*, 1:204.

12. Other notable bandits from the same period, such as El Tigre de Santa Julia and Heraclio Bernal, were famous for barbaric acts of violence.

13. At least one other article mentions a wife by the name of Maria Bermeo who supposedly aided Chucho in his heists (*El Monitor Republicano*, June 21, 1884;

Rodríguez Familiar, *Efemérides queretanas*, 1:202, in a gloss of 1884 arrest reports), while other articles list a daughter by the name of Delfina (Rodríguez Familiar, 202).

14. *El Tiempo* took pains to confirm that it was acute dysentery—and not abuse from prison guards, as circulated in rumors—that caused Arriaga's demise (November 5 and 13, 1885).

15. The first known piece dates to 1888: *Chucho el Roto, o La nobleza de un bandido: Ensayo dramático en dos actas y prosa* was attributed to Juan C. Maya and first performed in Mexico City in 1889.

16. These protests were alluded to in the play's reviews in contemporary Mexico City newspapers, such as *La Voz de España* (A. Robinson, "Mexican Banditry," 16).

17. Chucho's mother's house was "violated" by robbery, and upon her death Chucho vows justice. This is a frequent motif in the stories of bandit heroes such as Pancho Villa (i.e., avenging the rape of his sister), in which affronts to the family are posed as legitimate reasons for acts of revenge.

18. Chucho is not given his second chance in this play: he is instead carried away to Ulúa while repentantly entreating Isabel to prepare their daughter Angela to honor his memory as a redeemed version of his former self.

19. This play was written by Antonio Fuentes and produced in San Antonio by the Carlos Villalongín troupe. It was the first play to be presented by the group, less than one month after their arrival from Mexico, declaring on the playbill that "Our Company is pleased to announce . . . the play that has caused such a sensation in all theaters where it has appeared, because it stars a personage so well known throughout the entire Republic for notorious robberies carried out with great astuteness due to the solid and kind character that distinguished him. As this Company is aware that another of the Companies that passed through this town staged a play in two acts entitled *Chucho el Roto*, we would like to inform our public that the one we announce today is the real one, written in Puebla by Mr. Fuentes, which has filled all the theaters where it has appeared with a select audience" (Ramírez, *Footlights*, 141). The playbill also indicates a certain "serialization" of performance, with the first three acts scheduled for Monday, May 22, and the second three acts for Tuesday, May 23.

20. This addition of the Frizacs to Chucho's fictional storyline is indicated by the cast's roles as listed on the 1911 playbill (Ramírez, 141).

21. The copy of the 1916 novel (published by Editorial Quiroga) available in UNAM's Biblioteca Nacional is anonymously authored. Citations of the 1916 edition refer to this copy. (Authors Fernando Ferrari Pérez and Alfonso López Flores are indeterminately associated with later editions of the novel.) Amy Robinson offers this useful summary: "Chucho el Roto was a humble carpenter who fell in love with Matilde de Frizac, the niece of wealthy aristocrat Don Diego de Frizac. Matilde fell in love with Chucho, rejected him because of their unequal status, and then gave birth to their daughter Dolores (Lolita) in secrecy.

Chucho later kidnapped Lolita, and the de Frizac family used their influence to have him arrested for the crime of kidnapping. After escaping from jail, Chucho and his bandit gang episodically used disguises and ingenuity to rob wealthy targets, all the while finding ways to distribute the stolen riches to the poor. He was famously nonviolent, vowing [in a promise to his mother on her deathbed] to maintain his honor by never staining his hands with blood" ("Chucho," 452–53).

22. The author goes on to explain the possible reasons for a good man's turn to crime: "Society, in which man is forced to live in order to satisfy his needs, is sometimes so cruel and unjust that those beings endowed with ingenuity and character, honest but poor, are rejected from its bosom for these reasons alone, when they could instead stand out for their aptitudes, for being useful to their peers, they are instead pushed into crime and shame, only to be scandalized later on by their acts, and then, in the name of society and in its redress, redeem themselves in the dungeons of a prison or in facing the gallows" (2). He then issues a challenge to his readers to pass their own verdict: "It is therefore up to our readers to give their verdict according to their conscience, by either absolving or condemning Jesús Arriaga (a.k.a.) 'Chucho el Roto,' the lead character in this short play, or the society in which he lived, giving to each what is just, because it is not our goal in taking on this work to disturb the memory of a man whose name deserves the utmost respect . . . Rather, we try to contribute, in our small way, to the improvement of social conventions, drawing from the events that occurred in the past, to find the lessons we should use in the future" (3). The author closes this lengthy diatribe with an indictment, not of the individual criminal but of society at large: "Man has never wished to discover in himself the origin and source of all his own evils, but rather selfishly looks to causes that have nothing to do with him; and though words like 'charity,' 'philanthropy,' and others (with no applicability, in practice) are constantly invoked, anywhere and everywhere, what we instead find at the bottom of every society, and in each of its components, is nothing more than selfishness, greed, ambition!" (2).

23. In preparation for the sequel, the novel's epilogue shows young Dolores (Lola) longing to move to Mexico City so that she can continue her deceased father's work: "'I want to live out in the world, in a big city, where I can help more people, where the good that my hands may do reaches an entire *pueblo.*' The soul of Jesús Arriaga lives on in those words. Lola's father also wanted to increase the numbers of those he helped; he too wanted to go through the countryside and all the villages, spreading good and delivering justice" (117–18).

24. Though both are currently irretrievable, the 1919 silent film (starring Leopoldo de Cerro) and the 1921 film are thought to follow the basic plot of the 1916 novel, which soon became the canonical storyline (A. Robinson, "Chucho el Roto," 452). Neither appears, however, in Emilio García Riera's compendium of Mexican films from these years.

25. The 95-minute film was one of 1934's "super-productions," according to García Riera (*Historia documental*, 1:119), with publicity advertising it as the most expensive film in Mexico to date (123). It launched the international careers of debut director Gabriel Soria and title actor Fernando Soler (with Adriana Lamar in the role of Matilde), proving a critical as well as a popular success in its weeklong showing at Mexico City's Palacio Chino, followed by its export to international markets (122). García Riera attributed this film's popularity, as evidenced by its numerous remakes and parodies, to the Mexican public's penchant for heroes in disguise (i.e., Chucho's capacity to disguise his origins): "I suppose that the ability to hide behind a disguise, related to his personality, was very attractive to a broad popular audience. This explains the future reappearance of Chucho the Urban Bandit in a dozen other Mexican films, not counting parodies or derivations; there was an obvious relationship between his appeal and the one that masked heroes would have for that same audience" (122).The prologue to the tie-in edition states that the novel is crucial to a full understanding of the famous bandit hero: "We want to contribute by publishing this small work, a necessary addition for whomever wants to experience and fully understand the seductive, abundant and adventurous life of the one who, due to his elegance and popularity, was called 'Chucho el Roto' by his contemporaries" (3). It is possible that editors were also encouraging reading: at the time of the film's release, to a market of 16 million residents, two-thirds of the Mexican population was illiterate (García Riera, 22).

26. The UNAM library catalogue attributes the 1935 first edition of the illustrated *novela de aventuras* to Fernando Ferrari Pérez, who had died in 1933, and there is no attribution to any author (or date) in any of the available "episodes" (*cuadernos*) that came out every Thursday as part of Editorial Tolteca's illustrated "adventure series," in which Mexican Chucho appeared in the company of other series' heroes such as Sherlock Holmes. Episodes sold for ten *centavos* apiece, were available in newspaper stands and bookstores, and were advertised as part of a potential set of twenty total: "Collecting our notebooks, the reader will get a work of 400 profusely illustrated pages for just 2 pesos, a book whose store value is no less than 4 pesos a copy."

27. *Pepín* was advertised as an "illustrated bi-weekly" that would appear every Tuesday and Thursday, beginning in 1936 (undated episodes), for 10 *centavos* an episode "en todo México" according to 1936 advertisements. *Pepín*'s associated imprint, La Editorial Juventud, was obviously geared toward working-class youth, sponsoring clubs, contests, and prizes for young readers (such as scholarships to study to be a mechanic or an electrician), as well as progressive raffles with participation dependent on buying a certain number of episodes, seen in advertisements throughout 1936. *Pepín* sets *Chucho*'s initial episode quite early, in 1850, with the hero's controversial theft of his daughter Dolores. Each episode consisted of two double-page spreads of eight large frames each, for a total of sixteen frames per episode, and illustrated ample visual

intermediality in the form of handwritten notes, reward posters, etc., embedded within the imagery of the strip itself.

28. Agrasánchez, *Mexican Movies*, 27–28. The film was censored in two major US cities (New York and Chicago), and then revised and released in an altered form. It was successfully exported to Spain, however, in its original version.

29. The narrator serves as a mouthpiece for Chucho's class perspective and goals: "The real bandits . . . walk the metropolitan streets with impunity, while the middle and popular classes are consumed in misery or rot in prisons, with no hope of salvation. Taking revenge on that social caste, wounding it where it hurts most: in its coffers. Using money to wipe away the the helpless classes' tears. Having money, a lot of money, to earn respect; and, as far as [Chucho] was concerned, to educate his daughter brilliantly, in order to assure her place in society" (1:5–6).

30. In this speech from a later episode, a character described by the narration as "sensible" holds forth on the Revolution's injustices: "¡Anyone would have money upon finding themselves in those gentlemen's circumstances! Who were they before the Revolution? Nothing. They were glorified by that movement, elevated to political positions that they have now used to get rich. These are the new feudal lords who suck up both public and private wealth but take no responsibility onto their shoulders of providing for the needs of the masses of society who depend on them. If I may speak frankly, it disgusts me to extend my hand to those men, who are incapable of generous behavior" (5:12–13).

31. Quoted in Rubenstein, *Bad Language*, 30.

32. In the first decade of Mexico's so-called Golden Age, Chucho's popularity scarcely waned. 1944 saw a new edition of the 1916 novel (*Ediciones Populares Mexicanas*), just prior to a fourth film, *La sombra de Chucho el Roto* (1945), its progeny-based plotline revolving around Chucho's supposed son (screenplay by Raúl de Anda, under the direction of Alejandro Galindo). 1945 also saw a two-volume set issued by Editorial Amado Nervo: *Chucho el Roto, el bandido generoso* followed by *Chucho el Roto, segunda parte: La herencia de Lolita Frizac; La hermana de la caridad*, varyingly attributed to authors Fernando Ferrari Pérez or Alfonso López Flores. In the 1950s there were several other films: Tin Tan's comic knock-off, *Chucho el remendado* (1952), as well as Luis Aguilar's *Chucho el Roto, el bandido generoso* (1954, produced by Reforma Films, under the direction of Miguel M. Delgado); *El tesoro de Chucho el Roto* (1960), showcasing another family-based plotline centered around Chucho's daughter; and *Chucho el Roto* (1960–1962) starring Carlos Baena.

33. Here we use the term *melodrama* to indicate the heightened emotional quality of a family story that appeals to sentimentalism.

34. Fonoteca National, 6/28/2012, 15:30–17:00. Almeida recalls learning about the production from Cardozo (14:00), and Anne Rubenstein also mentions its existence (*Bad Language*, 30).

35. In the words of historian John Mraz, "1940 has been identified, retrospectively, in elite memoirs and mainstream histories alike as the beginning of Mexico's

Golden Age. This rubric is often used by scholars in connection with Mexico's 'classic' period of cinematic production, which roughly spanned the years from 1940 to 1960 . . . We propose to extend the metaphor to encompass other aspects of cultural production and reception—consumer culture, print journalism, television, and tourism" (in Joseph et al., *Fragments*, 8–9).

36. On the non-recording of *radionovelas*: O'Farrill, conversation with the author. Many such as *Anita de Montemar* were remade at a later date, when their second version was taped.

37. That it was produced is perhaps indicative of the era's renewed interest in Mexico's popular oral traditions, many dating from the nineteenth century, as a goldmine of relevant and recognizable material for the Mexican public. During this same period, *El Periquillo Sarniento* and *Martín Garatuza* were also made into *radionovelas* of which we have no recordings and have been lost to posterity (Fonoteca National, 6/28/2012, 18:00).

38. "Illustrated magazines from this period [1920–1930] often carried advertisements for radio service depicting what was surely an ideal for many middle-class consumers: a prosperous family gathered in the living room around the radio receiver, enjoying a musical program that came into their home from a distant station" (Gallo, *Mexican Modernity*, 120).

39. In contrast to the quintessential Golden Age family movies of Sara García, for example, these plots were *serialized*, though Ramírez Berg's commentary on those movies also speaks to the importance of the family in film productions of that era (*Cinema of Solitude*, 17–28).

40. In the United States, in contrast, the large professional conglomerates of RCA and NBC, not families, were predominant.

41. Indeed, Mexico's first commercial radio transmission in 1923 was led by Azcárraga Vidaurreta's uncle, Raúl Azcárraga (owner of a radio shop on Avenida Juárez). He and his brother Luis persuaded newspaper editor Carlos Noriega Hope, of the weekly literary magazine *El Universal Ilustrado*, to put up the money for a commercial radio station. Together they founded "*El Universal Ilustrado / La Casa del Radio*." Transmitting every Tuesday and Friday evening (Granados, *XEW*, 15), this effort constituted the first radio station in Mexico City (Gallo, *Mexican Modernity*, 123). By 1926 Mexico City had thirteen stations (Rubenstein, "Mass Media," 645). See also Gallo, 141–42, for the Azcárragas' role at Mexico's 1923 Radio Fair; Granados, *XEW*, 28–29; and Rubenstein, "Mass Media," 644–45.

42. Granados, *XEW*, 30–31. See also Esquivel Puerto, *Anecdotario*, 192–93, on the maintenance of former employees' gravesites.

43. On the signification of modernity, see Gallo, *Mexican Modernity*, 117–67.

44. Quoted in Granados, XEW, 33.

45. "La Voz": *El Excélsior*, September 18, 1930; quoted in Granados, *XEW*, 33. "Radio, in contrast, was the perfect medium for a country with a high illiteracy rate. Everyone—literate or illiterate—could listen to the radio. Peasants in distant regions who had never been able to read a newspaper could now tune into

the news, hear the latest reports from the capital, and even enjoy music from other parts of the world—all without leaving their villages. Postrevolutionary governments soon realized that radio was the perfect medium to educate the masses, and in 1924 the Ministry of Education launched its own radio station, CYE. The inaugural program featured a conference by Bernardo Gastélum, the new minister, echoing Vasconcelo's theories as he extolled radio as the most powerful weapon in the country's battle against illiteracy" (Gallo, *Mexican Modernity*, 125–26).

46. Rubenstein, "Mass Media," 639.

47. Rubenstein, 644.

48. "The W began to have a very strong, almost monopolizing influence on Mexican society; Don Emilio Azcárraga's dream was always for the W to be a nationwide station" (Alejandro Quintero, who had started in radio dramas as director of communications with Colgate-Palmolive in the 1950s, and then became Radiópolis' vice president of planning and development in the 1970s, participating in the merger of Grupo Televisa to become general director of Televisa Radio, as quoted in Granados, *XEW*, 277). Azcárraga from the start showed particular interest in broadcasting to the populations of Mexican immigrants in the United States.

49. XEW was the only station at this moment with such reach: by 1938, for example, Emilio Azcárraga's radio network included fifteen stations total (Rubenstein, "Mass Media," 645).

50. Broadcast media was politicized from the moment of its inception, and Mexico was no exception, with its earliest radio programming in 1923 including speeches by President Obregón and president-to-be Calles.

51. According to a 1942 edition of *Radiolandia*, music still made up 80 percent of XEW's programming. Informational programs/news were at 13 percent, comic series/*radionovelas* at 3 percent, and dialogues at 3 percent, followed by sports at 1 percent (Granados, *XEW*, 268–69). "In that political situation, XEW becomes Pan-American: its banner is now that of an American union or, at least, of the spiritual union offered by the songs that it broadcasts. During these times—and also in more peaceful ones—XEW unifies. The voices coming from the radio chanted their announcements, their counsel, their allegiances" (271).

52. Azcárraga cultivated direct connections with NBC and was directly affiliated with the United States' RCA network from the start (Rubenstein, "Mass Media," 645). The privileging of national content was to the exclusion of languages other than Spanish, by a series of laws first passed in 1932 and 1936, dictating, for example, that at least one-fourth of the music in stations' rotation consisted of Mexican music in Spanish representing the various regions: "In the north one could hear the music of the south and in Oaxaca you could listen to music from Nuevo León, and that was a feature of national unity that remains unparalleled" (Almeida, quoted in Granados, *XEW*, 280).

53. On the station's thirteenth-year anniversary, Azcárraga laid the cornerstone for Radiópolis, his strikingly modern headquarters for Mexican sound. Poet Ricardo López Méndez waxed lyrical for the occasion on the XEW family's communal efforts to broaden Mexico's cultural "soul" and standing, now proudly aggrandized into a city unto itself that would represent *mexicanidad* beyond Mexico's national borders. Engineer José Albarrán y Pliego, illustrious architect of the project located on the corner of Avenida Chapultepec and Doctor Río de la Loza, commented during the ceremony's broadcast on the honor of being selected by Azcárraga to serve as the designer of "this great City of Radio, Radiópolis" (quoted in Granados, *XEW*, 264–65): "Thirteen years have gone by since a handful of workers joined efforts in a common cause: for our radio station's call numbers to chart a course to be followed, to praise the name of Mexico name to the depths of its hinterlands by way of art, culture, commerce, and industry" (quoted in Granados, 265).

54. XEW's achievement was heralded on this occasion in hyperbolic terms by well-known radio announcer Pedro de Lille Aizpuru (1899–1964) as "yet another victory of those caravels of dreams known as XEW and XEWW, brave both in combat and in triumph. . ." (quoted in Granados, *XEW*, 264).

55. Almeida, quoted in Granados, *XEW*, 280.

56. Fonoteca National, 6/28/2012, 53:45–59:17.

57. Rubenstein also notes this tendency in the comic books of the 1930s–1940s, which were also serialized: "The basic plot of these melodramas, no matter what their settings, nearly always involved the destiny of a family. This family may be threatened or challenged by economic adversity, the greed or selfishness of some of its members, or sexual predations by powerful outsiders. [. . .] Stories like these appealed strongly to Mexican audiences because they resonated with the difficulties, dangers, and pleasures of postrevolutionary life. [. . .] Small wonder, then, that by 1940 a seemingly insatiable demand had developed for mass-media melodramas, whether in periodicals, on the radio, or in the movies. [. . .] The stories told by comic books and tabloid newspapers closely matched the narratives of *radionovelas*. [. . .] Useful plots or characters often passed back and forth among historietas, radio dramas, movies, and eventually televised soap operas, too" ("Mass Media," 642–44).

58. On the symbiotic relationship between the two stations, Vicente Morales quips that "the W was the original [master recording] and the Q was the laboratory" (n.d., 1:14:34).

59. Fonoteca Nacional, 6/28/2012, 15:30–17:00.

60. These long narratives were *radiophonic*, not *radiogenic* (Gallo, *Mexican Modernity*, 157–60): "XEW took on nineteenth century novels' sentimental discourse. That Romantic structure continues to live on in radio dramas" (Granados, *XEW*, 95). *Folletines*, broken down into parts, provided ritualized reading opportunities, many times *en voz alta* (out loud), fostering community participation for nonliterates in public spaces. Capitalizing on sound, as would the

radionovela, as far as we know the sharers of such stories in public spaces or in private homes were not designated readers, or specialized actors, but rather those who possessed the skill of literacy. (We have few records of such readings—only passing references, images, or anecdotes—to let us know that they did, in fact, occur.)

61. The first purported *radioteatro* in Mexico was an adaptation of Dumas's classic French *folletín, Los tres mosqueteros* circa 1932, produced by XEW and adapted by filmmaker Alejandro Galindo (Murillo Rivas, "El radiodrama," chapter 4; Fonoteca Nacional, *Radionovelas legendarias,* 6/28/2012). (No known recordings were made or preserved.) Other specifically Mexican plotlines soon appeared, such as those of *El baisano Jalil* and *Pancho Villa.* In the use of skilled readers, Mexico was developing an incipient "star system" in figures such as the classically trained actress Pura Córdova.

62. Di Lauro, quoted in Granados, *XEW,* 249–50, was privy to the industry, growing up in a household in which his mother worked as a *radionovela* actress and his uncle as a Colgate-Palmolive executive. Llenero's essay corrects some apparent errors in Di Lauro's story, such as the name of the Cuban station (CMQ, not CBQ; 272), and the incorrect attribution of *Anita de Montemar* to Caignet (the author was Leandro Blanco). According to Llenero, *El derecho* arrived in 1950 and aired on XEX (not XEW), stating very specifically that this was the only case in which XEX was able to best XEW in the ratings ("*El derecho,*" 276). In his version of the history of radio, however, Mejía Prieto places *Chucho el Roto*'s author Carlos Chacón at the epicenter of the earliest action: "In those years there were dramatic scenes, often presented on Sundays, complete works that were not adapted for radio, which came from Spanish theater. But it was not until 1934, and thanks to the work of [Carlos] Chacón Jr., that the first radio drama was made: *El proceso de Mary Dugan,* consisting of twenty 15-minute chapters, recorded on large discs, on wax matrix, by Guillermo Kornhausser and Eduardo Baptista. From there a specialized field of radio of incalculable importance began its brilliant trajectory. Of the many successes we can remember there are *Corona de espinas, ¿Quién es esa mujer?, Chucho el Roto, San Martín de Porres, La vida de Monseñor Rafael Guízar y Valencia, Juan Diego, El hermano Pedro* and so many others that would take too long to mention here, as well as *La sagrada familia,* which is now reaching record audience ratings" (Mejía Prieto, 280).

63. Charly Cardozo elaborates: "Soap-making companies were the first sponsors of radio dramas . . . Colgate-Palmolive in Mexico, Procter & Gamble . . . they began to draw attention on the air to their 'soap operas,' a genre born in Cuba . . . Of course, we can say that radio dramas came out of *la novela por entregas* . . . and Colgate-Palmolive had the monopoly on that structure and the formula for their production for about ten years, from the '40s to about 1957 or 1958. They even had a production director and . . . a group of female editors, very talented people, we should say, for writing" (Fonoteca Nacional, 5/25/2012, 45:00–48:00).

64. Cardozo says, "In fact, here in Mexico that was also happening. Colgate-Palmolive had its own shows, schedules, and exclusive actors, both in The W and The Q . . . We are talking now about the '40s and '50s" (6/28/2012, 43:20–43:40).

65. These were classic family melodramas such as *Anita de Montemar: Ave sin nido, El derecho de nacer* (featuring Mamá Dolores in what some called "the most human *novela* ever written"), and *Angelitos negros* (also known as a heartwarming story).

66. Cardozo says, "By the end of the '40s the two stations were very strong and started to search for more quality: new soap operas that would attract bigger audiences, and the two were now in competition" (Fonoteca Nacional, 6/28/2012, 17:00–20:00).

67. Fonoteca Nacional, 6/28/2012, 9:00–11:00.

68. Juan Pablo O'Farrill states that when he first went to work in the industry at XEW in the mid-1950s, Colgate-Palmolive and Proctor & Gamble were still the principal sponsors of *radionovela* production in México (conversation with the author, August 2016). Cardozo recalls that by the end of the 1950s, XEQ "stopped being a big station, stopped producing radio dramas, and continued on as a small radio station, a record label" (Fonoteca Nacional, 6/28/2012, 19:50–20:50).

69. Juan Pablo O'Farrill, conversation with the author, August 2016.

70. Fonoteca Nacional, 6/28/2012, 18:00.

71. Rey, quoted in Zacatecas, *Vidas en el aire*, 189. Rey also remembers being reviled by listeners on the street who recognized and confused her voice with that of her villainous characters (Granados, *XEW*, 251; Zacatecas, 185). Anecdotes abound regarding confusions caused by the Orwellian metafictional effect of radio events—sometimes calculated, sometimes not (Esquivel Puerto, *Anecdotario*, 46–47). There were 10–12 letters sent to XEW each month, full of signatures, in which *ejidatarios* (Indigenous farmers) petitioned the station to send fictional hero Rayo de Plata ("el vengador del Bajío," avenger of the heartland) to free them from their overlords, or *caciques* (Fonoteca Nacional, 6/28/2012, 1:09:00). There was also Cardozo's story of how *Chucho*'s main competitor, *Kalimán*, affected listeners' active imaginations. a Mexico City *pesera* (bus) driver was convinced that Kalimán was in the *centro histórico* (city center) while listening to a Tuesday episode. The driver and his passengers imagined that the car blocking Reforma was Kalimán's, and some passengers thought they had seen Kalimán himself (1:06:00–1:08:00, about *Kalimán*, episode 4, chapter 1, "Los misterios de Bonampak").

72. On the marketing of home sets, see Spigel, *Make Room for TV*, 27 and 29. "La programación": Granados, *XEW*, 272.

73. Granados, *XEW*, 253. On radio supplanting other forms of entertainment: "The family would gather around [the piano], daily life revolved around it. Any gathering included music and poetry. Little by little the piano is replaced; now the whole family will gather in front of the radio. It is a

classic scene: the children play, the mother knits, the father reads the newspaper, in the meantime bringing into existence those terms that today seem like anthropological technicalities: social coexistence, family life, popular traditions" (95).

74. O'Farrill, conversation with the author, August 2016.

75. Loviglio has argued that mass media technologies catalyzed affective sensorial revolutions that enabled the creation of newly inclusive national, local, and transnational communities. See *Radio's Intimate Public*, 133n2 and n4. Cardozo explains that the ratings of the early Golden Age period look deceptively low in comparison with television's later ratings, due to habits of shared listening—not every family could afford a radio set at home. At the same time he notes that, for the period, the ratings were very high (30–40 points, with very few reruns issued; Fonoteca Nacional, 6/28/2012, 18:00).

76. There are numerous anecdotes of public spaces becoming listening sites in the 1920–1930s (Gallo, *Mexican Modernity*, 125; regarding *El Mundo*'s radio broadcasts), but the tendency persisted for decades more, as we see in this colorful description from the 1940s: "With its epicenter in the room of the neighborhood doorwoman, a carnival of indomitable decibels crossed over clotheslines, laundry rooms, gazebos, curtains, chicken pens, dogs lying in the sun and flowerpots, with the preamble to an endless drama, the gnashing of teeth, the cursing of the villain: *The Unfortunate Story of Anita de Montemar, a Woman Who Cried Her Eyes Dry[La historia desventurada de Anita de Montemar, una mujer a quien se le agotaron las lágrimas]*. In the silence of the night, the instructions of Arturo de Córdova were awaited: *"Turn Off the Light and Listen" [Apague la luz y escuche]*. The grandmother, aunt, mother, father, and offspring all sat in a compact circle around an enormous RCA Victor, whose overheated bulbs ran down the minutes to the episode's end" (Barranco, "Apague," 102).

77. Fonoteca Nacional, 5/25/2012, 49:15–52:15.

78. Fonoteca Nacional, 6/28/2012. This family aura affected not only listeners but staff as well. XEW radio technicians (Juan Pablo O'Farrill and Vicente Morales) and producers (Carlos González Cardozo and Jaime Almeida Pérez) alike describe an almost magical sense of family emerging from the regularity and intensity of work rhythms dictated by *radionovela* production. The episodes were complex, live works of art that demanded teamwork (5/25/2012, 2:00) as well as immense talent and professionalism on a daily basis; there was a healthy sense of competition inspired by ratings and rival stations (6:00). O'Farrill, who participated in this world from age fourteen until retirement, speaks of "sharing the space with great actors, radio technicians . . . an infinity of exceptional persons . . . cohabiting the magical world of radio" (conversation with the author, August 2016).

79. By 1950, 56 percent of Mexicans over the age of six were minimally literate (Rubenstein "Mass Media," 639). There is some indication that later *radionovelas* may have fomented literacy in the form of numerous comic strips (*paquines*)

that arose transmedially out of a principal radio text (i.e., later examples of Chucho and Kalimán).

80. Vaughan, *Portrait*, 50.

81. Vaughan, 49. As opposed to more public forms of entertainment that involved recurring costs of admission, such as going to the theatre or the movies, radio could be seen as an investment in family life and the home.

82. Mejía Barquera, "La industria," 650. The LFRT in 1960 eliminated censorship and granted liberty of expression in radio and TV. To compensate for any loss of control, the government depended on deepening its relationship with media magnates and discourse about civic responsibility (643).

83. Mejía Barquera, 695–96. Television was close to 190 million pesos' worth of investment in 1968—up from over 130 million pesos in 1961.

84. The number of TV stations had also doubled, from 21 in 1960 to 47 in 1968 (Mejía Barquera, 695–96).

85. RPM "continued the growth it had maintained during the previous two de-cades. In those years, RPM had grown into a major business complex encom-passing companies that were connected in various ways through broadcasting" (Mejía Barquera, 699–701).

86. "This was all achieved through the complete integration of the leading group of radio broadcasters into a financial oligarchy through their close relationship with the ruling bureaucracy whose policy was one of absolute support for the interests of the radio broadcasters, during practically the entire period" (Me-jía Barquera, 702–3).

87. The Spanish edition, *Los hijos de Sánchez*, was published by Fondo de Cultura Económica. The director of the FCE, Arnaldo Orfila, lost his job a year later because of the lawsuit brought forth against Orfila and Lewis by the Sociedad Mexicana de Geografía y Estadística (Virginia Bautista, "Los hijos de Sánchez, un escándalo de medio siglo," *Excelsior*, July 8, 2011, http://www.excelsior.com.mx/node/759087).

88. US anthropologist Lewis's contention was that novelists of that period had not given "an adequate portrayal of the inner lives of the poor in the contemporary world" (*Children*, xii), with most of them "so busy probing the middle-class soul that they have lost touch with the problems of poverty" (xxiv). Lewis's work consisted of oral testimony taken separately from five family members from 1956 until 1962.

89. In Lewis's words, this was a "culture of poverty" applying "only to those at the very bottom of the socioeconomic scale," including "that large heterogeneous mass of small artisans and tradesmen usually referred to as the lumpenprole-tariat" whose members are "only partially integrated into national institutions and are marginal people even when they live in the heart of a great city" (xxv).

90. According to Lewis, the Miracle brought with it a chronic inflation that squeezed the real income of the poor; the cost of living for Mexico City's work-ing class had risen some five times over since 1939 (xviii) at the same time as

population had increased by over 13 million since 1940 to reach a high of 34 million in 1960 (xxviii).

91. Lewis, xviii. Lewis observed that "despite the increased production and apparent prosperity [since 1940], the uneven distribution of the growing national wealth has made the disparity between incomes of the rich and poor more striking than ever before" (xxviii).

92. On sense of family, see Lewis, xviii.

93. Mejía Barquera, "La industria," 637. The late 1950s saw López Mateos's first acts of repression against popular movements (Mejía Barquera, 641).

94. Ramírez Berg, *Cinema of Solitude*, 4. This relationship is defined by Charles Ramírez Berg as the *essence* of machismo—"a reciprocal ideological agreement between the individual male and the Mexican state, empowering each . . . The male receives a secure identity and the state receives his allegiance; the male gains a favored place in the patriarchal system, while the state accumulates might" (23). Amy Robinson has argued that these protests were not present in the *radionovela*, which she sees from the first episode as a romanticization of Chucho ("Chucho el Roto," 456). I argue, however, that these issues are as present in the *radionovela* (pre-dating 1968) as they are in the films, which were in fact based on the *radionovela*, which also provided that "vehicle for critical reflection about the state's abuse of power, as well as the importance of combatting it" (A. Robinson, 460, regarding the 1970s films). The radio version predates the films as well as Tlatelolco, in fact reinforcing the idea that this was an ongoing problem that culminated in 1968. Like in the films (but unlike the 1916 novel), the *radionovela* shows that "the state's use of violence against their criminal nemesis is a regular occurrence" (468).

95. Díaz Ordaz was president from 1964 to 1970, a time characterized by a highly authoritarian state and crackdown on social unrest that included imprisonment and torture, coinciding with a tide of popular social movements experienced worldwide. Lewis observed various contradictions: in spite of demographic realities that tended toward mother-centered households, he concluded that the culture of the urban poor was based in the importance of father models (*Children*, xxi) and the solidarity of a nuclear family to fall back on in the absence of effective institutions (xxvii). Lewis also noted critical attitudes toward the patriarchal, authoritarian institutions created by the dominant classes (such as the police), and a general cynicism and mistrust of government and those in high positions (xvii).

96. Fonoteca Nacional, 6/28/2012, 43:53.

97. Cardozo, 6/28/2012, 19:50–20:50; emphases transcribed based on vocal expression. RCN, producer of *Kalimán*, was a result of the Cuban Revolution's displacement of Cuban producers. A CBQ expat had fled the Revolution by way of Miami, come to Mexico, and started a small station that specialized in *radionovelas*, broadcasting twelve per day—six in the morning and six after noon, from Monday to Saturday (Cardozo, 6/28/2012, 1:03:40). *Kalimán* was a part of this initiative, first appearing as a Mexican radio drama in 1963. A war of

ratings shaped up in this period between XEW's *Chucho* and RCN's *Kalimán* (Cardozo 6/28/2012, 1:00:50), as the invented hero-orphan of mysterious origins fascinated listeners.

98. Fonoteca Nacional, 6/28/2012, 19:50–21:50; 44:45–47:00.

99. Chacón was best known for his recent hit from 1962, an autobiographical *radionovela* about a Peruvian saint popular with the poor and a known racial hybrid: *La vida de San Martín de Porres.* Starring Amparo Garrido and José Antonio Cossio, it was so successful that it was exported with acclaim to other countries, principally Peru.

100. Jesús's dying wish in the novel is that his remaining "earnings" be used toward Dolores's education, in a scene evocative of the martyred Christ's passion: "Neither Lola nor Matilde had said a word; but when they saw the haggard face of Jesús and the innumerable bandages and shrouding which covered him, they burst into deep sobs . . . Matilde also leaned over the bed and placed a kiss of love and forgiveness on the forehead of that man, whom she had loved with all her heart, perhaps the only one she had ever loved" (Editorial Quiroga, 115–16). Dolores promises her dying father that she will continue his philosophy of helping the poor ("I swear to you, my father, that I will be kind, modest; and that I will dedicate my whole life to good deeds"), while Matilde plays the role of a repentant Eve (not Mary), assuming responsibility for Jesús's banditry and promising to assist Dolores in her good works: "I am responsible for your having chosen a life that separated you from society and from good. Forgive me, Jesús. I am dedicated to ensuring the education of your daughter, of our Lolita, and I will dedicate my existence to her" (116). The novel's final scenes add a further biblical touch in the illustration of the loyalty of Jesús's followers, demonstrating the support of his band of six reformed disciples (particularly the ex-bandit Lebrija). Riffing off the US radio drama *The Greatest Story Ever Told* (1947), Chucho echoes the epic of the suffering Jesus of Nazareth. As faithful disciple Lebrija heads to his own execution, he declares: "I am going to die right now; I'm going to follow dear Jesús to the grave . . . Long live Jesús (Arriaga)!" (116). In closing with the atonement of Matilde and the future of Dolores, the novel's words resoundingly predict the future: Arriaga's name will not easily be forgotten.

101. Fonoteca Nacional, 6/28/2012, 19:50–21:50.

102. Fonoteca Nacional, 6/28/2012, 11:00–13:00; emphases transcribed based on vocal expression.

103. In this way, XEW's last hurrah was in a sense a tribute, to itself and its (family's) achievements in the dying age of radio, at the cusp of a point in which television was about to take over that family's efforts (as Radiópolis' *radionovelas'* storylines gradually morphed into Televisa's *telenovelas*).

104. Fonoteca Nacional, 6/28/2012, 2:00:15–2:01:15

105. That said, the *radionovela* would take its characters to many sites across the Republic in its extension of Chucho's adventures. As for the temporal aspect: while the historical Chucho existed in the late years of Juárez/early years of Díaz, the

setting of Chucho later came to be understood (first through the 1916 novel) as the Porfiriato leading into the Revolution.

106. Ricardo Castro Herrera (1864–1907). Calle de Aldaco and the Barrio de la Candelario, Jesús's workshop and home, versus El Puente de Alvarado and Plateros, the Frizacs' mansion and stomping grounds.

107. Fonoteca Nacional, 5/25/2012, 7:30.

108. Populist Victorian melodramas went on to add the stock characters and the Manichean opposition between good and evil that led to stereotyping of the genre.

109. Up until the 1960s, these interventions were fully live.

110. Fonoteca Nacional, 5/25/2012, 18:00–20:00; 6/28/2012, 1:17:00–1:18:00. See also the theses of Berenice Ponce Capdeville (2004 and 2018) on sound effects and *musicalizadores* in *radionovelas*.

111. The same juncture in a written text (even in a script meant for sound production or replay) will not likely produce any similar corporal (or collective) response.

112. Fonoteca Nacional, 5/25/2012, 10:30–11:45, emphases transcribed based on vocal expression.

113. 5/25/2012, 22:45–25:45. Cardozo adds that for a producer, radio allows for the idealization of characters more than any visual medium: "The image that I can offer on TV or in film is an image limited to an actress's face. If I describe her on the radio without them seeing her and if she has a very beautiful voice . . . if I describe the most marvelous woman, what happens? Each listener is going to create her in their imagination . . . without being subject to and limited by an image that we are presenting to them . . . in other words, in that sense radio has an advantage: everyone is effectively seeing and hearing the most ideal being that they could imagine, or an ideal situation for them that could not be created by anyone else" (25:50–26:15).

114. The *tabasqueño* López Ochoa (1933–2011) began his career in the capital in 1957/58 as a model in live television commercials (as there was still no recording) and enjoyed his early fame as the handsome "Sonrisa Colgate" who punctuated the live *telenovelas* that were already taking off. He began to do voicework and readings around the age of twenty-five, when Colgate-Palmolive recognized his vocal qualities as those of a potential "soap opera" actor and brought him into their permanent cast of actors by the end of the 1950s. López Ochoa made it through that transition into the last era of the XEW as a member of its star system. López Ochoa worked in various *radionovelas* before landing the role of his lifetime in *Chucho el Roto*.

115. According to Cardozo, the figure became real to López Ochoa: "His figure changes and he begins to evolve, and by the end of the radio drama, he is himself dressing up as a *charro* on television, he was starting to sing, and then it all ended: the radio show, the soap opera, but he was still performing live in different concert halls in other states—well, I don't know, for at least ten

more years—he would perform, he would sing, and people would ask him for '¡Chucho el Roto, Chucho el Roto!' and he would begin to speak like Chucho and tell Chucho stories on live shows he was doing with other people . . . And he did very well, he was a man truly attached to the character he played for many, *many* years!" (6/28/2012, 47:45–48:20). López Ochoa starred in many roles in his long career, but he is most beloved for his portrayal of the classic Chucho.

116. Consider, for example, Rita Rey's numerous anecdotes about being regarded as a villainess in real life—or, more important, Manuel López Ochoa's professional association with Chucho el Roto until the end of his life. In some sense, López Ochoa "became" Chucho.

117. Almeida speaks directly to the particular effect that vernacular narration produced in listeners: "I do like such things . . . I don't know about you . . . Maybe I wouldn't admit that in a business context or something, you know? But I think it does provoke a series of colorful bubbles in one's imagination, no? One can perceive aromas, and emotions move with the selection of music; the radio drama is an art, I mean, it is too bad for the new generations to have missed it, because it is such a pleasure to be savored, am I right?" (5/25/2012, 58:30–59:30).

118. 32:00–32:45. Cardozo speaks of the preference—even after taping/editing/sequencing technologies were available—for the live orchestration of voices with sound, through the guidance of a director (as if conducting an orchestra), as it provided an entirely different and more realistic effect: "Of the last things we accomplished . . . there was the possibility of recording in sequence, we didn't want to make them that way, because all of us who were participating . . . and mainly me as a producer, felt that the sequential format was very cold, and it didn't feel the same. The important thing was that everyone was involved, that everyone came together—the actors, the director, the person who does the sound effects, the person who adds the music—all together at the same time, making a mix occurring at all levels, a mix of everything that was occurring to them at the moment" (5/25/2012, 18:30–20:30).

119. In Joseph et al., *Fragments*, 8–9.

120. Granados continues, "I cannot specify the social function of nostalgia, but I can approach it through one of its conditioning factors: the encounter with that which is irreplaceable ["el encuentro con lo insustituible"]. Nostalgia exists because we discover something that we cannot replace or recover" (*Apague*, 88).

121. The opposite is the case in *El derecho de nacer*, in which the woman is the victim, and the man the aggressor.

122. Chucho says to his mother, "Men cry too—one of these days, your son will also cry, ma'am" (episode 9). To Matilde, he says, "I need to be by your side, by our child's side when she is born . . . I will steal money if needed . . . That is my child—I will not allow her to be taken away from me, I will not let them do that" (episode 11).

123. In this dramatic confrontation, Chucho appears unsummoned in Matilde's bedroom: "You are going to be the mother of my child. They can send me to San Juan de Ulúa [but] I come to claim what is mine, my love, my child. Our child will have rights. Give me your word that I will be our child's protector. I came to find what belongs to me. I will leave now to avoid something irreparable. This child is mine, and I will come to claim it" (episode 13).

124. Ramírez Berg has argued that these commonly held values affirm the patriarchy and its correspondent *machismo* and capitalism: in order for things to work out, it is the poor person's responsibility to stay in their humble place and accept the status quo (*Cinema of Solitude*, 25).

125. For example, he laments, "I am crying now like cowards cry . . . I am crying blood straight from my heart. Why does that have to happen to us, to the poor? What fault do we have for being born carpenters, or masons, or shoemakers? We have the same heart as a lawyer or a doctor, no? . . . Why should we be denied the right to love?" His mother remains a saintly foil, insisting to Chucho that rewards are left to God to bestow in the afterlife and gently recommending that he resign himself as she has done: "Do not despair, son, life is like that. There are social differences, there are surnames, names, titles, and poor people like us have only one name: the nobility of labor, honesty, our calloused hands . . . Do not attempt to reform the world, son. It was made like this, and poor Jesús Arriaga won't be the one to change it" (episode 14).

126. "It is just that life is unfair . . . While there are millionaires who spend their millions to hide a niece's mistake . . . there are many honest but very poor men who do not have enough money to earn the right to take care of their daughter. Why do some have so much, while others don't even get love? Why is this, mother? There must be a reason" (episode 16).

127. In all versions—the 1916 novel, the *radionovela*, and the first subsequent movie—Chucho takes his child back for himself when he finds he has no recourse. In all versions, this is justified by the storyline—i.e., it is shown as justifiable for a father to have access to his child.

128. She tells him that he had been "a quiet, peaceful boy . . . incapable of feeling resentment; you didn't hate anyone, and until recently you wished no-one ill will . . . You are my son, and mothers know more than their children realize" (episode 24).

129. These representations predate the films, to which Amy Robinson ("Chucho," 462) attributes groundbreaking socialist qualities. Robinson believes that the 1970 film particularly denounced the social order after 1968. Many of these elements were present, however, from the initial episodes of the *radionovela* dating back to 1965.

130. "To those who think that the poor have no culture, the concept of a culture of poverty may seem like a contradiction in terms . . . It has a structure, a rationale, and defense mechanisms without which the poor could hardly carry on" (Lewis, xxxvi).

131. See Lewis, *Children*, 25, 94, 110, 114, and 123 for family stories involving radio. TV, on the other hand, was rarely mentioned, and movies, with their admission fees, seem to have been reserved for special occasions or romantic dates as opposed to daily life (43, 149, 164, 236, 408). See other anecdotes in Vaughan, Llenero, and Granados (*Apague*). With regards to the ubiquity of popular media in the tenements, Lewis says that "in this day and age, even illiterate slum-dwellers pick up advanced ideas and terminology from TV, radio, and movies" (xxii).

132. Lewis, *Children*, xvi.

133. "Anger made Jesus forget the miserable conditions in which he found himself. Furiously he lifted his fists, as a threat against those belittling him. And he delivered this curse: he would go against *all* injustice because he sensed that someday he would have to be free. Suddenly, he collapsed on the floor unconscious, convulsing, seized by a fit of madness. Three jailers carried him and put him in the dungeon, dark as pitch, and left him lying on a damp filthy floor. He stayed there for who knows how long, until perhaps the cold or the anger that he felt, helped him regain consciousness."

134. "My mother, my queen, where are you? In heaven ... That is where you belong, mother dearest, there with God, with the angels. My child, Dolores, where is she? Who has her? Why, Mother? Bring her to me! Little Dolores, my dearest daughter, can you hear me? Can you hear me, my little girl? Come, come closer to me, I want you to sit on my lap. What happened to your doll, where did you leave it? Lupe? Lupe, my sister? Where is my daughter's doll? No! [*crescendoing agitation*] No! This darkness is hell, it is hell, I have been plunged deep into hell" (episode 28).

135. As it turns out, the *radionovela* anachronistically presents the prisons as full of "dissidents" and paints a picture of the times that seems more closely aligned with the twentieth century than the Porfiriato, an impression aided by modern elements such as the sounds of a typewriter in the background of the court scenes, and the use of a telephone after the torture scenes to contact interested parties (episode 36).

136. The figure of the ex-*plateado* Lebrija from the 1916 novel has since disappeared.

137. Chucho says to this family, "Let's work helping the poor, distributing whatever we have stolen among the people of the *pueblo* so that they no longer go hungry, so that children don't die of illness, and can go to school; we will seek out the elderly and we will give them something so that their old age may be more joyful ... We will do so many things, many very good things ... We will teach the rich what money can be used for, that same money now rotting in safes, calcifying and decaying in the banks" (episode 39).

138. Quoted in Mejía Barquera, "La industria," 646. José Antonio Padilla Segura, secretary of communications, offered a similar discourse in a 1969 speech, stating that the broadcasting industry "is obliged to avoid any kind of influence that would harm or disturb the harmonious development of children and youth, as well as to contribute to the *pueblo*'s cultural growth, to the preservation of

our nation's characteristics and values, our country's customs, its traditions, its proper language and the strengthening of its democratic convictions" (quoted in Mejía Barquera, 647–48).

139. Mejía Barquera, 655.

140. Mejía Barquera, 661. The government was forced to be content with 12.5 percent of each radio station's airtime, with the state reserving certain rights: "Upon issuing any subject matter that may disturb the peace or public order, cause alarm, bewilderment or alteration of the country's peaceful operations or serenity, the franchise shall come under scrutiny as a consequence" (670).

141. Mejía Barquera, 680. Until this juncture, broadcasters had become "accustomed to receiving ample allowances from the State and to solving problems directly with the State's personnel through top-level negotiations or supported in their close ties to the bureaucratic sector controlling the national Congress's operations" (681).

142. At the same time, RPM continued to grow, having signed a 1969 accord with the Sociedad Española de Radiodifusión (SER) to export *radionovelas* to Spain, Central America, and South America as well as the United States. It additionally signed an accord in the same year for a project of mutual distribution with Radio Programas de Perú (Mejía Barquera, 699–701), where the *radionovela* industry was booming. They also used the occasion to set up their own newsrooms, whereas before they had partnered with newspapers, claiming the need for independence (to avoid error): in 1969 Telesistema established its own newsroom under Miguel Alemán Velasco.

143. Quoted in Mejía Barquera, 691–92.

144. Industry spokesperson Guillermo Morales Blumenkron is quoted in Mejía Barquera, 694–95.

145. Fonoteca Nacional, 5/25/2012, 5:40.

146. 6/28/2012, 48:00–51:30. "Of course, radio dramas, especially once they were recorded, were broadcast not just once, but several times, as reruns, or sold to other Spanish-speaking countries, etc. in order to recoup investment costs, because radio dramas were made with the top actors, who charged more money than others, and went beyond the usual criteria. These were costs that other radio broadcasters didn't have because they didn't make these kinds of productions" (49:00–52:30).

147. 44:45–46:00. This was a common practice for successful *radionovelas*: *Kalimán* became a comic book and a movie, and *El derecho de nacer* was also adapted into a film.

148. First appearing in episode 1,950, the chorus goes: "I will sing to you now, kind sirs, the verses of Chucho el Roto / here in the *pueblo* he is named the generous bandit / King to all our ladies . . . never leave your sons without bread and without freedom" (*Voy a cantarles, señores, las coplas de Chucho el Roto / aquí en el pueblo nombrado, el bandido generoso / rey de todas las reinas . . . / nunca dejes a tus hijos sin pan y sin libertad*).

149. According to Cardozo, "*Telenovelas* had an enormous impact, everyone you could imagine was watching them" (6/28/2012, 41:30).

150. On the popularity of the *telenovela*, see the Blanca Sánchez obituary cited in A. Robinson, "Chucho el Roto," 455n18, as well as multiple testimonies given by radio announcers on the occasion of Manuel López Ochoa's death (preserved in a video on the YouTube channel of Hector Martinez Serrano of the 690AM program *Buenos Días*, uploaded on October 26, 2011: https://www.youtube.com/watch?v=7HWoiuecgBY&t=3s).

151. Ruffinelli, review of *Tiempo de ladrones: La historia de Chucho el Roto* (in *Latin American Theatre Review*, 1985), Mexican playwright Emilio Carballido's 1983 play. It is interesting that one of the story's latest iterations returns the Chucho legend full circle a century later to its original orality as a play (this was the initial literary iteration of Jesús Arriaga's story, the first records of which appear some three years after the historical figure's 1885 death).

152. Carballido, *Tiempo de ladrones*, 252.

CHAPTER 5

Epigraphs. Cueva (current Mexican film and radio critic), *Lágrimas*, 71. Jara, quoted in Nariman, "Televisa," 47. At the time of this statement (February 25, 1986), Jara was the director of Televisa's Institute of Communication Studies, a public opinion research organization.

1. Another indicator of "remediality" is the proliferation of versions manifesting across multiple media platforms.

2. Moser, "Introduction," 16.

3. See Moser, "Introduction," and Ndalianis, *Neo-Baroque Aesthetics*, for a discussion of the entire range of qualities associated with the neobaroque.

4. Ndalianis defines "serial logic" as the basis for contemporary culture. She does not, however, discuss soap operas—film and video games are her principal examples.

5. Ndalianis argues that serial logic is the product not of "an era steeped in sterile repetition and unoriginality," but is instead a neobaroque aesthetics of repetition concerned with the variation inherent in serialized form (*Neo-Baroque Aesthetics*, 33).

6. Emphasis on the intensity of viewer experience is considered by both Moser and Ndalianis to be a central neobaroque characteristic.

7. Cide Hamete Benengeli is a fictional Arab Muslim historian whom, in the 1605 preface, Cervantes positions as the intradiegetic author of *Don Quixote*, in a credibility-creating metafictional device that encourages readers to believe that Quixote and his story were real. Cervantes indicates that he is not the original author but is simply passing on information he found in a cliffhanger-filled manuscript from "the archives of La Mancha."

8. On intensification, see Ndalianis, *Neo-Baroque Aesthetics*, 4–5. Jim Collins states that "what audiences now conceive of as entertainment has changed so

thoroughly that 'the cultural function of popular storytelling appears to be in a process of profound redefinition'" (*Uncommon Cultures*, 16).

9.   "In few countries as in Mexico can one observe the clear historical dependence that television owes to radio" (Cueva, *Lágrimas*, 32).

10. That complicated father-son dynamic and transition are laid out by Claudia Fernández and Andrew Paxman in chapters 1–4 of *El Tigre: Emilio Azcárraga y su imperio Televisa*, first published in 2010. As Fabrizio Mejía Madrid describes it, "Connecting movie actors with radio, starting with XEW and ending now, connecting their voices with their images on television" was the elder Azcárraga's life work (*Nación TV*, 20).

11. Fernández and Paxman, *El Tigre*, 117 and 155–56.

12. With *Senda prohibida*'s fifty episodes of thirty minutes each, "the soap opera appears, a genre that would revolutionize Mexican television, putting it at the forefront of the Spanish-speaking world" (Fernández and Paxman, *El Tigre*, 99). Soap operas had appeared in Mexico before 1958, but they were a relative rarity, and weekly rather than daily productions, mostly from foreign-based businesses like Colgate or Procter and Gamble looking to sell their wares and expand their markets. Cueva believes that "the first Mexican soap opera was made in 1950 under the pompous title of *Roulletabile's Adventures*." He characterizes it as "a classic mega-drama from melodrama's most dramatic years." There was also an "original French melodrama, a sort of Robin Hood" (*Lágrimas*, 38). In 1956, Colgate-Palmolive had begun producing *La Telenovela Palmolive de la Semana*, in which each story lasted just a week.

13. Cueva reports that "Mexican soap operas would tend toward adaptations of titles previously tested on the radio, and would be broadcast with the mechanical and exaggerated tone of the tele-theaters [televised theater]. If there is one thing that characterized the Telesistema Mexicano executives, it was that they never took on a project unless they were sure of its commercial success, and with the launch of soap operas they were not going to put even the tiniest part of their investment at risk" (*Lágrimas*, 36–37).

14. Cueva, 63.

15. It was during this period that young literatos such as Sabido and Reyes, fresh out of UNAM, became censors as a means of making their living (Reyes de la Maza, *Memorias*, 93–128).

16. This was Mexico's first evening soap, leaving plenty of space for reruns (Cueva, *Lágrimas*, 99–100). To give an idea of these serial stories' rich potential for remediation, *El derecho de nacer* (initially issued from Havana in 1948) has been adapted into various formats throughout Latin America, including a 1952 Mexican film; 1960s soap operas in Puerto Rico, Perú, and Venezuela; and finally three different soap operas in Mexico (1966, 1981–1982, 2001), at a cyclical rate of every twenty years.

17. Cueva, *Lágrimas*, 67.

18. Quoted in Nariman, "Televisa," 17.

19. On Echeverría's demands, see Fernández and Paxman, *El Tigre*, chapter 4.
20. Cueva, *Lágrimas*, 127. Azcárraga Milmo had inherited control of the family businesses in 1972, upon Azcárraga Vidaurreta's death.
21. Fernández and Paxman, *El Tigre*, 229–30,
22. Cueva, *Lágrimas*, 106–7.
23. On the debate, see Fernández and Paxman, *El Tigre*, 241–42.
24. On the "important young film actor," see Cueva, *Lágrimas*, 67. Alonso's work was commercially successful: he enjoyed a long and varied career that would continue into the 1980s, by which time he had become known as "El Señor Telenovela" or "Míster Telenovela." As for Pimstein's reactions, Mejía Madrid writes that he "tolerated the existence of other soap opera producers. In particular, he attacked the didactic series of Miguel Sabido . . . and Ernesto Alonso's blockbuster historical episodes . . . Pimstein hated them" (*Nación TV*, 74).
25. Fernández and Paxman, *El Tigre*, 158. Premiering in March 1968, the series of ten episodes included popular colonial legends specific to Mexico, such as "La Llorona," "La Mulata de Córdoba," "El Caballero de la Noche," "Doña Beatriz la Sinventura," "El Callejón del Beso," and "La Calle de Don Juan Manuel."
26. Fernández and Paxman, *El Tigre*, 162–63. Alemán, a friend of Azcárraga Milmo's since their adolescence, was a son of former president Miguel Alemán Valdés (in office from 1946 to 1952) and a general television industry enthusiast who went on to become governor of Veracruz.
27. On Alemán Velasco working with Echeverria, see Fernández and Paxman, *El Tigre*, 221.
28. Fernández and Paxman report that "when his team did its poll in the Zócalo [Mexico City's central square] to survey folks' knowledge of Mexico's history, Alemán was stunned by the poor outcomes" (166).
29. Many historical *telenovelas* came directly out of this serialized trajectory of remediation: history, then *folletín*, then *radionovela*, then soap opera.
30. Fernández and Paxman, *El Tigre*, 162–64.
31. The *telenovela* is referred to by Vaughan as a source from which the Zúñiga family learned history (*Portrait*, 50 and 120).
32. As Cueva quips, "There is nothing more dangerous ideologically than presenting national history as a melodrama of the good guys versus the bad guys" (*Lágrimas*, 50).
33. Fernández and Paxman, *El Tigre*, 166–67.
34. As the longest Mexican *telenovela* at that time, *La tormenta* had some ninety-one episodes—thirty more than the average contemporary soap.
35. Fernández and Paxman, *El Tigre*, 168. Fernández and Paxman assert that "many parents sat their children down to watch that soap opera in order to improve their grades in history" (168).
36. Fernández and Paxman, 166. The same team soon went to work on *Los caudillos* (1968), about the War for Independence; the super-production *La constitución* (1970), produced by Alonso and starring María Félix; and *El carruaje*

(1972), commissioned by politicians to revisit the life and legacy of Juárez on an important national occasion. According to Cueva, these were soap operas that went "beyond ordinary budgets in their high spending on locations, costumes and cast, some taking a long time to shoot due to the sophistication of their scenes" (*Lágrimas*, 55).

37. Quoted in Fernández and Paxman, *El Tigre*, 167.
38. Fernández and Paxman, *El Tigre*, 166–67.
39. Sabido's thesis was "Three Thousand Years of Sacred Theater Representation in Mexico" (1952), to be later published as *Los coloquios del siglo XVI*. In 1961, he was named a scholar with the Centro Mexicano de Escritores.
40. Sabido was a founding member of Mexico's Teatro Pedagógico and of a civil association called El Teatro de México, which promoted plays from the baroque Golden Age as well as the popular dramas known as *pastorelas*, derived from oral traditions deeply rooted in Mexico's Indigenous cultures and the baroque spectacle of the struggle between good and evil. His work with the *pastorelas* constituted a twentieth-century baroque revival. Sabido traveled to small Mexican towns such as Tepotzotlán and Apoplán in 1962–1964, writing scripts based in the millennial traditions he had researched while at UNAM. The public was invited to take part in the spectacles—some involving as many as two hundred local actors—held in some of Mexico's most emblematic baroque churches. Sabido's productions were monumental, and intentionally foregrounded the cultural contributions of Mexico's Indigenous communities.
41. 1972 was also the premiere of Televisa's *Plaza Sésamo*.
42. Fernández and Paxman, *El Tigre*, 244.
43. Nariman, "Televisa," 20–22; Cueva, *Lágrimas*, 127.
44. Fernández and Paxman, *El Tigre*, 241.
45. Fernández and Paxman, 236.
46. Mérida, "Sabido."
47. Sabido found inspiration in the Peruvian example of *Simplemente María* (1969), written by Celia Alcántara, which inspired social change in female populations across Latin America.
48. Fernández and Paxman, *El Tigre*, 284–85.
49. Later on, Sabido would say that all of his theater pieces were written for and about Mexican women (Mérida, "Sabido").
50. Cueva, *Lágrimas*, 135. In 1979, IMEC would become the autonomous Instituto de Investigaciones de la Comunicación (IIC) de Televisa (Fernández and Paxman, *El Tigre*, 267).
51. The United Nations invited Sabido to collaborate on a similar project on the social uses of soaps, to be implemented in India under Prime Minister Indira Gandhi circa 1982.
52. These quotes are from *Revista Somos*, "El Mundo," 16.
53. Cueva, *Lágrimas*, 135–37.

54. According to Cueva, "Whenever Mexicans feel increased instability, their pre-disposition toward watching *telenovelas* increases" (*Lágrimas*, 144).

55. Fernández and Paxman, *El Tigre*, 282.

56. Nariman, "Televisa," 42.

57. Nariman, 42.

58. Cueva, *Lágrimas*, 190. Cueva also observes that with Televisa's network of ninety-five stations around the country, "the regional television stations prac-tically disappeared."

59. Riding, *Distant Neighbors*, 311–15.

60. On imports and quality, see Cueva, *Lágrimas*, 167; Nariman, "Televisa," 34.

61. During the 1980s, Sabido was responsible for such literary and intellectual programming initiatives as "Vida y voz con Arreola" and "México en la cul-tura." The commercial-free channel registered significant levels of viewership throughout the decade.

62. Protele, Televisa's exportation arm, was formed in 1987 (Cueva, *Lágrimas*, 205).

63. Cueva, 198.

64. Mejía Madrid, *Nación TV*, 74–75.

65. Fernández and Paxman, *El Tigre*, 260.

66. Cueva, *Lágrimas*, 199.

67. The successful *Rina* was actually an adaptation of a Cuban radionovela by Inés Rodena that Pimstein had recommended to Reyes for adaption and that was announced as "Teatro Seriado" in order to make it into the 9 p.m. slot (Cueva, *Lágrimas*, 163). With respect to his process of adapting many of Rodena's works to television, Reyes explains, "Seeing that they were almost identical made my blood boil and so I began to intersperse situations and characters of my own creation, leaving Doña Inés' pages behind. . ." (*Memorias*, 159–60).

68. Mejía Madrid, *Nación TV*, 74–75.

69. Cueva, *Lágrimas*, 163.

70. Cueva, 198.

71. Reyes, *Memorias*, 71. In the early 1970s, Alonso and others had also approached him about writing historical *telenovelas*. Reyes jokingly tells how he would fin-ish commissions again and again that were then rejected because producing them would be too expensive. After commissioning a soap opera on Enrique XVIII that would never be made, de Llano Palmer told Reyes: "Better to write something else . . . Something Mexican . . . I mean, grab yourself a novelist who has already died and adapt their stories." In response, Reyes happily returned to Riva Palacio: "I began to devour once more those novels by Don Chente, which are very amusing to me. During all of 1971 I did nothing other than write 276 chapters" (*Memorias*, 146).

72. In 1984, Sabido wrote a prologue to Reyes's theater chronicles entitled *En el nombre de Dios hablo de los teatros*. Over the years, Reyes had written a fourteen-volume history of "spectacles" (1810–1910) in Mexico for UNAM's

Instituto de Investigaciones Estéticas, where he served for thirty-five years as a research scholar. Reyes wrote extensively on nineteenth-century writers such as Lizardi, Prieto, Mateos, Gamboa, and Altamirano, as well as on the baroque. In 1985, renowned UNAM literature professor Clementina Díaz de Ovando lauded Reyes's achievements in that field. Upon his death in 2014, *Milenio* called him "one of the most important theater researchers of the second half of the twentieth century, in love with the nineteenth century . . . who practiced historiography with unbridled passion for the theater shows and spectacles of nineteenth-century Mexico . . . In the 14 volumes of pages he dedicates to that period one can see that reading about a country's theater demonstrates its political and historical evolution" (Chabaud Magnus, "Luis Reyes").

73. Besides his academic research, Reyes's greatest passions were Televisa and the TV medium: "I have loved television more than anything else in this world" (Reyes, *Memorias*, 134).

74. Reyes, 149. Like Sabido, Reyes's successful career in soap operas corresponded with a government position. Reyes and Sabido, like other young scholars, met as censors in the early 1960s, under the government of López Mateos. Reyes first served as director of radio and television in the RTC (1976–1980) during the López Portillo presidency, working directly under the president's sister (Margaret López Portillo) in the censorship offices—a position that came with power: "Luis decided what was authorized and what was not authorized on this country's public and private television. More than one powerful personage was afraid of him: this man did not mince words. He was very critical and that, of course, brought him any number of enemies" (Cueva, "Las telenovelas están de luto"). Having served for many years, Reyes enjoyed a conflictive and provocative relationship with government censorship, which at times he compared to the Inquisition. Reyes like Lizardi took irreverent delight in exposing hypocrisies and leveling classes: "To fancy oneself the arbiter of good and evil is the privilege of conceited jerks" (Reyes, *Memorias*, 93). Writing in 1988, Nariman reported that censorship within Televisa remained real, because the government could take away the conglomerate's privileges at any time, thus Televisa could not "provide an open forum for political debate, regardless of the potential benefits to viewers." Nariman also noted that "the government has access to 12.5 percent of Televisa broadcasting time" and that "other than citing broad areas such as religion and politics as off limits to Televisa, refrains from enacting a specific censorship code. Instead it relies on Televisa to protect its government-granted concessions by avoiding controversy" ("Televisa," 30–32).

75. This soap starred Reyes's then-wife, María Rubio, as villainess Doña Rafaela, and was successfully exported in English to the United States. *Rina* was part of Televisa's experimentation to attract both men and women to *telenovelas*, using Channel 2 in the evening exclusively for national soaps (Fernández and Paxman, *El Tigre*, 262–63; Cueva, *Lágrimas*, 163).

76. This was Lucía Méndez's first starring role in an international hit, alongside leading man Héctor Bonilla.

77. Cueva considers him "one of the most important men in the history of Mexican television," adding that "if anyone changed the way we made soap operas in this country, it was [Reyes]" ("Las telenovelas").

78. Cueva states that Reyes "fought like no one else to make soap operas that were different." Reyes's strategies included championing new writers and producers and period pieces ("Las telenovelas").

79. *Sesame Street* had started in Mexico with Televisa's creation in 1972. Rosy Ocampo was working on *Plaza Sésamo* when Moret approached her about his *Martín Garatuza* project. She had been a student in communications at La Universidad Iberoamericana when in 1981 she began with Televisa as an intern on the set of super-production *Toda una vida*, a soap opera biography (*telecrónica*) of actress María Conesa, written by Reyes. Later Televisa's vice president of content, Ocampo has stated that one of her greatest passions was cultural television for young people and families. She worked in the 1980s with Channel 8 on *El laberinto interior*, another television series about Mexico's colonial era: "Always surrounded by a multidisciplinary team of specialists and collaborators, Rosy offered a twist to the educational entertainment model of soap operas founded by Miguel Sabido" (Friederichsen, "Rosy Ocampo").

80. Cueva, *Lágrimas*, 160.

81. "Children and young people really liked them for their swashbuckling and intrigue" (actress Surya MacGrégor, conversation with the author, 2017). It was rerun on Mexico's Cablevision (Channel 27) in 1993, and again in 1994 on Channel 9.

82. Along with fiction by other *folletinistas* such as Dumas, Sue, and Hugo, these were works that Reyes mentions having read and enjoyed in his youth (*Memorias*, 29).

83. Reyes, 146–49. Reyes also amused himself by "drafting nonsense," joking that "although it may not seem like it, that is a demonically difficult professional task" (137).

84. This was a moral free-for-all that included men taking advantage of women, women taking advantage of men, women taking advantage of women, long scenes of swashbuckling between good and evil, and a completely original subplot about Princess Éboli and her son (as a contrasting family story to the Garatuzas).

85. Moser, "Introduction," 4.

86. At the end of the day, Reyes seems to have drawn heavily on the essence of *Les Pardaillan*'s hero: his many similarities to Garatuza support the themes of loyalty to family (and the importance of the father-son relationship above all), the unimportance of material possessions, the duty to help others in need, and the ability of a common man to change the nation's course.

87. Like the historical figure, the soap opera's Éboli is attractive and blind in one eye, sporting an eyepatch. In her television avatar, the eyepatch (reminiscent of villainess Catalina Creel) is gold, and Reyes gives her the name Micaela de los Arcángeles. The television Éboli had been born in New Spain and married to Ramón de Araujo of Taxco; as a widow, she now devotes herself to palace intrigue (per episode 47, 9/2/1986). The historical Princesa Éboli (née Ana de Mendoza y de Silva, 1540–1592) has more recently captivated audiences as the subject of a popular miniseries airing in Spain in 2010.

88. He leaves with these words: "Maybe I will catch up with you one day, Fernando, but for now I still have a lot to do." The hero is about to throw his sword away then sheathes it. Through the ending credits, he is seen patting his horse and riding into a notably cloudy plain (though not a sunset).

89. Even Reyes's memoirs are open-ended, gesturing the reader toward a next installment. It should be noted here that Mexican soap operas typically had closed endings and were not infinitely renewable as in countries such as the United States: in fact, when US soap operas such as the highly successful *Peyton Place* (1968) were first imported to Mexico, Mexican audiences were said to tire quickly of their excessive duration (Cueva, *Lágrimas*, 103).

90. See episode 7 (7/8/1986) in particular for comments on mores in Mexico's capital.

91. See episode 3 (7/2/1986) for examples of all these actions.

92. Blanca, for example, is punished by the Inquisition for disobeying her uncle Pedro in episode 22, 7/29/1986.

93. In episode 4 (7/3/1986), Alonso reminds Beatriz of the importance of maintaining Mexico's caste hierarchies. He accuses of her of treating Teo the slave so well that he might want his freedom. Beatriz has to defend her servants against Alonso's threats to beat them (episode 5, 7/4/1986).

94. The bad women help each other (particularly against men) but pit themselves against the good women: Luisa works with the all-powerful Inquisition to falsely accuse her rival Blanca, but La Sarmiento helps Luisa with her love potions and gives her lodging while she is on the lam (episode 34, 8/14/1986). An outlier is the old maid Cleofas, who doesn't help other women at all but consistently serves the men in power (episode 35).

95. La Sarmiento holds power over many men through her potent spells, yet she is isolated and alone. Femme fatale Luisa wants class revenge: in her childhood she was despised as an orphan, so she will now step over anyone (episodes 22 and 24, 7/29/1986 and 7/31/1986), using multiple disguises and crossdressing to manipulate several men simultaneously (episode 33, 8/13/1986), get their money, and rise in social class.

96. When the vain Luisa is tied up, drugged, and painted black by a group of laughing men, including Don Pedro, they make clear that this is not just a gag but the supreme punishment of a bad woman: "She will be mistaken for one of those slaves from Cuba or Africa, sold in public squares." As they subject the

unconscious Luisa to "Satan's paint," the men cackle about how "this won't be erased for many years . . . disfiguring a person's face, contracting their muscles . . . frizzing their hair up like black people's . . . What a horrible way to wake up: to fall asleep as a beautiful lady and wake up as a servant . . . We will paint her entire body so that there is no doubt she's a slave" (episode 31, 8/11/1986).

97. "Por Blanca, por Beatriz, por Román . . . por Antonio, perrrrro!" Martín calls his beloved partner "Antonio" even as he learns that Antonio was born Catalina.

98. Martín, for example, speaks with Fernando about his ties to the popular classes, saying the *pueblo* makes the best ally—much better than the hypocritical rich.

99. In a conversation between Antonio and Román, the family is referenced as "the famous Carbajals who were burned by the Inquisition, not kindly looked upon by today's society" (episode 52, 9/9/1986), with Ana excoriated as a "descendant of those heretics, Luis de Carbajal the Elder and Luis the Younger, burned by the Inquisition in 1590." Society's attitude toward those condemned by the Inquisition is reflected in a declaration (by the secondary character Carlos de Arellano): "No one can erase the memory of those who died in those flames, never repenting, never embracing the Christian faith" (episode 62, 9/23/1986).

100. Román makes a disparaging comment about miscegenation when told the establishment's name: "The Zambo's Tavern? The owner must have that *defect*" (episode 70, 10/3/1986; emphasis mine). *Zambo* was a racial term historically used in colonial Spanish, referring to people of mixed Indigenous and African ancestry living in New Spain.

101. In that same episode, Martín is described by elites as "the best swordsman of New Spain," "a man of thorough education who can take his place at the table beside counts and marquises with no noticeable difference," and "cunning, brave, skillful, bold, courageous . . ." Fernando states that "above all he is a loyal friend and I would not how to manage without him" (episode 3, 7/2/1986).

102. Blanca's uncle Pedro confesses that, before meeting her, he had imagined her to be dark-skinned and ugly: "I do not know why it had gotten into my head, that because you were a girl born in distant Michoacán to a native mother, that you would be *mestiza* with Indigenous features, like so many others." Blanca's indignant response is to defend the Indigenous: "If you knew the authentic Indigenous people of Michoacan, you wouldn't think like that, uncle . . . The Tarascos are a beautiful race." Her uncle also makes his prejudice known regarding Indigenous names:

> Pedro: Well, to me, all those pagan names sound equally horrible, they should just change them all and give them Christian ones.
> Blanca: Unfortunately, they are already doing that.
> Pedro: Do you have a problem with Christian names, Blanca? You should be careful about what you say. Remember that you are in the capital of New Spain, and there are Inquisition spies everywhere,

who have taken some people prisoner for less than what you just uttered. (episode 6, 7/7/1986)

103. The *telenovela* shows that the categories of "good" and "bad" reach across class: no class is homogeneous, but contains individuals, good and bad, within it. In *Martín Garatuza*, for example, the worst elements of the aristocracy (embodied by Pedro) ally with worst elements of the *pueblo* (embodied by Ahuizote) in the grand climax to try to kill the good guys.

104. Unlike in history, Viceroy Gelves is not on the side of the *pueblo* and does not care about their opinion (episode 13, 7/16/1986); the king, of course, is similarly unconcerned with whether the viceroy pleases the *pueblo* (episode 41, 8/25/1986).

105. Blanca insists on the value of the Indigenous when she is asked if the Tarascos are light-skinned like her:

> Blanca: No, I inherited it from my father, whose skin was white, and from my mother I inherited patience and religious devotion.
> Pedro: I hope that your devotion is Christian, and not the worship of earthen idols, as in some parts of New Spain . . . I have noticed some strange ideas flitting through your head, and that is very dangerous here in the capital. Isn't that true, Alonso?
> Alonso: You must not speak with such exaltation of those pagan lands.
> Blanca: Excuse me, Alonso, how can you not want me to speak well of a race to which I am honored to belong, to which my mother and her parents belonged as well?
> Pedro: You are the daughter of a Christian, as are all of us who belong to the glorious Mejía side of the family.

He takes her aside to say, "I see you don't know much about the topic of religion," suggesting that she needs to spend time in a convent "in order to learn the roots of our religion through and through" (episode 7, 7/8/1986).

106. In the words of the seductress La Sarmiento to Martín: "Your name is repeated each day and all over in this capital of New Spain. Villains envy your swordsmanship, gentlemen envy Fernando for having you as the best bodyguard in the colony, women of all social classes shudder and sigh when they see you go by, Martín Garatuza . . . You are more famous than the viceroy" (episode 4, 7/3/1986).

107. Luisa leads a group of Indigenous women (*indias*) to do her bidding (episode 30, 8/8/1986). Luisa's capture and blackening by the men takes place during the rebellion, while no authorities are watching.

108. Cueva considers Reyes "a warrior who professionalized the business of melodramas as never before." Reyes had become increasingly interested in providing special-interest soap opera to niche populations, even allowing government consultants to work with Televisa content production, pushing the boundaries of what was acceptable content for a "tightly controlled" television industry.

According to Cueva, Reyes paid the price for innovating in the late 1980s: "Generating [new work] was such hell that Luis ended up banned from Televisa." Azcárraga Milmo hired him back in the early 1990s, however ("Las telenovelas").

109. Cruz went on in 1987 to further studies at Televisa's Centro de Capacitación para Escritores, where he took a course on scriptwriting under the direction of Alejandro Galindo and joined the SOGEM literary workshop run by Silvia Tomasa Rivera. Cruz did not work again with anyone from the Téllez-Olmos-Villaseñor team after *El extraño retorno*, but he did eventually write for TV Azteca (1996–1999). He became best known, however, as an eccentric writer of goth and science fiction tales, such as the successful vampire novel *Aleister* (also about a figure transported from the past and thrust into current times); its fourth printing was released in 2019. As of 2021, Cruz could be seen on the TV show *Infernalia*, based on his work *Obra del maligno*, a collection of stories and poems centered around evil, now in its tenth printing. The author of more than twenty books, Cruz is still active in Mexico City's "occult" scene, and some now refer to him as Mexico's modern Lovecraft.

110. Villaseñor Sanabria brought considerable literary and historical knowledge to bear on *El extraño retorno de Diana Salazar* as a poet, playwright, translator, theater promoter, and producer, as well as professor and critic (Ocampo et al., *Diccionario de escritores mexicanos*, 8:268–69). A native of Mexico City, Villaseñor received her BA in Hispanic literature from the University of Guanajuato before going on to earn her MA and PhD in literature from UNAM. She received a second PhD in comparative literature from the University of Paris. Throughout the 1980s, Villaseñor taught classes to actors and writers at UNAM, as well as at El Instituto Andrés Soler of the National Association of Actors (1986–87), the Writers School of the General Society of Mexican Writers (1988), and the Workshop of Creative Acting (1992–2001). From the 1970s on, she was consistently present at the intersection of media and culture, integrating literature and theater into her work at Televisa, first as a member of the Research Department (1972–1975), and then from 1978 to 1986 as a consultant to the vice president of research, Sabido, with whom she had previously collaborated on an award-winning film adaptation of *La Celestina* (1969), a Channel 2 show entitled *Ahora Silvia,* and Channel 9's *Comunicación*. Villaseñor's prize-winning adaptations of literary and dramatic works to radio and television included works by Quevedo, Cervantes, García Lorca, Rulfo, Pacheco, Paz, and Martín Luis Guzmán.

111. Cueva, *Lágrimas*, 205.

112. "Tellez and Olmos co-wrote some scenes, and, according to cast interviews, shared such an acidic black humor that together they would laugh aloud at their scenes of death and drama" (*Revista Somos*, "El Mundo," 20).

113. Olmos began acting in the 1960s, including in a production of José Triana's *Noche de los asesinos* while reporting to Chiapas on the 1968 student movement. In 1969 he moved to Mexico City to train at the Escuela de Arte Teatral

(Instituto Nacional de Bellas Artes y Literatura), then received a scholarship to the Centro Mexicano de Escritores, where he studied writing under Hugo Argüelles. Olmos was the author of numerous plays and winner of numerous awards (including the Premio Juan Ruiz, awarded by the Mexican Theater Critics Association, and the Sor Juana Prize by the Critics and Writers Union, as well as a lifetime creator's grant from the Mexican government).

114. Ocampo, *Diccionario de escritores mexicanos*, 6:128–29, For Sabido's didactic works, Olmos won the Premio Teleguía, the Premio del Consejo Latinoamericano de Población (UNESCO), and other prizes.

115. "[Téllez] is one of the few creatives who combined production with stage direction" (*Revista Somos*, "El Mundo," 25).

116. Actors cast in Téllez-Olmos projects were proud of being selected, and considered their works to be at a different level. *Cuna* and *Extraño* star Alejandro Camacho said: "Above all the fact that those productions worked well and gave status to the businesses that broadcast them and to us as actors, well, that is important . . . We came from the universities, I come from the Faculty of Philosophy and Letters at UNAM [National Autonomous University of Mexico], I was a scholarship holder in the United States and I did not get ahead just because I was on TV, I have a theater career, putting together a cast like that does not just happen" (ocho8, "Cuna de lobos").

117. Cueva, *Lágrimas*, 166–67.

118. *Cuna de lobos* "was not a love story but rather a drama of hatred and revenge in which a poor girl struggled to get her son back in a world of perverted millionaires" (Cueva, 203).

119. Cueva reports, "So exciting was the ending that the next day it was broadcast again and there were large signs proliferating in the streets that read 'Vote Catalina Creel for President.' The frenzy over its ending intensified in the Chihuahua area, because 'Creel' was the last name of some local newspaper owners and the day after the last episode they published a message offering condolences for the death of their 'aunt' Catalina" (Cueva, *Lágrimas*, 202).

120. Surpassing *Los ricos también lloran* (parodied in the 2014 film *La dictadura perfecta*), *Cuna* was the most prize-winning soap opera of that time (winning prizes for Best Soap Opera of 1987 and the Premio *TVyNovelas*), and was subsequently exported to 158 countries.

121. Fernández and Paxman, *El Tigre*, 367 and 372.

122. Riding, *Distant Neighbors*, 219.

123. Fernández and Paxman, *El Tigre*, 372.

124. Fernández and Paxman, 374.

125. "It took months to shoot . . . before going on air" (Cueva, *Lágrimas*, 204). Lucía Méndez's unexpected pregnancy also caused filming delays.

126. Cueva, *Lágrimas*, 195.

127. In this vein, *El extraño retorno* took up tendencies initiated by Ernesto Alonso's *El maleficio* (1983) and its sequel, *El maleficio 2* (1985–1986), which was also very successful. Some viewers thought *El extraño* was a continuation of that series, given the fact that both protagonists had amber eyes.

128. To prepare viewers, a voiceover announced "the surprise ending not to be missed . . . It goes beyond the supernatural, beyond the unbelievable, it rocks your senses" at the close of episode 194 (1/10/1989). Episode 195 ended with "What lies beyond death? . . . Get ready tomorrow for an outcome that will take you to another world!" at the close of episode 195 (1/12/1989).

129. *El extraño retorno*'s scope for transmedial success is evidenced in parodies and pastiches: in 2009 Lucía Mendéz appeared with her trademark amber eyes in several comedic sketches (such as "El extraño retoño de Diana Salazar" and "Diana Salazar contra Tunco Maclovich") in Televisa's *Desmadruga2*.

130. Gudinni laments that, after Téllez passed away, "other producers continued re-hashing their stories of Cinderellas who find a wealthy prince. The modernity of Carlos Téllez never returned" (*El castillo*, 423).

131. *El castillo*, 423.

132. Díaz y Ovando, *Vicente Riva Palacio*, 34–36.

133. Among the Inquisition documents in the Bancroft Library of the University of California, Berkeley, we find the trial of Leonor de Carvajal, sister of the more famous Luis de Carvajal. The songs and poems recorded in her trial, such as an iteration of the Mosaic Law in verse and other examples of the crypto-Jewish oral tradition, were used as damning evidence against Leonor and her family.

134. We see this in the soap's frequent references to contemporary unemployment (1988). From the first episode (4/8/1988), there is an emphasis on Diana's inability to find a decent job, particularly one that does not sexualize her: in episode 3 (4/12/1988) she mentions being offered "a job that included taking her clothes off to show her qualifications," which she turned down.

135. Many superstitions arose during the filming of *El extraño retorno*, as a result of eerie events such as the set inexplicably catching fire, or the female protagonists hearing curses they had aimed at each other during earlier fights.

136. The on-location filming of the seventeenth-century bonfire scene in Zacatecas's central square required some seven hundred extras. The use of amber eyes to represent an altered state, made popular by Robert De Niro in the movie *Angel Heart* (1987), was the responsibility of a young Guillermo del Toro, in charge of the movie's special effects.

137. *Cuna de lobos* was the first soap opera to receive an award from the Instituto Nacional de Bellas Artes Mexicano for musical composition: "Plascencia Salinas knew how to set the avant-garde tone and there his best work lives on" (Gudinni 423).

138. Fernández and Paxman, *El Tigre*, 261. Juan Gabriel wrote an original song for the show, "Un alma en pena," which Azcárraga switched out because of its reference to "god-forsaken priests" (*sacerdotes infames*), an overt criticism of the Church. It became one of Mexico's greatest hits of the 1980s. Azcárraga changed it for "A Little Death" ("Morir un poco"), a tune also sung by La Méndez, which became nearly as popular.

139. Cueva, *Lágrimas*, 173.

140. Ndalianis, *Neo-Baroque Aesthetics*, 1–30.

CONTINUARÁ

Epigraph. Rincón (Colombian media professor), "Nuevas narrativas televisivas," 147.

1. Romano, "Who Killed Literary Reading," B13.

2. Romano, B13.

3. This has not resulted in the "erosion in cultural and civic participation" that Romano also predicted.

4. What exactly is the contemporary difference between a series and a *telenovela*? Is it the quotient of melodrama? Between both, we see a fusion, or hybridization, permitting each to adopt some qualities of the soap opera, and vice versa, with melodrama again functioning as a unifying common denominator, and family melodramas still present.

5. Onishi, "Thumbs Race."

6. See anecdotes from the 1980s in the sociological study by Covarrubias et al. on Mexican television soaps and the family.

7. This observation was made by Mexican-Polish actress Ludwika Paleta (b. 1978), of the *telenovela* homage *Los hijos también lloran* (2018–2020), in EnPOPados, "*Los hijos*."

8. Instituto Federal de Telecomunicaciones, *Encuesta Nacional de Consumo* (2016), 14. Since the writing of this epilogue, new statistics have become available ("Encuesta Nacional de Consumo de Contenidos Audiovisuales. Reporte especial 2020-2021" and "Segunda encuesta 2021 de Usuarios de Servicios de Telecomunicaciones"). These statistics, however, reveal aberrations caused by the 2020-2022 Covid pandemic such as increased religious viewing (for self-help); news viewing (up from 49 to 64 percent for crisis information); and educational viewing (up to third place after news and movies; for home schooling). In-person schooling was suspended during 2020 and 2021 and during that time basic education classes were transmitted through free-to-air television services. Thus, new IFT statistics from 2020-2021 do not reflect normal trends and cannot be used in this book's argument. Stay tuned to the progression in future reports from the Instituto Federal de Telecomunicaciones.

9. Televisa is now seen in its home country as a poor copy of its former self. TV Azteca appeared in the 1990s as challenger to the stale conservatism of Televisa, and particularly so after the death of Azcárraga Milmo in 1997; Argos took advantage of that opening to become Mexico's most innovative independent TV producer. In heritage "new *telenovelas*," miniseries, sequel series, and TV dramas, TV Azteca and Argos incorporated advances in genre, more controversial social topics, and renewed aesthetics. In 1997–1998, TV Azteca and Argos worked together to produce the acclaimed *Mirada de mujer*, attracting viewers who were tired of Televisa's worn offerings, and pioneering the transformation of the Mexican *telenovela*.

10. Rachel Oaks (Ana Corona, translator), "Netflix: Lo que el mundo está viendo" (blog entry), HighSpeedInternet.com, June 20, 2017, https://www.highspeedinternet.com/resources/netflix-lo-que-el-mundo-esta-viendo. Netflix doesn't offer

viewing statistics. Oaks's independent study provided a list of the most-searched-for Netflix series by country, across the world.

11. The anti-*telenovela* sentiments surfaced strongly circa 2015 when Televisa first streamed its *telenovelas* with Netflix, with hundreds of reactions voiced via memes along the lines of *no big loss, who cares, good riddance, who wants to perpetuate that aspect of our culture anyway?* (see Llamas-Rodríguez, "Blim and Chill"). By 2016 Televisa had created their own platform, Blim, to take their online products back, which seems to have been increasing in importance since that time.

12. For one of the first studies in this direction, see Smith, *Multiplatform Media.*

13. The teleseries was picked up by Netflix in 2019 (Cooper, "Paco Taibo's Republic").

14. "Montaje rompe. . .": event listing on the México es Cultura website, May 30, 2018, https://www.mexicoescultura.com/actividad/190746/los-hijos-tambien-lloran.html. In Mijares, "*Los hijos,*" when asked about the shows that "educated" his generation, playwright Andrés Zuno admits that he was "a child of soap operas and cartoons" (*un niño telenovelero y de caricaturas*) and names a half-dozen titles that influenced him, including *Cuna de lobos* and *El extraño retorno de Diana Salazar.*

15. EnPOPados, "*Los hijos.*"

16. *Los ricos también lloran* was also parodied in the 2014 film *La dictadura perfecta.*

17. Mijares, "*Los hijos.*"

18. Zárate, "*Los hijos.*"

19. "Las redes sociales. See also Bravo Torres Coto, "La sociedad inalámbrica."

20. "Las redes sociales," 11.

21. "Las redes sociales," 8, 10–11. The figure of 172 million blogs comes from 2014; for comparison, the number was 34 million in 2006.

22. See Erick Yañez Navarro, "Podcasting in Mexico: Quality or Quantity?" *Medium,* June 8, 2019, https://medium.com/@AdondeMedia/podcasting-in-mexico-quality-or-quantity-90d95cecb954. See also Fernando Hernández Becerra, "Why the Podcast Boom Has Yet to Hit Mexico—and Why It needs to," *Current,* March 7, 2017, https://current.org/2017/03/why-the-podcast-boom-has-yet-to-hit-mexico-and-why-it-needs-to.

23. Sughey Baños, "A sus 83 años, Miguel Sabido aprende a manejar el streaming para compartir sus pastorelas," *El Universal,* December 24, 2020, https://www.eluniversal.com.mx/espectaculos/miguel-sabido-aprende-manejar-el-streaming-para-compartir-sus-pastorelas.

Bibliography

ARTICLES, BOOKS, AND THESES

Acevedo Valdés, Esther. *Constantino Escalante: Una mirada irónica*. Mexico City: Consejo Nacional para la Cultura y las Artes, 1996.

———. *Una historia en quinientas caricaturas: Constantino Escalante y "La Orquesta."* Mexico City: Instituto Nacional de Antropología e Historia, 1994.

Agrasánchez, Rogelio. *Mexican Movies in the United States: A History of the Films, Theaters and Audiences, 1920–1960*. Jefferson, NC: McFarland, 2006.

Albarrán, Elena Jackson. "Children of the Revolution: Constructing the Mexican Citizen, 1920–1940." PhD diss., University of Arizona, 2008.

Alfaro Cuevas, Martha Eugenia. "Revisión histórica del semanario *El Mundo Ilustrado* (1894–1914) en sus diez etapas a partir del análisis de sus carátulas y portadas." *Diseño y Sociedad*, Fall 2013–Spring 2014, 35–36.

Alfie, David, et al. *El cómic es algo serio*. Mexico City: Eufesa, 1982.

Algaba Martínez, Leticia. *Las licencias del novelista y las máscaras del crítico*. Mexico City: Universidad Autonoma Metropolitana-Azcapotzalco, 1997.

Allen, Rob, and Thijs van den Berg, eds. *Serialization in Popular Culture*. London: Routledge, 2014.

Altamirano, Ignacio. "Dos palabras" (prólogo). In *Calvario y tabor*, by Vicente Riva Palacio, 5–6. Mexico City: Manuel C. de Villegas, 1868.

———. *Revistas Literarias de México*. Mexico City: T. F. Neve, 1868–1869.

Anderson, Benedict. *Imagined Communities*. Rev. ed. New York: Verso, 2006.

Anderson-Imbert, Enrique. "El telar de una novela histórica: 'Enriquillo,' de Galván." *Revista Iberoamericana* 15, no. 30 (1950): 213–29.

Aurrecoechea, Juan Manuel. *El episodio perdido: Historia del cine mexicano de animación*. Mexico City: Cineteca Nacional, 2004.

Aurrecoechea, Juan Manuel, and Armando Bartra. *Puros cuentos: La historia de la historieta en México, 1874–1934*. Mexico City: Consejo Nacional para la Cultura y las Artes, 1988.

Azuela, Mariano. *Cien años de novela mexicana*. Mexico City: Botas, 1947.

Barragán, José. *Juan A. Mateos: Periodista liberal*. Mexico City: Dept. del Distrito Federal, 1983.

Barranco, Alberto. "Apague la luz y escuche." *Revista Contenido*, June 30, 2016.

Bedoya Sánchez, Gustavo Adolfo. "Ignacio Manuel Altamirano (1834–1893): Mediador cultural de la vida literaria (México: 1867–1889)." *Anales de Literatura Hispanoamericano* 45 (2016): 301–23.

Beezley, William H. *Mexican National Identity: Memory, Innuendo, and Popular Culture*. Tucson: University of Arizona Press, 2008.

Beezley, William H., and Michael C. Meyer. *The Oxford History of Mexico*. New York: Oxford University Press, 2000.

Benjamin, Walter. *Illuminations*. Translated by Harry Zohn. New York: Schocken, 1969.

———. "Theses on the Philosophy of History" (1940). In *German 20th Century Philosophy: The Frankfurt School*, edited by Wolfgang Schirmacher, 71–80. New York: Continuum, 2000.

Borrás, Leopoldo. *Historia de periodismo mexicano del ocaso porfirista al derecho de la información*. Mexico City: UNAM, 1983.

Brandenburg, Frank Ralph. *The Making of Modern Mexico*. Englewood Cliffs, NJ: Prentice Hall, 1964.

Bravo Torres Coto, Jorge Enrique. "La sociedad inalámbrica: La telefonía móvil desde las industriales culturales." Doctoral thesis, UNAM, 2015.

Bravo Ugarte, José. *Periodistas y periódicos mexicanos*. Mexico City: Editorial Jus, 1966.

Bustillo Oro, Juan. *Vida cinematográfica*. Mexico City: Cineteca Nacional, 1984.

Carballido, Emilio. *Tiempo de ladrones: La historia de Chucho el Roto*. Mexico City: Editorial Grijalbo, 1983

Carbó, Anna Ribera. *La Casa del Obrero Mundial: Anarcosindicalismo y revolución en México*. Mexico City: Instituto Nacional de Antropología e Historia, 2010.

Carey, Elaine. *Plaza of Sacrifices: Gender Power and Terror in 1968 Mexico*. Albuquerque: University of New Mexico Press, 2005.

Carrasco Puente, Rafael. *La caricatura en México*. Mexico City: Imprenta Universitaria, 1953.

Carreño King, Tania. *El charro: La construcción de un estereotipo nacional (1920–1940)*. Mexico City: Federación Mexicana de Charrería, 2000.

Castillo, Debra Ann, and Edmundo Paz-Soldán, eds. *Latin America Literature and the Mass Media*. London: Garland/Routledge, 2000.

Castro, J. Justin. *Apostle of Progress: Modesto C. Rolland, Global Progressivism, and the Engineering of Revolutionary Mexico*. Lincoln: University of Nebraska Press, 2019.

———. *Radio in Revolution: Wireless Technology and State Power in Mexico, 1897–1938*. Lincoln: University of Nebraska Press, 2016.

Castro Martínez, Pedro Fernando. *Adolfo de la Huerta: La integridad como arma de la Revolución*. Mexico City: Siglo XXI Editores, 1998.

Chabaud Magnus, Jaime. "Luis Reyes de la Maza (1932–2014)." *Milenio*, October 3, 2014, https://www.milenio.com/cultura/luis-reyes-de-la-maza-1932-2014.

Charrería: Origen e historia de una tradición popular. Mexico City: Federación Mexicana de Charrería, 2010.

Chasteen, John. *Americanos: Latin America's Struggle for Independence*. Oxford: Oxford University Press, 2008.

Chucho el Roto, o La nobleza de un bandido mexicano. San Antonio: Editorial Quiroga, 1916.

Chucho el Roto. Novela de aventuras. 10 episodes. Mexico City: Editorial Tolteca, 1935.

Cinematográfica Mexicana. *Chucho el Roto: El bandido generoso; Una vida de nobles hazaña*s. Movie tie-in edition. Mexico City: Estudios Neolito, 1934.

Collins, Jim. *Uncommon Cultures: Popular Culture and Post-Modernism*. New York: Routledge, 1989.

Cooper, Marc. "Paco Taibo's Republic of Readers." *Nation*, April 15, 2019, https://www.thenation.com/article/archive/paco-taibo-mexico-culture-books/.

Coronado, Eligio Moisés. "Modesto C. Rolland Mejía." *Personajes célebres sudcalifornios*, June 12, 2020, http://www.sudcalifornios.com/item/personajes-celebres-sudcalifornios-modesto-c-rolland-mejia

Cosío Villegas, Daniel. *Historia moderna de México: La república restaurada; Vida política*. Mexico City: Hermes, 1973.

Covarrubias, Karla Yolanda, M. Angélica Bautista, and Bertha A. Uribe. *Cuéntame en qué se quedó: La telenovela como fenómeno social*. Mexico City: Editorial Trillas, 1992.

Cox, Jim. *The Great Radio Soap Operas*. Jefferson, NC: McFarland, 2008.

Cueva, Álvaro. *Lágrimas de cocodrilo*. Mexico City: Tres Lunas, 1998.

———. "Las telenovelas están de luto." *Milenio*, September 30, 2014, https://www.milenio.com/opinion/alvaro-cueva/el-pozo-de-los-deseos-reprimidos/las-telenovelas-estan-de-luto.

Dalevuelta, Jacobo. *El charro-símbolo*. Mexico City: Edicion Particular, 1932.

Dávila, Mariano [Alguien, pseud.]. *Breves observaciones sobre la moderna novela titulada "Monja y casada, vírgen y mártir: Historia de los tiempos de la Inquisición": Aceptación de un tremebundo reto*. Mexico City: Imprenta Literaria, 1869.

Díaz y Ovando, Clementina. *Vicente Riva Palacio y la identidad nacional*. Mexico City: UNAM, 1985.

Dolores, o La hermana de la caridad: Continuación de Chucho el Roto. San Antonio: Editorial Quiroga, n.d.

Eiji, Otsuka, and Marc Steinberg. "World and Variation: The Reproduction and Consumption of Narrative." *Mechademia* 5 (2010): 99–116.

Eiss, Paul K. *In the Name of El Pueblo: Place, Community, and the Politics of History in Yucatán*. Durham, NC: Duke University Press, 2010.

El Colegio de México. *Historia de la alfabetización y de la educación de adultos en México.* Mexico City: El Colegio de México, 1994.

El Mosaico Mexicano: ó Colección de Amenidades Curiosas e Instructivas. Mexico City: Isidro Rafael Gondra; Ignacio Cumplido, 1836–1842.

Escalante Gonzalbo, Pablo. *Nueva historia mínima de México.* Mexico City: El Colegio de México, 2005.

Esquivel Obregón, Toribio. *Recordatorios públicos y privados: León, 1864–1908.* Edited by Guillermo Zermeño Padilla. Mexico City: Universidad Iberoamericana, 1992.

Esquivel Puerto, Emilio. *Anecdotario de radio y televisión.* Mexico City: Publicidad Latina, 1970.

Estill, Adriana. "The Mexican *Telenovela* and Its Foundational Fictions." In Castillo and Paz-Soldán, 169–89.

Fernández, Claudia, and Andrew Paxman. *El Tigre: Emilio Azcárraga y su imperio Televisa.* Mexico City: Grijalbo, 2013.

Fernández L'Hoeste, Héctor, and Juan Poblete, eds. *Redrawing the Nation: National Identity in Latin/o American Comics.* London: Palgrave Macmillan, 2009.

Florescano, Enrique. *Historia de las historias de la nación mexicana.* Mexico City: Taurus, 2002.

———. "México a través de los siglos: Un nuevo modelo para relatar el pasado." *La Jornada,* March 9, 2001, http://www.jornada.com.mx/2001/03/09/suple. html.

Flores Magón, Ricardo." 'Exposición de Motivos' del Programa del Partido Liberal." *Regeneración,* 1906.

Friederichsen, Brenda. "Rosy Ocampo: Innovar en television." *Lideres Mexicanos,* December 21, 2017, https://lideresmexicanos.com/entrevistas/rosy-ocampo-innovar-en-television.

Fuller, Andrew C. S. "Jakarta Flânerie: Seno Gumira Ajidarma's Writing of Urban Indonesia." Doctoral thesis, University of Tasmania, 2010.

Gallo, Rubén. *Mexican Modernity: The Avant-Garde and the Technological Revolution.* Cambridge, MA: MIT Press, 2005.

García Cubas, Antonio. *Diccionario geográfico, histórico y biográfico de los Estados Unidos Mexicanos.* Vol. 2. Mexico City: Oficina Tipográfica de la Secretaría de Fomento, 1888.

García Riera, Emilio. *Historia documental del cine mexicano.* Guadalajara: Universidad de Guadalajara, 1992.

Gillingham, Paul, and Benjamin T. Smith, eds. *Dictablanda: Politics, Work and Culture in Mexico, 1938–1968.* Durham, NC: Duke University Press, 2014.

Giron, Nicole. "Ignacio Manuel Altamirano y Vicente Riva Palacio: Una amistad con fondo de parentesco tixtleco." *Secuencia* 35 (1996): 7–22.

———. "Reseña de México en el *Diccionario universal de historia y de geografía.*" Secuencia 63 (2005): 231–37.

González, Aníbal. "Journalism and (Dis)Simulation in *El Periquillo Sarniento*." In *Journalism and the Development of Spanish American Narrative*, 21–41. Cambridge: Cambridge University Press, 1993.

González de Bustamante, Celeste. *Muy Buenas Noches: Mexico, Television, and the Cold War*. Lincoln: University of Nebraska Press, 2012.

Granados Chaparro, Pável. *Apague la luz . . . y escuche*. Mexico City: Biblioteca del ISSSTE, 1999.

―――. *XEW: 70 años en el aire*. Mexico City: Clío Editorial, 2000.

Granados, Pedro. *Carpas de México: Leyendas, anécdotas e historia del teatro popular*. Mexico City: Editorial Universo, 1984.

Grishakova, Marina, and Marie-Laure Ryan, eds. *Intermediality and Storytelling*. Berlin: De Gruyter, 2010.

Gudinni, Alfredo. *El castillo de las estrellas*. Mexico City: Grijalbo Mondadori, 2001.

Guerra, François-Xavier. *México del Antiguo Regimen a la Revolución*. 2 vols. Mexico City: Fondo de Cultura Económica, 1988.

Guerrero Viguri, Raquel. "La telenovela a la webnovela: La fase experimental; El nacimiento del formato en los casos de 'Historias de culpa' (2000) y 'Vidas cruzadas' (2009)." Master's thesis, Universidad Veracruzana, 2013.

Guzmán, Martín Luís. *Memoirs of Pancho Villa*. Translated by Virginia H. Taylor. Austin: University of Texas Press, 1966.

―――. *Memorias de Pancho Villa I: El hombre y sus armas*. Mexico: Ediciones Bota, 1938.

Hadatty Mora, Yanna. *Prensa y literatura para la Revolución: La novela semanal de "El Universal Ilustrado."* Mexico City: UNAM, 2016.

Hayes, Joy Elizabeth. "Radio Broadcasting and Nation-Building in Mexico and the United States, 1925–1945." Doctoral thesis, University of California, 1994.

Hilmes, Michele. *Only Connect: A Cultural History of Broadcasting in the United States*. Boston: Cengage Learning, 2014.

Illades, Carlos. "La representación del pueblo en el segundo romanticismo mexicano." *Signos Históricos* 10 (July–December 2003): 16–36.

Instituto Federal de Telecomunicaciones. *Encuesta nacional de consumo de contenidos audiovisuales 2016*. Mexico City: Instituto Federal de Telecomunicaciones, 2016. http://www.ift.org.mx/sites/default/files/contenidogeneral/comunicacion-y-medios/encca2016vf-compressed_1.pdf.

―――. *Encuesta nacional de consumo de contenidos audiovisuales, Reporte especial 2020-2021*. Mexico City: Instituto Federal de Telecomunicaciones, 2021. https://somosaudiencias.ift.org.mx/archivos/01Reporte_final_ENCCA2020-2021vp2_.pdf.

―――. *Segunda encuesta 2021 de Usuarios de Servicios de Telecomunicaciones*. Mexico City: Instituto Federal de Telecomunicaciones, 2021. http://www.ift.org.mx/sites/default/files/contenidogeneral/usuarios-y-audiencias/segundaencuesta2021acc.pdf.

Jenkins, Henry. "Transmedia Storytelling." *MIT Technology Review*, January 15, 2003.

Jiménez, Armando. *Picardía mexicana*. Mexico City: Editorial B. Costa-Amic, 1958.

Jiménez Rueda, Julio. *Vidas reales que parecen imaginarias*. Mexico City: Nueva Cultura, 1947.

Joseph, Gilbert, Anne Rubenstein, and Eric Zolov, eds. *Fragments of a Golden Age: The Politics of Culture in Mexico since 1940*. Durham, NC: Duke University Press, 2001.

Kelleter, Frank, ed. *The Media of Serial Narrative*. Columbus: The Ohio State University Press, 2017.

Lahr-Vivaz, Elena. *Mexican Melodrama: Film and Nation from the Golden Age to the New Wave*. Tucson: University of Arizona Press, 2016.

Landy, Marcia, ed. *Imitations of Life: A Reader on Film and Television Melodrama*. Detroit: Wayne State University Press, 1995.

"Las redes sociales: Vértigo y pasión." Special issue, *Proceso* 53 (2016).

Leal, Luis. "El contenido literario de *La Orquesta*." *Historia Mexicana* 7, no. 3 (January–March 1958): 329–67.

Lear, John. *Picturing the Proletariat: Artists and Labor in Revolutionary Mexico, 1908–1940*. Austin: University of Texas Press, 2017.

Lewis, Oscar. *The Children of Sánchez: Autobiography of a Mexican Family*. New York: Vintage, 1963.

Lizardi, José Joaquín Fernández de. *El Periquillo Sarniento*. Edited by Carmen Ruiz Barrionuevo. Madrid: Cátedra, 2008.

———. *Obras*. Edited by María Rosa Palazón and Jacobo Chencinsky. 14 vols. Mexico City: UNAM, 1963–1997.

Llamas-Rodríguez, Juan. "'Blim and Chill': *Telenovelas* and Class Ideologies in the Online Streaming Wars." *Flow*, November 28, 2016, https://www.flowjournal.org/2016/11/blim-and-chill-telenovelas-and-class-ideologies-in-the-online-streaming-wars-juan-llamas-rodriguez-university-of-california-santa-barbara.

Llenero, Vicente. "El derecho de llorar." In Monsiváis, *A ustedes les consta*, 271–79.

López, Ana. "Our Welcomed Guests: *Telenovelas* in Latin America," *To Be Continued . . . Soap Operas around the World*, Robert Allen, ed. (London/New York: Routledge, 1995), 256–75.

———. "The Melodrama in Latin America: *Telenovelas*, Film, and the Currency of Popular Form," *Wide Angle*, 7, no. 3 (1985), 4–13.

Losada Tomé, José. *La historieta mexicana*. Artes de México 158. Mexico City: Artes de México, 1960.

Loviglio, Jason. *Radio's Intimate Public: Network Broadcasting and Mass-Mediated Democracy*. Minneapolis: University of Minnesota Press, 2005.

Macías, Marco A. "Imagining Villa: An Examination of Francisco 'Pancho' Villa through Popular Culture and Collective Memory, 1910–2015." Doctoral thesis, University of Arizona, 2018.

Manguel, Alberto. *A History of Reading*. New York: Viking, 1996.

María y Campos, Armando de. *El teatro de género chico en la Revolución Mexicana*. Mexico City: Cien de México, 1956.

Martí-López, Elisa. *Borrowed Words: Translation, Imitation, and the Making of the Nineteenth-Century Novel in Spain*. Lewisburg, PA: Bucknell University Press, 2002.

Martín Barbero, Jesús. *De los medios a las mediaciones*. Barcelona: Gustavo Gili, 1987.

Martínez, Rafael. "*Rip Rip*: La Libertad de Imprenta". In *50 Discursos Doctrinales en el Congreso Constituyente de la Revolución Mexicana, 1916–1917*, edited by Raúl Noriega et al., 151–56. Mexico City: Instituto Nacional de Estudios Históricos de la Revolución Mexicana, 1967.

Matute, Álvaro. *México en el siglo XIX: Antología de fuentes e interpretaciones históricas*. Mexico City: UNAM, 1993.

McAllister, Matthew P., Edward H. Sewell, and Ian Gordon. *Comics and Ideology*. New York: Peter Lang, 2001.

Mejía Barquera, Fernando. "La industria de la radio y la televisión y la política del estado mexicano (orígenes y desarrollo)." Vol. 2. Doctoral thesis, UNAM, 1981.

Mejía Madrid, Fabrizio. *Nación TV: La Novela de Televisa*. Mexico City: Grijalbo, 2013.

Mejía Prieto, Jorge. *Historia de la radio y la T.V. en México*. Mexico City: O. Colmenares, 1972.

Méndez Lara, Francisco Iván. "Venustiano Carranza y la prensa: Un panorama periodístico, 1913–1919." *Caleidoscopio* 35/36 (2016–2017): 103–43.

Mérida, Janet. "Sabido va por más novelas históricas." *El Universal*, December 6, 2017, https://www.eluniversal.com.mx/espectaculos/television/sabido-desea-hacer-mas-novelas-historicas.

Merino, Ana. *El cómic hispánico*. Madrid: Càtedra, 2003.

Merlín, Socorro. *Vida y milagros de las carpas: La carpa en México, 1930–1950*. Mexico City: Instituto Nacional de Bellas Artes, 1995.

Mijares, Mariana. "*Los hijos también lloran*, un experimento valiente y autobiográfico." Cartelera de Teatro blog, February 7, 2018, https://carteleradeteatro.mx/2018/los-hijos-tambien-lloran-experimento-valiente-autobiografico.

Monsiváis, Carlos, ed. *A ustedes les consta: Antología de la crónica en México*. Mexico City: Ediciones Era, 1980.

———. "Gabriel Vargas." *La Jornada*, November 23, 2007, https://www.jornada.com.mx/2007/11/23/index.php?section=politica&article=024a1pol.

———. "Identidad nacional: Lo sagrado y lo profano." *Memoria Mexicana* (UAM-Xochimilco) 3 (1994): 37–43.

———. *Las herencias ocultas*. Mexico City: Debate, 2007.

———. "Vicente Riva Palacio: La evocación liberal contra la nostalgia reaccionaria." Prologue to *Monja y casada, vírgen y mártir*, by Vicente Riva Palacio, iii–xviii. Mexico City: Océano, 1986.

Moore, Ernest R. "Una bibliografía descriptiva: *El Periquillo Sarniento* de José Joaquín Fernández de Lizardi." *Revista Iberoamericana* 10 (1946): 383–403.

———. "Un manuscrito inédito de Fernández de Lizardi." *Ábside* 3, no. 12 (1939): 3–30.

Mora, Sonia Marta. *De la sujeción colonial a la patria criolla: "El Periquillo Sarniento" y los orígenes de la novela en Hispanoamérica.* Heredia, Costa Rica: EUNA, 1995.

Morales, Miguel Angel. *Cómicos de México.* Mexico City: Panorama Editorial, 1987.

Moreno, Julio. *Yankee, Don't Go Home! Mexican Nationalism, American Business Culture, and the Shaping of Modern Mexico, 1920–1950.* Chapel Hill: University of North Carolina Press, 2003.

Moser, Walter. "Introduction." In Moser, Ndalianis, and Krieger, *Neo-Baroques,* 1–24.

Moser, Walter, Angela Ndalianis, and Peter Krieger, eds. *Neo-Baroques: From Latin America to the Hollywood Blockbuster.* Leiden: Brill Rodopi, 2017.

Murillo Rivas, José Alfredo. "El radiodrama en el cuadrante: Fuente creativa en desuso en la radiodifusión sonorense." Master's thesis, Universidad de Sonora (Mexico), 1997.

Musacchio, Humberto. *Diccionario enciclopédico de México ilustrado.* Mexico City: Andrés León, 1989.

Museo Nacional de Culturas Populares. *El país de las tandas: Teatro de Revista, 1900–1940.* Mexico City: Consejo Nacional para la Cultura y las Artes, 2010.

Nariman, Heidi Noel. *Soap Operas for Social Change: Toward a Methodology for Entertainment-Education Television.* Foreword by Everett M. Rogers. Westport, CT: Praeger, 1993.

———. "Televisa: History and Operating Philosophies of Mexico's Private Commercial Television System, 1950–1988." Master's thesis, 1988.

Ndalianis, Angela. *Neo-Baroque Aesthetics and Contemporary Entertainment.* Cambridge, MA: MIT Press, 2004.

Noriega, Raúl et. al. *50 Discursos Doctrinales en el Congreso Constituyente de la Revolución Mexicana, 1916–1917.* Mexico City: Instituto Nacional de Estudios Históricos de la Revolución Mexicana, 1967.

Nuñez Monge, Francisco María. *Periódicos y periodistas.* San José, Costa Rica: Editorial Costa Rica, 1980.

Ocampo, Aurora Maura, et al. *Diccionario de escritores mexicanos, Siglo XX.* Mexico City: UNAM, 1988.

ocho3. "'Cuna de Lobos' revolucionó la TV en México: Alejandro Camacho." *Ocho Columnas,* October 17, 2016, https://8columnas.com.mx/espectaculos/cuna-de-lobos-revoluciono-la-tv-en-mexico-alejandro-camacho/.

Ochoa, John Andrés. *The Uses of Failure in Mexican Literature and Identity.* Austin: University of Texas Press, 2004.

Olea Franco, Rafael. *La lengua literaria mexicana: De la Independencia a la*

Revolución (1816–1920). Mexico City: El Colegio de México, 2019.

Onishi, Norimitsu. "Thumbs Race as Japan's Best Sellers Go Cellular." *New York Times*, January 20, 2008, https://www.nytimes.com/2008/01/20/world/asia/20japan.html.

Orozco y Berra, Manuel, ed. *Diccionario universal de historia y geografía: Colección de artículos relativos a la República Mexicana*. Mexico City: Tipografía de Rafael, 1853.

Ortega y Medina, Juan A. *Polémicas y ensayos mexicanos en torno a la historia*. Mexico City: UNAM, 1970.

Ortiz Gaitán, Julieta. *Imagenes del deseo: Arte y publicidad en la prensa ilustrada mexicana (1894–1939)*. Mexico City: UNAM, 2003.

Ortiz Monasterio, José. "Avatares del Archivo de la Inquisición de México." *Boletín del Archivo General de la Nación* 6, no. 5 (July–September 2004): 93–110.

———. "Dos discursos patrios de Vicente Riva Palacio: Un caso para evaluar la aportación de la novela histórica como método de conocimiento." *Historias* 69 (January–April 2008): 57–79.

———. *Historia y ficción: Los dramas y novelas de Vicente Riva Palacio*. Mexico City: Instituto Mora; Universidad Iberoamericana, 1993.

———. "*La Orquesta* (1861–1877): Periódico Omniscio, de Buen Humor y Con Caricaturas." *La Orquesta* 1, no. 7 (May–June 1987): 34–39.

———. "La revolución de la lectura durante el siglo XIX en México." *Historias* 60 (January–April 2005): 57–76.

———. *México eternamente: Vicente Riva Palacio ante la escritura de la historia*. Mexico City: Instituto Mora; Fondo de Cultura Económica, 2004.

———. "Rescate de un análisis de Edmundo O'Gorman sobre la novela *Calvario y tabor* de Vicente Riva Palacio." *Literatura Mexicana* 21, No. 1 (2010): 123–54.

Otsuka, Eiji, and Marc Steinberg. "World and Variation: The Reproduction and Consumption of Narrative." *Mechademia* 5 (2010): 99–116.

Pacheco, José Emilio. *La novela histórica y de folletín*. Mexico City: Promexa, 1985.

Pérez Montfort, Ricardo. "El charro como estereotipo mexicano." In *Charrería: Orígenes y historia de una tradición*, 86–170. Mexico City: Federación Mexicana de Charrería, 2010.

———. "'Esa no, porque me hiere': Semblanza superficial de treinta años de radio en México, 1925–1955." In *Avatares del nacionalismo cultural: Cinco ensayos*, 91–115. Mexico City: Centro de Investigación y Docencia en Humanidades del Estado de Morelos/Centro de Investigaciones y Estudios Superiores en Antropología Social, 2000.

Plasencia de la Parra, Enrique. *Independencia y nacionalismo a la luz del discurso conmemorativo, 1825–1867*. Mexico City: Consejo Nacional para la Cultura y las Artes, 1980.

———. *Personajes y escenarios de la rebelión delahuertista, 1923–24*. Mexico City: UNAM, 1998.

Poblete, Juan. "De la lectura como práctica histórica en América Latina: La primera época colonial y el siglo XIX." *Cuadernos de Literatura* 20, no. 39 (January–June 2016): 57–94.

Ponce Capdeville, Berenice. "Caravana de sonidos: Historias de radio, música y efectos." Bachelor's thesis, UNAM, 2004.

———. "Teatro del aire en México (1936–1940)." Master's thesis, Universidad Iberoamericana, 2018.

Pruneda, Salvador. *Huellas.* Mexico City: Editorial México Nuovo, 1936.

———. *La caricatura.* Mexico City: Arana, 1973.

———. *La caricatura como arma política—Caricaturas anónimas y de los artistas: J. G. Z., Constantino Escalante [et al.].* Mexico City: Octavo, 1958.

Puente, Ramón. *Villa: Sus auténticas memorias.* Los Angeles: Mexican American Publishing Co., 1931.

Quintana Navarrete, Jorge. "Eugenesia y sinofobia: Las campañas antichinas en Sonora." Mexico City: UNAM, forthcoming.

Quintanilla, Susana. "*El águila y la serpiente* de Martín Luis Guzmán." *Letras Libres,* April 30, 2010, https://www.letraslibres.com/mexico/revista/iv-el-aguila-y-la-serpiente-martin-luis-guzman.

Radin, Paul. *An Annotated Bibliography of the Poems and Pamphlets of J. J. Fernández de Lizardi: The First Period (1808–1819).* San Francisco: Sutro Library, 1940.

Ramirez, Elizabeth C. *Footlights across the Border: A History of Spanish-Language Professional Theatre on the Texas Stage.* New York: Peter Lang, 1990.

Ramírez Aparicio, Manuel. *Los conventos suprimidos en Méjico: Estudios biográficos, históricos y arqueológicos.* Mexico City: J. M. Aguilar, 1861–1862.

Ramírez Berg, Charles. *A Cinema of Solitude: A Critical Study of Mexican Film, 1967–1983.* Austin: University of Texas Press, 1992.

Rea, Lauren. *Argentine Serialised Radio Drama in the Infamous Decade, 1930–1943.* Farnham, UK: Ashgate, 2013.

Revista Somos. "El mundo de las telenovelas." Special Issue, 1991.

Reyes de la Maza, Luis. *Crónica de la telenovela: México sentimental.* Mexico City: Clío, 1999.

———. *Memorias de un pentonto.* Mexico City: Editorial Posada, 1984.

Riding, Alan. *Distant Neighbors.* New York: Knopf, 1985.

Rincón, Omar. "Nuevas narrativas televisivas: Relajar, entretener, contar, ciudadanizar, experimentar." *Comunicar* 18, no. 36 (2011): 43–50.

Rincón Gallardo, Carlos. *El charro mexicano.* Mexico City: Porrúa, 1939.

Riva Palacio, Vicente. *Calvario y tabor.* Mexico City: M. C. de Villegas, 1868.

———. *Ensayos históricos.* Edited by José Ortiz Monasterio. Mexico City: Consejo Nacional para la Cultura y las Artes, 1997.

———. *Martín Garatuza.* Mexico City: Porrúa, 2001.

———. *México a través de los siglos,* vol. 2. Mexico City: Ballescá, 1884–1889.

———. *Monja y casada, vírgen y mártir.* Mexico City: Porrúa, 2001.

———. *Periodismo: Primera parte.* Edited by María Teresa Solórzano Ponce.

Vol. 10 of *Obras escogidas de Vicente Riva Palacio*. Mexico City: UNAM; CONACULTA; Instituto Mexiquense de Cultura; Instituto Mora, 2002.

Roberts, Marthe. "Origins of the Novel." In *Theory of the Novel: A Historical Approach*, edited by Michael McKeon, 57–70. Baltimore: Johns Hopkins University Press, 2000.

Robinson, Amy. "Chucho el Roto in Mexico's Post-1968 Cinema." *Mexican Studies/Estudios Mexicanos* 30, no. 2 (Summer 2014): 446–78.

———. "Mexican Banditry and Discourses of Class: The Case of Chucho el Roto." *Latin American Research Review* 44, no. 1 (2009): 5–31.

Robinson, Jerry. *The Comics: An Illustrated History of Comic Strip Art, 1895–2010*. Milwaukie, OR: Dark Horse Books, 2011.

Rodríguez, Richard. *Next of Kin: The Family in Chicano/a Cultural Politics*. Durham, NC: Duke University Press, 2009.

Rodríguez Familiar, José. *Efemérides queretanas: Acontecimientos notables en la vida de Querétaro*. Vols. 1–2. Querétaro, Mexico: Imprenta Salesiana, 1973.

Romano, Carlin. "Who Killed Literary Reading?" *Chronicle of Higher Education*, July 23, 2004, B13.

Ross, Stanley Robert, et al., eds. *Fuentes de la historia contemporánea de México: Periódicos y revistas*. Vols. 1–2. Mexico City: El Colegio de México, 1965.

Rowe, William, and Vivian Schelling. *Memory and Modernity: Popular Culture in Latin America*. London: Verso, 1991.

Rubenstein, Anne. *Bad Language, Naked Ladies, and Other Threats to the Nation: A Political History of Comic Books in Mexico*. Durham, NC: Duke University Press, 1998.

———. "Mass Media and Popular Culture in the Postrevolutionary Era." In Beezley and Michael C. Meyer, *Oxford History of Mexico*, 637–70. New York: Oxford University Press, 2000.

Ruiz Barrionuevo, Carmen. "*El Periquillo Sarniento* de Fernández de Lizardi y los problemas textuales de las cuatro primeras ediciones." *Siglo Diecinueve* 2 (1996): 147–62.

Ryan, Marie-Laure, ed. *Narrative across Media: The Languages of Storytelling*. Lincoln: University of Nebraska Press, 2004.

———. "Transmedial Storytelling and Transfictionality." *Poetics Today* 34 (Fall 2013): 361–88.

Schmitt, Marlène. "El folletinista y sus públicos: Notas acerca de la reedición de *El fistol del diablo*." In *Literatura mexicana del otro fin de siglo*, edited by Rafael Olea Franco, 311–26. Mexico City: El Colegio de México, 2001.

Scolari, Carlos. "Transmedia Storytelling: Implicit Consumers, Narrative Worlds, and Branding in Contemporary Media Production." *International Journal of Communication* 3 (2009): 586–606.

Scolari, Carlos, Paolo Bertetti, and Matthew Freeman. *Transmedia Archaeology: Storytelling in the Borderlines of Science Fiction, Comics and Pulp Magazines*. London: Palgrave Macmillan, 2014.

Serna Rodríguez, Ana María. "Prensa y sociedad en las décadas revolucionarias (1910–1940)." *Secuencia* 88 (2014): 111–49.

Sierra, Justo. *Evolución política del pueblo mexicano.* [Caracas]: Biblioteca Ayacucho, 1977.

Smith, Paul Julian. *Multiplatform Media in Mexico: Growth and Change since 2010.* London: Palgrave Macmillan, 2019.

Sol, Manuel. "Ignacio Manuel Altamirano: Intención e imagen de un crítico." *Literatura Mexicana* 9, no. 1 (1998): 45–65.

Solórzano Ponce, María Teresa. "La novela teatralizada de Vicente Riva Palacio." *Literatura Mexicana* 7, no. 2 (1996): 351–64.

———. "Una voz recuperada." In Riva Palacio, *Periodismo*, 13–37.

———. "Vicente Riva Palacio (1832–1896)." *Literatura Mexicana* 7, no. 2 (1996): 639–44.

Spell, Jefferson Rea. "The Genesis of the First Mexican Novel." *Bridging the Gap: Articles on Mexican Literature.* Mexico City: Editorial Libros de México, 1971.

———. *The Life and Works of José Joaquín Fernández de Lizardi.* Philadelphia: University of Pennsylvania Press, 1931.

Suárez de la Torre, Laura. *Constructores de un cambio cultural: Impresores-editores y libreros en la ciudad de México, 1830–1855.* Mexico City: Instituto de Investigaciones Dr. José María Luis Mora, 2003.

Taibo II, Paco Ignacio. *Pancho Villa.* Mexico City: Planeta, 2006.

Tenorio-Trillo, Mauricio. *Artilugio de la nación moderna: México en las Exposiciones Universales, 1880–1930.* Mexico City: Fondo de Cultura Económica, 1998.

———. *I Speak of the City: Mexico City at the Turn of the Twentieth Century.* Chicago: University of Chicago Press, 2013.

Thelen, David. "Mexico's Cultural Landscapes: A Conversation with Carlos Monsiváis." *Journal of American History* 86, no. 2 (September 1999): 613–22.

Trujillo Muñoz, Gabriel. "La literatura policiaca mexicana: Un caso abierto." *Acequias* 55 (Spring/Summer 2011): 34–38.

Unzueta, Fernando. "The Nineteenth-Century Novel: Toward a Public Sphere or a Mass Media?" In Castillo and Paz-Soldán, 21–40.

Valenzuela, Georgette José. "Campaña, rebelión y elecciones presidenciales de 1923 a 1924 en México." *Estudios de Historia Moderna y Contemporánea de México* 23 (January–June 2022).

Vanderwood, Paul J. *Disorder and Progress: Bandits, Police, and Mexican Development.* Lincoln: University of Nebraska Press, 1981.

Vaughan, Mary Kay. *Portrait of a Young Painter: Pepe Zúñiga and Mexico City's Rebel Generation.* Durham, NC: Duke University Press, 2015.

Vaughan, Mary Kay, and Stephen E. Lewis. *The Eagle and the Virgin: National and Cultural Revolution in Mexico, 1920–1940.* Durham, NC: Duke University Press, 2006.

Vázquez Valle, Irene. *La cultura popular vista por las élites*. Mexico City: UNAM, 1989.

Vigil, José María. "Necesidad y conveniencia de estudiar la historia patria." In Ortega y Medina, *Polémicas y ensayos mexicanos*, 265–78.

Vogeley, Nancy. "The Concept of 'the People' in *El Periquillo Sarniento*." *Hispania* 70 (1987): 457–67.

———. "José Joaquín Fernández de Lizardi: Nuevos lentes para observar su obra." Conferencia Magistral (Zacatecas, *Primer Coloquio Internacional de Cultura Literaria Virreinal*, 2015), https://ljz.mx/2015/10/08/primer-coloquio-internacional-de-cultura-literaria-virreinal-con-participacion-de-mas-de-15-universidades-e-instituciones-nacionales-y-extranjeras/

———. *Lizardi and the Birth of the Novel in Spanish America*. Gainesville: University Press of Florida, 2001.

Wold, Ruth. *"El Diario de México": Primer cotidiano de Nueva España*. Madrid: Editorial Gredos, 1970.

Wright, Amy E. "The Closest Layer of the Palimpsest: Unearthing the Nineteenth-Century Serial Novel in Serna's *Angeles del abismo* (2004)." *Latin American Literary Review* 81 (2013): 91–108.

———. "Genaro García's *Leona Vicario, heroína insurgente* (1910), or, A Centennial-Year Revision of the Mexican Woman's Place in the Public Sphere." *Iberoamericana* 39 (2010): 145–60.

———. "Serialization and the Novel." In *Cambridge History of the Mexican Novel*, edited by Anna M. Nogar, José Ramon Ruisánchez Serra, and Ignacio M. Sánchez Prado. Cambridge: Cambridge University Press, forthcoming.

———. "Subscribing Identities: The Serial Novel in the Development of Novel and Nation; Spain and Mexico from the 1840s to the 1860." Doctoral thesis, Brown University, 2006.

Zacatecas, Bertha. *Vidas en el aire: Pioneros de la radio en México*. Mexico City: Editorial Diana, 1996.

Zárate, Eder. "*Los hijos también lloran* abrirá el telón nuevamente pero esta vez de manera virtual." *Voces del Periodista*, March 24, 2020.

BROADCASTS, PERFORMANCES, AND RECORDINGS

Serial presentations are generally cited in this book with episode date and time marker.

EnPOPados. "Los hijos también lloran conferencia completa." Zoom interview of the author, cast, and creative crew. Canal EnPOPados, October 26, 2020, https://www.youtube.com/watch?v=2KBlrQ5xuRo.

Fonoteca National. *Radionovelas legendarias*. Interview series. Mexico City, 2012.

Index

Page numbers in italic refer to images.

Touissant, Cecilia, 177
Tovar, Pantaleón, 49, 210n11, 216n13
transmediality, 8, 12, 16–18, 23, 43
  of Chucho el Roto, 115–16, 120, 133,
    139–41, 153–57, 243n79
  definition of, 3, 209n2
  of *El extraño retorno*, 263n129
  of Riva Palacio's works, 75, 159–60,
    196–97
  in twenty-first century, 203, 211n31
TV Azteca, 203, 206, 261n109, 264n9

UNAM (Universidad Nacional
    Autónoma de México)
  alumni, 165, 167, 171, 252n15,
    254n40, 255–56n72, 261n110,
    262n116
  faculty, 166, 190, 215n49, 261n110
  Televisa and, 170, 182
Universal, El, 12, 13, 84, 112, 231n82
Universal Ilustrado, El, 12, 13, 210n21,
    237n41
uprisings. *See* rebellions

van den Berg, Thijs, 3
Vasconcelos, José, 78, 125, 230n77,
    238n45
Vigil, José Maria, 223n102
Villa, Pancho, 12, 13, 80–84, 108–11,
    111, 230–31nn80–81
Villaseñor Sanabria, María Margarita,
    182, 261n110

Villegas, Manuel C. de, 11, 49, 55, 71
Vogeley, Nancy J., 30, 35, 38, 212n2,
    213n22, 214nn47–48

Wagner, Fernando, 154
Weingartshofer, C'Cañak, 172

XEQ, 128–29, 241n68
XEW, 122–34, *139*, 238n49, 238–
    39nn51–54, 239n58, 239n60,
    245n103
  ratings and rivalries, 130, 138,
    240n62, 241n66, 242n78, 245n97
  star system, 240n61, 246n114
  See also Cardozo, Charly (Carlos
    González); *Chucho el Roto*
    (*radionovelas*); O'Farrill, Juan
    Pablo
XEX, 211n26, 240n62

Zapata, Emiliano, 80–81, 83, 84
Zapata, Luis, 16
Zarco, El (Altamirano), 82–83, 210n15
Zarco, Francisco, 49
Zayas Enríquez, Rafael, 116–18
Zendejas, Hipolito (Carlos Fernández
    Benedicto), 79, 91–94, 103, 105,
    107–8, 226nn27–28, 229n64,
    230n78
Zevaco, Michel, 172–73
Zuno, Andy, 205–6, 265n14

CPSIA information can be obtained
at www.ICGtesting.com
Printed in the USA
LVHW071932080723
751906LV00003B/30